PENGUIN BOOKS

THE NASHOS' WAR

Mark Dapin is the editor of *From the Trenches* and *The Penguin Book of Australian War Writing*. His novel, *Spirit House*, set on the Burma Railway during World War Two, was shortlisted for the Royal Society of Literature's Ondaatje Prize and *The Age* Book of the Year Award, and longlisted for the Miles Franklin Literary Award. In 2015, *The Nashos' War* was the winner of the People's Choice Award and the Alex Buzo Shortlist Prize in the national Nib Waverley Library Awards for Literature; and in 2016, it was shortlisted in the NSW Premier's Literary Awards for the Douglas Stewart Prize for Non-Fiction.

ALSO BY MARK DAPIN

From the Trenches

The Penguin Book of Australian War Writing

Spirit House

King of the Cross

Strange Country

Fridge Magnets are Bastards

Sex & Money

THE NASHOS' WAR

Australia's national servicemen and Vietnam

MARK DAPIN

PENGUIN BOOKS

PENGUIN BOOKS

UK | USA | Canada | Ireland | Australia
India | New Zealand | South Africa | China

Penguin Books is part of the Penguin Random House group of companies whose addresses can be found at global.penguinrandomhouse.com.

First published by Penguin Group, 2014
This edition published by Penguin Random House Australia Pty Ltd, 2017

10 9 8 7 6 5 4 3 2 1

Cover and text design by Adam Laszczuk © Penguin Random House Australia Pty Ltd
Cover photography by James Evan Jones
Typeset in Adobe Garamond by Samantha Jayaweera, Penguin Random House Australia Pty Ltd
Colour separation by Splitting Image Colour Studio, Clayton, Victoria
Printed and bound in Australia by Griffin Press,
an accredited ISO AS/NZS 14001 Environmental Management Systems printer.

National Library of Australia
Cataloguing-in-Publication data:

Dapin, Mark, author
The nashos' war : Australia's national servicemen and Vietnam/Mark Dapin
9780670078622 (paperback)
National service—Personal narratives, Australian.
National service—Australia.
Vietnam War, 1961-1975—Personal narratives, Australian.
Vietnam War, 1961-1975—Participation, Australian.
Australia—Armed Forces—Recruiting, enlistment, etc.
Australia—Armed Forces—Military life—History.

penguin.com.au

CONTENTS

PART 2

No one is fool enough to choose war instead of peace – in peace, sons bury fathers, but in war, fathers bury sons.

HERODOTUS C.450 BC

Courtesy of the Department of Veterans' Affairs

Phuoc Tuy Province

Province boundary
District boundary
Minefield
Rubber plantations

PREFACE

This is not the book I thought I would write. When I became interested in the Australian national service scheme of 1964–72, I believed a number of things that have turned out to be false. Firstly, I assumed most men marched into the army having made a deliberate choice between military service and conscientious objection. In retrospect, my naiveté seems almost grotesque. The great majority of young Australians in the mid-1960s considered obedience to the law to be an obligation rather than an option, and would no more have resisted military service than burgled a neighbour's home. Secondly, I imagined the national servicemen who went to Vietnam resented being sent to war. While some did, many others welcomed the chance to escape from boring jobs, see some of the world and perhaps take the mateship of a footy trip into battle. I also thought that, within the logic of the 'domino principle' and the doctrine of forward defence, there must have been some desperate military requirement for conscription. I now believe, in the words of the magisterial *Official History of Australia's Involvement in Southeast Asian Conflicts, 1948–75*, the Menzies government was 'determined to introduce and to maintain conscription, including a commitment for overseas service, for its own sake'.[1]

The reason I supposed national service had a primarily military purpose was my presumption that the scheme was broadly unpopular. It was, in fact, applauded by the majority of the people, press and politicians, even if the prospect of sending conscripts off to war left an astringent taste in more sensitive palates. I imagined the scheme was reviled in part because I thought the radical movements of the times led public opinion. But it was the actions of national servicemen, in accepting discipline and following orders, which most closely reflected the values of the society that had produced them. Most of Australia was conservative, patriotic and law-abiding throughout the Vietnam period. Anti-war protesters, even at the peak of their numbers, were often thought of as deviants, ratbags, idiots and traitors. Outside of the university campuses – and sometimes inside them, too – they could be abused, harassed and ridiculed. While a revolutionary minority adopted the cause of the Viet Cong, the mothers and fathers in the moratorium protests were marching to stop the killing and to keep Australian troops out of harm's way. But the clergymen and schoolteachers, pacifists and students may not have understood that the soldiers – national servicemen included – did not necessarily want to be out of harm's way. The women of the Save Our Sons movement, who tirelessly picketed the army inductions of thousands of young men, perhaps did not realise that many had not asked to be saved. And if the demonstrators had been told some of the national servicemen felt the protests were against a choice they had made, they would have been mystified. Because who would choose to go to war?

Perhaps the last of the illusions I shed was that mainstream public opinion turned against the war under the weight of evidence of US war crimes. Australia's troop commitment actually became more popular in the wake of the My Lai massacre trials. And, while the facts of Australia's Vietnam War can be marshalled in support of virtually any thesis, if this book establishes nothing else, it should at least put paid to the myth whose naiveté seems almost grotesque, that every conscript in Vietnam was actually a volunteer.

I began to write this book after I had edited *The Penguin Book of Australian War Writing*, because I felt there had been curiously little attempt made to understand the reality of the experience of Australian national servicemen both at home and in Vietnam. In its place had grown an apologetic consideration for their treatment when they came home and were supposedly doused in spit and blood, and met at airports by demonstrators waving placards accusing them of raping women and killing babies. A picture of the 'home front', clouded with half-truths and misconceptions, had virtually become the story of the war. I wanted to return combat, bravery, boredom, hardship and grief to the centre of the narrative, to give the war back to the national servicemen.

But military history is as much about the way a war is remembered as the conflict itself. This book tells of events recalled almost fifty years on, through filters of battalion reunions, long nights at the RSL, further study, earlier history books, TV mini-series, Hollywood movies and the myopia of hindsight. While I have tried to check men's stories against the public record, service records, newspaper reports and their friends' corroborations, some details will inevitably have become confused – not least by the author. In more martial cultures, I imagine, there is a tendency for men to covet the role of war hero, and place themselves at the centre of the action. In the stories of Australian ex-soldiers, the teller often drifts to the periphery, as nobody wants to be heard saying he did more than his mates.

Initially, I hoped to recount each event as it might have appeared to the individual at the time, stripped of anything but the most basic geopolitical and military contexts as understood by a twenty-year-old in the 1960s. In the end, I had to tell a little extra, so the reader could more clearly see what was being shown. But to the average national serviceman, the war often looked like a series of chaotic incidents triggered by arbitrary orders issued for inexplicable reasons and conjoined only by his own bemused participation. If the reader requires a command history that explains exactly how and why each incident occurred, the aforementioned *Official History* is peerless.

This is a book about men who performed at least part of their national service. It does not overly concern itself with those conscientious objectors who did not spend time in uniform. Theirs is another important, sometimes heroic story, but the only objectors interviewed for *The Nashos' War* were those who changed their minds once they were in the army. There has been a lot written about the fissures in society during the war but not much about the divisions within individuals. The lines between objector and enthusiast, and participant and observer, are not as defined as they first appear. In this book are the stories of Australian Communist sympathisers who fought the Viet Cong, and a refugee from Communists who decided he could not raise a gun against them. In history delivered as soap opera, there were stark divisions between 'the journalists', 'the students', 'the protesters' and 'the nashos', but plenty of journalists were national servicemen, arts students ended up as infantrymen, and many erstwhile protesters put duty, patriotism and sometimes expediency before political principle, and acquiesced to military service. These men do not necessarily live easily with their decisions, and it seems a great unfairness to have foisted these choices upon them when the majority of un-balloted youth were free to grow their hair to their shoulders, pack their surfboards in the back of a Kombi and drink Bundy on a beach. I spoke to men who regret their actions on the battlefield when no other course could have led to a better outcome, to men who have been haunted their whole lives because they went out into the bush on a particular day, and others who remain tormented by the fact they stayed behind that same morning.

Just as I have not looked much at the protesters and objectors who spent the war as civilians, I have paid no attention to those military-age members of pro-war organisations who chose the Robert Menzies route and, while campaigning in favour of conscription, did not themselves join the thousands who volunteered for national service. No doubt they suffered their own internal struggles, and could provide a missing piece of this incomplete picture of 1960s Australian masculinity.

I have concentrated on the way national servicemen viewed the army, rather than how the army as an institution experienced the national service scheme. That is one more book to be written. I also struggled with my title. In calling this *The Nashos' War*, I do not mean to imply that Australia's Vietnam was simply a 'nashos' war', only that the war as lived by national servicemen is my focus. *The Regs' War* is a further volume to be added to the imaginary shelf of important work yet to be done. I wrestled also with terminology: I have called the National Liberation Front 'the VC', the People's Army of Vietnam 'the NVA' and the conflation of their forces 'the enemy' so as to echo the language used by national servicemen, not as judgement upon their military or political character.

Finally, I hope this book can offer a different narrative to national servicemen than the partially folkloric saga of victimhood and rejection which has grown up since the war. Mentally and physically, Australia's national servicemen were something of an elite, who did what society demanded of them with the support of most of the people most of the time. The book I thought I would write would have been packed full of lessons about protest, conformity, rebellion and discipline. The book I have written ultimately exalts a single confounded banality: nothing about history is as simple as it might first seem.

PROLOGUE

When the first national servicemen of the new scheme gingerly stepped off their buses and into recruit training battalions in July 1965, Robert Menzies was prime minister of Australia in much the same way as Elizabeth II was Queen of England. A generation had grown up knowing no other person in either office. If anything, Menzies' permanence was more established than the Queen's. She had only reigned since 1952, whereas he had led the Liberal–Country Party coalition government since 1949, and had earlier served as prime minister from 1939–41.

Menzies exuded authority, promised security, and had presided over a long period of economic growth in a peaceful, homogenous, conservative nation, where every white Australian was also a British citizen. From the Tasman Sea to the Indian Ocean, there was something close to full employment – an unskilled man could walk off a job on a Monday and into another on Tuesday – and not much incentive for an ambitious boy to join the army.

The Australian Labor Party (ALP), led by the abrasive, uncharming Arthur Calwell, was accustomed to humiliation and defeat. While Menzies seemed born to rule, Calwell, the son of a police officer, appeared at best fated to serve, at worst simply to protest the perfidy of his betters. The ALP had not recovered from its split of 1955, after which a number of highly organised, implacably anti-Communist, mainly Catholic members formed the original Democratic Labor Party (DLP).

The Communist Party of Australia (CPA) seemed destined to die of old age. A 1965 study of political attitudes among young Australians found 'with no class differentiation whatever, our adolescents decreed that the Communist Party should be "cut out of our democracy"'. The frustrated investigator, a Dr DJ Drinkwater of the University of Queensland, said 'our adolescents are shockingly and wilfully ignorant of political matters. Not only do they know little or nothing about our current political parties but they think that is how the world should be.'[1]

The voice of eighteen-year-old Melbourne pop singer Normie Rowe was the brash, reverberating sound of young Australia in 1965, and teenage women seemed gripped by a kind of Normie-mania. A concert in Bathurst, NSW, ended early when about thirty yelling girls rushed the stage and chased Rowe behind the curtains. Sydney radio station 2UW announced a Normie Rowe Day, but a gang of teenagers broke through security and stormed the function. In Brisbane in December, Rowe had reached the last song of his short set when police cleared the stage. Hundreds of fans lined up outside and marched to Rowe's hotel, chanting, 'We want Normie', blocking traffic with their parade. Rowe promised the Sydney *Sun* he would never start thinking like an adult. 'The teenage world is a lot happier than the adult world,' he said. 'I mean I have never heard of a group of Red Chinese 13-year-olds fighting Nationalist Chinese 13-year-olds.'[2]

On smaller stages, among more earnest youths, Australian folk singers were quietly admired. In Sydney, Sean Cullip and Sonja Tallis, performing as Sean and Sonja, harmonised with ecclesiastic grace. They played the Troubadour cafe in Edgecliff, which could hold a hundred people at street level and perhaps a hundred more in the basement. Their audience would queue for an hour to get in and sit on hard benches drinking indifferent coffee in silence, out of respect for the performers.

But music and dancing were for girls and women. Australian men were supposed to play ball games, and the growing number of boys who enjoyed pop music were viewed with unveiled suspicion. Cricketers and footballers were the heroes of the healthy-minded: taciturn, undemonstrative men such as batsman Doug Walters, who played his Test debut at nineteen years old, and scored 155 in his first innings.

In 1965, Essendon won their eleventh VFL premiership, with Keith Gent striving to carve a place for himself on the half-forward flank. In the west, East Fremantle's Harry Neesham, winner of the Caris Medal for best and fairest first-year player, was the rising star of the WANFL. In League, the absurdly skilled Bob Fulton was signed to Wests Illawarra, who finished eighth on the ladder.

Unusually among the men of their time, none of the dominant political figures of 1965 had seen active military service. As a student at the start of the First World War, Menzies had held a commission in the Melbourne University Regiment but, despite his support for universal conscription, never actually joined the Australian Imperial Force (AIF). This apparent paradox has sent sympathetic biographers gimbling and gyring around the facts, searching for a congenial explanation, but Menzies himself always declined to give the reasons behind his decision. When in 1939, a political rival, Earle Page, inaccurately accused him of having 'resigned' his commission to avoid overseas service, Menzies told parliament, 'I did not resign anything. I served the ordinary term of a compulsory trainee. I was in exactly the same position as any other person who at that time had to answer the extremely important questions – is it my duty to go to war, or is it my duty not to go. The answer to those questions cannot be made on the public platform.'[3]

Calwell, who, like Menzies, was born in the last decade of the nineteenth century, had applied for a commission in the AIF when war broke out in 1914, but was rejected as too young. He, too, saw out the war in the militia, but became a fierce voice against conscription. Bartholomew Augustine Santamaria, whose official position was president of the National Civic Council (NCC), the brain which informed the body of the DLP, had kept out of the military in the Second World War. Although he had just turned twenty-four when the fighting broke out in 1939, Santamaria won exemption from military service to work for the Catholic Action movement, an organisation with no military purpose.

Despite its unmilitary leadership and outward calm, Australia had been at war continuously since 1950. But the fact the nation had sent 17 000 men to fight in Korea in 1950–53, and lost 339 dead and 1200 wounded – a far greater casualty rate proportionately than the country was to suffer in the Vietnam War – went comparatively unremarked, as all were volunteer soldiers. Australian regular forces had also fought in the Malayan Emergency from 1950–63, losing thirty-nine men with twenty-seven wounded, with no particular public reaction. The Korean War finished in a stalemate which led to the division of the country between north and south. The Emergency ended with the defeat of a Communist insurgency and the formation of the Federation of Malaysia in September 1963. The new state comprised peninsula Malaysia and also Sabah and Sarawak on Borneo, an island which the territories shared with the sultanate of Brunei and the five Indonesian provinces of Kalimantan. Even before Malaysian independence, Indonesia, under President Sukarno, had supported an uprising in Brunei, and begun attacking targets and infiltrating troops into Sabah and Sarawak. Indonesia's sustained harassment was dubbed 'Confrontation' by the Indonesian foreign minister. It was aimed at weakening and ultimately wrecking the federation: in Indonesian, the word 'Kalimantan' means all of Borneo, not just the southern portion of the island. A series of Indonesian cross-border raids drew in British and Commonwealth forces, and in 1965, Australian infantry, engineers and Special Air Service (SAS) were all sent to Borneo.

Australia had also taken sides in the First Vietnam War, which ended in 1954 when the Communist Viet Minh, led by Ho Chi Minh, drove out the French Empire. Although the French and their colonial troops fought the war, by 1953, 70 per cent of their military effort was bankrolled by the US. Australia too had begun to ship weapons to the French, but by the time the ordnance arrived the warring parties were in peace talks, so they were never used. At a conference table in Geneva, the Viet Minh and the French agreed to divide Vietnam into two 'regroupment zones'. Ho's forces would consolidate in the north, the army of France's puppet emperor Bao Dai in the south. This was simply a ceasefire line, and the Geneva conference's political declaration stated it 'should not in any way be interpreted as constituting a political or territorial boundary'.[4] The declaration further called for general elections to be held in both zones in July 1956, to allow the people of Vietnam to decide their future. The US president, Dwight Eisenhower, wrote later, 'I have never talked or corresponded with a person knowledgeable in Indochinese affairs who did not agree that had elections been held as of the time of the fighting, possibly 80 per cent of the population would have voted for the Communist Ho Chi Minh as their leader rather than Chief of State Bao Dai.'[5]

The Viet Minh withdrew ninety thousand of their one hundred thousand soldiers and forty-five thousand of their sixty thousand political activists from the south, but left ten thousand mostly local fighters behind in the jungles and fifteen thousand cadres in the villages. An estimated nine hundred thousand Vietnamese fled the Communist-controlled zone in the north, two-thirds of whom were Catholics, the human legacy of the French Empire. North and south became de facto states when the first president of the south, the dictator Ngo Dinh Diem, refused to hold elections. Instead, Diem cut the strings of the puppet Bao Dai in a fraudulent referendum. In October, he asked the people to choose a head of state between himself and the emperor, who now lived in Paris and did not bother to join the contest. Diem won with 98 per cent of the vote, in many places polling more votes than there were voters.

Diem governed the south from the ravenous port of Saigon. Ho controlled the north from Hanoi, an ancient city of lakes on the banks of the Red River. Ho was preoccupied with building 'socialism' in his police state. His 'land reforms' claimed the lives of perhaps fifteen thousand of his own people, but Ho was like Stalin's own Vietnamese Jesus, walking over lakes of blood to demonstrate his divinity. He cultivated an air of sanctity, and an almost holy asceticism, but he was less a socialist saint than a Comintern King Herod, a slaughterer of innocents.

In the south, communists were hunted down, imprisoned, tortured and often executed. In 1957, the hungry and impatient fighters left behind in the jungles began to strike back with assassinations of southern government officials. In 1960 North Vietnam, now led by Communist Party First Secretary Le Duan, with Ho only a figurehead, authorised the guerrillas to launch a new campaign. The National Liberation Front (NLF) was formed from the fighters and cadres of the south in alliance with a number of non-communist groups also opposed to Diem's rule. The NLF became widely known as the 'Viet Cong' (VC), an initially pejorative contraction of 'Vietnamese Communist', and their insurgency quickly escalated into a civil war. In 1962, the Menzies government sent a team of thirty military advisers, designated the Australian Army Training Team Vietnam (AATTV) to help train the Army of the Republic of South Vietnam (ARVN) to fight the rebels. The ARVN was a direct descendant of French-raised military forces, and not widely supported in the Vietnamese countryside. The increasingly heavy-handed and murderous Diem was overthrown in a US-backed military coup in November 1963. A succession of unstable, unpopular and corrupt juntas followed him and, by the middle of 1965, real political power in Saigon was held by the unelected prime minister Air Vice Marshal Nguyen Cao Ky.

Premier Ky's position looked hopeless – some ARVN units couldn't or wouldn't fight – and his government would have fallen if not for a massive upsurge in US military intervention. In March 1965, the US began to flood the south with troops – there were one hundred and eighty thousand in the country by the end of the year – and bomb the north from the skies. The US Army was joined by smaller numbers of soldiers from a handful of allies (styled the Free World Military Forces) including South Korea, New Zealand and Australia. The Menzies government felt it needed a powerful friend in the region. The prime minister told parliament, 'The takeover of South Vietnam would be a direct military threat to Australia and all the countries of South and South East Asia. It must be seen as part of a thrust by Communist China between the Indian and Pacific Oceans.'[6] Australia, which had encouraged the US to become more deeply involved in the conflict, despatched the 1st Battalion Royal Australian Regiment (1RAR) to South Vietnam, with Logistics and Signals troops in support.

The Australian press was generally supportive of the move, with the notable exception of Rupert Murdoch's year-old national newspaper, *The Australian*, which warned, 'Australia has lined up her generations against the hatred and contempt of resurgent Asian peoples – without adding one iota of confidence or strength to the tragically embroiled American nation. It could be that our historians will recall this day with tears.'[7]

The main body of Australian troops arrived in June 1965, and were made part of the US 173rd Airborne Brigade at the Long Binh base at Bien Hoa, twenty-five kilometres north-east of Saigon. 1RAR began its initial operation as a battalion in South Vietnam on 23 June, one week before the first national servicemen turned up at the gates of Puckapunyal and Kapooka in Australia, nervous and determined, twenty years old and impossibly young.

PART 1

I

THE ERROL NOACK LETTERS

Terracotta-tiled columns climbed the soaring facade of the Century Building in Swanston Street, Melbourne, reaching for the cupola like fingers stretched to pluck a dome from the sky. From the mid-1960s to the early 1970s, the Art Deco tower was a temple of chance, home to the offices of both Tattersall's Lottery and the Department of Labour and National Service (DLNS).

In a boardroom on the second floor, at nine-thirty a.m. on 10 March 1965, Victorian Liberal MP Ewen Daniel Mackinnon, under the supervision of fellow Liberal member Donald Chipp, thrust a stick like a pronged baton into a nest of coloured marbles, and began to pick out the balls from the open side of an antique blackwood Tattersall's barrel. Each of the 181 marbles bore a number corresponding to a date between 1 January and 30 June 1945, and ninety-six were selected. Men whose birthdays fell on the dates matched by the marbles had to either make themselves available for two years' national service in the Australian Army, or give a valid reason why they should defer. Two young men paraded outside the Century Building, wearing like sandwich boards hand-written placards reading 'We Don't Want To Kill' and 'Don't Ballot Our Lives'. A woman marched behind them.

Ewen Mackinnon's late father, the Liberal MP Donald Mackinnon, had been director general of Australian recruiting in the First World

War, when he'd despaired of the demands of conscriptionists to press young men into service. They had split the country, he said, and hampered his efforts to persuade volunteers to enlist. His son Ewen had volunteered for the 2nd AIF in 1940, at the age of thirty-seven, and served as an officer in the Middle East, whereas Chipp had joined the Royal Australian Air Force (RAAF) in 1943 but saw out the war in Benalla, near Wangaratta, Victoria.

According to the traditions of Vietnamese astrology, a man's destiny is determined by his date of birth. A son, Errol, was born to Walter and Dorothy Noack in North Adelaide, SA, on 28 March 1945. If he'd arrived two days earlier, or five days later, Errol might have lived a longer life and died a different kind of death.

Dorothy shot through when Errol was a baby, leaving Walter, a man with a jaw like an axe blade, to bring up their boy. In Vietnamese folklore, Errol was a rooster, held to be handsome, stylish, loyal and honest, bearing the elemental sign of wood. A wood rooster is tireless in the service of a good cause. He must especially guard his liver.

Errol was his father's pride. Walter called him 'such a terrific kid',[1] and hoarded every birthday, Christmas and Father's Day card, storing all the spidery promises of love. He kept his son's yabby log, where the catches were carefully recorded in Errol's neat blue script, and each weighty detail underlined twice in red. Father and son worked together: on Sunday, 6 March 1960, they caught sixty large yabbies and three hundred and fifty smaller specimens. Errol estimated the value of their catch at 'over £5.0.0'. He paid Walter a pound for his yabby meat and ten shillings for his labour.[2]

In 1960, Walter was working at the SAFCOL fish-canning factory in Port Lincoln. Errol moved to Marleston, an inner suburb of Adelaide, to live with his uncle, Herb Noack, and his aunt Loris, and finish school with the Lutherans at Concordia College, Highgate. He was an indifferent student, and worked harder on the wall bars and rings in the school gymnasium than in the classroom. He left after taking his Intermediate Certificate in 1963, then travelled west to join his father at SAFCOL. When the Port Lincoln fishing fleet hauled in the tuna, Errol worked with filleting knives on the butchery team, but at the end of the season, the SAFCOL plant largely closed down, and Walter and Errol would look for labouring jobs, in Tumby Bay or Port Neill. Both men liked a drink and a bet, and were always lending each other money. They moved around, renting units in Port Lincoln, but were living in a caravan at Kirton Point when Mackinnon pulled Errol's birthdate marble from the barrel.

At twenty years old, Errol stood 185 centimetres tall, with handsome woodcut features and hair like golden wattle. He dressed sharply, in narrow-collared shirts, pointed-toed shoes and thin dark ties. He had the muscles of a bodybuilder. He trained against his own strength with isometric exercises, and supplemented his diet with caffeinal protein. He loved to get out in the ocean, swimming and spear-fishing, and once dived into the sea from the top of the Port Lincoln shark tower. Some nights, Errol would borrow Walter's big black 1939 Hudson, and cruise the quiet streets of Port Lincoln with a car full of friends. They'd stop at the beach to light a campfire and pass around bottles of beer. The legal drinking age in South Australia was twenty-one, but Errol and his sometime workmate Robin 'Binny' Mattner looked old enough to get served in the local pubs. At weekends, they'd sit at the bar in the Pier Hotel or the Tasman, if they weren't chasing girls at the dances around town.

The last time Mattner worked with Errol, he and Walter were building Port Lincoln's imposing grain silos. Walter drove a semitrailer heavy with cement sacks, which Errol carried across the site from the truck to a mixer. 'He had one bag on each shoulder,' said Mattner, 'and he'd just do that all day.'

Errol rarely swore. He could sail and he could sing. In black-and-white photographs, he has a fisherman's eyes, from squinting into the sun. 'He was a nice fellow, with a gentle nature, very respectful to other people,' said Mattner. 'He was a good mate of mine, probably one of the best mates I ever had.'

Errol did not know his birthday had come up in the ballot. The opening of the draw was shown on television, but the winning numbers were never announced. Reporters and cameramen were ushered out of the room after Mackinnon had raised the first marble in the air. A spokesman for the DLNS said the occasion would be closed to onlookers 'because the boardroom where it took place was not big enough and also because the drawing "is not a public affair"'. Chipp defended the decision to keep the ballot secret. The DLNS, he said, was 'experienced in this matter and was well aware of the pitfalls which might come from the publication of names of people likely to be called up'. He offered the example of 'a well-known public figure, such as a footballer' whose date of birth might be known to the public who could then 'infer from this that he was likely to be called up'.

'If this man happened to be a conscientious objector,' said Chipp, 'or did not pass the required medical or aptitude tests, there would be a certain odium.'[3] However, conscientious objectors had to argue their case in open court, and their names were duly reported in the press. And throughout the scheme, many people wrongly believed football clubs could use their influence to get exemption for their players, that the life of a good ruckman or halfback was considered more valuable than a tuna-cannery worker, or a builder.

Errol was a reluctant conscript. When he received his call-up papers, he visited the Adelaide Labor MP Clyde Cameron to ask what he should do. Cameron, who remembered him as 'a fine young man'[4], asked whether the Lutheran faith allowed Errol to kill another human being. When Errol said it did not, Cameron advised him to register as a conscientious objector.

In the end, Errol chose not to take that path. 'Since there was nothing he could do about it,' said his uncle Herb, 'he decided to make the most of it.'[5] Errol passed his medical examinations. His interviewer at the DLNS described him as a 'clean athletic type of person'.[6] Errol received a letter confirming he had been found fit and was required to commence 'national service with the Army during the week beginning 28 June, 1965'.[7] Later in the post came a 'Circular to National Servicemen', attached to a military form which, he was instructed, 'should be filled out by you with your parents' assistance'. As Errol was under twenty-one, the law required parental consent 'to the administration of anaesthetic for the performance of surgical operations'.[8] He was also too young to vote in an election.

The barrel from which Errol's marble had been plucked had last seen action in an earlier national service scheme, which had been introduced by a previous Liberal administration in 1951. That arrangement had provided a short period of compulsory basic military training for all eighteen-year-old men, followed by at first two and later three years' part-time service alongside volunteers in the Citizens Military Force (CMF). While CMF members were not required to serve outside Australia, recruits could choose to train for longer periods with the navy or air force, if they agreed to go overseas.

The scheme was modified in 1957, with the annual number of trainees cut from thirty-three thousand across the three services to only twelve thousand, all of whom would serve in army CMF units. These youths were chosen by ballot and barrel, and so the pattern was set. On 26 November 1959, the minister for defence, Athol Townley, announced the scheme would be suspended 'because of the excessive demands it made on both money and manpower, without compensatory military advantages'. National service cost Australia more than £9 million a year, and tied up almost three thousand regular soldiers in training the CMF.[9] But the system had been very popular with the public and, throughout the early 1960s, groups such as the Returned Services League (RSL) and, less predictably, the Queensland Women's Electoral League had lobbied for its reintroduction. In August 1964, the minister for the army, Dr

Alexander James 'Jim' Forbes, said national service training would not return, as military advisers unanimously agreed 'that it would detract from our effective defences'.[10] Less than three months later, in November, a new national service scheme was announced, in which conscripted men would be taken into the army for two years, and be liable for overseas service. It was widely assumed this meant they might go to Borneo, to defend Malaysia's borders against Indonesia.

Early in 1965, the US began to bomb North Vietnam. An escalation of the war looked likely, but it was unclear what form it might take. The US did not want to go in to the ground fighting alone and, for its part, Australia was 'looking for a way in and not a way out', said Menzies. Australia might have sent another one hundred and fifty instructors to the AATTV but, ironically, experienced warrant officers and NCOs such as these were now required at home to train national servicemen. On 29 April, Menzies told Parliament that Australia would dispatch an infantry battalion to Vietnam, in response to a request from the government of South Vietnam. In fact, it transpired, Australia had petitioned the initially unenthusiastic South Vietnamese to make their 'request', and it took the US to convince them. Menzies claimed the fighting in Vietnam was not a civil conflict, but a cover for Chinese expansion.

The war was never as popular as national service. In September 1965, the closest opinion poll to the June deployment of 1RAR showed only 56 per cent of Australians believed Australia should continue to fight in Vietnam, whereas 28 per cent thought the troops should come home. However, 69 per cent were in favour of conscription, with only 25 per cent opposed.

Errol Noack enlisted at Keswick Barracks, SA, on 30 June 1965, and was sent to 2nd Recruit Training Battalion (2RTB) at Puckapunyal, Victoria. Walter received a form letter from Errol's company commanding officer (CO), informing him his son had arrived, and would spend ten weeks learning basic military skills before being transferred to a corps training unit. 'He will be encouraged to write home regularly, to attend Church and to take part in sports,' wrote the CO. 'Should the change from civilian to service life unsettle your son I would be grateful if you could use your influence to help him over the initial period of his training.'[11] It was as if Errol were going away on a school camp.

Two thousand one hundred men who turned twenty in 1965 marched in with the first intake of national servicemen. Trainees from South Australia, Tasmania, Victoria and Western Australia, and some from New South Wales, went to Puckapunyal, an unaccommodating camp ten kilometres west of Seymour, Victoria, freezing in the winter and often unbearably hot during the summer. The remaining men, including virtually all the Queenslanders, trained at 1RTB at Kapooka, NSW, a base which seemed to have been chosen for precisely the same characteristics.

Like infantry battalions, the RTBs were divided into companies, which were separated into platoons. The four companies – A, B, C and D – were known as Alfa, Bravo, Charlie and Delta, after the NATO phonetic alphabet. Errol was in C Company. He always wrote home clearly and honestly, with humour and doubt, his good nature shining through his careful, church-school copperplate and erratic punctuation. He told Loris Noack about his sixteen-hour days, rising at five-thirty a.m. to shower, dress, polish his boots, make his bed and clean his rifle, to be on mess parade an hour later. He spoke of marching parades, rifle drill, bayonet practice, target shooting, cross-country marches and physical training (PT).

'They keep us amused,' he wrote, wryly. 'Thursdays is sports day, and most South Aussies and Vic's play Aussie Rules . . . The only day off is Sunday, but you do not actually get the day off until all your boots, brass, clothes, rifle, kit, webbings etc. is up to scratch. Most of the guys in my platoon are bonzer blokes. The wet canteen (Pub) is an enormous size (colossal) the size of the MAJESTIC Theatre or bigger, and it is packed every night . . . '[12] The Majestic Theatre, a nineteenth-century auditorium on King William Street, Adelaide, was the biggest known venue in Errol's world. Anything larger was simply bigger than the Majestic.

All the recruits in Errol's unit were national servicemen but, after Puckapunyal, they would be integrated into the regular army. In August, Jim Forbes announced that some were 'almost certain' to serve overseas.[13] If the battalion to which they were posted was selected to relieve forces already stationed in Vietnam or Malaysia, national servicemen would go alongside the regulars. This would mark the first time conscripts had been sent out of Australian territory since the Second World War, when a single brigade of the CMF had fought in the Dutch East Indies in 1943–44.

After recruit training, every national serviceman was assigned to a corps. Conscripts could be posted almost anywhere in the army, from a field canteen to a topographical troop, but the largest proportion ended up in Infantry. Errol was assessed by an army psychologist as 'suitable for training to a moderately skilled level in most army postings'.[14] He was sent to Infantry. This meant the Royal Australian Regiment, which had been formed in 1948 as three battalions, and seen service in the occupation of Japan, the Korean War and the Malayan Emergency. A fourth battalion, 4RAR, had been officially raised in 1964, and three more battalions had to be established in 1965 to accommodate the influx of national servicemen and the expansion of Australia's regional commitments: 7RAR was formed in Victoria, 6RAR in Queensland and 5RAR in New South Wales.

Errol marched out of Puckapunyal on 5 September 1965 and was sent to B Company 5RAR for infantry training at Holsworthy camp, which sprawled through woodlands, gullies and creeks about thirty kilometres south-west of Sydney. At Holsworthy, national servicemen and regulars trained together, just as they would remain in mixed units for the rest of their time in the army.

Every soldier in the Australian Army was expected to be able to act as an infantryman and pick up a weapon if the need arose, but in corps training the diggers of the Royal Australian Regiment endlessly drilled to fight. They learned to move as a section within a platoon, a platoon within a company, and a company within the battalion. They sharpened their weapons skills, took on combat roles such as machine gunner or platoon medic, and most pushed their fitness to the limits. By this time, Errol's mate Mattner had been called to report for his national service medical. 'RECRUIT training is hard,' Errol wrote to Mattner, 'if your [sic] not used to rushing around and jumping to every little beck and call. And failure to take notice of any order or command given, results in a fine – quite stiff sometimes, or else several days or a week's C.B. [confined to barracks] They make that tough too.

'But still you might enjoy it,' he added, doubtfully.

'We are just starting to get leave,' he told Mattner. 'When we get it – which is every second weekend and three weeknights we have a ball – hit the town in style. Piss on in glory, as long as we are back for REVAILLE at 6am next morning . . . I've cottoned on to several nice "birds" since leaving Adelaide . . . and one lives here at Bondi, near Sydney (she's keen too). Gambling takes a bit of our dough. TROTS, dogs, races, poker machines etc. any left spent on booze and women.'[15] He wrote again to his aunt and uncle when he returned from an exercise in December: 'It was pure hell! . . . We were flown by Caribou to Singleton, from where we were flown by chopper (HELICOPTER) up into Queensland to the fringe of the jungle. We then penetrated deep into the hot steamy jungle – with everything we had for the month carried on us physically (ie. water, rations, equipment, bedroll, hutchie (tent) (2 man) + machine gun GPMG and 700 rounds of belt ammunition. I am the gunner in my section – so I carry the gun which weighs far more than the SLR rifles and Owen guns.' The infantry tended to pick the biggest men as machine gunners, since they had to haul perhaps twenty-six kilograms of weapon and ammunition in addition to an infantryman's ordinary load.

'We hacked our way through the jungle with machettes [sic],' wrote Errol, 'slow tedious going – up and down steep jungle covered hills. Making our way up non-perennial streams covered in leeches and tick. The leeches made a real mess of our boots and socks, blood everywhere – the tick had to be pulled out with tweezers. The place was lousy with snakes – all varieties . . . Our platoon killed on an average 5 snakes a day while many more were seen. Three chaps in another platoon were bitten by black snakes and the emergency helicopter was called in by our radio signals operator and they were rushed to Singleton Hospital. I think they are all recovering O.K. now.'[16]

Through it all, Errol retained his cheery ambivalence about the army. 'Training is quite tough in many respects here,' he wrote, 'but somehow one can get used to it.' Whenever he wrote to his relatives, he remembered to ask about the rest of the family, the dog and Loris's mother, 'Mrs Boehm', and assured his aunt and uncle he was sending letters to his father, too.

Culturally, the sixties stopped for 5RAR, crawling through the Queensland bush in short-back-and-sides, making camps without women. In the cities, would-be bohemians in duffle coats and goatee beards sipped coffee and shared cigarettes with long-haired girls, growing up another way. In November, eighteen-year-old Normie Rowe became the youngest Australian to win a gold record, when 'Que Sera Sera' with 'Shakin' All Over' sold more than fifty thousand copies. But the Beatles topped the hit parade with 'We Can Work It Out' and 'Day Tripper' on Australia Day, 25 January 1966, when Robert Menzies, the father of the national service scheme, retired as Australia's longest-serving prime minister. In March, his successor, Harold Holt, confirmed for the first time that national servicemen would definitely be sent to fight in South Vietnam.

But Errol Noack had already written home months before to say his commanding officer had told him he would 'probably (quite on the cards) be going to Thailand (Saigon) and later Vietnam'. Errol was not wholly enthusiastic. 'There is of course no hope in the world of getting out of it,' he wrote to Herb. 'Wherever my unit goes – I go too. Besides I have never been to Saigon, Vietnam or Thailand so it will be something new . . . '[17]

Errol seemed to believe Saigon was a country of its own and also a place in Thailand.

2

THE FRIENDS OF ERROL NOACK

'I hadn't thought of Saigon as another country,' said Grant Collins. 'I didn't even know that fucking Saigon was there.' Collins was born in Adelaide on 23 May 1945, another of the dates pulled out of the Tattersall's barrel in March 1965. His father had been a flight sergeant in the Royal Air Force in England in the Second World War, and his mother a member of the Women's Royal Air Force. In Australia they moved up to the country and took over the Imperial Hotel in Terowie, SA, the last station on the broad-gauge railway line from Adelaide and the first stop on the narrow-gauge track northbound. Collins' father walked out when his son was seven years old, and the boy never saw him again. His mother stayed in town but couldn't keep the pub.

Collins left home at fourteen, and found a job pre-testing television sets in Adelaide. He joined the judo club at St Clair Youth Centre in Woodville, and eventually finished runner-up in the state judo championships. When Collins was called up, he weighed seventy-six kilos. He was 183 centimetres tall and extremely fit. He thought the army would offer him an adventure. He imagined he'd travel and see a bit of Australia.

Collins did his recruit training at Puckapunyal. Like Noack, he was easy around machinery. He understood the way weapons worked, and could dismantle and reassemble them easily. He felt the instructors initially disdained the national servicemen, whom the camp CO had declared would not be referred to as 'conscripts' or 'nashos' by his staff.[1] 'They weren't really allowed to swear at us,' said Collins, 'so they'd yell out, "Cons, get your arms up or you'll be sexually intercoursed!" There was a perception that, because we weren't people who had volunteered to go in, we were probably sissies, mummy's boys.'

The national servicemen didn't share the regulars' ingrained deference to rank. In bayonet practice, 'I disarmed our section 2IC with a typical judo throw,' said Collins. 'He was putting all his weight on his front foot. If he'd've charged somebody who was really skilled at martial arts, he was gonna be up shit creek. He found that out, but he landed on a rock on his back, so we didn't see him again.'

The first intake's basic training was almost a public performance. 'Right from day one, the press would come in and see us eating breakfast,' said Collins. 'Well, obviously the breakfast was specially put on for that press thing to happen.' If anyone from the outside was watching the trainees, 'We were suddenly treated as if we were human,' he said, 'and that's definitely not recruit training.

'Journalists were our biggest enemy in the early stages. We probably said too much, and didn't think about what we were saying . . . The media seemed to pick up on the tiniest little things, and didn't seem to realise that would reflect on the soldier. One of our people said something about the food, then the army put an investigation into it. These comments were very, very sensitive. It was almost like we were behind the Iron Curtain.'

At the end of recruit training, Collins applied to be posted to the Royal Australian Corps of Signals, because he had worked with electronics, and the Royal Australian Electrical and Mechanical Engineers (RAEME) since he had also been a motor mechanic. 'But it didn't really matter,' he said. 'Really the choices were Infantry, Infantry, Infantry.'

Collins drew Infantry, and was offered the option of going to 2RAR in Enoggera, Queensland, or 5RAR at Holsworthy. 'So I went to Queensland,' he said, 'because I thought, I've never been to Queensland. It wasn't Enoggera: I didn't even know that existed.'

At Enoggera, his training followed the same direction as Errol Noack's. He was selected as a machine gunner on the basis of his size and strength. The divide between national servicemen and regulars became blurred during corps training, said Collins. 'We'd already had the stuffing knocked out of us, so we were starting to look a bit like military. I think the thing that swung it over very quick with the regular army, though, was that many of us had aptitudes way above theirs for certain things. Where they'd probably spent weeks learning, we'd pick it up in a day. I also think there became more of a mutual respect in corps training, because we could start to see skills that they had, whereas recruit training is not really skills, it's just scream at one another and see who wins.

'We knew who the nashos and regs were,' said Collins. 'You hung out in groups. Regular soldiers had their regular lifestyle and, at twenty, there wasn't a huge number of nashos that were real pissheads, but there were a lot of regular soldiers that were. By the end of orders of a night, they were at the canteen. The rest of us went on leave or would do whatever we were gonna do, but we didn't just go to the boozer.'

After Christmas, Collins was transferred to Holsworthy, to join B Company 5RAR as a replacement. He was posted as the gunner of a two-man machine-gun team. Noack was his number two, who had to carry the spare barrels and ammunition and take over if Collins was hurt.

Collins and Noack shared a tent. 'He was very straight,' said Collins, 'had a good sense of humour, and we called him Flex, for when the bodybuilders used to flex and show their muscles. He started off very embarrassed about it, but after that, if you said, "Give us a flex," he sort of cut the arm up. He was a character, a very complex person. He had a whole lot of facets about him. He could be anything he wanted to be.'

Noack had once modelled clothes for the Myer department store, and was worried at first the other men would find out, because that 'kind of meant you were some sort of poof', said Collins, 'and he definitely wasn't that'. Noack told Collins his mother had died when he was very young, 'and everything was always about the aunts, the uncle and Walter'.

The men of 5RAR knew they were bound for war when they were sent on a Battle Efficiency Course at the Jungle Training Centre in Canungra, Queensland. Almost every recruit going to Vietnam, from cooks to engineers, had to pass a similar course. Collins and Noack were fitter than most soldiers, usually finishing first and second on forced marches and distance runs. The circuits of the parade ground handed out as penalties by the Physical Training Instructors (PTIs) had always been meaningless to them. In March, the two men were separated when Noack flew to Western Australia to try out for the SAS, an elite regiment based in Swanbourne, on the beach to the west of Perth. He roomed with three other men who hoped to get into the regiment, including Ron Canlan, a regular army cook. 'Anything to do with the unarmed combat, the physical side of it, he was one of the top ones,' said Canlan. 'I was always running second-last or last. I was one of the worst.

'They had a buddy system,' said Canlan. If a soldier received a punishment, his 'buddy' had to do half of it for him. Noack was 'giving one of the instructors a bit of back-chat', said Canlan, 'and the instructor said, "Right, you can do forty push-ups." I was his buddy, and the instructor said, "No, you don't have to do them, he can do them." So he made him do the forty push-ups, and the instructor said, "What've you got to say now, Private Noack?" and Flex said, "Could've done a hundred." So the instructor said, "Righto, smartie. Down and do another hundred." [Errol] did the hundred, then the instructor said, "What've you got to say now, Private Noack?" He said, "I could've done a hundred one-handed." So Flex got down and did them, no problem at all. He was the perfect physical specimen. If you were having a poster of a soldier you'd want in the army, Flex would be it.'

Noack was by now leaner and harder, his hair shorter, his appetites bigger. And he was tearing through life, as if he knew it might be running out. 'He was the party boy,' said Canlan. 'He liked hitting the Savoy Hotel in Perth. Every morning we used to have to go and do a ten-mile run before breakfast, and I'd know Flex to come in at three or four o'clock in the morning, and we'd have to go out at half-past five or six o'clock, and he'd gone out and done the run, and beat all of us in by about half a mile.'

Noack failed the SAS 'cadre'. His instructors reported he 'appeared to lack enthusiasm and application throughout the course' and 'did not measure up to the standards of self discipline' required by the unit.[2] When he returned to 5RAR, Noack was no longer Collins' number two on the machine gun, but the pair remained close friends.

Neither Collins nor Noack fully understood Australia's war aims in Vietnam. 'One side of us was saying, "This is doing the right thing, because it's our country,"' said Collins. 'On the other hand, shit, you could get hurt and – more importantly – we could never get a straight answer out of anybody on what we were going to do when we got there. What was the objective? It's like they didn't know. Then they said it was only gonna be a police action anyway, and I thought we were gonna be like coppers.'

Errol wrote to tell Loris he would be leaving for Vietnam in May 1966. For his pre-embarkation leave, he made his way to Port Lincoln to stay with his father in the caravan. It was a cold morning on their last day at Kirton Point, but Walter and Errol Noack took a swim together before they drove to Adelaide. Errol's twenty-first birthday had passed forgotten while he was on the SAS cadre course, so Herb and Loris held a small party for him at their home. The only other guest was Walter. That same month, troops under twenty-one years old serving in war zones overseas were given the right to vote in Australian elections.

On his last day of leave, Errol presented himself for Holy Communion. He read from his grandfather's Bible the family devotion,

John 16:22, 'Ye now therefore have sorrow, but I will see you again and your heart shall rejoice.' That night, Walter and Errol drove to West Beach Airport, and Errol boarded the plane back to Sydney. He flew out to Saigon at midnight on Friday, 13 May, to become part of the first Australian battalion to include national servicemen in Vietnam. A week later, he wrote his first letter home to Loris, apologising for the writing and grammar 'as we have had quite a few beers since arriving back from patrol'.

'It's really not so bad after all,' he wrote, echoing his equivocal assessment of every military situation. B Company had been sent first to the port of Vung Tau, a faded French beach resort to the south-east of Saigon. 'At the moment, we are in what is regarded as a rest area but still carry loaded rifles everywhere we go. We are living in tents on the beach with barbed-wire entanglements everywhere – constant guard post and piquets are manned 24 hours a day . . . We will be moving inland to search and destroy Viet Cong strongholds within the next nine days.' Characteristically stoic and mildly unimpressed, he wrote, 'Oh well! Less than a year to go now.'[3]

Errol was concerned about a suitcase he had left at Adelaide Railway Station. He said it contained 'some clothes, shoes etc.' and asked Herb to pick it up as 'I may have need of some of those when I come home'. He signed off with 'lots of love' and six kisses. 'The last said,' he wrote, 'includes Uncle, Mrs Boehm and yourself.'[4]

When Loris Noack received the letter, on 2 June 1966, Errol had been dead for nine days.

3

THE BODY OF ERROL NOACK

Grant Collins had his twenty-first birthday in Vung Tau on 23 May 1966. He and Errol Noack talked about taking a swim in the South China Sea, which broke on the sand below the dunes, where the Australians had raised their tents like beach campers in the hot breeze. Early the next day, A and B companies of 5RAR were choppered north of Vung Tau to Nui Dat in Phuoc Tuy province, to begin to secure the rubber plantations and scrub around the hill the Australian Task Force had chosen for its base. Up until then, 1RAR, the sole Australian infantry battalion in the country, had continued to operate from the US base at Bien Hoa.

It was a vague, gloomy morning, as the men moved from a rubber plantation through bananas and into the scrub. The heat of the monsoon season left them saturated in their uniforms. B Company's Intelligence officer, Major Robert O'Neill, said the regulars were worried about the way the national servicemen would perform under fire, concerned that 'a group of newcomers might not be able to stand the pace'.[1]

A Company set off first from the helicopter landing zone, frightened and alert, patrolling in truly hostile country for the first time. With the plantations behind them, the country in their arc of vision all looked the same. They were searching for signs of an enemy they had never seen, pictured in the pocketbook issued to each man as cartoon Orientals in black pyjamas and conical hats, and painted in training as cruel little terrorists, castrators and beheaders, bus-bombers and man-trappers, with their punji pits and mines.

The Australians padded through the long grass like millipedes, treading softly with hundreds of pairs of feet. They snaked in platoons of about twenty-eight men, with a forward scout at the head, manoeuvring in sections of eight, each led by a corporal. The platoon itself was commanded by a lieutenant, with a sergeant – always a regular soldier – as his 2IC (second-in-command), and a medic and a signaller travelling with them. It was 5RAR's first real operation, in country largely outside government control and barely known even to the Australians who'd been in Bien Hoa.

The newcomers quickly became disorientated, confused and extremely hot. Unsure exactly what they were looking for, they turned back on themselves to make certain they hadn't missed it. They spotted what they thought were guerrillas and fired, but lost sight of them in the bush. Although A Company had been the first to land, B Company eventually passed them, as A Company tried to follow the footsteps of the VC. At five p.m., the gathering dusk meant they had to stop and 'harbour up' for the night.

Both companies took up positions and set up radio contact. B Company's commander, Major Bruce McQualter, sent a party, including Noack, to collect water from a creek when suddenly, said Collins, 'Firing seemed to come from everywhere. We gave covering fire over the top of our people. Unfortunately, we were firing across a creek, so the people embedded in the creek and people further along the creek could still fire at one another.'[2] Noack rose and was shot down. 'I saw him get up to change position,' said Collins. 'You don't know why he was getting up. It was our first contact. We were really shitting ourselves.'

Tony White, 5RAR's doctor, was camped only a kilometre away but, he wrote, 'It was now dark and too risky to organise an escort for me to go over to B Company's position.'[3] Medic Ron Nichols had given him some morphine, wrote O'Neill, 'but he was still in pain and complained of lack of feeling in his legs. Bruce spent several minutes talking with Noack and giving him what comfort he could'.[4]

'I did the wrong thing,' said Collins. 'I broke ranks after they got him from the creek back up to dry land, and the shooting had stopped. I went off to talk to him and, of course, I got my arm chewed off about that. For a start, a machine gunner doesn't leave his gun. But he had a hole in the side of his stomach that you could've put your little finger in, and I thought, Well, fuck it, he's gonna go home. He's right. But he was complaining, because the round had gone around and around and cut up his stomach.

'Noack had a single nine-mil bullet in his side,' said Collins, 'and, of course, he looked fine. He had a tiny bit of blood coming out.' A landing zone had to be cut for the helicopter and 'he was carried out in less time than it would have taken me to get there', wrote White.[5]

The bullet that hit Noack had 'churned around his insides and cut up his liver'.[6] On the outside, he was barely damaged. 'All of his vital organs were stuffed,' said Collins. 'But he was alive when we put him on the dustoff, and I had just basically put it out of my mind that he was in any trouble.' But Noack died soon after admission to the US 36th Evacuation Hospital in Vung Tau, his life seeping out through a single bullet hole. 'The word quickly passed from digger to digger,' wrote White, 'out to the farthest sentry. It had a crushing effect on all. Our day had begun with elation as we set forth on our great adventure. It ended in shock and dismay.'[7]

'For a fellow that big to die from what appeared to be almost nothing, like walking into a stick, it just devastated us,' said Collins. Thirty-six regular soldiers had died in Vietnam since 1963, but Noack was the first national serviceman to be killed in action. He'd been in country for ten days and 'his combat time was really four hours', said Collins. At first, it was hard for the men to grasp what had happened. An invisible enemy had inflicted a single casualty from an unknown position, then disappeared. 'The belief was at the time that the Viet Cong came through the creek,' said Collins, 'and got between B Company and A Company, opened fire on our water party, realised there was a much bigger force there than just those people, and pissed off.'

But the company commanders quickly understood the situation. The first man killed in B Company had been cut down by A Company. Noack was a victim of friendly fire. This was not the version that reached the Australian public. The reporting of Noack's death was confused by the army's initial refusal to confirm or deny what had occurred. The Task Force commander, Brigadier Oliver Jackson, initially assured Canberra that Noack had been killed by the VC, and the Adelaide *Advertiser* duly offered a jumbled account of the day's action: 'B Company reported contact with a number of Viet Cong early on Tuesday evening. The guerrillas broke contact after a 20-minute fight. Trapped, the Viet Cong began firing in both directions, and it was during this fight that Pte Noack was hit from extremely close range by automatic rifle fire.'[8]

The true story did not publicly emerge until long after the end of the war.

Walter Noack was at work at SAFCOL when he received a cable from the minister for the army, Malcolm Fraser, delivered by an army captain accompanied by a Lutheran minister and a policeman. 'It is with deep regret that I have learned that your son 4717546 Private Errol Wayne Noack has died of wounds received in action on 24 May in Vietnam.'[9] Walter had lost his housemate, his workmate, his best friend, the son who lent him money to back horses and shared a bottle of West End with him at the end of the day. In place of Errol, he was given letters and telegrams, scraps of paper, unevenly typed. Fraser's memoirs made clear he 'does not weep over Vietnam', but Harold Holt's biographer heard Holt was 'in tears when informed of Noack's death'.[11] Holt 'hated the idea of conscription', wrote Fraser – although there seems evidence to the contrary. 'He just believed it was necessary and I think he really worried about sending conscripts into war.' Fraser never did. 'I thought it was the only solution,' he wrote. 'The decision had to be made and therefore the decision was made, and there is not a great deal of purpose lying awake about it at night.'[11]

Holt immediately issued a statement offering his 'personal sympathy' to the Noack family.[12] Even General Westmoreland, head of the US Military Assistance Command Vietnam, communicated to Walter his 'feeling of close personal loss'. He wrote, 'I know it must be especially difficult for you because of the fact your son was serving so far from home and family . . . You may rest assured that all of us will continue do our utmost to bring eventual victory so your son's sacrifice will not have been in vain.'[13]

Herb told journalists Errol had been like a son to him. He said, 'I know we should be prepared to defend Australia, but I'm very much against the idea of a lottery being used to pick those who have to defend us. When a man's life is at stake, it doesn't seem quite fair.' But Errol had died in Vietnam for the good of his country. 'None of us is happy about it,' said Herb. 'Nobody could be. But I don't want any attack on Government policy to be made out of this. It wouldn't be right, using the boy's life for propaganda.'[14]

Herb's wishes were ignored, and Labor Party leader Arthur Calwell said Errol's death 'need never have happened. Every member of the Liberal and Country Parties and every member of the DLP who voted for or supports the Government's conscription policy must share the terrible responsibility for sending voteless 20-year-old youths into action . . . The Opposition calls on the Australian Government to urge our American Allies to halt this useless, senseless, lunatic war.'[15]

The Australian Students' Labor Federation was in conference in Adelaide, and a short time after the announcement of Noack's death, students began to gather around the National War Memorial on North

Terrace. 'Bareheaded in drizzling rain', they milled beneath marble reliefs of the Spirit of Duty calling the youth of South Australia to war, and the Spirit of Compassion holding a dead soldier to her breast. Later in the evening, they held placards reading 'Who Killed Noack?' and 'Fight For Holt and Be An Angel'.[16]

The Cross of Sacrifice in Pennington Gardens – originally a women's war memorial – was daubed with the words:

Errol Wayne Noack
aged 21
His was not to reason why

The police pointed out this was a contravention of section 113c of the Criminal Law Consolidation Act, under which offenders 'may be whipped'.[17] The Youth Campaign Against Conscription held a small vigil outside the prime minister's home in Melbourne, but Holt was away in Canberra. 'Passing motorists sounded their horns,' noted the Adelaide *Advertiser*. 'Some called out rude remarks.'[18]

When Walter arrived in Adelaide to receive Errol's body, he said, 'It's all like a rotten dream. I keep thinking that I'm going to wake up from it. Only a couple of weeks ago I shook hands with him at Adelaide Airport. I can still feel it.' He had not slept since he had received Fraser's telegram, which he carried crumpled in his pocket. 'I don't know how long it takes to sleep again after something like this,' he said.[19]

Twenty-eight white-sashed women from the anti-conscriptionist Save Our Sons movement stood vigil for Noack with their heads bowed outside Melbourne Town Hall, and later handed out flyers for a protest rally. 'A young man burned one of the leaflets,' reported the Melbourne *Sun*. 'But a National Serviceman bought a bunch of chrysanthemums at a nearby stall and gave it to Mrs Jean McLean, of Beaumaris, Victorian secretary of the movement.'[20]

While they may have been saddened by Noack's death, most

Australians were unshaken. Less than a week after Noack died, a Gallup poll showed opposition to sending conscripts to Vietnam had actually declined by 8 per cent since February. The third most cited reason for supporting national service for young men was that 'discipline does them good'.

The media found Errol's mother, Dorothy Carpenter, living on a dairy farm in Burra in the Mount Lofty Ranges. 'His father had custody and would not let me see him,' she said. She had only learned from a friend that he was going to Vietnam and had first heard of his death on the Channel Nine News. 'I'm against this conscription of lads for Vietnam from here,' she said. 'My view is that if we were at a state of declared war they would not have to conscript men. They would go voluntarily to defend the country.'[21]

Errol came back to Walter, drained of blood, rigid and cold, and Walter visited his son's body at the funeral parlour several times as he lay waiting for the grave. 'Errol looked as though he was just sleeping,' he wrote, 'with all his natural colour . . . The American specialists embalmed Errol using a new process. Soon as Errol died they pumped a special liquid into his veins, and they say that in 25 years Errol will be the same as when he died.'[22]

A grieving Perth shop assistant named Sandra Harrison was desperate to come to the burial. 'I expected a wedding when Errol came home,' she said, 'not a funeral.' But she felt she 'couldn't just barge in on the mourning party', so she approached the army's Western Command for help. According to a jaunty newspaper piece published on 30 May, 'An Army despatch was flashed from Perth to Adelaide . . . and now Sandra has been allocated a special place with the family party.'

Harrison said this was 'very kind of the Army',[23] and the story was a rare piece of good publicity in the wake of Errol's death. However, when Walter saw the news, he contacted the army to say the family didn't want Harrison to come as she 'would prove an embarrassment both to them and herself', and 'another girl who had been friendly' with Errol in Adelaide would be there.

The small kindness threatened to become a greater injury, and the military panicked. According to army files, a Staff Captain Gent 'went to Perth Airport after unsuccessful attempts to find the girl at home and in the City. The girl was already at the ticket counter accompanied by her parent. Mr. Gent spoke to the father, then Miss Harrison, and persuaded them it would not be wise for her to attend the funeral. The airline ticket was cancelled, and the Harrison family went home.'[24]

The truth behind the story was never reported.

No bells rang to call the bereaved to Errol's funeral. The spire of the bluestone Bethlehem Lutheran Church on Flinders Street, Adelaide, reached thirty-seven metres into the sky, but its belfry was empty. A set of three church bells had been sent over to the German-speaking congregation by the Kaiser in 1879. The bells landed in Sydney, but were stolen before they reached South Australia, leaving the Lutherans of Adelaide with a silent tower.

Errol Noack's coffin, draped in an Australian flag, was carried into the church at twelve-thirty p.m. on 1 June 1966. The church doors were opened at one forty-five p.m., by which time the crowd outside had grown almost one thousand strong. Film of the funeral showed grim-faced and pale elderly mourners in heavy coats, tearless in their grief. Errol's slouch hat and bayonet were laid across the lid of his casket, which was flanked by an army catafalque party. Pastor Fischer, who had known the boy well, reprised the verse Errol had read to his family the night he'd left Adelaide: 'I will see you again and your heart shall rejoice.' The coffin was mounted on a gun carriage and escorted in slow procession to Derrick Gardens, the services section of Centennial Park Cemetery, by two army motorcyclists, twenty-four soldiers and the Southern Command Band, playing muffled drums.

Errol's slouch hat and bayonet were replaced by a wreath before the casket was lowered into the ground, and a firing party from 3RAR let loose a three-volley salute for the only child of Walter Noack, who died on 24 May 1966 because he was born on 28 March 1945.

On the day after Errol was buried, Loris and Herb Noack received the letter from their nephew, asking them to pick up his suitcase from Adelaide Railway Station.

4

THE REALITY OF NATIONAL SERVICE

The army had opposed the reintroduction of national service from the start. The fifties program had been a disaster and, although the army was finding it difficult to recruit in a time of full employment, its greatest shortages were of tradesmen, non-commissioned officers (NCOs) and junior officers, not the ragtag selection of unskilled, semi-trained men it had come to expect from national service. Instead of immediately introducing conscription in 1964, the government raised army pay by 30 per cent, improved service conditions, and all but doubled its recruiting budget. Soldiers' income, however, still 'fell short of comparable civilian earnings',[1] and there were no opportunities for the manual workers' traditional supplement of overtime. On 1 August, the minister for the army, Jim Forbes, who had won a Military Cross in the Second World War, said the government accepted the unanimous advice of its military advisers that national service should not be introduced. By late September, the US was creeping closer to a deeper involvement in Vietnam, and Indonesian troops had landed in peninsular Malaysia, but it was again indicated that the government 'would certainly not agree to a return to a full-scale national service scheme'.[2] But the improvements to pay and conditions had not immediately brought the army close to its recruiting target, and there was public talk of a limited national training scheme involving a few thousand men a year.

In October, the *Sydney Morning Herald*, while acknowledging the army had a shortfall in recruits, said the government hadn't 'made any serious effort' to find volunteers: 'The tempo and organisation of recruiting remain unaltered. It is still a part-time job for the Commonwealth Loans organisation; no one of national stature has been appointed to run a recruiting campaign; there has been no appeal from the Prime Minister for young men to join the Army.'[3]

The minister for defence, Shane Paltridge, who had served with the 2nd AIF in South-East Asia, reported to cabinet recommending against the immediate introduction of national service. 'It is too early for the effects of the recently approved conditions of service to be fully seen,' he wrote. 'The next 6 months are the most favourable for recruiting and should be exploited to the maximum extent. By intensive measures being planned . . . recruiting forecasts might well be considerably improved.' But he conceded, 'It is unlikely that the improvement would be sufficient to enable Army objectives to be completely achieved.'[4] Paltridge's thinking was informed by his 'Services' Manpower Review' commissioned in September, which found, 'The months January–April are the best for recruiting, with an upward trend in November, and it is in the early months of the New Year that the real effect of the recent decisions will require to be felt. Accordingly this is the appropriate time for a recruiting drive, with the advertising build-up commencing in November.'[5]

The review suggested recruiting tours, displays and bands, government statements, an increase in the number of apprentices trained, and other measures such as lowering the army's minimum entry age and selectively raising the retirement age. It was remembered that from October 1950, with a highly intensive recruitment campaign – conducted against the background of a warning by Menzies of the need to prepare for war within three years and an actual war being fought in Korea – total enlistments reached more than ten thousand in the first twelve months and thirteen thousand the following year. This was compared with about seven thousand five hundred enlistments in the year 1963–64, when there was neither campaign nor warning of war but the manpower goal was more than one-third greater. Paltridge believed national service 'should be introduced only as a last resort, and a final intensive effort should be made to build up Army strengths by voluntary recruiting'. He felt the government should begin to plan carefully for the implementation of the scheme, and make clear its intention to introduce conscription – with the liability for overseas service – in the event of a future 'defence emergency', or even a situation that fell short of a defence emergency, if voluntary recruitment didn't work.[6]

Menzies' minister for air, Peter Howson, kept a diary throughout his career in government. Howson, who was Mentioned in Dispatches as a Royal Navy pilot during the Second World War, felt his government had no legitimate military reason to impose conscription in 1964. On 4 November, he wrote in his diaries it was 'obvious that PM and Harold Holt want national service training and were going to move in that direction . . . PM skilfully reassessed the strategic basis to accord with the need for national service. Harold stated that SE Asia might fall within a few months, and that New Guinea might be attacked. Therefore we needed a large army. For the rest of the day and night he carried on, using this premise. It is a false argument. But the PM chiefly for political reasons (to win the Senate especially in NSW) wants National Service. Then he twists the military need to accord with the political need.'[7]

The chief of the general staff, Lieutenant General Sir John Wilton, was virtually forced by cabinet to support the decision to reintroduce national service and 'only came to accept its inevitability with extreme reluctance'.[8] Wilton's capitulation was expressed in a 'Statement of Military View' which was, in fact, partly drafted by the cabinet secretary Sir John Bunting. This, along with the manpower review, was presented to Menzies' cabinet, which promptly concluded 'on the basis of the professional military advice provided and for more effective national defence having regard to the current strategic appreciation, to take steps to introduce a compulsory selective national service scheme'.[9]

'The decision was not based on military advice in the sense in which that term was generally used,' said the head of the Australian War Memorial's Official History Unit, Dr Peter Edwards.[10] The cabinet had more or less consulted itself on its own inclinations and decided it had been right all along. 'It is a terribly bad decision,' wrote Howson in his diary, 'but there was no point in trying to stem the tide.'[11]

In November, only fifteen days after Forbes had last publicly rejected the idea, the minister for labour and national service, William 'Billy' McMahon, said, 'In the changed circumstances announced by the prime minister . . . selective National Service training has become inescapable.' The new conditions included 'aggressive Communism' in the region, and 'recent Indonesian policies and actions'.[12] Politically, it was an astute move. An opinion poll found 71 per cent of Australians were in favour of conscription, and, *The Age* reported, Liberal Party strategists believed the national service scheme would 'define defence as the main issue in the coming Senate election . . . answer all of the Labor party's criticisms of the Government's defence preparations and at the same time provoke dissension within the Labor party over the conscription of men for overseas service'.[13]

The idea that Australians should be conscripted into the services and compelled to fight in foreign lands had been defeated twice in referenda during the First World War. In October 1916, 51 per cent of Australians voted against the proposal, in a defeat for the government which led the Labor prime minister Billy Hughes to split the party and enter a coalition with the Liberals rather than govern with his own anti-conscriptionist comrades. In December 1917, after Hughes and his supporters had merged with the Liberal Party to form the Nationalist Party of Australia, a more limited proposal (under which men were to be selected for service by ballot) was rejected by almost 54 per cent of voters. In the Second World War, another Labor prime minister, John Curtin, slipped in conscription by first requiring every eligible male to join the CMF, and then expanding the area in which the CMF could serve from Australia to most of the South West Pacific.

The Menzies government's 1964 national service scheme differed from anything which had existed in Australia. Its initial aim was to quickly raise the strength of the army from 22500 to 37500 troops, by calling up 4200 youths in the last half of 1965, and 6900 every subsequent year (although from 1966, the number of conscripts was raised to 8400 a year, increasing the army's size to 40 000). All male British (that is, Australian) citizens had to register for national service when they turned twenty years old. Recruits would first be chosen by ballot, before further selection through medical examination, intelligence testing and security vetting. The men who passed faced a commitment of five years' service – two of them full-time and three in a reserve capacity (although the reserve training requirement was never activated). Those in full-time study or working to complete an apprenticeship could defer their entry into the army until they'd completed their qualification. Cases of exceptional hardship could also apply for deferral but, like students and apprentices, they remained liable for call-up until the age of twenty-six, or in some cases, such as men completing medical or law degrees with a further professional training requirement, the age of thirty.

Diplomats, Aborigines 'except any class prescribed by regulations', and members of the Permanent Forces were exempt. Resident 'aliens' – that is, unnaturalised immigrants – were not, at first, required to register. 'There would be little virtue and much administrative effort would be involved for no good reason if action to call them up was not intended,' wrote the secretary of the DLNS, Henry Bland. 'We could expect, from earlier experience, strong diplomatic protests if we even registered.' Besides, 'Some of those 20 year olds who are aliens would not be attractive recruits from the Army viewpoint. Language difficulties and security considerations are relevant factors.'[1] But there were no occupational exemptions for Australian citizens, no way out for men in primary industries, no resort to 'war work' as an alternative to taking up arms. Only ministers of religion and theological students were automatically excused – along with the mentally and physically disabled, and proclaimed conscientious objectors who could satisfy the courts their convictions were genuinely held (although objectors might be expected to perform non-combatant duties).

Aliens, nineteen-year-olds and men whose birthdates were not drawn in the ballots could voluntarily register for national service – and consistently, through the life of the scheme, more men voluntarily registered than ever sought to become conscientious objectors. Each year there would be two registrations, and four intakes to the army. Men who failed to register were liable to be fined $100. Men who were out of the country on the date their age group was expected to register had to register upon their return, and go into a later ballot. All national servicemen would be required to serve overseas if necessary.

Men who married before their ballot – that is, before they knew if they had been called up – would be deferred indefinitely which, practically speaking, meant they were exempt. But, after an early loophole was closed, men who married after their birthdate had been drawn would have to see out their service. Similarly, men who joined the CMF in advance of the draw were, subject to conditions, relieved of their national service obligations, but nobody could join the CMF after they'd been called up and expect to stay out of the regular army.

The government maintained that high levels of voluntary enlistment in the CMF remained essential. It hoped the CMF option would encourage this and stressed 'there should be no suggestion that young men joining the CMF in this way are "draft dodgers"'.[15] But ordinary CMF soldiers never had to go to Vietnam, and efficient CMF service was the only way – short of joining the priesthood or rabbinate – a single man could ensure he wasn't sent overseas to fight. This meant the CMF evolved from being an organisation for the citizens who were most interested in joining the military into a larger body including those who were least enthusiastic about the idea.

Since the national servicemen couldn't initially be expected to train each other, regular soldiers had to be posted to the RTBs and to training jobs within battalions and at the various specialist army schools. The need to employ regulars to make soldiers out of national servicemen meant that men who had volunteered to fight wars were instead engaged in drilling conscripts who may have held quite different hopes for their lives.

In compensation, the army won a huge public works program worth £23 million, the biggest ever undertaken for the military. Forbes said it was needed because of the introduction of national service training, and £19 million would provide barracks and camps for units to which national servicemen would be posted. Money would be required to build a new officer-cadet training unit, increased accommodation at Kapooka, new barracks at Puckapunyal and a third recruit training battalion in Singleton, NSW.

Half a century later, Forbes remembered national service was 'very good for the army. Its pre-war barracks had not been maintained or improved since the Second World War because of various economic restraints. Now, the army realised that the government was edgy enough about introducing national service without the added risk of facing accusations that the conscripted soldiers were being put into inferior accommodation. Treasury resistance was brushed aside and substantial building programs took place.'[16]

The government tried to provide for the national serviceman too. If he had a permanent job, his employer was obliged to take him back after he had finished in the army. If his skills required supplementing, he was entitled to a year's free training or education, including a living allowance for full-time students. He was eligible for low-interest business loans and, more importantly, if he served overseas in certain circumstances, a war-service home loan – and, for some young men, this was to prove incentive enough to go to war.

The national service scheme was ushered in hurriedly and with little preparation. Registration opened on 25 January 1965 and continued until 8 February. All those who complied were given a certificate of registration, which their employers could ask to see, since it was an offence to employ men who had failed to register. 'The registration went remarkably smoothly,' wrote Henry Bland to the prime minister's private secretary. 'In fact, a much higher percentage of our estimated number of registrants had registered on 8th February than was our experience under the earlier Scheme.'[17]

A total of 40989 men registered, and only about one hundred cases of default were initially detected. Of those registered, 21777 men were balloted in. They were examined by 681 medical boards, including 586 medical practitioners, in all parts of Australia, mostly in the evenings. The doctors were to screen out those suffering from problems including poor hearing or vision, heart conditions, asthma, severe hayfever, pulmonary tuberculosis, congenital diseases, ulcers, chronic diarrhoea, diabetes, gout, dizzy turns, severe migraines, motion sickness and homosexuality.[18] Each doctor was issued with a booklet specifying that only men who could carry out all kinds of field duties, with weapons, in all climates and conditions, should be passed as fit, and the army could not 'undertake to correct, through training, any medical, nervous or mental disabilities that a recruit might show'.[19]

A recruit had to be at least five foot two, have the mental and emotional fortitude to live away from home, stand up to stress and fear, get along with other people and learn at an average rate. And so disappeared, as far as they could be detected, the most extreme eccentrics and oddballs, the most socially awkward and emotionally immature – along with the illiterate, men with learning difficulties, and anybody prepared to admit he was gay.

All the men called in for medical examination were also interviewed by DLNS officers to assist in determining their suitability to various army postings, to identify – by their education – those fit for officer training, and to screen out those who might not make satisfactory soldiers. Some were given a series of psychological tests. Of the 969 passed medically fit who were psychologically tested, the DLNS reported, 218 immediately failed. The results of all the examinations, tests and interviews were shared with the army.

It was a vast, complex and expensive national project, and it remains unclear why national service had to be implemented so urgently in November 1964. In a later essay, Menzies wrote, 'American conscripts were engaged in South Vietnam and, therefore, in the long view, in the defence of Australia. Great Britain then had national service, which provided many of her troops in Malaya. How could we possibly take up the attitude that whereas conscription for military service might be all right for our allies and protectors, it was no good for us, for local political reasons.'[20] But the call-up had officially ended in Britain on 31 December 1960, and the last national serviceman in the British army had been demobbed on 16 May 1963 – and conscription was very good for the government, for 'local political reasons'.

Menzies disdained to explain himself further and, in his later years, seemed to regard questions as impertinent. His government tended to present its decisions as consequences. It reacted in a rational manner to perverse and often incomprehensible provocations. The mechanics of the process were simply that the government did what needed to be done in the light of the circumstances. But on 2 June 1965, the Save Our Sons movement had presented an 1100-signature petition to Menzies' office, asking the prime minister to assure them that if any young man called up for national service 'should object to military service, they will have the right to refuse to serve for private and personal reasons.

'According to your own statement you exercised this right yourself in 1916. Do you deny it to our sons?'[21]

5

THE MYTHS AND MEANING OF NATIONAL SERVICE

Feathers are to a bird, as fur is to what?
(1) A coat, (2) a swan, (3) a rabbit, (4) a glove, (5) an ostrich.
Which word means the opposite of pretty?
(1) good, (2) ugly, (3) bad, (4) crooked, (5) nice.[1]

In 1963, 11079 men had applied to join the army and only 2839 were accepted. Of the remainder, 1417 were rejected for their low educational standard. Many could not pass an intelligence test which included the two questions above. Recruits were expected to have a mental age of twelve and a reading age of ten. It wasn't the quantity of potential soldiers that bedevilled the army, it was their quality.

An old optimism that the army would provide a kind of finishing school for the less mentally able had years ago proved unfounded. Although the military could carry dullards in the fifties scheme, they had little value as soldiers. A government document prepared in 1964 said studies had shown 'a recruit with a mental age of less than 11 years and 9 months is unable to learn basic military skills or to adjust to the Army environment. Illiterate or near-illiterate recruits, particularly those with a below-average intelligence, have extreme difficulty in absorbing instruction.' Even the lowest level of acceptable recruit posed problems. They often couldn't do their job, they tended not to stay in the services and, given the choice, the army would have turned them away. 'The absorptive capacity of the Army for minimal-standard recruits is limited,' said the paper. 'Almost two-thirds of an educationally-backward group will make no improvement under further educational instruction.'[2]

By September 1965, only 133 men had registered as conscientious objectors, while 657 had volunteered for national service irrespective of whether their birthdate was drawn. However, a number of these volunteers ended up among the 4421 men rejected by the army from the first batch balloted in. As soon as it became known that large numbers of young men failed to meet the army's entry requirements, the press began to wonder if the army was being too choosy or a generation had grown up sickly and weak. There was little public understanding that the scheme was searching for the fittest and brightest, and there was an underlying idea that the army should take what it was given and mould it into something better – a promise many believed to be at the heart of national service.

But the scheme was never going to pull men from the bottom of the heap. It wasn't designed to help the hopeless or teach the unteachable. It was devised to provide a fully trained peacetime army that could respond immediately to a defence emergency or the threat of war. For many Australian parents, however, national service had meanings unrelated to defence. It offered hope their sons would grow up into clean-shaven, short-haired young men in the images of their fathers. The army would show the boys hardship (within reason) and discipline (but not brutality). It would make them robust and outdoorsy, but also smart and tidy. It would teach them the value of obedience and working together as a team. National service was the opposite of pop music and foppery, tight pants and patterned shirts, bodgies and jazzers with their marijuana cigarettes. It was the old ways against the new, the barber against the beatniks. It gave boys a small taste of what their fathers had faced in El Alamein or Madang, and what their grandfathers had lived through at Gallipoli and the Somme.

National service was the old songs against the new music, 'Waltzing Matilda' against pop and rock'n'roll. It was security against confusion, masculinity against the androgynous. In the early 1960s, the sons of men were learning the ways of women, growing hair past their collars – but also little continental beards. Time and again, reporters covering the early days of national service refer to young men shaven and shorn, forced to wear haircuts instead of hairstyles, as if this were the biggest change the army would bring to their lives.

For some parents, the army was also the opposite of violence. It would channel their boys' aggression, see it tamed and sated, left behind on long runs at sunrise, or released with bullets on a firing range in the scrub. It would cure juvenile delinquents of their nascent criminality by exposing them to the arts of war.

Two mildly opposed ideas – a boy's effeminacy born of wearing both women's hair and men's beards – were synthesised into one. Young men were simultaneously too hard and too soft. They could be sneering, grass-fighting, gimlet-eyed rockers or limp-wristed, guitar-strumming, coffee-sipping wimps. Either way, the army would push them from the edges to the middle, where normal boys played with rifles, swam in waterholes, respected their parents and marched in step. The discipline would be for the good of everyone, because boys like these – the pansies and the hoons – could not be relied upon to defend their homes and farms when the Asians streamed down from the north, as they had poured through the Pacific only twenty-three years before. There was nothing illusory or paranoid about the threat from Asia to women who'd waited at home for letters from their husbands in New Guinea, to the thousands of families whose men had disappeared into Changi with the fall of Singapore, or the people who remembered the bombing of Darwin and midget submarines in Sydney Harbour. Australia needed strong men to defend her, trained soldiers at her borders, loyal allies by her side. The war generation had seen Thailand, Malaya and the Dutch East Indies fall like dominoes before the Japanese, with their martial will and unifying ideology of a Greater East Asia Co-Prosperity Sphere, an Asia for the Asians. The men whose names marked the cenotaphs in country towns, or cascaded like tears down plaques in memoriam were once their playmates, brothers, cousins and lovers and their absence would always be a presence – and a warning.

But national service had other meanings for the young. Many of those born in 1945, the last year of the last war, had grown up believing their fathers and grandfathers were, if not heroes, then at least men who'd been in battle, kept their nerve and stuck by their mates. But the younger generation had no way to prove themselves as men beyond bare knuckles in the pub car park. They'd grow old, the lucky ones, with memories of great days on the football field, a punch-up at a piss-up, a kiss and grope with a girl they never planned to marry, and nothing more. The structure of the economy was changing, and some men who might have once have expected to labour outdoors and grow trim and bronzed under the sun found themselves confined to offices, trapped within walls between files and ledgers, doing women's work, tamed and angry and desperately bored.

For them, the army meant freedom, and the chance of a bigger, more heroic life. It was an opportunity to measure up to the Anzacs, to march out of the banks and insurance offices and into history, and make their parents proud. It was a chance to bury the disappointment of work and return to the safety of school, and the raucous comfort of a mob of men their own age, dealing cards, passing footballs, camping out and chasing skirt, while they learned to use weapons, drive vehicles, read signals and fight.

This was true in particular for the first intake of national servicemen. None had graduated from university and only a few had finished an apprenticeship. There were some, such as police officers, who'd completed their training and were starting their careers, and others, such as sportsmen who, at twenty, were the best they were ever going to be, but many of the first intake hadn't yet found a focus. They'd been drifting between jobs, or confined in an occupation they regretted ever entering. They'd made a mistake, but the army offered them the possibility of release.

There were others, of course, who were happy and settled, who'd sprung a lucky position as a TV cameraman or played guitar in a band. And there were the quiet, sensitive boys, who never wanted to be turned into soldiers and liked their lives and themselves just the way they were. The nature of selective conscription meant many of them escaped – failing the medical, the interview or the army's aptitude tests – but others were caught in the crowd of second-grade footballers and swept along to the barracks, fearful of everything, from the jostling of sweaty shoulders to the sergeant major's oaths, and their time in the army turned out to be either a misery or a revelation, a ruination or a salvation. And, for some, it brought their death.

There were early doubts expressed about the scheme, a nagging feeling things didn't quite add up. The press reported 'larrikins' might not be reformed by national service because the army was to ask balloted men if they'd ever appeared before or been adjudged uncontrollable by a children's court, committed to an institution by magisterial order, or sentenced to imprisonment. The *Sun-Herald* quoted 'the Army' as saying: 'If we have to have conscription, we don't have to fill the Army with criminals.' But this was precisely what the public wanted. LR Johnson, a Labor MP, criticised the government on the grounds that 'bodgies, larrikins, people with long hair-dos and those who frequented milk bars could not be conscripted'. Johnson said, 'They are the ones who will be exempted, just as many young men have been exempted in the past because they have had insufficient academic qualifications.'[3]

Nor was national service ever going to provide a cure for Communism and force political deviants into line. In a secret government document, in a discrete section marked 'highly confidential', Minister for Labour and National Service Leslie Bury wrote that the army insisted, 'Those who are enlisted should not have criminal records of a character which would make them unsuitable soldiers nor constitute security risks.' Men balloted in would undergo security checks by ASIO and the Commonwealth Police, but those who failed never knew why. 'For security reasons, despite the fact that those with adverse records will not be called up, they are subjected to the process of medical examination, interview, and, if necessary, psychological test, and are then notified that they are granted indefinite deferment.'[4]

As of 31 December 1965, 177 young men had been rejected solely because of their criminal records, and another sixty excluded as security risks. The sensitivity of this information was noted over and again in government documents. 'We have been extremely chary about saying anything about these checks,' DLNS secretary Bland wrote to the secretary of the prime minister's department. 'And for reasons which I am sure you will understand.'[5]

The National Service Act transformed the magistrates courts into a theatre of the bizarre, where the older generation sat in judgement on the convictions of youth. At first, the courts seemed only to grant conscientious-objector status to men who had some kind of supernatural opposition to military service. In Melbourne in June, sheetmetal worker Brian Gray, a Christian Israelite who believed the British were the direct descendants of the lost tribes of Israel, said he would 'sooner go to gaol than fight in the Army' but was passed for non-combatant duties. Warehouseman Jeffrey Ross Foley of the pacifist Church of God was exempted after he said he wouldn't take up arms even if his family or church were in danger, because, 'All those who live by the sword, die by the sword.' Wool clerk Martin Walter-Heinz Ernst was exempted as a Jehovah's Witness.[6] His church had already predicted man's dominion on earth would end in 1914 and 1925, and now believed the Messiah would return in 1975.

But in Sydney in July, builder's labourer Robin Peter Kitching was refused conscientious-objector status as the former chairman of the peace committee of the Eureka Youth League. During the hearing, he admitted to also being a member of the Communist Party. The army would not accept Kitching anyway, and he won a later appeal based on pacifist convictions not in line with CPA policy.[7] In August, a magistrate refused exemption to Chinese-born Chu Benedict Bun Gee, who stated it was 'completely against my will, principle and conscience to fight against people of my own race in South-east Asia'. He said, 'I am sure no Australian would ever think of fighting against fellow Australians, even though he may be naturalised elsewhere.'[8]

Not every member of a Christian sect received an equally sympathetic hearing. Shoemaker John William Thompson of the missionary-oriented Open Brethren was refused exemption.[9] And, as all over the world, certain authorities felt compelled to argue theology with Jehovah's Witnesses, and lure them into conceding that whatever they were doing for a job was somehow equivalent to soldiering. Postal officer Brian William Spillane was refused total exemption in the Special Federal Court after an exchange with a Mr G Halliday for the minister for labour and national service.

Halliday: 'Didn't you affirm when you joined the P.M.G. [Post-Master General's Department] in 1961 that you would obey lawful commands and serve the Queen?'

Spillane: 'That is true.'

Halliday: 'Wouldn't that mean that by working for the P.M.G., you could easily be, and probably are, helping to deliver Servicemen's mail?'

Spillane: 'Yes, but I am not contributing to the war effort.'[10]

Their argument took on a different flavour in the light of the later mistaken belief held by soldiers in Vietnam that postal workers refused to deliver their mail as a gesture against the war.

Each exemption of a Millenarian, a cultist or a Communist – few though they were – chipped away imperceptibly at the truth that the group of men chosen for national service included representatives of the entire population. Slowly and smoothly, the various stages of the selection process shaved off the demographic edges. Recent migrants and many Aboriginal men were already excluded, then small religious minorities and elements of the radical political fringe. But folk singers never had a chance: on 24 September, a magistrate in the Special Federal Court in Sydney refused to listen to a record by the duo Sean and Sonja offered in evidence for Sean Cullip's hardship deferral. He was prepared to accept they were a very good team, but was concerned he might not be able to appreciate their music.[11]

There has always been an abundance of myths, a treasury of fool's gold, clouding our understanding of national service and the Vietnam War, and the myths of 1964 were different from those of today. National service did not straighten out delinquent youths; it was never meant to, and it didn't try. The ballot was not fixed, certain occupations were not favoured over others, and footballers were not exempt from war service. But nor did the national servicemen represent a true cross-section of Australian society. Non-naturalised migrants were only included in the ballot in 1967. The problems of Aboriginal conscription were such that few Indigenous people ever ended up with a national service number. The sons of the very poorest families were largely absent – they couldn't pass the literacy tests or the physical exams. As to postwar misconceptions, fewer than a quarter of the sixty-three thousand men conscripted ever went to Vietnam, and many of those never saw combat. Outside of the infantry, the armoured corps and the engineers, Vietnam was usually a fairly safe place for most Australian soldiers. Vung Tau, where the 1st Australian Logistics Support Group (1ALSG) was based, was one of the most secure towns in the south, and not a rest and recreation centre for the Viet Cong, as has often been claimed. More men volunteered for national service than ever refused to register. Draft-resistance was the pursuit of only a tiny minority. All but one infantry battalion had a homecoming parade and the welcome was, in the main, riotously enthusiastic. There were very few protests against returning soldiers, and none of them seem to have taken place at airports. Soldiers were more likely to assault demonstrators than the other way around. While many national servicemen volunteered to go to Vietnam, many others seem not to have been given the opportunity, and still others who baulked were told they had to go.

The majority of the mainstream media supported both the Vietnam War and national service and, while its enthusiasm for the conflict faded with the years the popular press hardly ever criticised the diggers, nor lost its happy zeal for the idea of conscription.

6

THE HAPPY MEDIA

There would be no more washing dishes or peeling potatoes: Australian newspapers sold the idea of national service through a frozen smile like Chesty Bond's, with the same stilted optimism of the front-page advertisements that promised housewives they need never again wash woollens by hand, and they would find the 'world's finest trousers' for their husbands at Fletcher Jones.

The pattern was set when the first postwar national service scheme was introduced in 1951, to be greeted with a flush of earnest newspaper features designed to allay fears of barracks life, and convince a generation of returned servicemen that their sons would be entering a very different organisation from the army their fathers had so recently left behind. There would be no more futile discipline, arbitrary punishment, indigestible rations, arrogant inefficiency, or soldiers' time squandered in unmilitary pursuits such as gardening. And if any gardening did happen to occur, it would be horticulture with a strictly strategic purpose. The same assurances were given, point by point, when national service was born again in 1965.

The 1951 national service scheme initially provided for universal conscription. Every eighteen-year-old male was liable to register for

176 days' training with either the army, the navy or the air force. If they chose the army, they served only the first three months consecutively, with an additional seventy-eight days in the CMF. There was no requirement to go overseas unless they were accepted by the navy or the air force, where they were obliged to serve the full period in a single block, and leave Australia if necessary. From May 1951 to January 1957, thirty-three thousand men completed training every year, twenty-eight thousand of them in the army.

Before the first trainees were even encamped, the defence correspondent of the *Sunday Herald* was quick to promise readers that army catering had improved. 'Food has perhaps top priority,' he wrote, 'for the post-war Services live well.' Also, the modern 1950s army, cleaned up and stripped down like the lines on a space rocket, had 'washing machines and washing-up machines',[1] so trainees would not have to waste their brief but busy time in the services scrubbing pans and laundering shirts. A week later, the paper's leader writers promised that even marching and shouting were on their way out. 'The old conception of "square-bashing", of the loud-voiced N.C.O., and drill for the sake of drill, has gone into the discard,' they wrote. 'The approach will be through co-operation rather than compulsion.'[2]

There are few memoirs written of that first army scheme, but what literature there is contains no reference to the new collegiate spirit or the taming of the drill sergeant. Its most able chronicler, the urbane Clive James, remembered, 'When we stepped off the bus at Ingleburn, they were already screaming at us. Screaming sergeants and corporals appeared suddenly out of huts.'[3] James was given extra duties in a kitchen where, he claimed, the smallest dixies took ninety minutes each to clean, and the biggest was so large he had to be lowered into it by a rope. Nothing much of importance seemed to have altered since the 1940s. His late father, who had joined the army in the Second World War, would have recognised the hours he spent on parade – although, James wrote, 'since most of one's time in the army is wasted anyway, I preferred to waste it by moving about in a precise manner'.[4] Two years into the scheme, coverage of the joys of basic training had taken on a wounded tone. The first deck of a *Sydney Morning Herald* headline whispered, 'Army scheme far from perfect, but . . . ' The next line screamed, 'N.S. Training Has A Good Basic Purpose' in letters twice the size. 'A special correspondent' had been charged with answering criticisms of the scheme. He chose the method of an imaginary dialogue between youth who thought they knew best – styled as 'the young intelligentsia'– and the army. As was the custom in these pieces, he first addressed the catering question. 'The food,' he wrote, 'whatever some epicures may say, is ample and good . . . Cabbage, it is true, is still not well cooked, but how many restaurants cook it well?' There was no time to waste time. 'There is too much to be taught, and too little time available for it,' wrote the special correspondent, 'for any recruit to be non-productively employed at any stage.' Curiously, two paragraphs later, he agreed (with a phantom third party) that 'undoubtedly a certain amount of time is wasted'. He finally came to the heart of a matter which was to trouble both defenders and detractors of national service for many years to come. 'Another criticism which can be dismissed,' he wrote, ' . . . is levelled at what is called "grounds maintenance and improvement".' He then launched into a furious defence of military gardening: 'Two years ago the present camp outside Liverpool was an unsightly scar on the countryside. There are many gardens there to-day, and N.S. trainees have made most of them. "We're not doing National Service training just to put in the time making gardens," complain some of the lads. "Of course not," replies the Army. "But after all, who lives in these barracks? You do." . . . And in terms of citizenship and morale,' the special correspondent decided, 'the few hours spent weekly on "grounds maintenance and improvement" seem to be well spent.'[5]

In 1954, the scheme was revised to give an exemption to any youth who lived outside an eight kilometre radius of a CMF training establishment or worked in rural production, effectively sending farm boys back to the land. In parliament, the minister for defence, Sir Philip McBride, 'argued unconvincingly that the principle of universality extended only as far as the obligation for all eligible youths to register'.[6] A Gallup poll showed two-thirds of the Australian people preferred national service to be every young man's obligation.

The Sydney *Daily Telegraph* admitted in 1955 that 'criticisms and suspicion about the Services' capacity to provide worthwhile training for the annual intake of trainees have been confirmed . . . National Service not only has been a waste of defence funds it has been a waste, too, of many trainees' time and industrial ability.'[7] A defence review in 1957 abolished universal service and replaced it with a system of selective conscription based on a birthdate ballot, which would train only twelve thousand young men each year, all of whom would go into the army. 'We have, quite frankly, disturbing deficiencies on the equipment side,' admitted Menzies. 'Such, however, have been the immense social advantages of national service training that we have been reluctant to modify that great scheme. I say "modify" because we have never thought of abandoning it!'[8] The scheme was abandoned in November 1959, but it had been hugely popular, maintaining the approval of 83–88 per cent of voters.[9] Perhaps its only drawback was that it was no real use to the army.

When the government announced the return of national service, it prompted another flood of stories about good food, comfortable beds and friendly NCOs. In January 1965, the *Sun-Herald*'s Bob Johnson recapped all the reassurances of fourteen years before. 'In camp,' he wrote, in the uplifting tones of a public-information film, 'waiting for each recruit – no lining up at the quartermaster's store – will be a steel-framed bed each with £10 foam-rubber mattress. Laid out neatly on the mattress will be sheets (yes – sheets) pillow and pillowcases and up to six blankets. Beside the bed will be a floor-rug and a steel wardrobe. There will be four beds to each sizable room in the big brick dormitories. The wet canteen will serve beer; and down in the recreation hall will be television and a heated indoor swimming-pool.'

Johnson noted that only about one in twenty eligible men would be chosen from the first draft, although, 'The odds will be shortened when a £23-million military installations expansion program is completed next year and the Army is able to accept almost twice the number of conscripted men each half-year.'[10]

Johnson was wrong. Men who took part in the first ballot had a much higher chance than any subsequent group of ending up in the army. Apprentices and students whose birthdates were drawn in the first ballot were automatically called up when they completed their courses. This meant the DLNS needed to draw fewer marbles in later ballots because – until at least 1969 when newly qualified doctors were conscripted in large numbers – there was always a reserve left over from the first ballot. While ninety-six marbles were drawn for the first national service intake in March 1965, only thirty were pulled out of the barrel for the fourth intake in September 1966.

In Victoria, 2RTB in Puckapunyal was set to become the largest unit in the Australian Army, with about 400 staff and 1350 national servicemen. Scot Palmer of the Melbourne *Sun* took a tour of the renovated camp, which the army chiefs called 'the best accommodation ever provided for basic military training in Australia'. The recruits' huts were divided into four cubicles and Palmer noted they were furnished with 'pink-and-white curtains, a light fawn vinyl floor covering, mustard-colored bedside mats and radiators'. Food, Palmer predicted, would no longer be a source of complaint among recruits. 'The only complaint they will have at Puckapunyal is how to put it all away.'[11]

Perhaps the sole hardship the newspapers would concede the recruits might face was an army haircut, and over this they shed crocodile tears. Tony Boothey of the Victorian Men's Hair Fashion Council appealed to the army to 'evolve a form of acceptable haircut that is neither an extreme "Beatle" cut or a harsh short-back-and-sides cut'. Although Boothey predicted 'some heartbreaks' if the crop did not 'lean towards a more moderate style that will be liked by the younger generation', the army insisted it would stick by its dress manual. While a soldier might sport a neat moustache, the 'face must be clean shaven to the level of the corners of the eyes, and hair showing below the head dress is to be kept short'.[12] The army would ensure obedience and uniformity with the teeth of clippers and the blade of a razor. The 1960s would not be permitted to penetrate the gates of the training battalions under the Trojan hats of national servicemen.

On the morning of 30 June, the first intake reported for duty in New South Wales. 'Fatherly sergeant-majors, kindly sergeants and corporals with beaming smiles greeted new National Servicemen at the Army's Marrickville training depot,' noted the *Sydney Morning Herald*, with a certain ironic glee. After two three-course meals, the recruits cheered when the Eastern Command Band played the Beatles' 'I Want to Hold Your Hand'. A small number of protesters from Save Our Sons and the Youth Campaign Against Conscription stood vigil at Central Railway Station as the conscripts said goodbye to their families and those bound for Victoria boarded the train to Puckapunyal. According to the *Sydney Morning Herald*, they 'swarmed forward with cardboard posters held over their heads' to be halted by plainclothes detectives including men from 'the C.I.B Special Branch, two sections of the Army's detective force, Commonwealth Security and Railway detectives'.[13] A report in *The Age* claimed 'many conscripts aboard the train began singing Waltzing Matilda as it pulled out'.[14] A second troop train left for Wagga Wagga, to no protests, later in the evening, carrying recruits to Kapooka. The *Sun-Herald* dispatched the redoubtable Bob Johnson to shadow them on a train journey that lasted '11 cold, wearying hours' when it should have taken less than seven, and saw three hundred and forty youths struggle to grab breakfast in a dining car that seated thirty. As was customary, however, both journalist and the recruits (quoted collectively and anonymously) conceded 'probably . . . the train was heaven compared with some of the emergency transport of 20 years ago'. Johnson spoke to a trainee named Philip Reed, the only twenty-year-old drafted from his home town of Scone, who'd 'already made friends' with Michael Birchell from Tamworth. Both men agreed they had to simply accept their fate. 'Yes,' said Birchell, 'the Government says you go, so we go.'[15] He would be dead within eight months of leaving Australia.

The day before the first trainees arrived at Puckapunyal, the Melbourne *Herald* promised they would be served ice-cream twice a week and 'spared much of the worst of army bugbears, fatigues'. A new generation was assured that 'in today's modern army there are even automatic "spud barbers" and dishwashing machines'.[16] Melbourne men reported to the Army Engineers Depot at Swan Street, Richmond, the next morning, where the gates opened at eight a.m. While girlfriends may have looked glum and two middle-aged women held up signs saying 'We oppose the call-up', 'the happiest faces belonged to the recruits', reported the *Herald*. The *Sun*'s Barrie Watts noticed 'a couple of beardies and weirdies, a few who trembled and a few who grumbled. One brought out his guitar and sang a ban-the-bomb refrain.' But Victoria's first national service trainee was Frankston bank teller Gerry Bruin, who had arrived at seven thirty-five a.m. The fates smiled, as 'besides being first, he also seemed the perfect recruit', wrote the *Herald*.[17] Bruin was five feet eleven, ten stone and played back pocket for Pines Estate football club in Frankston. He was looking forward to military service, and hoped to join the infantry. At Puckapunyal, a contingent of trainees from Sydney was met by the Headquarters Southern Command Band playing the strange wartime ballad 'You'd Be Far Better Off in a Home', and the *Sun*'s Watts noted some recruits had actually been given *three* cups of tea by the time they were issued with their 'brand-new equipment' at 2RTB.[18]

Only one young man seemed out of touch with the spirit of the day: the *Sun* reported that in Bendigo a youth had failed to turn up at the drill hall for the bus to Puckapunyal, and army officers had found him hiding under his house. A staff reporter for *The Age* saw the day characterised by 'a typical ultra-efficiency but an un-Army gentleness'. 'The clothing issue denied all the old jokes about the army and sizes,' he wrote. 'Tailors were there to ensure proper fitting.'[19] Oddly, the *Sydney Morning Herald*'s RTB correspondent noticed most of the trainees 'struggled to fit on Army hats which for many seemed the wrong size. One platoon of 64 sent back 23 recruits whose pants were too long or whose jackets were too wide . . . Several trainees said their clothes would require severe tailoring.'[20]

The next day, Robert Coleman for the *Herald* observed that the recruits, now wearing uniform and marching around, were 'somehow . . . beginning to look like soldiers', whereas they hadn't looked like soldiers when they'd been wearing civilian clothes and sitting on a bus. Coleman went back to see Gerry Bruin, to discover he'd 'slept like a log'. Unfortunately, Bruin's first day was spent in the camp kitchen. 'He was allocated to prepare vegetables,' Coleman admitted, 'but the days of "spud barbering" are gone. The Army has automatic potato peelers now.'

There were at least two professional footballers in the first intake at Puckapunyal, Western Australian Harry Neesham, an East Fremantle player who'd been signed up by Geelong, and John Perry, who had played three games on a half-forward flank for Richmond in 1965. Perry told Coleman, after only two days in camp, that the army was 'mighty'. 'I think I'm going to enjoy it,' he predicted.[21] Sadly, Perry was on kitchen duty too, and had spent the day making tea, refilling sugar basins and cleaning tables.

By 3 July, the tone of Coleman's dispatches had become hysterical, if not insane. For the first time, he styled himself as 'ex-VX Robert Coleman' in his byline (VX was the Second World War prefix for Victorian servicemen's army numbers) and posed for a photo in a slouch hat, the strap of which lent him an unduly prominent double chin. His story, which seemed to be addressed to his former comrades, began, 'Fair dinkum, Digger, you'd never believe it. Up here at

Pucka where you sweated out your rookie training in the early 40s the National Servicemen have got washing machines now . . . And the fang-farriers! They've got a dental surgery here equal, they say, to anything in Australia. It's enough to make you want your molars mauled.'[22]

This was how the media prepared young men for recruit training.

7

SILVER CITY

Few first-intake national servicemen at Kapooka in July 1965 would have recognised their experience from the press reports. In the freezing Wagga Wagga winter, the trainees were bawled out, bullied, abused, given mess duties and fatigues, and subjected to most of the other frightening, boring, toughening, bonding processes their fathers and grandfathers had been through before them. The majority came to accept the pain as a necessary part of military training, and look back with pride at the fact they'd survived.

Many of the national servicemen who went on to form 6RAR came down from Queensland on troop trains to New South Wales. Among them was John Robbins, a big, capable man, with eyes that twinkled even as they squinted into the sun. Robbins' father was a Queensland bank manager, and the family had moved from branch to branch. Robbins had started school in St George in the west and finished in Townsville in the north. Like many of the knockabout sons of professional men, he had spent some time as a jackaroo, but left the bush for Brisbane in September 1964, and a job as a clerk in the livestock department of Elders.

'I wasn't concerned when I got called up,' said Robbins. 'I was actually looking forward to it. I'd been in the cadets at school. I had bush skills. When I first went jackarooing, my boss said, "Well, you'd better learn how to ride a horse and sleep on the ground," so he sent me on the road with a drover for three or four months.' Robbins was a yarner, a desert-dry gee-up merchant, a salesman and a showman, a Crown and Anchor gambler. He recalled his first day at Kapooka, when instructors barked orders at the bewildered recruits in language far more savage than Grant Collins remembered at Puckapunyal: 'Get over there, you dickhead; not there, you stupid arsehole. What are you, a fuckwit or something? Answer me, you penis-with-ears, and call me sir or I'll come down on you so fucking hard you won't get up for a month. Stop laughing, you stupid shit-for-brains. What's your name, you dopey prick?'[1]

Recruit training was designed to frighten, disorient and exhaust young men, to take away the marks of their individuality, from their clothing to their hairstyle to their first name, and replace them with a standard disguise: a uniform, a shaved head and a number. Recruits were harangued and terrorised and subjected to ludicrous injustices by angry little regular army corporals who laid waste to perfectly made beds, and theatrically furious sergeant majors who had tired youths parade naked but for overcoats in the darkness of a freezing night. The idea was to bond the men through a shared sense of hardship and injustice, to unite them against the manufactured enemy of NCOs, to have them realise that the only way to survive was to act together, with the more robust helping the fragile, the faster men carrying the slow, and the sharpest and brightest passing down their knowledge to the dullards and the inept. They had to learn to move and think as sections and platoons, and bury their own interests for the good of the collective. They had to embrace pure Communism. If they were ambushed, the recruits were taught, they could not run away, they had to face the enemy and charge towards them. One man fleeing might preserve his own life, but every man fighting might save the rest. It did not matter who died, as long as the platoon, the company, the battalion, the army survived, so a man's unit had to become his identity. The recruits grew stronger through loathing their NCOs, but were slowly coaxed into seeking their approval, to try to prove to the bastards that they too were men with skills and courage, not pricks with ears with shit for brains.

Bevan Beitzel, a boilermaker from Ipswich, Queensland, said, 'They purposefully set out to break you, to mentally bring you down, and they succeeded. The first five or six weeks was a living hell. They didn't give you time to scratch yourself or sit down and think about anything, they just kept you going the whole time, and they drained you. But after that, they became more civilised with it, and by the end, they were your best friends.'

Every hour of the day was filled with artificial deadlines. The trainees were always tired and nodding off in afternoon lectures, while their instructors were fresh because they worked in shifts. The national servicemen had to keep their clothes neat, folded and square, and make a bed with a sheet pulled so tightly a dropped coin would bounce. They learned the army way, by repetition and rote, dividing every process into the smallest, mechanical steps – swivel, pull, twist, repeat and reverse – the polishing of the brass, the cleaning of the weapon, the naming of the parts.

John Robbins quickly made friends with a hut mate, John Heslewood, who had been working at the Commonwealth Bank in Wynnum, a southern suburb of Brisbane on the shores of Moreton Bay. Heslewood said he 'wasn't bothered' by going into the army: 'I'd applied for a transfer from Brisbane and I didn't have enough experience, so when this came up, I thought, Oh well, this might be something different anyway.' His journey to Kapooka marked the first time he had been south of the Queensland border. Also in their barracks was a young racing driver named Dick Johnson, who wrote, 'I was the only motor mechanic or vaguely mechanically minded person in our hut . . . but three huts farther down, part of the same intake, at the same time, was . . . Peter Brock! And I never knew him.'[2]

'It was a piece of piss, the army, to me,' said Robbins, 'being out there in the bush. Because I'd been shooting roos: we used to kill a roo a day for the dogs, and cut them up, butcher them. And I knew where we were. You just learn which way you're going; even without a compass you know where the sun is. I'd left home when I was seventeen, and you go into the army at twenty. I had probably a bit of an advantage over most of the others because I'd been looking after myself.'

Another young Queenslander in the first intake at Kapooka was Norm Wotherspoon, who watched Robbins from a distance. 'I'd never had a lot of confidence,' said Wotherspoon. 'I was pretty much in awe of most people. But he was a bit of a character. It's probably why I didn't get too close to him, because you think, Why would these people want to talk to me?'

Wotherspoon came from Bowen, Queensland, the only place in Australia to have elected a Communist MP. His stepfather, Ern, a mattress maker and upholsterer, was a Communist of sorts. 'I suspect his view of Communism was if you had more than you needed and somebody had less than they needed, you gave it away,' said Wotherspoon. 'We had a big vegetable garden and, when neighbours were sick and people were out of work, we'd be giving vegetables away.'

Ern continually denigrated Wotherspoon, until the boy felt worthless. 'My stepfather basically convinced me from the time I was two that I was pretty lazy and stupid and wouldn't achieve anything,' said Wotherspoon. 'I think he was a little jealous of me being the baby, and he wanted my mother to himself.' At sixteen, Wotherspoon found a position as a clerk at the Department of Machinery, Scaffolding, Weights and Measures, and left home. His stepfather's parting words about the job were, '"You'd better keep it. It's the only one you'll ever get." Being a child who believed what he was told, I thought that was just my lot,' he said.

Wotherspoon never thought about conscription until he was called up. 'I paid very little attention to news,' he said. 'I had very little interests, few social skills because I didn't play sport at school and wasn't allowed to fraternise with anyone after school. Nobody ever came over to play and I never went over anywhere to play.' When he was told to go into the army, he said, 'I had been brought up to obey the law, so I just went. I felt a bit of foolish excitement since I was the only one at work that got called up. It made me a momentary celebrity, and that's always good when you're a nothing.'

Wotherspoon found recruit training 'quite difficult but sort of exciting in a scary way. For the first time in my life I had a few people who I actually interacted with – and they were my own age. And I got myself fitter than I'd ever been, with lots of running and marching and keeping organised. And the more I got into it, the more I liked it. All told, it was a sort of unexpected adventure – and, after all, I'd been told I couldn't think for myself, and I was following orders, so it sort of fitted.

'I wasn't a real good soldier at Kapooka. They used to always make fun of me very loudly. I was always second- or third-last to get up on parade, and I marched funny and I had trouble firing rifles because I was left-handed and they were right-handed. And even when we played compulsory sports, I thought I'd try soccer and they realised fairly quickly I was pretty hopeless, so I didn't play any sport in the army either. I just wandered around watching other people play sport, and no one seemed to give a stuff.'

One of Wotherspoon's hut-mates was Bill Winterford from West End, Brisbane. Winterford said he left school when he was about eleven years old, and went up to Mount Larcom in Queensland, where he worked on a farm, then started an apprenticeship in a garage until he 'got sacked for thumping the boss's son'. Back in Brisbane, he loaded ice-cream trucks, then worked as a driver for an electrical-industrial cable company.

'I tried to join the army when I was about eighteen,' said Winterford, but he failed the entrance tests. 'My spelling wasn't real bright,' he said. 'I used to write phonetically.' At twenty, he was called up, and this time they let him in. 'I'm only about five foot three,' he said, 'and I was about the littlest in the platoon, but I loved it.' A soldier, he said, 'was the thing in my life I most wanted to be'.

Other men arrived at Kapooka from country New South Wales. Michael George travelled down from Dubbo with a handful of local boys. He'd originally come off a farm in Holbrook, NSW, where his father, a former RAAF ground crewman, had been a soldier settler. George was educated at the Lutheran College at Walla Walla, about one hundred and thirty kilometres from Wagga Wagga. He'd been drifting between seasonal jobs, and was working as an unqualified diesel mechanic in Dubbo when he was called up. The men in his family carried the weight of the disasters of Australian military history. His grandfather had fought at Gallipoli and lost a leg at the Somme, and his uncle had been a prisoner of the Japanese in Changi. But George, like so many other boys, wanted to be a soldier too. 'I'd actually done two and a half years in the CMF,' he said. 'When I got called up, I resigned from the CMF so I could go.'

Another of the Dubbo lads was Alan Parr, a tough boy, fast with his fists, who'd been born in Sydney and apprenticed as a sheetmetal worker, but never finished his time. In his first job at a Heinz Bros factory, two of the tradesmen had tried to blacken his balls with boot polish as an initiation. 'After I nearly cleaned them up throwing hammers at them,' wrote Parr, 'one grabbed me and had me on the ground. I kicked out at him and he smashed into a pile of guards that came crashing down on top of him . . . they never bothered me again.'[3] He'd gone up to Dubbo and was working on a sheep property when his number came up.

Peter Doyle was born in Newcastle. His grandfather had fought in the trenches in the First World War. 'He was gassed but he lived,' said Doyle. 'The gas knocked him about a bit. He ended up dying of a heart attack.' Doyle went to live in Belmont, Lake Macquarie, to keep an eye on his grandmother, mow the lawn and look after her house. He finished high school there, then moved back home, and his grandmother sold up and moved to Newcastle too. Doyle took a job in a wool store, displaying and cataloguing yarn, and said he wasn't worried one way or the other about national service: 'If I went in, that was fine; if I didn't go in, that was fine.'

Doyle was quartered near Beitzel in the old part of Kapooka, where reporters rarely trod. Soldiers called it 'Silver City' because it was made up of corrugated metal huts left over from the Second World War with 'no water, no toilets, no heating in the middle of winter', said Doyle. When the media came to Kapooka, Beitzel said, 'They concentrated on filming the new area. I don't think they wanted to see the igloos we were in.'

Not all of the press reporting of the first national service intake was asinine. *The Bulletin* sent its correspondent Sam Lipski to Puckapunyal in July, and Lipski reported that 'surprisingly few of the recruits have expressed anything negative about the Army', and he wondered if this might have 'something to do with the nature of the first intake'. He said the unsayable – that these men didn't seem like a true cross-section of society, and included 'a disproportionately high number of white-collar workers, especially bank and insurance company clerks.

'Too ready to accept the "company policy"?' he speculated. 'It will be interesting to compare the general reactions of future intakes which will include large numbers of university students, technical school students, and apprentices.'[4]

Lipski saw the first intake for what it was – clean-cut, clever, law-abiding and conservative, and representative of little but itself.

At the end of their ten weeks at Kapooka or Puckapunyal, the trainees had learned drill, map-reading and field craft, and they had prepared themselves to kill, by shooting targets on the range, bowling grenades from a pit, and fixing bayonets to skewer dummies hanging like bodies on a gallows. It's not an easy thing to slay a man you don't hate, when you didn't kill the priest who strapped you or the fat boy who bullied you or the dad who punched the daylights out of you, the corporal who humiliated you, or even the hoon who jumped you after the dance. But you don't do it for yourself, you do it for the good of the unit, to preserve it from threat, and you learn to call that 'mateship' and it comes to replace any idea of friendship you might have had in the past. That's what the recruits learned: that true friendship needs a foe.

On parade at the end of recruit training, they paced straight-backed and in time, heads held high, because they were desperate to impress the same men who'd bowed and browbeaten them, abused and punished them, scorned and ridiculed them such a short time ago. They were ready for a new enemy now. When the first batch of 1250 trainees passed out of Puckapunyal on 5 September 1965, Minister for the Army Jim Forbes declared the ten-week-old national service scheme had 'already proved itself a success'. *The Age* agreed. The first national servicemen 'came through with flying colours', wrote the paper's correspondent. 'Their handling of weapons on parade, slow and quick time marching was a pleasure to see.' Forbes told the trainees, 'I will be very surprised if you do not go further in your life than those who have not served their country in the Army.' Among them, in brilliant sunshine after morning rain, stood Errol Noack.

The Age, always prepared to go one step beyond even the government, assured its readers the recruits would 'go into a specialist corps of their own choice'.[5] This was never part of the bargain. The 'Information Booklet for National Servicemen' issued to every conscript told recruits their corps allocation would 'take account of the civil skills and experience which you already possess and which might usefully be employed in the Army', ability and aptitude, existing vacancies and, finally, 'your own preference'. The closest the army came to matching *The Age*'s promise was the laboriously shackled: 'Although no guarantee can be given, those recruits who do best during recruit training can normally expect to be allotted to the Corps of their choice if this is practicable.'[6]

The regulars had more control. An army booklet for junior officers explained a recruit should ideally choose his corps on enlistment, and should be given the job he requested within the unit. But there were limits: 'You can't make a silk purse from a sow's ear, and there is no sense in agreeing with a man he could be a radio mechanic when he has never built even a crystal wireless set, and his education is only primary.'[7]

Every national serviceman filled out a form on which he could nominate his corps preferences. Some believed they were offered three choices, ranked in descending order. But it seems there were only two options, and the third space was meant to be filled in by the army, with the name of the corps allocated. Many men were posted to their favoured corps. Dick Johnson became a mechanic in the RAEME and stayed in Australia throughout his service ('I was supposed to go to Vietnam,' he said, 'but because I broke a piece of cartilage off in my knee, they deemed me medically unfit . . . I wouldn't have minded going').[8] Peter Brock asked for and was given a posting to the Royal Australian Army Medical Corps (RAAMC), and he too served his time in Australia.

But Sam Lipski, the journalist with the eye of an anthropologist, puzzled over the 'ease' with which the army 'filled the quotas for the "fighting" corps like Infantry, Artillery and Armored'. Infantry was the first choice for about half of the first national service intake, he was told, which was a higher percentage than was normal among regular troops. He found this odd when, 'The most consistently found attitude among recruits has been, "I'm in the Army for two years. I might as well make the most of it." With such an attitude it could be expected that corps like Engineers, Signals, Surveyors, Service Corps and others which offer training more directly useful on return to civilian life would get a much higher percentage of volunteers.'[9] But many men, despite their broader ambitions, hoped to join the infantry just because it seemed to offer the most authentic army experience. If they were going to be a soldier, they wanted to be a real one, and not just a clerk in a uniform with army-issue stationery, a bed in a barracks and a shiny pair of boots.

More than eight hundred trainees from the first intake of national service were sent to infantry battalions: 250 to 2RAR, and 280 each to 5RAR and 6RAR. The Royal Australian Engineers got 264 men; the service corps, 182; the artillery, 145; the RAAMC, 140; ordnance, 105; the RAEME, 85; the catering corps, 75; the armoured corps, 62; signals, 60; dental, 30; and provosts, 15. A further 140 men were sent to specialist corps such as Education and Psychology. Most units offered three months' specialised corps training, at schools scattered throughout the country. The majority of engineers were sent to the School of Military Engineering in Casula, NSW; artillerymen joined field regiments in Holsworthy, NSW, and Wacol, Queensland. The Armoured Corps Centre was in Puckapunyal. Medical and dental corpsmen marched into the School of Army Health, Healesville, Victoria.

John Robbins chose to join the infantry, although, 'At the end of the day,' he said, 'I don't think it mattered what you put down. If you put in you wanted to be a dentist, I'm sure you would've ended up in the infantry, because that's where they had to get the numbers.' Whereas later intakes would attend the new Infantry Training Centre at Singleton, the first national servicemen did their corps training within their battalions. Robbins was posted to 6RAR with 'at least twenty' of his mates. Together, they went north to El Alamein Barracks in Enoggera, where the conscripts, who were concentrated in D and B companies, drilled alongside regular soldiers. Some of the regulars were 'a fair bit younger than us', said Robbins. 'There was quite a few that were only just seventeen. They wanted to be in the army, so they joined as soon as they could.'

At Enoggera, Alan Parr, who had asked to be posted to Infantry or Artillery, led the kind of army life journalists swore had passed forever. As well as sentry duties, 'They'd have us picking up cigarette butts and that kind of thing around our huts,' he said. 'I either mowed the lawn or did a bit of gardening.' Norm Wotherspoon chose Intelligence, then Infantry. 'I was vaguely given the impression that whatever else I tried for, I was going to get Infantry anyhow,' he said, 'because I wasn't considered much good at anything else.' But Bevan Beitzel, the boilermaker, said, 'I put Infantry first and Engineers second. The only reason I put Infantry was I knew they were coming back to Brisbane. But I actually got Engineers, and I appealed against it . . . They said, "Oh well, if you want to be in Infantry, there's plenty of vacancies."'

Peter Moore, once a 'bitsa boy' in a Holden garage in Roma, Queensland, had asked for the RAEME as his first preference and the Royal Australian Armoured Corps as his second, but he was posted to Infantry. 'At that stage, not knowing we were going to Vietnam, it didn't worry me too much,' he said. After Kapooka, Moore had spent a month in the kitchens at Puckapunyal with 7RAR. 'There was about six of us in a platoon and we had one corporal looking after us,' he said. 'They were still waiting for the second intake to come out and fill [the battalion] up, so we did bugger all really. We did all the mess duties – the sergeants' mess and the officers' mess – you'd clean up in the mornings and, if you were on the detail at night you had to serve, you'd work in the kitchen washing the dishes. They had some dishwashers but the big pots and pans – they were cooking for forty or fifty – all had to be scrubbed.' Puckapunyal is only about 125 kilometres from the Victorian Alps, and the Timbertop campus of Geelong Grammar School. 'I was there when Prince Charles was at Timbertop,' said Moore, 'and we went up to Timbertop on manoeuvres. Our platoon was the enemy platoon so we virtually did what we liked. We just ran around, made fools of ourselves and annoyed everyone. We used to take it in turns to go down and get a couple of slabs at the town, and have a few beers every night.' When the army asked for volunteers to go up to Brisbane and join 6RAR, Moore put up his hand because he wanted to be closer to home. If he hadn't, he would never have gone to Vietnam.

Most men enjoyed corps training far more than recruit training. The NCOs were kinder. The work was more interesting. The initial shock of being in the army had worn off, and the fear of the unknown had largely drained away. They were always with their mates, bush-camping, hunting, shooting, playing sports and drinking. They were growing fitter and stronger, sharper and more worldly, forced to adapt to sudden arbitrary changes, to rise to the kind of life-or-death challenges that rarely came up in bank offices or shearing sheds.

8

OFFICER TRAINING

Every educated national serviceman was offered the opportunity to become a junior officer, if not a young gentleman. At the newly opened Scheyville Officer Training Unit (OTU) near Windsor, NSW, the army hoped to turn conscripts into second lieutenants in twenty-two weeks, less than half the time it took to train regular officers on the one-year course at Portsea Officer Cadet School, Victoria. At Scheyville, the curriculum would be bled dry of anything not immediately useful to an infantry platoon commander in the field. The traditional 'finishing' lessons in manners and deportment were kept to a minimum. Scheyville graduates were not expected to spend much of their two-year military career at formal dinners.

Dave Rae Sabben, a graphic artist from Cremorne, NSW, was the last national serviceman of the first intake to go into recruit training. He received his call-up notice at one-fifteen p.m. on Friday and was on the train from Central to Wagga Wagga eight hours and thirty-five minutes later. Sabben had been given his medical examination in May, but wasn't among the men chosen to go into the army in June. He said he'd had a letter from the DLNS notifying him he was being considered for the second intake in September, but was worried he might end up being rejected, either because he was born in Fiji, or because of a football injury to his hand. He'd already told his boss he was leaving, so he made his way to the York Street recruiting centre to find out if there was a problem. The centre didn't know anything about it, so Sabben went to the national service registration office. He phoned them twice to follow up and finally 'this lad pestered us so much we thought we had better get him in', said the assistant registrar.[1] 'They were pretty shocked, actually,' said Sabben.

Sabben was a handsome, dark-haired youth with a dangerous smile. He'd been a sergeant in his school cadet corps and had been determined to become an officer in the Australian Army. He didn't want to commit to six years as a regular, so he'd decided to follow his brother into the CMF, and begin part-time officer training once he turned twenty. But national service offered him a better option: a two-year posting with the possibility of a second lieutenant's rank.

Sabben arrived at Kapooka a day after the rest of his intake, carrying a biscuit tin packed with his shaving gear, toothbrush and Bible. A couple of weeks into recruit training, he had the chance to try out for a place on the new scheme at Scheyville. 'The whole group was paraded by companies,' said Sabben, 'and the question was asked, "Have you passed your leaving certificate? Put up your hand." Then the officer out the front said, "Okay, you guys are qualified to apply for officer training." Those who wanted to apply left the parade ground and formed up on the side. There was probably twenty or so out of the hundred in the company I was in.'

They were told the training would prepare them to fight a jungle war. That war, they believed, would be in Malaya. Both Sabben and Norm Wotherspoon put in for Scheyville. 'They said if you wanted to be an officer, they'd give you a day off drill and everything,' said Wotherspoon. 'We did some problem-solving stuff: you've got this piece of wood and you've got to go over the crocodile-infested water – and I stood back and had no idea what was going on.'

Sam Lipski reported on the selection process for *The Bulletin*: 'The officer selection board, which in the case of Scheyville candidates consisted of a colonel assisted by two other officers as well as psychologists, observed recruits for a whole day as they gave lectures, participated in group discussions and were confronted with tasks like building a bridge across an imaginary stream with some planks and a piece of string. Here the board looked for the emergent leader, for how he establishes relations between members of the group, for qualities of initiative and persistence.'[2]

Wotherspoon failed selection but Sabben passed, and was flown with the other successful candidates from Kapooka to the RAAF base at Richmond. They were taken by bus – 'embussed', in army English – through Richmond's imperial Georgian town and Windsor on the Hawkesbury River, past the old Macquarie Arms Hotel, into slate and shale hills and open, rolling bush. The bus turned down an ornamental approach, through the Scheyville gates and onto the parade ground, where the national servicemen were told to get off.

'"Told" is a nice word for it,' said Sabben. 'We were shouted and screamed at and yelled at: "Fall in line!" "Put your kitbag down here!" "Arrange yourselves by height!" "What's your number?" It was just absolute panic and bedlam from the time the bus door opened. I had been forewarned that it was extremely intensive, but nothing could possibly forearm you for the experience.

'Being the first of the nashos put pressure on everybody,' said Sabben. The hastily assembled staff had little idea what to expect from the national servicemen. They couldn't be certain if the course would be too hard, or the conscripts too soft. Every subsequent intake would run a 'father-and-son' system, in which each junior cadet was paired with a senior student (a man who had passed the first eleven weeks of the course). But the first Scheyville intake was formed from dust, and the earliest cadets' 'fathers' were the camp NCOs. For national-service role models, the cadets had nobody but each other.

There were two twenty-year-old men from the New England city of Tamworth in the first intake: tall, smiling Gordon Sharp and pitbull-fit

John O'Halloran. Sharp's father ran a garage in town, O'Halloran was the son of a stock and station agent. Their boys had been in the same classes at St Nicholas Primary School and then at the Christian Brothers College, right through to the Leaving Certificate, which they both failed. They played rugby league and hockey in the same school teams. Sharp's parents, Eric and Roma, were married on the same day as O'Halloran's mother and father, and they celebrated their wedding anniversaries together every year. Each couple had two children, both of them boys, and O'Halloran's brother went through school with Sharp's brother, Tony. Both Sharp and O'Halloran were called up for national service in the first intake. They were both selected for Scheyville. And, because the Christian Brothers forged good soldiers, and footballers made the best infantrymen, and because history is an inveterate ironist, with none of the novelist's disdain for coincidence, both Sharp and Halloran became platoon commanders in the same battalion, 6RAR.

Sharp was named after his uncle, a fighter pilot who flew missions over the Mediterranean in the Second World War. 'He married an English girl over there and, in the last weeks of the war, he got shot down and killed,' said Sharp's elder brother, Tony. One of Sharp's mates in Tamworth, Cec Bayliss, used to deliver spare parts to the Sharps' garage. The two youths kicked around town at the weekends and raced their old cars along the Peel River. Boys in Tamworth would take their transistor radios to the pool and play rock'n'roll while they watched the girls.

The young Gordon Sharp left home once he'd retaken his Leaving Certificate, and headed for Sydney, where his cousin, Don Sharp, ran a hotel in Neutral Bay. 'He was only a bloody kid straight out of school,' said Don. 'He only stayed a few days. He was a very confident young man in his own way, with a very good sense of humour.' Don had spent twelve years in the CMF, 'although I never saw an enemy shot fired in my bloody life', he said. He remembered Gordon as 'the greatest Romeo this side of the Black Stump. He had a terrific personality. He used to keep us all greatly amused. He loved cars, cards and women.'

Sharp went around the TV stations looking for a job, and quickly landed a position as a trainee cameraman with Channel Seven. 'He went home to get a change of socks and everything,' said Don, 'and came back to Sydney to live.' Tony said his brother 'thoroughly enjoyed himself' at Channel Seven. 'He had a real good job and a girlfriend and he was going up to the football and the cricket up in Queensland. The only hiccup he ever had in his life was when he got called up.'

While Sharp didn't want to go into the army, O'Halloran did. 'I failed the Leaving the same day as he did,' said O'Halloran, 'but I thought, Oh well, that'll do me, because I'd got a job even before the results came out, at the bank. So I never went back to school.'

The course at Scheyville was the Portsea year with all the easy parts cut out: twenty-two weeks broken into 1430 periods, with twelve periods a day, five days a week, and five periods on a Saturday. In reality, for most men, the commitment was heavier than this. Almost every day for almost six months, Scheyville was their life, and they spent almost every minute fighting to stay there.

'If you put a foot out of place, you got put on a charge,' said Sabben, 'and that meant extra drills first thing in the morning, usually before dawn: you'd have to do another half an hour of parade-ground bashing or something. There was always pressure. Two-minute showers, and usually lukewarm if not cold, so no incentive to stay there anyway. There was nothing relaxing, nothing. Even in your relaxed time, you were under observation, being monitored, marked, assessed on everything. At the end of the day, you'd march into the mess hall, sit down and have dinner, and they were watching you. They were taking notes. How do you relate to your mates? Are you a drinker? Do you smoke? Does this rule your life, or can you take it or leave it? If you have access to alcohol, do you take one and be happy, or do you take one and sneak two?'

'There is an emphasis,' wrote Lipski, 'in everything the cadets do, on the likelihood of service in South-East Asia. Military history is concerned with one subject – the Indo-China war, and Bernard Fall's book, *Street Without Joy*, is the Clausewitz.' *Street Without Joy* is a stern, poetic analysis of France's military failure in Indochina, written by a French journalist who was angrily opposed to the Viet Minh but nursed a wary acceptance of their strengths. It had been published in 1961, before the US had any significant military presence in Vietnam, but came to serve as a warning of almost every disaster that was to come. It was often studied, but rarely heeded. 'The bottomless pit the South Vietnamese insurgency has become [proves] that the Viet-Minh and its allies throughout the Indochinese peninsula have lost nothing of their fearsome ability to fight and win a prolonged jungle and swamp war against superior forces slow to throw away the traditional "book",' wrote Fall.[3]

'Because of the premium on time the cadets do not do normal camp duties,' wrote Lipski.[4] 'There was no paperwork,' said Sabben. 'We had to fill out one form, and that was our own charge sheets.' The emphasis was strongly on physical fitness, training and drill but 'physically they didn't ask any of us to do anything we couldn't do', said Sabben, 'and, typically, the instructors did it first. It was very tough, very rugged, you were as fit as bloody nails, they fed you really well, but they took it out of you too. You were always deliberately led to the belief that you weren't doing well enough, and everybody else was doing better: "Come on, Sabben, you're pulling the chain." If you did your ten mile hike in x minutes, the next time you did it, it'd be x-minus-one minutes. Nobody ever stopped you and said, "You did that. Well done. You're coasting the course." I had the impression that I was cycling just as hard to keep up with the mob and, talking to the others, that's exactly how they felt.'

The lessons of Scheyville weren't always explicitly taught. 'You boil everyone down to the bottom line,' said Sabben, 'you deprive them of sleep, you overload them with work, and the subliminal mechanism is to make you understand that you can't do everything. You've got to prioritise. So if you're standing there at two o'clock in the morning, studying your books under the infrared heating strip, and you've got this lesson to learn or that pair of boots to polish, which are you going to do first?'

The entire Scheyville experience was also a tutorial on management. Every man was given a rank within a platoon for each exercise, but there was also a fixed rank structure among the cadets. For example, the West Australian footballer Harry Neesham was colour sergeant. 'We all got the shits with Harry,' said O'Halloran, 'because in the first three months at Scheyville, no one was allowed a day off. Then, all of a sudden, Neesham was flown home from Sydney to Western Australia to play bloody Australian Rules. Rod Hatcher couldn't even get leave to go to his sister's wedding.'

'Come September,' said Neesham, 'East Fremantle rang me on the Tuesday before the first semi-final and said would I come home and play football and, of course, I hadn't played for eleven weeks. The team we were playing was West Perth, and they'd beaten us in the three preliminary games. I said, "Absolutely, but I don't know as I'll get leave from the army."'

Scheyville commandant Brigadier Ian Geddes was a rugby union man, and initially reluctant, but he was persuaded that allowing Neesham to play would make for good publicity for the army. So, on Saturday, 18 September, Neesham left the barracks at about five-fifteen a.m., 'flew off at about seven-thirty from Sydney Airport, landed in Perth at twelve-ten West Australian time, went straight from the airport to the oval, had a shower and a rubdown, and went out and played in the semi-final.'

East Fremantle won the game and Neesham won best on ground, and was back on the plane at ten a.m. on Sunday. 'It had a very positive impact in terms of the attitude towards national service in Western Australia,' said Neesham, 'because the army had done the right thing, Neesham had come back, East Fremantle had won, national service can't be all the bad.'

Two weeks later, when Neesham asked for leave to play Claremont – the team that had beaten the Sharks in the 1964 Grand Final – Geddes was less inclined to turn him down, although 'a couple of the blokes were a bit upset', said Neesham.

He was given approval to play in the preliminary final, and East Fremantle won again. But Geddes told him he had missed too much training, and shouldn't bother to apply for leave a third time. So East Fremantle approached a sympathetic government minister – 'This is only hearsay,' said Neesham – and on the Friday before the grand final against Swan Districts, Neesham was told he could go. 'We kicked seven goals in the last quarter, against the breeze, and won the grand final.' He returned to Scheyville the next day.

Don Sharp saw Gordon only once while he was at Scheyville, when he came back to Sydney with his wrists in bandages. 'He was climbing up a bloody rope and he had his wrists around the wrong way,' said Don. 'I said, "There's your way out, if you don't want to go on." He said, "No, I'm staying in and doing my time." He would've been a good bloke, probably too good.'

O'Halloran had assumed Sharp would have to leave the course because of his injury, which happened on the scramble nets, 'where you go up, throw yourself over and come down'. O'Halloran said, 'You do it in full battledress, with your tin hat and your rifle. Well, he went up, threw himself over, and went headfirst straight down. He forgot to hang on, and he broke his wrist and got concussion. And they put him into Concord Hospital. At far as we were concerned that was the finish of Gordon, but he got back. He convinced the powers that be at Scheyville that he was all right, and he could still graduate, and he did.'

The first Scheyville intakes differed from those that followed in that there were no graduates or professional men, and every officer was exactly the same age as his national service peers in the ranks. Later cohorts would include qualified accountants and engineers, a flood of teachers and, as their deferments expired, lawyers and men with postgraduate degrees. But the class of 1966 was dominated by athletes – golfers, footballers, rugby players and cricketers. 'A hell of a lot of the blokes were good sportsmen and not brilliant academically,' said O'Halloran.

In a camp where it was difficult to make the time for friendships, O'Halloran, Sharp and Neesham were mates. 'We were all Micks,' said Neesham, 'so we'd all go to Mass together. And O'Halloran, Sharp and myself had all been taught by the Christian Brothers.' Sharp finished fiftieth in the class, O'Halloran twenty-eighth – 'I was tickled pink for a bloke who'd failed his Leaving,' he said – Sabben came twenty-second, and Neesham sixth.

But among all the footballers beaten into shape by the nuns and the brothers, and the athletes from the Anglican private schools, and the churchgoing farmers' sons toughened by boarding, was a single declared Jew, David John Roubin. Roubin's grandfather, Sidney Rosebery, has served in both world wars. Family tradition has it that he raised his age to enlist in the first and lowered it to take part in the second. Rosebery graduated from medical school in 1915, then spent six years with the British Royal Army Medical Corps in the Near and Middle East, and was twice Mentioned in Dispatches. In the Second World War, he joined the AIF, survived the New Guinea and Borneo campaigns, but died on 1 February 1946.[5]

Roubin's mother served during the Second World War, although his father, the owner of a menswear business, had a protected occupation. When Roubin was ten, they moved to Brookfield in Western Brisbane. There was only one other Jewish family in the area, but the Roubins belonged to the Orthodox Brisbane Hebrew Congregation, and Roubin was bar mitzvahed in its Byzantine-revival synagogue in Margaret Street, as were his two younger brothers – one of whom, Loris, was also to serve in Vietnam.

Roubin was working as a trainee manager at Coles when he was called up. He did a fortnight at Kapooka – 'the worst two weeks of my life up until then' – and applied for officer selection. He thought, 'Officers are managers in the army. Maybe I could do that.' At Scheyville, he said, 'There were lots of visits from senior military people, lots of visits from politicians. I can remember being visited by so many different chaplains – they'd come and knock on my door and most of them had never seen a Jew before, particularly not in the army. They'd want to know how I was, was I having any difficulties, did I need any special food, all that type of thing. They all came to have a look at me. They were amazed I didn't have horns growing out of my head or a long beard.'

Roubin had suffered a severe speech defect throughout his childhood and teens. 'I would stutter and stammer,' he said, 'particularly when I was nervous. I'd open my mouth and go, 'Ah- ah- ah — ' and nothing would come out. The speech at my bar mitzvah was a bit like that. It was so bad that if there was a knock on the door I would run and hide. If the phone rang, I would run and hide. So the army was the best thing for me. You had no option – you had to stand up in front of the class and talk. Out in the parade ground, you had to be in command of a platoon. One day, I couldn't get the words out, and they marched right off the end of the parade ground into the grass.'

Scheyville helped cure his stammer and when Roubin graduated, 'Mum and Dad came down from Brisbane,' he said. 'My grandmother was there. The graduation parade was really something. The graduation ball was something. It was a relief to know that the training was finally over. There was a lot of satisfaction. Even forty-odd years afterwards, when there's military music, I want to get up and march around. I love it.'

Four hundred first-intake national servicemen applied for officer selection, but only 106 men marched into Scheyville OTU in July 1965 – ninety-nine national servicemen and seven army aviation air cadets. Twenty-two weeks later, there were only seventy-six men left. Scheyville had a failure rate of about 30 per cent. 'You'd wake up one morning and the guy in the next room wasn't there,' said Roubin. 'He'd gone. You'd go out on a short exercise for two or three days, you'd come back and go to bed and the next morning there'd be five or six gone. The guys that didn't make it were just sent off.'

All those who passed the course became junior officers, but only a small minority ended up as infantry commanders in Vietnam. Most remained in Australia, often in training roles, scattered through every unit in army, from the ordnance corps to the legal corps. Other Scheyvillians ended up in every theatre from New Guinea to Singapore. But Neesham, O'Halloran, Sharp, and Roubin all went to Vietnam – although one of them didn't come home.

9

READY TO GO

In January 1966, the Scheyville graduates took up their postings. Gordon Sharp and Dave Sabben were both sent to D Company 6RAR. John O'Halloran was given a platoon in B Company. Together in the battalion, officers and men slogged through exercises in the bush, armed camping trips, mock battles fought in the vast military training area north-east of Rockhampton. They fought their way through the battle efficiency course at the Jungle Training Centre at Canungra in south-east Queensland, almost more frightened of having to repeat the course than its fearful tyranny of shimmying up ropes, clambering over obstacles and jumping from a tower into water far below.

Canungra was largely steep old dairy farming country, with rugged eucalypt and casuarina bushland, as well as some true jungle and deep rainforest. It did not have the South-East Asian climate or vegetation. Much of the training had to take place further out, as far as the chocolate-soil country of the Lamington Plateau, with its bandicoots and stinging bushes. Grant Collins said, 'It's difficult country and the training there is intense, but it is quite possible. It's not like a lot of the exercises when you're basically hitting a brick wall and you just don't know how you're going to get through it. At Canungra, it's just a case of persevering. But Canungra obviously was tough, and it was at least something that semi-simulated Vietnam, but the jungle was quite different. And the way they were setting it up with ambushes and so on, in Vietnam, that type of fighting just wasn't there. For a starter, we were always the ones that were doing the ambush.' Bill Winterford said, 'They had a Vietnam village made up with all tunnels in it, and they had their own VC, and we had to go and clean the joint up. I think I got killed about three times.' If it wasn't entirely realistic, the jungle training at least served to build up – or break down – the confidence of men.

Robbins enjoyed every exercise but, he said, 'There were fellas in there who weren't real good at being a soldier, and we used to carry them a bit. You knew who they were, and you had to make allowances for it. There's fellas that just find ways to trip and fall: they'll trip over a branch or something, and it makes a lot of noise when you've got all your gear, and there's a chance that the rifle might go off.

'At Shoalwater Bay there was a couple of nashos who didn't want to be there,' said Robbins, 'and it was hard to get them to take it seriously. One fella, who actually died at Long Tan, he hated every bit of it. You'd say, "We've got to put this ambush in," and they'd say, "Oh, fuck the ambush. Why don't we just stay here?"'

Cec Bayliss's father died when his son was one year old, and Bayliss had grown up in Bendemeer, on the Macdonald River north of Tamworth. He'd had a gutful of selling motor spare parts by the time he was called up, and 'was quite happy to go in the army', he said. Bayliss was posted to 6RAR and, when his infantry training at Enoggera was nearing its end, a call went out for volunteers for a battalion band to play music for the men while they marched. Experienced bandsmen were coming over from 2RAR, but recruits were needed to make up the numbers. Bayliss had played tenor horn in the Tamworth Police Boys' Band, so he put his name down and forgot about it. At the end of corps training, he was told to pack his bags and leave his mates for the unknown ranks of Admin Company, where the band was based.

There were about a dozen in the band when Bayliss joined, including half a drum corps, and it doubled in size when the recruits arrived. Bayliss was taught the side drum. Also in the band was national serviceman Albert McCormack from Launceston, Tasmania, who'd worked in the offices of an insurance company before he was called up. The others called McCormack 'Lionel' because they thought he looked like the country-folk singer Lionel Long. McCormack was 'a real comedian', said Bayliss, 'a slack soldier but a real great bloke'. He didn't like the army. 'He didn't really want to be there.'

The band was 'pretty ordinary', said Bayliss. 'Our bandmaster said it was the worst one he'd ever had.' The bandsmen were also trained as company medics, which came as a surprise to Bayliss. 'I just thought I was going to get a bludgy job playing in the band,' he said. Bayliss got married before he was posted overseas. His best man was Mick Birchell, a local panel beater and captain of the high-school rugby league team, who had been interviewed by Bob Johnson at Kapooka, and who would be dead before the year was out.

D Company's Barry Vassella had been a professional golfer in Brisbane, training under Charlie Earp, who was later to become Greg Norman's coach. Vassella had recently won a junior PGA championship in Queensland when he was conscripted. 'I was just about to start playing tournament golf,' he said. 'I was ready. What can you do? Go to jail for two years? No thanks. It was a big adventure. A far bigger adventure than I thought at the time.'

Smiling, friendly Vassella was determined to be a good soldier. 'I didn't care how hard they pushed,' he said. 'I just loved that physical challenge. Some of the exercises we did were physically tougher than anything we did in Vietnam. The last exercise at Shoalwater Bay, we'd be doing twenty kilometres a day, chasing enemy. And that was hard work, for two or three weeks nonstop.' Vassella was in Twelve Platoon, in the same section as Alan Parr, with whom he shared a birthday. Parr, he said, was 'a bit of a wildman. He had red hair and a fiery temper, and you could stir him up pretty easily if you tried.

'The whole platoon seemed to come together pretty quickly,' said Vassella. 'There were just a few outsiders, NCOs, who we thought were absolute pricks. And being national servicemen, at that time we'd rile up if we thought we were being hard done by. We didn't know you were supposed to shut up.'

Norm Wotherspoon was initially in Vassella's platoon, but when the national servicemen of D Company merged with the rest of 6RAR, Wotherspoon was posted to C Company. No longer completely on the outside, buoyed by months of shared experience, Wotherspoon had begun to make friends. He'd been out with Barry Vassella to watch Barry Humphries in Brisbane, and in C Company he got on well with little Bill Winterford. But 'Billy had a hasty temper,' said Wotherspoon, 'and he was engaged to a girl called Jacqueline, and I liked her but I liked her as a friend. And he took that ill one night and chased me all along Hill End until I had to hide up a tree for an hour. After that, he told me I had to watch my back overseas, but he decided not to pursue that.'

In the end, D Company believed they got the best out of their training. Their company commander, Harry Smith, was known for pushing men as far as they could go, but by this time they'd come to believe that all the hardship was for their own good.

'He'd run us and he'd run us,' said Peter Doyle. 'We were as lucky as Dicky Cox. We were, without a shadow of a doubt, the fittest company in the battalion. And the endurance then proved its worth later on. Harry Smith was an outstanding company commander. He was a great bloke. He wanted his pound of flesh, but he looked after the troops, too.'

'He had us that fit that Canungra was a pushover,' said Robbins. 'We were doing nine-mile runs in full gear in the mornings.'

When the time came to leave for Vietnam, most of 6RAR felt they were ready. 'We were all very patriotic,' said Wotherspoon. 'One of the news channels came by and they asked me what I thought. I said, "It's our duty to go and I'm happy to go." I believed the government was guiding our nation gently into the future, and if we had to fight the yellow peril, we had to fight them. It was the pattern of my life. I went along with what people in authority told me to do.'

Although the government repeatedly made it clear that, if a unit was sent overseas, its national servicemen would move with it, the myth that every national serviceman was a volunteer – even if their acquiescence was reached through peer pressure – runs through much Australian writing about the Vietnam War. It seems likely that at least some of the men of 5RAR were given public opportunities to refuse overseas service. Irvine Brooks of A Company said, 'We were never asked. I'm positive of that. We always knew we were going, but eventually they just turned around and said we were preparing to go.' But Gerry Coret of D Company remembered: 'When I went into the battalion, they told us on the parade ground a couple of months before that we were going to Vietnam, if you don't want to go or something's wrong . . . tell us now. There were quite a few guys who didn't want to go or couldn't go for one reason or another . . . I don't think they stepped forward as such, they just went and saw the OC.' Colin Poyser, also of D Company, said, 'We were asked, and I told the family, and I said I wanted to go.'

Many of the national servicemen of 6RAR were emphatic they were not asked. 'At no stage did anyone give us the choice,' said Wotherspoon. 'Nobody asked us, we just assumed we were going, because that was why we'd been called up.'

'I have got no memory of being asked,' said Doyle, 'no memory of that ever happening. It was a case of, "The battalion's going to Vietnam." I am absolutely 100 per cent unequivocal that I never filled in a form.'

'I can't specifically remember being asked,' said Beitzel, 'but I know the general feeling – and my belief – was we were given the option. We had one bloke in our platoon, he didn't want to go and he didn't go.

I don't know what his reasons were. He was sort of blacklisted a bit, and he was actually taken away from us. I know he was still in the command at Enoggera, because I remember him being a sentry on the gate when I got back from Vietnam to get my discharge papers.' D Company's John Heslewood said, 'The army says they were given the option of pulling out if they didn't want to go, but that's bullshit. It just didn't happen.'

'I don't recall that they ever asked us,' said Robbins. 'But I don't recall anyone saying, "I'm not going." I think we were just expected. You were in there and you had to go.'

In the history of the Vietnam War, the exception doesn't prove the rule, and nor does it verify the opposite. Only a hero or a fool would make too many generalisations. In May 1966, the government explicitly and specifically banned the army from asking national servicemen if they would serve overseas. In a confusing reply to a question in parliament, the minister for the army, Malcolm Fraser, said some units had prepared 'of their own volition, questionnaires asking national servicemen . . . which corps training they would prefer.' These were not issued by the government or army headquarters, but contained 'one or two' questions about overseas service which had been withdrawn to prevent 'misunderstanding'. Fraser had been asked whether national servicemen were being asked to sign a declaration that they were prepared to serve overseas. The government was adamant they were not. 'There is no Government or Army Headquarters requirement for any national serviceman to sign any document saying that he is willing, or that he would like, to serve overseas,' said Fraser.[1]

Menzies retired on 26 January 1966. On 8 March, in response to US pressure for more troops, and in fulfilment of the army's aspiration for an independently operating Australian force, the new prime minister, Harold Holt, announced the government would treble Australia's military contribution in Vietnam. By the middle of the year the battalion group currently at Bien Hoa and under US command would be replaced by a 'self-contained military task force of 4500 men – including more than 500 national servicemen'. The 1st Australian Task Force Vietnam (1ATF) would be under Australian command and made up of two infantry battalions, an SAS squadron and eight RAAF Iroquois helicopters, as well as combat and logistical support units and the six Caribou cargo aircraft and one hundred men of the training team already in Vietnam. 5RAR and 6RAR would replace 1RAR, which would come home in June, after a year in Vietnam, and both of the replacement battalions would include national servicemen. The normal tour of duty in Vietnam would be twelve months, and the national service intake would continue at eight thousand four hundred a year.[2] A day later 'more than 500 national servicemen' had become 'about 1400'.[3]

Malcolm Fraser briefed cabinet that each rifle section of 5RAR would comprise seven national servicemen to three regulars. Soon after the battalion arrived in South Vietnam, with the absorption of the second national service intake, 5RAR should be made up of 400 national servicemen and 379 regulars. Similar ratios were planned for 6RAR and all subsequent battalions. This had stark implications for the mortality of national servicemen. The job of a rifleman on patrol was one of the most dangerous in Vietnam: in 1966, when nobody had foreseen the casualties which would be inflicted on Australian engineers by Australian mines, the rifleman was the soldier most likely to die. And although national servicemen made up only about one-third of the entire Task Force, 70 per cent of riflemen in Vietnam would be conscripts.

The Liberal candidate in the by-election for Menzies' former seat of Kooyong in Victoria was twenty-seven-year-old Andrew Peacock, who said he had told his secretary to rip up 'snide and insincere letters' sent to him about conscription. 'I won't give the writers . . . the satisfaction of having me read them,' he said. He claimed he had not heard from one person sincerely worried about national service, and the issue was being used 'almost purely for political purposes'.[4] Peacock won the seat with a comfortable majority on 2 April.

The first national serviceman to go to Vietnam left Australia by air on 4 April. He was Sergeant Alan Watson, a former Brisbane court reporter posted to the Eastern Command provost corps, who was detailed to take shorthand notes at an Australian court-martial in Saigon. Watson was home before the week was out, but returned three times to Vietnam.

The US newspaper *Newsday* looked at Australian preparations with a quizzical eye. A *Newsday* 'special correspondent' said the Australian government dreaded the death of the first conscript, but showed a 'remarkable willingness' to have its hand forced in the direction of greater military commitments overseas. This was despite the country's urgent need for development funds, and due to the 'irrational' fear that an underpopulated Australia would one day be taken over by 'a horde of yellow men invading from the north'.[5]

The Australian tabloid press enjoyed the idea that a majority of national servicemen were happy to go to Vietnam. The *Sun-Herald*'s Bob Johnson was a specialist in going places, finding nothing, and then reporting on things that weren't there. On the eve of the departure of elements of 5RAR for Vietnam, he visited Holsworthy to find no last-minute packing, no frenzied activity, no rivalry between conscripts and regulars, and nobody with any truck with the anti-war movement. Furthermore, 'malcontents, if any, just weren't around'.[6]

Earlier, Geoff Jones of the Melbourne *Sun* had visited troopers of the 1st Armoured Personnel Carrier Squadron in Puckapunyal, some of whom would be going to Vietnam. Under the headline 'Morale High at Puckapunyal', Jones had reported that, inside the squadron, 'probably the only long faces the day the names go up on the board will belong to those lads who are NOT in the 1400 trainees to make up Australia's increased task force'.[7] Among those men whose optimism was noted by Jones was Vic Pomroy of Melbourne, who had less than a year to live.

In the infantry, officers and men were now bonded in their platoons, perhaps nowhere so tightly as Eleven Platoon D Company 6RAR, whose second lieutenant, Gordon Sharp, did not always keep the traditional distance from his troops. Before they left Australia, some of the men from D Company went out on the town with Sharp, who 'never drank alcohol', wrote Robbins later, 'but could be the life of the party; he could get pissed on lemonade . . . We were in the city in his MGB sports car at about 5.00am when he noticed a big sign on a building – Delta Company Construction. Sharpie says, "I've gotta have that sign." So he swings around, pulls into the kerb, walks onto the road, stops a passing truck, tells the driver the story, gets up on top of the truck and acquires the sign. He converted it to Delta Company Destruction and that sign went with us to Vietnam along with a nude photo in a frame from a hotel in George Street.'[8] Sharp was 'a mate of ours', said Robbins. 'We always respected his rank, but he was able to mix with us, him coming in as an officer through nasho, and us being nashos.'

On 20 April 1966, a prayer vigil was held by the Canberra Vietnam Vigil Committee at Wynyard Park. The chairman of the organising committee, the Reverend Alan Walker, said, 'The vigil has been arranged as a protest against conscription and the war in Vietnam. We are not condemning the young soldiers . . . We recognise they are the victims of wrong policy by the Australian Government.'[9] It's an important tenet of post-war folklore that protesters blamed soldiers for the war. It's difficult to find any contemporary statement that supports this idea. Most demonstrations actually used the war as an issue to attack the government.

On 21 April, thirteen hundred troops bound for Vietnam, including most of 5RAR, marched through Sydney. There were no protests, although hundreds of police had turned out to deal with any possible demonstrators. Cheering crowds ten deep lined Macquarie Street. Almost every building flew a flag. Workers shredded phone books and sent flakes of paper falling like confetti onto the parade. The crowds were leafleted not by Communists but by BA Santamaria's

National Civic Council, which had produced thirty thousand flyers supporting Australia's involvement in Vietnam.

In Tamworth, the *Northern Daily Leader* had interviewed six local national servicemen set to leave for the war, including John O'Halloran, Mick Birchell, Cec Bayliss and Gordon Sharp. 'Except for Gordon, the group seemed resigned about leaving their jobs to join the Army,' wrote the newspaper. Gordon Sharp said he would lose a lot of experience while away, and would not have volunteered for overseas service.[10]

Sharp flew to Vietnam on 8 June, the same day on which a crowd estimated at about three hundred thousand people gave the returned men of 1RAR a 'Mardi Gras' welcome home. 'In Martin Place,' wrote the *Sydney Morning Herald*, 'office girls tore up telephone directories and office paper to shower the troops with confetti. One elderly woman dashed into the marching ranks and began kissing the cheeks of the soldiers. Young girls repeatedly ran up to the soldiers and threw streamers into their ranks. PMG employees in Martin Place sent down a thick hail of ticker tape.' NSW premier Robert Askin had appealed to city employers to allow their staff time off to watch the march.

There were isolated dissenters among the spectators. An elderly man with a metal crutch knocked 'one long-haired protester almost senseless. A woman with an umbrella beat two demonstrators over the head. One youth who broke towards the saluting dais clutching a placard was knocked flying by a detective.' But 'barristers in Macquarie Street, splendid in their gowns and wigs, lined the footpath to applaud' and 'building labourers perched on scaffolding opposite the town hall to join in the welcome'. The commanding officer of 1RAR, Lieutenant Colonel Alexander Preece, approached the dais outside Sydney Town Hall, straight-backed and in-step, the model of discipline. Suddenly Nadine Jensen, a twenty-one-year-old typist from Campbelltown, ran at Preece and threw her arms around him, smearing him with red paint, kerosene and turpentine, 'symbolic', she later said, 'of the blood being shed in Vietnam'.[11]

Preece handled the incident with dignity, his composure unaffected, as if he'd been expecting something like this, as if he'd always seen it coming. He shrugged her off, kept his eyes fixed on the dais, salute tight to the brim of his slouch hat, palm turned outwards, as she moved on to the next man in the parade. Police pulled Jensen out of the way, dragged her off and took her to hospital 'for a clean-up' before charging her with offensive behaviour. Jensen said she would plead guilty with an explanation. 'I wanted to make the politicians realise that some people in Australia are opposed to our sending the troops to fight in Vietnam.' The next day in court, Jensen, her blonde hair stained red, waived her right to a first offender's closed hearing and was fined $6 and given a $100 good-behaviour bond for a year. She said she'd felt it was her personal responsibility to do something about Vietnam, the protest had been her own idea, she didn't belong to any party or organisation, and her actions were not directed against the soldiers, whom she called 'the instrument of high authority', but against the authority itself.[12]

Jensen's one-woman demonstration was not thought of as important by the *Sydney Morning Herald* at the time. The front page on 9 June featured large photographs of marching soldiers, and welcome-home banners, while the report of Jensen's actions appeared on page five. It was preceded by domestic news judged more pressing: the first eighty national servicemen had been sent to Borneo; Australian National Line was still trying to find a crew to take the cargo ship MV *Jeparit* to Vietnam; 203 of the old £100 notes were missing from the banking system and might be under someone's carpet; and the state cabinet had shelved plans for Sunday drinking in hotels.[13]

Yet today, the three hundred thousand welcoming citizens have disappeared from memory – along with the eighty engineers, the first of hundreds of forgotten Australian national servicemen who served in Malaysia and Singapore – to be replaced by flights of swooping, vampiric Nadine Jensens, soaked in plasma. Throughout the Vietnam War, there was no other reported example of returned soldiers in

Australia being doused in red paint, blood, entrails or anything else. There were no reported incidents at all of national servicemen being treated this way.

All these stories came later, after the fall of Saigon.

10

IN COUNTRY

The new Australian Task Force set up its base in the poor and rural Phuoc Tuy province, south-east of Saigon. The camp at Nui Dat was built by the men who were to occupy it, dug out of the ground – and almost out of South Vietnam itself – by national servicemen and regulars, infantrymen, engineers and all the rest: men from Brisbane and Dubbo, Adelaide and Armidale. The Australians were joined by 161 Battery of the Royal New Zealand Artillery, and a small number of US troops, but few Vietnamese ever walked through the gates of the Dat, except as interpreters or prisoners.

Phuoc Tuy, with a local population of about one hundred thousand, was chosen as the Australians' tactical area of operation in part because it was a centre for enemy activity. Wherever green hills or mountains rose from the paddy fields and rubber plantations, guerrilla bases looked down upon the villagers below. The area had been a centre of resistance throughout the French War. The villages of Long Tan (which had been emptied by US troops before 1ATF arrived) and Long Phuoc were VC strongholds, just as they had once supported the Viet Minh. But there were cadres and organisers and part-time guerrillas throughout the province, as well as professional 'main-force' soldiers. The 'local-force' peasants of the D445 Provincial Mobile Battalion – raised from Hoa Long, a little west of 1ATF;

Dat Do to the east; and Long Dien to the south – proved a tireless adversary to the Australians, along with the regularly constituted 274 and 275 Main Force Regiments. The VC were the local people in arms, but the Australians had come to Phuoc Tuy to disrupt their supply routes, to separate the guerrillas from their villages, the sons from their mothers, the legs from their lungs.

In the years to come, most Australian engagements in Phuoc Tuy would happen over a very small area. The Battle of Long Tan in 1966 took place in a rubber plantation only five kilometres from Nui Dat. The worst fighting of the 1968 Tet Offensive raged through Long Dien, about eight kilometres south of 1ATF. The Battle of Binh Ba in 1969 was fought six kilometres to the north of the base. The killing in Phuoc Tuy was an intimate, family affair.

Australian troops arrived in Vietnam either by ship or by air. Dave Sabben flew with D Company 6RAR from RAAF Amberley to Saigon's huge Tan Son Nhut Air Base. 'Tan Son Nhut was like bedlam,' said Sabben, 'breakfast in a lunatic asylum. Everywhere you looked there were planes landing and taking off, buses and jeeps. There was ammo dumps and fuel dumps, the whole bloody works. Half the runways were crowded with helicopters and jets, just parked, not taking off. There were thousands of war machines, acres and acres of Hueys and Phantoms. We'd not seen anything like it in the whole Australian Army. Tan Son Nhut airport contained more choppers and aircraft than the whole of Australia. We got off the aircraft, out of air-conditioned luxury into an oven, a furnace.'

They were flown to Vung Tau, a port city about one hundred kilometres from Saigon, where they had 'about five days of acclimatisation', said Sabben, 'because these guys had come out of temperate Australia to tropical Vietnam in the middle of their summer. We were sitting there in June and the water bottles were warm.'

'As we were going through Vung Tau, I saw a woman sit down

and she was having a shit in the street,' said John Robbins. 'I thought, Shit, that's different.'

'Suddenly there was no restriction on ammo,' said Sabben. 'However much you wanted to shoot, you could shoot. Finally, for the first time, everyone had a shot at the M60 [machine gun]. They'd only ever been on the range and fired a couple of shots from the SLR [self-loading rifle]. Now they fired two magazines from the SLR. It was just getting them used to the noise and the kickback and the firing positions and so on. It was hectic. There were helicopters overhead the whole time, and Armoured Personnel Carriers [APCs] trundling around the place, but conditions were very primitive. We were living in canvas tents on the beach. Nothing was developed there – no electricity, no telephones.'

A Company's Bevan Beitzel, the boilermaker from Ipswich, who ended up on a Vietnamese language course, said 'We did short patrols, mainly to acclimatise, and I remember walking along Back Beach, and we got strafed by a US jet. It was only a joke. He frightened the shit out of us. Our platoon commander was a little bit of an edgy type of bloke. He got fanatical about picking up intelligence about where the enemy might be. Any piece of paper that was on the ground, if it had Vietnamese writing on, it could be the missing key. It was a bit of a joke with us that we were more like litter collectors, picking up paper.'

Kenny Gant, a butcher from Brisbane, wrote home to his parents, 'If you could see where we are camped, you would never think there was a war on. The camp is right on the beach front and we are living on the sand. I've got sand in everything – gets on your goat after a while. There's stacks of kids running around trying to sell pineapples and bananas to us, funny little things they are – smell like the chook house though. They call us cheap Charlie number 10 because we won't pay their price for anything. They call us number 10 and the VC are number one.' Later in the week, he wrote, 'Had a riot in town last night. Two Yanks were killed and a few wounded when someone threw a grenade in the street . . . Had a striptease show on Friday night. Two tarts from Kings Cross came over and took their gear off, nothing real exciting.'[1]

5RAR was the first of the new battalions to leave Vung Tau to work on the Task Force base, thirty kilometres north-east. 'We flew into Nui Dat by helicopter,' said 5RAR's Gerry Coret, who'd been working as a shoe-shop relief manager in Victoria when he was called up. 'It was one of the many times I was very frightened, because when we arrived there were bombs going off and there was shooting. I thought, Oh shit, what are we letting ourselves in for here? But all it was was the Americans clearing the area.'

After 5RAR had secured their part of Nui Dat, 6RAR followed them up to the hill. 'There were absolutely no defences,' said John Heslewood, 'no barbed wire, no pits, nothing. From the minute you get there, you were putting up barbed wire and digging pits, and we also had to start patrolling straight away, to make sure that area around the place was clear. When you weren't patrolling or doing ambushes at night-time, you were in camp digging holes in the ground or putting up barbed wire. And there was no tents or anything, so you were sleeping under two-man hutchies. All your gear got wet every day. It got dry the next day, then got wet again, so it was pretty ordinary at first.'

'I remember thinking, We're going to be here for a long time,' said Beitzel, 'so you ground your ideas on what your pit's going to be like. Once I came back from the language course, I can't remember ever getting into the pit. The only ones you'd get in there were rats and snakes.' Beitzel said 6RAR 'more or less joined up with 5RAR, completed virtually three-quarters of the circle, then we started putting up the concertina wire, the Claymore mines and all this. You'd be up before the sun in the morning for stand-to.' The circumference of the fence was twelve kilometres. 'Our wire was thirty or forty metres wide,' said Peter Moore, 'and ten or twelve coils high, and if you weren't doing that you'd be digging the gunpits, and the coverings over those all had to be done. The only hot meals we got was when they brought them down in the hotboxes probably once a week, and the rest of the time was hard rations. We got a couple of tents: one was for the Q store and one we could either have for the boozer or a dining area. Of course, the first one was the boozer.'

'The wire was a cattle fence, initially,' said Peter Doyle, 'just a couple of squares of barbed wire and a few metal pickets. It piss-poured with rain. What gear we had in our kitbags went mouldy. We were just living like animals. We worked seven days a week, month in, month out. We had to put in command posts, and they were all dug by hand.'

'The day we moved up there,' said Norm Wotherspoon, 'we had to dig our weapon pits chest high, and that was the day the monsoon started. When it was stand-to at dusk, we were up to our chests in water when we were standing in the pits. Some guy had blown up his li-lo and I saw it floating away through the rubber. We just seemed to be completely wet and rained on for about six weeks.'

'So you're working all day in that heat,' said Robbins, 'plus patrolling, and at night you had to have all-night ambushes. They'd tell you to sleep, because you're going out on an all-night ambush. Well, you couldn't bloody sleep. You can't sleep during the day, in that sort of heat, particularly if Artillery are putting rounds off all the time. It was bloody hard. And the morale was probably at a low point, because of the rain and the mud. The mud was bloody awful.'

Cec Bayliss, the bandsman from Tamworth who had discovered he was also the platoon medic, said the band pitched a tent near battalion HQ, filled it with their instruments, and touched them only once in the next ten months. As a medic, he said, he was simply a rifleman with a 'pretty ordinary' medical pack. 'All our bandages were from 1942,' Bayliss said. 'My medical pack was ripped. It was old when I got it. There was nothing to carry our morphine in. I ended up getting a box that artillery shells come in and put my morphine in that, because at that stage we had needles and they'd just get broken. We ended up getting a drip, but in the early days we never had that.' Traditionally, the bandsmen/medics were known as stretcher bearers. 'But we never carried a stretcher,' said Bayliss. 'All we had was a stretcher that you fold up. You had to find bits of timber to put up each side of it. She was pretty bloody basic.'

It was the *Daily Mirror* in London, rather than any Australian newspaper, which reported the 'incredible' news that Australian combat medical teams in Vietnam were using British First World War field dressings, 'clearly marked "Made by Arthur Berton Ltd., London, June, 1917"'. A spokesman for the army didn't deny the charge, but said, 'Because of its composition, the age of a field dressing is of no importance.'[2] Bayliss said the bandsmen had better musical instruments than medical implements: 'I don't think the medical pack I carried was up to scratch, but the drums were pretty good.'

'After a while,' said Doyle, 'we had a couple of tents – which, I might add, had been in storage since the Second World War or Korea – and when we unpacked them they were full of holes.'

'At one stage the sergeant cook came around our hutchies to see if we had any supplies,' said Irvine Brooks of 5RAR, 'because you'd get your rations, and you wouldn't take them all out on patrol with you, because there was stuff you didn't want to take, stuff you didn't like – and he came around to see if we had anything they could cook up for meals.'

Some of the boys already wished they'd stayed at home, away from the storms and the bugs, the sand and the heat, but plenty had come looking for a blue and were impatient for the battle to start. But there were few national servicemen who were keen to fight a counterinsurgency, or even understood what it meant. The regulars with experience in Malaya knew, to a degree, but Malaya wasn't Vietnam: the 'bandits' or 'Communist Terrorists' in Perak and Kedah had little support outside the minority Chinese community. Whereas the Viet Cong and their 'sympathisers' – their mothers and fathers, wives and sisters, aunts and uncles, cousins and brothers, school friends and comrades – were popular in every town and village in

Phuoc Tuy, with the exceptions of the provincial capital of Ba Ria and Binh Gia, a Catholic settlement of refugees from the north.

It was a difficult situation for Australian troops to comprehend. They were supposed to be defending the people of the south from infiltration from the north, but most of the locals who wholeheartedly backed their efforts were northerners, whereas the infiltrators were largely men who'd been born and brought up in Phuoc Tuy. In 1966, the people of the province had been infiltrated not yet by a military force but by a political idea, which the Australians had agreed was alien and must be expelled.

The village of Long Phuoc, 1.2 kilometres south-east of Nui Dat, had been a 'fighting village' of the Viet Minh, and a source of sanctuary and recruits for the VC. Long Phuoc was inside the Australians' Line Alpha, a cordon of land within four kilometres of Nui Dat to be cleared of locals and so keep the base out of range of fixed mortars. US troops had driven out the villagers but, after their families had been resettled, the old men, women and children returned to tend their cattle and their gardens, and the graves of their ancestors buried in the ground, and the young men still carried arms against the enemy.

If Nui Dat was going to come under fire, the chances were the shells would swoop out of Long Phuoc. So on 21 June 1966, the Australians went in to destroy it and, for some of the men, it broke their hearts. Pat Burgess, one of the finest of the Australian war correspondents in Vietnam, recorded the demolition of Long Phuoc. 'Long Phuoc was a village of deep, cool wells, of fishponds shaded by flowering shrubs, of verandahs made for children to play around and to shade the old from the Phuoc Tuy sun. In almost every yard there were wood shavings. It was a village of craftsmen, who made their own furniture, who carved even their own candlesticks. It was a village of subsistence farmers and fishermen. It was also, it turned out, a village of riflemen . . . honeycombed with tunnels . . . The people of Long Phuoc were told by loud hailer and pamphlet that it was to be destroyed. Destruction by napalm and bomb would have been less hazardous but the Australians cleared it house by house, tunnel by tunnel. But they still burned it. On to the flames they still had to throw the hand-carved candlesticks, the old exercise book, the flimsy parasol, the tiny rubber thong.'[3]

This was Operation Enoggera, one week's work. It's the image of that 'tiny rubber thong' that lingers. Without it, there would be less of a memory of Long Phuoc. The Australians made no habit of destroying villages, and perhaps that's another reason why the ghost of the place of deep cool wells and shaded fishponds continues to haunt the history books.

Operation Enoggera included 6RAR and 1 Field Squadron, the engineers. They ruined the entire settlement. 'We finished it off,' said Heslewood. 'Just razed it.' Peter Moore said, 'I really wondered what we were doing putting all these beautiful big homes down and destroying houses. I wouldn't've thought anyone would do that.' But once an Australian soldier was wounded by a sniper, 'your thoughts change', said Moore.

'There was a wooden structure, and it had a little Buddha in it,' said Wotherspoon. 'I said to the platoon commander, "Look, this is a school. It's a Buddhist shrine. We don't have to burn it." He said, "Of course you do. This is how they indoctrinate people." I remember watching that Buddha burning and thinking, This isn't right. I saved a little certificate that some kid had been given, or was going to be given.'

The Australians recovered rice and salt, rifles, punji stakes and unexploded shells. 'I was watching people dismantle buildings and set them to the torch,' said Wotherspoon. 'There were crops around the village, bananas and rice, and I wondered how it would be to be moved unwillingly away from your home, and told that anyone found in that area would be considered enemy and shot. That was a pretty tough call. Because people did try to go back, for whatever reason, and some of them were shot. They weren't combatants at all. They were just villagers.'

'We cleared that,' said Moore, 'and we did a lot of heavy patrolling in that area, moving people out of there, and there was still a lot of stragglers from the places that we'd pushed them out of, who were going back in there to their fruit farms and all that, and we'd catch them in there and escort them back out to where there should be, and interpreters would tell them they weren't supposed to be there and not to come back in. Which was another thing a bit funny to me: they're not letting people go and gather their food.'

Kenny Gant wrote home, 'I was a bit scared before we went as the Yanks tried to take it a few months ago and they had 23 killed and 96 wounded so I didn't know what to expect. Before we went in, the Yanks bombed it a few times and that must have cleaned out all the people because when we went through we didn't see a soul . . . One of our blokes shot a woman the other day. She was walking through the bush and he fired a few shots over her head and called for her to stop but she kept running, so with his next shot he shot her dead as a doornail.'

Gant, the fifth of thirteen children, was worried for his brother, Ron. 'Sure hope Ronnie doesn't get called up,' he wrote later, 'If you do, don't have anything to do with infantry. Believe me, there's no glory in shooting women and kids and burning their houses.'[4]

The Australians had not come to Phuoc Tuy to drive civilians out of their homes. They were in Vietnam to stop a North Vietnamese idea from marching south, just as they believed the Japanese idea of imperial domination had been halted, turned back and eventually crushed at the end of the Second World War, before it could reach Australia. But they wanted to see Communism given flesh and blood by yellow men in khaki, uniformed and armed, and confront it on the battlefield man to man, like a gunfight on the main street of a windblown town, where marshals faced down outlaws and victory went to the side with the quickest draw and the keenest eye, but also the purest heart. And the Australians believed they had all those things. 'It was frustrating,' said Robbins. 'We'd had all this training, and we were gonna run into some of them, try ourselves out and see if we were any good – and where are they?'

The correspondent Burgess never discovered what he was looking for while he was in Vietnam, the transcendent truth of the conflict, but his eyes caught clues wherever they rested. 'Every time I went back to the Task Force I went out to Long Phuoc,' he wrote. 'On each occasion I found a dignified Vietnamese lady collecting the roof tiles and piling them carefully one on top of the other against the day when the war would end and she would be able to rebuild her house and move back among the woodworking chisels and the flowers and vegetables in tins.'[5]

On the evening the destruction of Long Phuoc began in Phuoc Tuy, Arthur Calwell addressed a meeting against government policy on conscription and Vietnam at Mosman Town Hall, Sydney. He was jeered by pro-war hecklers and responded, 'You think you can deflect an idea with a bullet. You cannot.'[6] When the rally was over, and the Labor leader about to be driven away, nineteen-year-old Peter Kocan walked up to his car and fired a sawn-off .22 rifle through the window at point-blank range. 'Oh, I've been shot,' Calwell cried, and, according to the *Sydney Morning Herald*, 'with blood streaming down his face, he slumped across the lap of his driver'.[7]

Barry Robinson and Wayne Haylen, Australia's first two 'draft-card' burners, chased Kocan for about one hundred metres and overpowered him. An ambulance took Calwell to the Royal North Shore Hospital, where a doctor said Calwell had been hit by splinters when the car window had shattered. A number of glass fragments were removed from his face, throat and jaw, but he was in a satisfactory condition. The bullet was found lodged in his lapel.

It was the first attempted assassination of a federal political leader in Australian history, by a man later judged to be mentally ill, who admitted he wanted to kill any public figure but it was easier to shoot Calwell because he didn't like his policies. Although Peter Kocan and his rifle are barely remembered, while Nadine Jensen and her paint are never forgotten, the shooting of Calwell was as much an aberration as Jensen's swooping flight. While there had been some sensational reports of rowdy clashes at political meetings, *The Bulletin* editorialised, 'however offensive to nearly all Australians the anti-Vietnam demonstrations may have been, they have been on the whole scrupulously law-abiding – only outdone in this respect by the calm response of most emotionally committed Government supporters. The debate has been passionate but in no way conducive to violence . . . we live in a world marked by insane violence and instability. And what has happened in Australia, until last week's shooting? A few demonstrations, a girl pouring red paint on herself to symbolise blood . . . '[8]

But all the muffled sound and fury at home was as nothing compared to the cheering news from overseas where, in that same edition of the *Bulletin* the Australian public was reassured, the battle was almost over. In a piece headed 'After the Viet Cong Collapse', the journalist Peter Samuel wrote 'It is now abundantly clear to all except those who live in dreamworlds, that the war in Vietnam is being won.' Samuels mocked those who'd claimed the Free World Forces would need vast numbers of troops to beat the VC, or the communist reinforcements were inexhaustible. 'Those ratios turned out to be bunk,' wrote Samuel. 'The Viet Cong may yet pull off a few spectacular feats, but the war is increasingly taking the form of a series of mopping-up exercises. These will be a bloody and horrible business but there is little doubt that it can now be successfully accomplished.'[9]

It would not be last time the VC had been finally defeated – in the media, if not actually on the ground.

Norm Wotherspoon was now a signaller, but his company 2IC, Captain Peter Harris, enjoyed his sense of humour, and seconded him to be his batman, or orderly. Wotherspoon was serving at Harris's side when his platoon mate and friend since recruit training, Bill

Winterford, lost an arm during Operation Hobart, a search-and-destroy mission to clear VC from the area around Nui Dat.

'Hobart was absolutely stupid,' said John O'Halloran. 'I think it was our first major battalion operation, and we moved out of a night-time. Well, Christ almighty, you couldn't find any bastard. It was a long patrol, heading out north of Long Tan, but then sweeping down one side of the paddy fields, coming down beside Long Tan, and sweeping down the other side.'

Winterford was with C Company, patrolling the edge of an area of bamboo on 25 July 1966. 'It was supposed to be about five days out in the scrub,' said Winterford. 'I only lasted one day. I think we were on a left flank, coming up towards this clearing, which spread out about one hundred to two hundred metres. There was trees and bush on the other side, and as we came up to it, the sergeant opened fire. A radio message came back, "Cease fire, you're shooting at your own people," and he said, "Well, tell them they've changed their uniforms." '

The patrol had crossed paths with VC who had already exchanged fire with D and A companies, altered their direction of movement and run into C Company. 'Then all hell broke loose,' said Winterford, 'machine-gun firing and bugles blowing and whistles. It put the fear of Christ into you. I was a machine gunner, and where I went down, I couldn't bring my gun into fire, so I moved up, and this sapper – who I didn't know from a bar of soap – came up beside me with ammunition and we got in a bit of a blue. We were being hammered by this machine gun. We quietened that down. I must've been a better shot than him.'

'Captain Harris was in charge of the company that day,' said Wotherspoon, 'and he was a real gung-ho hero type. He'd stroll around like Rambo, and I had to stroll around with him. He had a fierce temper, and I sort of liked him and hated him. He could be an absolute prick. But, once he worked out the enemy had mortars, he was running around and calling in artillery support, and when it came they got the range wrong.'

'They fired two shots,' said Winterford. 'The first one came in all right, and the second one landed about twenty-five feet from me. The shrapnel took my arm off. Well, it was hanging there. The rest of it's a bit blank. They said I kept standing there firing, like an idiot. That's apparently why they gave the medal. I was the first nasho to get the Military Medal.'

'He got his arm basically shredded,' said Wotherspoon. 'So Harris said, "Come on, Wothery," and went over there, and there were people shooting everywhere, and Bill was lying there. He must've been in enormous pain, and he was cracking these weak jokes while he was bleeding all over the grey dust with this arm hanging by a thread.'

'The medic was very fast,' said Winterford. 'He got to me. I think I only yelled out about three times. He tied my hand onto the side of my arm. He reckoned they might be able to save it, but when I saw it, I knew it had gone. The American choppers came in and pulled out me and Sapper [Leslie] Prowse. He got hit in the head with small-arms fire. He died on the chopper going in. I never lost consciousness. I apparently abused the forward observer, he was a Kiwi. I told him the only people out here who're safe are the ones we're fighting.'

Under fire, Wotherspoon realised he was 'absolutely more afraid of Captain Harris' than the enemy. 'I had wondered how I'd be in a combat situation and I found that I just obeyed orders, and afterwards my knees shook and my lips trembled.'

The VC 'bounced off Charlie Company', said O'Halloran. 'By this stage, we'd gone into a harbour position around the fence, right on the side of the crop, about five metres in from the paddy fields. And they hit us.'

The enemy began mortaring the Australians – and blowing bugles. 'It was the first time any of us had ever heard of this type of thing,' said O'Halloran. 'They'd blow the bugles and hit us, then they'd blow again and not a shot, and they'd pull back – I was shit scared, we were all shit scared, and "Bluey" Bartsch, a national serviceman, tough as guts, a redheaded truck driver from Queensland, but solid as rock, says, "Hey, boss, these cunts've got a fucking band out here, eh?"'

O'Halloran's Five Platoon escaped without casualties, but Six Platoon B Company was hit much harder. Pat Burgess sent home a cheery report of B Company's battle, which saw the deaths of three Australians. But Burgess saw the bright side: 'The whole battalion knows that the three soldiers all died gamely and that 19 wounded fought on while they were able,' he wrote. 'One Australian machine-gun changed hands four times during the action as soldiers took over from their dying or badly wounded mates . . . In this Australian platoon the old men were the National Servicemen. Most of the others were younger than the National Servicemen, 19 years old or 20. Only one man in the platoon had ever been fired on before.

'The Australians came under heavy machine-gun fire from three sides. It was low and withering. Also, every man in the platoon who was not wounded felt the mortar bullets [sic] slam into the trees behind him like axe blows, every man was hit by earth from exploding mortar bombs . . . Tony Purcell . . . was wounded in the arm. He killed a Vietcong scout, and then was killed himself. He was a National Serviceman from the second intake, and although wounded had continued to throw grenades.'[10]

Bill Winterford completed his national service back in Australia, with only one arm. 'I was sent back to Enoggera,' he said, 'to a holding area, and I worked in the sergeants' mess, polishing brass. I used to do phone duties and shit like that, but no more carrying rifles or anything. I did my two years.'

When Winterford's time was over, he tried to re-enlist. 'I had to write a letter of sympathy, as they called it, saying why I wanted to stay in. In the end, I said I didn't want sympathy, I just wanted to stay in the army, and took my discharge. Then I got married. I couldn't get a job, because you'd let them know you only had one arm, and when you'd go in they'd wind up saying, "No, you wouldn't be able to handle the job." So I fronted the army and they gave me a job at RAEME Workshops at Bulimba.'

He passed his fitter's certificate, qualified to work on any weapon from air rifles to artillery, and stayed with the RAEME for twenty-eight years, as a civilian governed by army rules and regulations. 'I designed my own jigs,' he said. 'If there was a way to do it, I could do it. I could put together a machine gun faster than anyone.'

While Nui Dat was still under construction, the army asked for volunteers to take Vietnamese-language training back in Vung Tau. They needed one man from each infantry platoon, one from each company headquarters, and one from battalion headquarters.

'I thought it might beat sitting around digging holes and putting wire up,' said Beitzel, 'so I volunteered. It was run by an Australian Army major, but all the instructors were in the ARVN and they spoke pretty good English. They didn't expect us to learn the Vietnamese language. They wanted us to be able to pick up some of it, and they paired us off with a Vietnamese lad. They were usually university students who'd done English through their education. At the end of the course, my bloke would come back to my platoon, and the idea was him and I would work together as interpreters.

'They'd bring out these Vietnamese lads of a daytime, and we'd mingle with them, ask them a few questions, get to know them a bit, just trying to see if we could match with somebody we could get on with. I don't know how I ended up with Dinghi Dong. He was a quiet lad. He had some problems when he first came back with us. If he wanted to go to the toilet, he went to the toilet there. He didn't cover it up. It took us quite a while to train him into digging a hole and burying it. He had problems with hygiene, but the platoon sergeant absolutely loved him. They let him go home to his family every so often, and he used to bring me back Vietnamese records that were on the hit parade in Vietnam at the time.

'They put them in uniform, but when they came to us they were wearing Aussie greens and a bush hat, and the same webbing that we had. At Nui Dat, he slept in the same tent I did. On patrol, he just slept with me, because him and I were in platoon HQ. The only time when I was in Vietnam that I really needed translation, he wasn't there. After I went back to the unit, we went out to guard the main highway from Vung Tau to Saigon for the Yanks. They were moving equipment through, and the ARVN were doing the patrol, and they tripped on a booby trap and one of them was seriously injured. They took him to the US military hospital and they wanted his family to be advised of what had happened. So they took me to the village and I had to try and translate to them exactly what had happened to him and where he was. We got through it. It was more hand signs than anything.'

Most of the Australians on the course were not linguists, but Netherlands-born Gerry Coret already spoke Dutch, English and German, and perhaps absorbed a little more Vietnamese than most. 'I got to speak with the Vietnamese people and find they were more interested in getting on with their life than having wars around them,' he said. 'I found them very pleasant.'

Barry Vassella, who was also on the first course, described it as 'totally and absolutely useless. Really. I don't know who dreamed it up. We all learned some Vietnamese and we could interpret a little bit, but it was absolutely useless as far as use of manpower was concerned. Maybe I interpreted on three or four occasions over a year. They put on a big show. We graduated. The bloody brigadier came down and gave us parchment scrolls. We were totally out of our depth. So I learned a few phrases: "Where's your ID card?" I got that off pat.'

In May, when the fatally wounded Errol Noack had been lifted by helicopter into the skies over Phuoc Tuy, like a soul carried to heaven in the belly of a dragonfly, his mates in the battalion, whose job had been to keep him alive, couldn't think about what they couldn't change. Either Noack would live – and they always believed any man who was intact would get through – or he would die, but the rest had to carry on for the sake of those who remained. 'When anyone got hit, they disappeared,' said Grant Collins. 'They were put into a chopper and they were gone. You didn't spend any time with your wounded and, when they died, you didn't have time to even think back and start some sort of grieving process.'

There was never much of a camp life for most infantrymen at Nui Dat. While troops such as cooks remained at the base most of the time, for the diggers operation followed quickly upon operation, with men often sweating for five weeks at a stretch in the bush. A man had little time to get to know anyone outside of his own platoon, or even his own section. Unless he had met them in training, the rest of his company might be strangers. At the end of an operation, the infantry returned briefly to their hutchies and makeshift bars, to the task of building the camp, and to drink their beer ration of 'two cans per man per day perhaps', which accumulated during the course of the operation into enough grog to stop a shearing shed.

Physically, the once fit Collins began to fade, with 'the constant patrolling and carrying the weight of the gun and everything else. When I couldn't go any further, the weight was just too much, I wouldn't give up,' he said, 'because I felt you don't let your mates down. I lost too much weight. I was about seven or eight stone, very, very thin, skinny, there was nothing left. All my cheeks stuck out, ribs, the collarbones were all forward. All of a sudden, I'm taken out, had to be sent home, and then I'm back to Australia. I never in my dreams thought that was gonna happen.'

Collins arrived home on 14 August 1966. 'I was met by reporters at Adelaide Airport,' he said, 'where a photograph was taken of me, followed up the next day with a photograph of me having breakfast in bed. Now, I couldn't eat, so mum put two raw eggs on a plate with a piece of bread and made it look like I was having boiled eggs and toast.'

The story appeared on the front page of the Adelaide *News*. Collins was sitting up in bed, his pyjamas buttoned up to his neck, a wireless behind his head, while his mother served him breakfast on a tray. He was described as 'South Australia's first National Serviceman to come home from Vietnam', whose friend Errol Noack had been 'cut down by a burst of enemy gunfire'. Collins told the paper, 'We are often fighting a war we cannot see. But we are there for a purpose. And we are a big morale lifter for the Americans.'[11]

After the story was published, Collins said, he had a visit from the military police at Keswick Barracks, asking what other information he might have revealed. 'I said, "Nothing. What you saw in the picture and what was said in the paper was all there was,"' said Collins. But the piece had included a line that indicated Collins was 'outspoken about the war in Vietnam', and the MPs wanted to know what that meant.

When he heard Collins was home, Walter Noack tried to contact him, to talk about his son. 'He got in touch with my mother,' said Collins. 'I told her I didn't want anything to do with anybody. The army had warned us, over and over and over, if we so much as used the word "Vietnam" we'd end up with ninety days in the stockade.'

After the war had ended, many veterans would blame public hostility or indifference for their reluctance to talk about what really happened in Vietnam – and the silence of the soldiers would breed rumour and suspicion about the way they'd fought – but, at the time, it was said repeatedly that the army had ordered them not to comment.

'We were in a free country,' said Collins, 'but there was no freedom for us to talk to the press at all, and there was no way that I could've sat down after Vietnam and talked about Noack's death. We all signed the Official Secrets Act, that document that said we wouldn't give any military information to anybody.' Collins spent some time in hospital in Adelaide before he returned to barracks.

'When I left the army,' he said, 'I was now trained as a machine gunner. There wasn't any jobs available for me as a machine gunner at home. I don't know why, but there just wasn't. So I went back to being a motor mechanic. Now, I was two models of cars behind everyone else

– Holden used to release a new model every year – and I really didn't fit in with the people any more, because they weren't disciplined. The apprentices used to call me "The General" because I gave them orders or something, I don't know . . . '

11

THE BATTLE OF LONG TAN

The Battle of Long Tan is a story now, and the men who lived through it are like actors on a stage. It's the best known and best rehearsed episode of Australia's Vietnam War, and every man has learned his lines. They know their parts, even the villains. History and memory have lent D Company 6RAR a cast of characters drawn from war movies and westerns, the comic books the younger men read in their bunks at Kapooka. There are the firm-jawed and the glass-chinned, the lovable larrikins and gnarled old soldiers, the boss with a backbone of steel and a heart of gold.

The company commander, Harry Smith was, inevitably, a disciplinarian with a purpose, a moulder of men. Smith was a veteran of the Malayan Emergency, who ensured D Company trained until the fat melted off them like a roast in a drip tray. Smith's NCOs included Sergeant Bob Buick, another Malaya man. Buick had been born in South Africa, enlisted in the Australian Army from 1959–65, spent six months lost as a civilian then turned himself back in to the army to fight in Vietnam. In some respects, Buick was a national serviceman's nightmare – a fierce authoritarian with the bearing of an angry wrestler, itching for a fight. 'He was a very gung ho type of man,' said Alan Parr, 'and for us, only just being national servicemen, it was very off-putting.'

Then there was the company's Sergeant Major Jack Kirby, who has become a kind of anti-Buick, clever, fatherly and funny but unfailingly, unflinchingly brave, a diggers' NCO. Kirby, who had fought in both Korea and Malaya, was as big and hard as a bronze statue.

But the old soldiers Buick and Kirby were outranked by younger men with no battlefield experience. An Australian infantry company was typically divided into three rifle platoons and a headquarters platoon. D Company's Ten Platoon was led by Second Lieutenant Geoff Kendall, a regular soldier and Portsea graduate, and Eleven and Twelve were under the command of national servicemen: Twelve had Second Lieutenant Dave Sabben, and Eleven belonged to Second Lieutenant Gordon Sharp.

Sharp was 'just a genuine good bloke', said John Robbins. 'He loved life. He wasn't particularly keen on the army. He said to me a couple of times, "This is bullshit, you know." Then he would've shut up.'

In retrospect, it was obvious which officer would die.

Among the men under Sharp's command were Robbins, his partner in Crown and Anchor, bank clerk John Heslewood, and Albert McCormack, the stretcher bearer who looked like Lionel Long. Before he left Australia, McCormack had told a friend he had a feeling he would not come home.[1] They were joined by Jack Jewry of St Marys, NSW, a clerk and salesman for a timber company, who had married his wife Susanne three weeks before he left for Vietnam. They'd been going out since she was thirteen years old and he was fourteen. Their honeymoon was cut short so Jewry could complete his jungle training, and Susanne couldn't afford to go up to Brisbane to see off her husband, but she wrote every night and he replied almost every day. The other boys would rib him because her letters were sprinkled with perfume. She was pregnant with his child.

There was Kenny Gant, the butcher from Queensland, always worried he would 'cop one', who wrote to his mum saying he hadn't taken off his protective medal. 'As a matter of fact, I've got three of them on me all the time; one on my watch, one on my dog tags and one in my wallet. Also, I've got that Troll Doll in my pocket that Doll gave me (all of its hair is falling out too).'[2]

Glenn Drabble, also of Eleven Platoon, a blinds installer from Zillmere, Brisbane, had written to his father, Ernie, telling him he hated the army. Ernie, a strong believer in national service, told his son he had to make the best of a bad job. Glenn had celebrated his twenty-first birthday in January, playing poker in the garage at home with his army mates. In August, he wrote to his girlfriend, Beverley Pilkington, asking her to make arrangements for their marriage the next year.

Under Sabben's command in Twelve Platoon were Alan Parr, forward scout Paul Large from Coolah, NSW, and his great mate Dave Beahan, a former clerk at the University of New England, Armidale. Large had just received news from home. 'We were in the canteen and our mail arrived,' said Beahan. 'The next minute I heard Largey yell out, "You beauty!" Later on, he came down to my tent and said his girlfriend had just accepted his engagement offer, and she wanted him to pick one of his army mates as best man. And he asked me. I said, "No, Paul. I don't even know her." He said, "No, she wants me to pick an army bloke, and I want you."'

With hindsight, it was also clear which men would die.

The newly built Australian base at Nui Dat sat in the centre of Phuoc Tuy province like a nonchalant provocation. In guerrilla country in the midst of an armed uprising, the Australians had constructed a tiny overseas territory, where men from Tamworth smoked Winfield cigarettes and drank Foster's beer in a warren of sandbagged hutchies, mess tents and unit bars. They ate meat and potatoes, talked cricket and cars, and played scratch games of Australian Rules and rugby league where there was space to pass a ball. It was a corner of South

Vietnam where English was the only spoken language, where the Vietnamese weren't permitted even to take away the garbage.

On 18 August 1966, Nui Dat would be more like Australia than on any other wet season evening in the rubber. There would be a concert party led by Col Joye, a tamed rock'n'roller who'd released a spirited version of 'Stagger Lee' in 1959, but by 1963 had been reduced to covering 'Waltzing Matilda'. The bill included seventeen-year-old Little Pattie singing 'He's My Blonde Headed, Stompie Wompie, Real Gone Surfer Boy'. If the troops closed their eyes, they could imagine the beach at Maroubra, the waves between the flags. If they opened their eyes, they could see a pretty young blonde in a short skirt, the life they were missing by serving overseas.

The night before the entertainers were set to perform, Nui Dat came under mortar and recoilless rifle fire for the first time, and a man who had been whole was suddenly in parts. Every night, the Australian and New Zealand artillery loosed routine harassment and interdiction fire into the darkness, peppering the country with shells to aggravate any enemy who might be moving around. Until 17 August, the fire had gone only one way. At 2.43 a.m., the barrage was returned, by unseen Viet Cong. Their attack lasted twenty two minutes and wounded twenty-four Australians.

Sapper Michael George, the diesel mechanic from Dubbo, had just come off piquet duty when he was ordered back to herd the other engineers out of their beds and into their pits. 'Our captain at the time, a mortar landed just outside his tent,' he said. 'He was just getting up, and he lost a leg, and the other one was pretty mangled too.'

Tents were torn and scorched, vehicles battered and two men were crippled, the Engineers' Captain Doug Paine and Gunner Philip Norris of 1 Field Battery. The Australians expected the VC to follow up their bombardment with an infantry assault, but none came. Later on the morning of 17 August, B Company 6RAR sent out a fighting patrol to find the position from which the attack had been launched. They left before breakfast, expecting to be back within three hours.

They discovered rudimentary mortar base plates – simple holes with rocks in them – then split into platoons to search for tracks. They patrolled all day and found nothing.

B Company camped out the night, and on the morning of 18 August two of its platoons returned to base, to pick up transport for their rest and convalescence (R&C) leave in Vung Tau. Despite the threat to the Task Force, half the men were ferried off to the seaside. 'The tempo of operations in the first two months had been unrelenting,' explained Sabben. 'There'd been no time off at all. Every third night you didn't have any sleep because you were on an ambush, and the other two nights you had sentry duty on the perimeter, so you might've slept two hours on, two hours off. So everyone was bloody dog-tired. People were starting to faint on patrol, and fall asleep on sentry duty. It was really two months of super-intense activity. It was decided then that we would rotate by half-companies – send a half company down to the ALSG so they could have a couple of days on the beach. Half of B Company was due to go.'

R&C was a short break, distinct from the week-long overseas R&R (rest and recreation) leave which was every man's entitlement. R&C was generally taken in Vung Tau where, initially, the men stayed in tents in the sand near 1ALSG. The other Australian troops called Vung Tau's base-bound soldiers Pogos, supposedly for Personnel On Garrison Operations, and reviled, despised, envied or dismissed them. On R&C, Sabben said, 'You basically had nothing to do except turn up for meals – you were counted; you had your roll call at meal time – so you'd get to the meal and have breakfast, then you'd do your own thing. You stayed on base, so basically you took books, you took records, you had a swim, you played beach cricket. If you were able to, you could scrub up and go down to Vung Tau, if there were a lot of you. You weren't allowed to go alone, but the ALSG people had shuttle buses. You'd stick in the centre of town and you'd buy some souvenirs, go to a bar; most people ended up in a brothel somewhere. It got more lenient as time went on, but in the early days it was extremely strict.'

While other men waited for the resupply convoy to Vung Tau, Five Platoon B Company, commanded by Second Lieutenant John O'Halloran, stayed out with some of company HQ, and continued to search for signs of the enemy. O'Halloran and his men penetrated about one hundred metres into the rubber, then stopped and sent out small fan patrols. They came upon the spot from which the recoilless rifles had been fired, where the rubber trees had been cut down to give the rockets a clear shot. They were ordered to wait in the rubber for D Company to relieve them and, as they squatted to scrape their lunch rations out of their mess tins, they could hear Col Joye and the Joy Boys running through their sound check at Nui Dat, as if the very air was Australian.

Goondiwindi-born Dave Thomas had joined 6RAR only the night before. He had been working for an agent as a trainee stock assistant, north of Roma and south of the Carnarvon Range. He'd gone over to Vietnam as a replacement, and spent a month at 1 Australian Reinforcement Unit at the foot of the hill, before he'd been dispatched to B Company. 'I got there at last light the night Task Force got mortared,' said Thomas. 'All the fellas were down on the wire in the weapons pits, on stand-to. The sergeant told me that I'd be sleeping in that tent there, and our section commander would be Jock Rutherford. They gave me a stretcher. When I went to go to sleep on it, it was rotten, and I went straight through it and landed in a puddle underneath. There were no duckboards in the tents in those days, just the start of a bit of blast wall around the extremities. I thought, Oh well, I'm the new fella. You just lie there and cop that. When the mortars were popping, I thought, They're coming from the wrong direction. Unless I've turned around during the night, they're coming in. Next thing, Jock says, "They're incoming, get out of here and down to the wire."' Thomas did not meet the men on either side of him in his section until they left the base before dawn. 'I was basically just trying to fit in,' he said.

When they reached the VC's mortar plates, near a rubber-tapper's hut by a well, he said, 'There was a lot of rubbish, a few ammunition tins, a busted pair of Ho Chi Minh sandals and other things lying on the ground. We'd been up just past the well and everybody, without anybody saying anything, virtually all sat down. There was no wind, no birds, nothing. There was no noise. In the bush, you hear some noise, even if it's in the distance, but when it gets to that, it's a bit eerie.'

D Company left the base to relieve B Company with a certain reluctant truculence, expecting a boring, inconclusive patrol. As far as they were concerned, the mortaring of Nui Dat had been a VC shoot-and-scoot, and the enemy would long ago have returned to the hills. D Company thought only in terms of the village guerrillas. Although there had been reports of main-force VC in the area, these hadn't been passed down to the men, some of whom affected to despair even of ever finding the elusive local force D445 Provincial Mobile Battalion. 'There were jokes flying around,' said Robbins, 'saying they were going to fly 2RAR to be the enemy,' as they had been in training exercises back home.

An infantry platoon operated with three rifle sections and a headquarters. Robbins was in charge of Six Section of Eleven Platoon. 'I didn't care whether I saw Little Pattie or Col Joye or not,' said Robbins, 'but I know there were quite a few that wanted to, so as we left, they were saying, "Stuff the army, stuff Vietnam, stuff this, fuck that," and all the rest of it. "Why us? Why have we got to be doing this?" We'd been out two days before, through that Long Tan area, and we hadn't seen anything. So here we go again.'

D Company met B Company at the edge of the plantation. They stopped to eat and then, as B Company headed back towards Nui Dat, D Company moved forward. 'Of course, being the new fella, I was given the recoilless rifle base that we'd found,' said Thomas. 'Anything happens in the army, you just give it to the new bloke. I was a bit pissed off because it was bloody awkward, especially when you were going through and under branches and navigating.'

D Company examined the tracks as the other men headed back.

'There were two sets,' said Sabben. 'One set of human tracks, soldiers' tracks, skirted the rubber plantation, went around into the bush and headed north-east; the other tracks were bullock-cart tracks, heading into the rubber plantation. And they made very deep ruts in the mud. So we knew that they were heavily loaded and we assumed, therefore, that they were loaded with all the weapons that had bombarded us. It was now thirty-six hours after the shelling, so the people on foot would've been long, long gone. So Harry [Smith] decided to follow the cart tracks into the rubber, which is what we did. From about three o'clock on, we were following the tracks eastwards into the Long Tan rubber plantation . . . A small group of enemy approached from the south, from our right, not expecting us: just sort of chatting and smoking, with rifles over their shoulders. They were obviously doing a clearing patrol and didn't expect any trouble, so they walked into Buick and his rifle. Buick fired the first shots of the battle.'

The Australians wounded one enemy and killed another. Gordon Sharp picked up the dead VC's AK-47. 'Because there were only six or seven of them,' said Sabben, 'and we hit two of them, and Gordon Sharp's platoon had twenty-eight or thirty men, Harry said, "Detach yourself from company and chase them, follow them." So the enemy headed off eastwards, and Eleven Platoon headed after them. The other two platoons of Delta Company closed up and crossed the road, and kept following them at a reasonable patrol pace.'

D Company was at the edge of the Long Tan rubber plantation. Eleven Platoon reached a rubber-planters' hut, assumed the enemy were inside and mounted an attack, but the VC had already left. 'So we got into an extended line and just fired through this area,' said Heslewood, 'through the trees. Then the shit hit the fan – this huge, huge amount of bloody fire, automatic and single fire, and we were ordered to hit the ground. For the first four or five minutes, it was just chaos. No one knew what was going on. And then the orders started coming through – "you go there, you go there, you go there" – and all the fire started to be controlled.'

'You're thinking that there's only going to be half a dozen,' said Robbins. 'They're making a lot of noise for half a dozen. We all went to ground and we returned fire. With your eight or ten men, you're spread out a fair bit, and you're seeing these fellas and you're firing and, of course, it's different to shooting roos because when you shoot a roo, they drop. This time, you're not sure whether you got them. They come back at you. They're moving towards us, and I thought, Christ, this is nothing to do with what we were expecting. And the noise, the fire, was just unbelievable.

'I started to say the Lord's Prayer. I'd only get halfway through it and something else'd start and I'd have to start again. I couldn't remember where I was, at the end of it or the beginning. I was just saying it in my mind. I thought, Christ, I don't think we're gonna get out of this. It was just bloody ferocious, the rattling of machine guns, the mortars, the explosions.'

Gordon Sharp called in supporting fire from the New Zealand battery in Nui Dat. 'We were all sitting in the boozer,' said George, 'and the next minute all hell opened up, the artillery going left, right and centre. We said, "Hello, some bastard's copping it."'

'Then the artillery started landing,' said Heslewood, 'and it was beautiful. It was landing fifty to a hundred metres in front of us all the time, which kept [the VC] well back. The lieutenant brought the artillery closer and closer to us, and there was just a huge volume of artillery. You could hear it whistling over the top all the time, and whether it was luck or good management, every time you could see a large force of them getting together to go at us, as they moved in, all of sudden twelve rounds of artillery would fall on them, and that broke up every attack.'

Gordon Sharp was shot in the throat, and died holding the captured AK-47. Buick took over the radio and continued to direct the artillery, while in Nui Dat a squadron of APCs was making ready to relieve the besieged men. Norm Wotherspoon was on the C Company radio set, listening to the battle in camp. 'I felt, "Shit, this is really bad," because you couldn't do anything and it was pissing with rain and it seemed to be all chaos. There was all this happening on the radio, but absolute silence in the tent. It was just the enormity of it all. I think we were all stunned that this huge attack should be happening so close, only a couple of miles away. D Company, that was my company.'

O'Halloran and his men from B Company had stopped and waited to be called back to fight. They were on the battalion radio net, when O'Halloran heard the voice of Sharp disappear and another take its place. He knew then that his school friend was dead.

Robbins attempted to muster his section. 'I went for a run out to try and get the men back,' said Robbins. 'I was calling out, but you can't hear anything. It's hard to communicate with everyone because of the noise. So I went maybe fifty yards and every one I saw of our blokes, they were already dead. I was calling them back in, then someone yelled out, "No, they're dead!" Then he must've got shot. Then I was coming out because my 2IC was on the gun, Warren Mitchell, and he got shot. He was dead. The gunner, Glenn Drabble, was dead. Then, when I was coming across the gun, that's when I got shot. Shot in the right arm. And I just lay there, thinking, I don't know what I'm gonna do here.

'There was no one around. I couldn't use my right arm. I got a grenade out, because they'd showed us film about what they did to their prisoners, and I thought, I'm not going with them. I'll either take some with me or whatever, but I'm not going. I reckoned if I just lay there and did nothing, they'd assume I was dead,' he said.

'The rubber had been knocked down, and I could see them gathering behind that, and the next thing this bloody artillery shot had come and – *poom!* – away they were gone. It was getting close, this artillery, and that's when Buick said, "We're gonna get out of here."' The sergeant got up and ran towards the yellow plume of a smoke grenade thrown by Sabben's platoon to guide them back to company HQ. 'I turned around,' said Robbins, 'I saw him pissing off, going that way, and I thought, Fuck, I'm going to have to do it this side.

I had my backpack on but I left my rifle. I shouldn't've done that. I ran the way he went, and I went to ground. I ran into Ernie Grant, and he said, "Are you hit?" and I said, "Yeah," and he said, "I'll get rid of your backpack," and he was taking the backpack off and he got shot through the head.

'Then I saw [the VC] in front of me, going back, so I just took off. I just zigzagged, and I got into a bit of a gully and that's when I asked for some morphine off the medic, Graeme Davis. He said he didn't have any, and he was going to give me a bandage, and while he was doing something to me, he got shot. He got hit in the shoulder. Then he was bellyaching there, going off.'

Sabben's Twelve Platoon had started off at the rear, behind company HQ. To machine gunner Alan Parr, the first shots in the silence had sounded like a volley at a rifle range, then there was a moment of quiet. But when Eleven Platoon ran into the VC, the plantation erupted into a roar, like the rage of some giant animal. 'I can remember stopping,' he said, 'and we were sitting on the ground. Someone yelled out, "Mortars!" and there was a few falling around the area and they told us to dig in and get scraping holes, then we had to jump up and go.

'We travelled out into the rubber trees, where we were trying to get to Eleven Platoon, and we came under fire and everyone hit the deck. I was facing towards Eleven Platoon, and over to my right was the hut Eleven Platoon had cleared.' The planters' hut had been reoccupied. The VC 'had tried to circle around Eleven Platoon', said Parr, 'because they didn't know how many of us were there.'

Parr saw a tracer round with a pyrotechnic base and fired his machine gun for the first time in action. 'Until then, I didn't know they had tracer ammunition,' said Beahan. 'I thought the only tracer ammunition was ours. Between their tracers and our tracers, it virtually lit the place up. When there was a ceasefire, this long pause, fairly early in the piece, the rains started and Largey called out, "My smokes are wet!" So I pulled mine out, and threw them over to him. He took one and threw the packet back. We got separated after that.'

The VC 'looked as though they were coming out from behind the hut', said Parr. 'I reckon there was a couple of hundred Viet Cong marching away from Eleven Platoon, heading around behind company headquarters, dark figures moving through the trees in a line. Because I was facing Eleven Platoon, I ran across into the rubber trees and plonked down facing that group of men I could see, and fired another burst, and then someone yelled out, "Stop firing!" because no one really knew who was who.'

He returned to his original position, opposite Eleven Platoon, and a bullet smashed into his weapon and travelled straight though the point where the spare barrel fitted in. 'You couldn't fire it,' he said. 'It had a bloody big hole in the barrel. It would've blown up.' Now Parr was in a battle without a gun. 'You were just hugging the ground,' he said. 'I've never got so low in my life. You felt as though you melted into the ground. You couldn't get any lower.'

And the rain came down 'as heavy as you could possibly imagine', said Sabben. 'You can see the rain coming half a mile away in the open on the paddy fields, and it's just like a wall of water. You see the grey wall coming at you, and things behind it are obliterated. When it hits you, it's like stepping out from clear into a waterfall. This particular day, it was more than just a monsoon, it was a thunderstorm as well. So above us the thunderheads were lightning, and we had the effect of lightning subdued but under the clouds. It would be like flashbulbs going off, but not startling, just dimly. When the artillery flashed it was the same thing, except you could hear the noise and see the vapour of the blast. You could see the lightning and because we were right under it, you could hear the thunder straight away. But it was low rumbling, that feeling you have when you're sitting in the theatre and they put on the earthquake sounds, and your guts churn. Everything instantly is wet around you, and the rain is coming down so hard it's going straight through the leaf canopy, it pushes the canopy out of the way, and it's like little bullets hitting the ground. And once the ground was wet, once it was saturated – because it was level and there was nowhere for the water to go – it just lay there, so the pools formed within a few minutes. And once the pools formed, the rain was pelting into the pools, and the pools were dissolving the surface mud, and the pools then were splashing, and the rain was heavy enough to raise that little splash mist about a foot above the ground. So we were lying on the ground in that mist and, from twenty-five yards away, if you looked, you'd just see the uniform reddish-brown mist. But occasionally you'd see a hat sticking up out of it.'

The weather played both friend and foe to every man in the plantation. 'When the enemy went to ground, we couldn't find them,' said Sabben. 'They may well have crawled towards us, and we wouldn't have seen them until they could see us, but when they stood, and when they advanced on us – because they had to advance; we were in defence, almost all the time – we could see them standing above the mist, so we could hit them and they didn't know where the bullets were coming from. They could see the muzzle flashes but, so long as our aim was good, by the time they saw the flashes, it was too late for them.'

The rubber trees themselves seemed to suffer. 'There's latex sitting behind the bark of every rubber tree,' said Sabben. 'If you rupture the bark, latex will run out. Not gush out. It'll leak out. The latex doesn't dissolve readily so, despite the rain, a couple of minutes after a bullet has gone through a tree, this white latex will dribble down the bark, and it'll be pure white. There's no dust or mud at that level, and the water isn't going to dissolve it. It's just there, like blood. It looked like the rubber trees were standing there bleeding.'

It wasn't the war the Australians had prepared for but it was the best war they could have hoped for, those men who'd come to Vietnam wanting to fight. They weren't herding sullen, frightened villagers from their homes, interrogating old peasants on bullock carts, laying ambush to woodcutters in the forest. They were fighting off uniformed enemy soldiers against suffocating odds, in a battle their fathers and grandfathers would have recognised as war. And, in memory at least, they held the line with laconic sangfroid.

Ten Platoon were swung up on the left. 'The bloke beside me was a fella named Harry Esler,' said Doyle. 'We used to walk together. He was in my section. I was on the ground, trying to dig my way to China, and Harry Esler was kneeling up to get a better view. Bear in mind all our blokes that were killed were shot from the chest up. And I was yelling to Harry Esler, "Get down! Get down! You'll fucking get it! Get down!" And he was firing away, like, "Fucking got one of them! Fucking got one!" And I stopped looking at him, because I honestly and truly believed that if I looked across, he was going to be a crumpled heap on the ground. I thought, I'm not gonna look at him, and I didn't. And he's alive.'

'We were just hiding among the rubber trees, firing out,' said Eleven Platoon's Heslewood. 'Every time they saw you move or roll over or something, you attracted attention. But we were just lying there. We were talking, saying, "Mate, eight degrees down to your left, there's one in a tree," and they'd say, "Yeah, I've got him." That sort of stupid talk was going on all the time: "You have a go, it's your shot." "Yeah, all right." Then you'd say, "You missed him."'

At Twelve Platoon, Lance Corporal Neil Bextrum was lying next to Parr. 'He said, "I just knocked over another one,"' said Parr. 'I said, "Well, give us a bloody shot." He passed his rifle over to me and I fired a few shots at some Viet Cong then gave it back to him.'

This was the culmination of everything that had happened to the national servicemen since they'd turned up at the army depot with their hairstyles and shy smiles and little bags of LP records and black-and-white pictures of their sweethearts, and surrendered themselves to the process of being chipped into soldiers. All the yelling and stamping, the sneers and abuse, the late-night kit inspections and early-morning runs, it had all been for this. D Company had been pounded into a unit of platoons and sections in which every member knew what every other man was expected to do, and now they'd eaten together, slept together, showered together and shat together, they were going to fight together and perhaps die together because they were one single entity. They weren't men, they were the component parts of D Company, and only by being D Company did they have a chance to stay alive. No man could turn and run, nor dissolve into the mud or the mist. They all had to act like the soldiers they had become, and if last year – when they were bank clerks – they were selfish, stupid or scared, then today they must be selfless, cunning and brave. They had to believe they were not the men they used to be, because those men would have been massacred here. They would have been cut to shreds by the enemy, who poured out of the trees with their bugles blowing and their cries like strangled birdsong and their own fearsome unity built upon their single angry purpose and the stark, unassailable faith that whether they were from the north or the south, from Phuoc Tuy or Hanoi, the country belonged to them, and not the lanky, rangy white men with their beef smells and their beer smells, their surf music and soap.

For the Australians, the justifications came before and afterwards. Now there was only the killing. But even that was not the way they had imagined. 'In any film,' said Sabben, 'there's an explosion and people throw their hands up and get cast aside and dive for cover and so on, and there's always a split second between the shell exploding and the effect that you see. In reality, when you're looking at something, without any warning at all, suddenly it's gone. There is no halfway point. When an artillery shell lands, it explodes and, in an absolute instant, there's nothing there any more except steam and smoke. There's none of this arms flying everywhere and watching a soldier get picked up and thrown ten yards and so on. By and large, if you hit a killing shot on a soldier, it's just like a marionette, and you cut the strings. He just flops. If you hit something solid, a bone or something, you might push him backwards, but he's already moving forwards.

His momentum is forwards. And if you hit a killing shot, through the head or the top of the chest or something, he's standing one second and flat on his face the next second. He just slumps where he is. Either he's hurled backwards by the kinetic energy of the round – in which case he simply goes backwards and falls, or else his own momentum simply puts his nose in the dirt. Those sort of perceptions of detail came as a bit of a surprise. Fairly academically, I might add. Because after you've seen the first couple, and the next few minutes you see a few more, the novelty wears off very quickly. You're not looking at them as human beings. They're impersonal. They're enemy soldiers, and you're accounting for them like they were targets. It's not until afterwards when you replay it in your mind that you realise each of these guys had a girlfriend and maybe a kid and he'll never see them again. That sort of gut-wrench comes later, not when you're primed and the adrenalin's there and your finger's on the trigger and you know if you don't hit him he's going to hit you.'

Ten Platoon were trying to relieve the VC pressure on Eleven. 'That's when we got hit,' said Doyle. 'They stopped us. We took a few casualties. We were unable to get to [Eleven]. We had to stop our advance. Major Smith tried to swing Twelve Platoon around, to relieve from the other side. The same thing happened. For a fair while, Eleven Platoon were out there on their Pat Malone. We were getting hit, they were getting hit.'

The VC were trying to figure out the limits of the Australians' perimeter, but 'everywhere they went, they got hit', said Doyle, 'because we were covering such a big area, and they couldn't confine really where we were. They thought we were a battalion. It was piss-pouring with rain. When we were trying to scoot around, and we went to ground, I was thinking, Where's the biggest puddle of water, or the biggest puddle of mud? And I actually got into the biggest puddle I could find, simply because where the water was laying, that meant there was a depression in the ground. It would have been a depression maybe only two or three inches deep, but it made you a lower target.'

Sabben's Twelve Platoon had thrown the yellow smoke grenade to indicate a position the men could fall back to, in the hope that D Company could regroup. 'We just ran in,' said Heslewood. 'The gunfire after us was like a bloody drumbeat, getting louder and louder and louder. And then you might run thirty metres and someone would scream out, "Hit the deck!" then we would dive, turn around behind a tree again, get some breath back, and then the gunfire would drop off again – "Okay, let's go," – and then you'd go another fifty. We all got back doing that, but it was just luck. Every time we showed ourselves, the fire built up. The other two platoons were all back in a big area around company headquarters, so we all moved back to there, and Jack Kirby said, "Are you all right? Any wounds? You go over there." And he'd put you in a position somewhere. He came back, "Here's some ammunition for you." It kept coming, but he put us out the back, towards the rear, and the attack was going through the front, so he gave us a break there.'

'When we got back,' said Robbins, 'there was such a sense of relief for me. And Jack Kirby got all of the wounded into one area. I was walking around. I thought, Shit, I'm pleased to be here, and the next thing – *bang!* – he crash-tackled me, knocked me arse over head, and said, "You get down, you stupid bastard! Get down!"' Kirby, a big man and an easy target, was dashing around 'picking up people and carrying them back', said Beahan. 'To see that man run here and run there was just unbelievable.'

'We were on this little bit of a depression, a reverse slope,' said Doyle. 'The wounded were put in the middle. "Doc" Dobson, our medic – now, bear in mind he's a Band-Aid putter-on and "here's an Aspro" – every one of those people that he treated lived. Not bad when you've got blokes with severe gunshot wounds.' But the VC kept on coming, as if their numbers were inexhaustible, like they grew out of the soil and were replenished by the rain. 'When they confined us, they knew that we were in this small group, that's when they really hooked in,' said Doyle. 'They ran in a couple of hundred at a time, in waves, trying to overrun us. It was impossible to keep them out with rifle fire and machine-gun fire. And they were running through artillery barrages.'

Air strikes had been called in, but they were useless in the storm. From the clouds, they couldn't tell D Company from the VC. Everything was shadow. The ground had been given up to ghosts. Harry Smith sent them back, to give a clear run to the artillery.

The first man from Eleven Platoon whom Parr had seen retreat was the platoon sergeant. 'Buick had a stunned look on his face,' said Parr, 'but we most probably all looked like that. They went through shit up there.' Parr's weapon was still broken. He went to Kirby in anger. 'I held the gun up at him and said, "Look, this is fucked!" and threw it into the rubber trees. He just sort of looked at me, and maybe I had the look Buick did, and away he went and came back with a rifle for me.' Parr had to prise the bullets out of his machine-gun belt to load them into a single rifle magazine. 'At that time, I was feeling as though I'd never see another sunrise,' he said. 'I didn't think I'd go home.'

'I can remember having a leak while laying there in the mud and water,' Parr wrote later. 'The things that made you feel uncomfortable didn't seem to matter any more, your body seemed detached from your emotions – we could have done anything physical that day with ease and not been troubled by it.'[3]

Someone shouted that Paul Large had been shot. When Beahan heard his mate had been killed, 'It really knocked the shit out of me,' he said. 'I just cried and cried and cried. I think we all prayed and cried. I don't believe there's one that wouldn't have cried during the battle.'

'Then, of course, we ran out of ammunition,' said Doyle. A resupply was ordered at Nui Dat and came in by chopper through the storm. 'There was a bit of consternation with the Australian helicopters,' said Doyle, 'but a couple of blokes said, "Fuck this, we're going anyway," and they flew into an absolute tropical downpour – tree-height – and kicked the ammunition containers out of the door.' The aircraft drew fire from the VC. 'We noticed, dramatically, the change of fire coming to us,' said Doyle. 'They couldn't see the helicopter, but they could hear it, and they never brought it down.'

It was when the ammunition dropped from the sky that Kirby became the hero he had always promised to be, the man he had to be for the others, larger than life, larger than death. 'Jack Kirby was like a fireplug, as big wide as he was high,' said Doyle. 'I can still see him, running around like a pack horse, draped with ammunition for the machine guns, boxes of ammunition under his arms, going, "Here! Here!" throwing bullets at every man with a weapon. He was drawing a lot of fire, and he never got a Band-Aid.'

'It was nearly dark, piss-pouring with rain,' said Doyle. 'We were nearly out of ammunition again, we knew quite well that another helicopter wasn't going to get in.' The VC were massing for a fresh attack. 'If that assault had got underway, they would've walked right through us.' D Company knew APCs were supposed to be coming from Nui Dat, but they didn't know when. 'We were only about five thousand metres from the base,' said Doyle. 'We'd been out there for about three hours and they still hadn't shown up.'

'We kept saying, "Where the f– are they?"' said Beahan. 'You could hear them coming,' said Heslewood. 'It was a very thick scrub. You could hear the gunfire. Then, all of a sudden, they just burst out of the scrubland into our area.' At just after seven p.m., 3 Troop of the 1st Armoured Personnel Carrier Squadron (1APC), which had fought its way across from Nui Dat, rolled into the enemy. 'They actually drove through them,' said Doyle. 'They had to be careful about overshoots, so they weren't shooting up our positions. I can remember lying in the mud, using my elbows, my knees and my bloody chin, trying to dig a hole in the mud, and I heard the rise and fall of a diesel engine as it revved and dropped and revved and dropped, and I thought, F–, it's a carrier. All the artillery was still dropping down. They next thing I saw was this big grey shape coming through the rubber.' The APCs broke through the enemy and the enemy broke contact. 'As quick as the firing started, it finished,' said Doyle. It was 'the most beautiful sound you'd ever hear', said Robbins, 'the roar of these APCs and these big 50 cal machine guns up on the top, blasting away'.

The APCs brought A Company 6 RAR to continue the fight, but the battle was over. The enemy fled. 'That was when blokes started to realise how bad we'd been done,' said Heslewood. 'It was pretty dark then, and they'd had an aid post organised for the wounded. I wandered through there, and that's where Johnny Robbins had ended up; he was wounded through the arm. He was lying there with the other blokes, bandaged up and all that, and I said, "How did your lot go?" And he said, "They're all gone. The whole section."'

John O'Halloran's platoon had pulled up when they'd heard the first enemy shots. 'Then it just became a rolling drumbeat,' said Dave Thomas, 'a crescendo of rifle fire. We turned around and went back to another position where we were standing in a banana patch, and the overshoots were whistling over the top of us, but they weren't coming down below a certain height. Then it started to rain, and we were drinking water off the banana leaves. It was a fair while before we were told to go back in. I think they'd basically forgotten us.' O'Halloran's men came towards D Company in an extended line, and 'The Chinamen were running between us,' said Thomas. 'They were doing the bolt. They'd had enough. They weren't worried about us. But in the rain we couldn't tell friend from foe. We got back in there before A Company on the APCs. We were given a position facing west and told to dig in.' They used 'anything available, your hands or an entrenching tool or in my case a rubber-tapper's cup. It's amazing how quickly you can dig. But the soil was wet anyway.'

But by the time O'Halloran's platoon arrived, 'it was virtually like the last act of a play', said Thomas. 'It was curtains went down, and that was it. There was only the odd rifle shot. The APCs took the wounded out to the landing zone, and we then had to form a great conga line to get out of the place. It was as black as a dog's guts. You could stick your arm out and you couldn't even see it. There was no moon, everybody tripping over one another. You were basically hanging onto the webbing of the fella in front of you.'

'The armoured personnel carriers formed a defensive perimeter,' said Doyle, 'opened the top of their hatches so the interior lights would shine up – we had to be careful, there was still a couple of thousand crooks out there. American medevac choppers and some Australian choppers flew into the circle, loaded the wounded on first. The last couple of loads out was the dead. And that finished about midnight.' Robbins went out with the wounded. 'That was the most wonderful taxi ride I'd ever had,' he said. 'We harboured up for the night around the APCs,' said Thomas. 'I don't think anybody slept all that well.'

'I woke up in the mud,' Doyle said. 'All I had was the clothes that I stood up in, the webbing and an ammo belt. Our packs, we dropped in the initial contact. We were stuffed and far from home, rotten dirty, as usual. By then, the brass were flying in, in helicopters, there were APCs – there was more people there than you could point a stick at.'

'I honestly thought I'd never see another sunrise,' said Parr, 'and to be laying there near an APC and see that sun come up was the most glorious thing in my life at that time.'

The battalion commanding officer, Lieutenant Colonel Colin Townsend, wanted 6RAR to return to Nui Dat, said Doyle, but 'after a while, Harry Smith said, "Saddle up, D Company, we're going back in . . . first." And I was thinking, now that everybody was out there, they'd go in and we'd be tail-end Charlie. Harry's had an aneurysm. He's blown a piston in his head. In hindsight, it was a brilliant command decision. If we'd have gone back to base with our tails between our legs, it would've taken a bit to get back on the horse.'

At the time, however, Doyle was deeply unhappy. 'I got back into an APC with other blokes,' he said, 'and in an APC you sit against the wall, facing inwards with the rifle between your knees. Normally, you're talking shit, a bit of bravado.' But the journey into the rubber passed straight-backed and in silence. There was 'not one bit of black humour, bullshit, there was nothing,' said Doyle. 'I was more terrified than I was during the actual contact: I think because we didn't expect it, it erupted, it was on, then it finished. Whereas the next day we knew what we were walking into. The pins and needles started in my feet, went up through my legs, up through my body, up through my head, up through my ears, and I was numb. I believed 100 per cent, Okay, we got out yesterday by the skin of our teeth. We're going back in. There's heaps and heaps of them. We ain't gonna see the sun go down. When the back of the carrier dropped down, and we shot out, I thought, The shit is just gonna hit the fan.'

But nothing happened. 'There was not a shot fired,' said Doyle. 'We did our normal drills, got into defensive position, and all was quiet. The other side had done a magnificent job – because the area was still peppered with artillery through the night – and gathered up hundreds of wounded and untold amounts of dead. We followed blood trails through the rubber where they were carting bodies off. You've got to give them credit for what they did: if we were hurt, we were on a chopper, and in thirty minutes we would be in a major surgical hospital; they crawled off into the bush like mongrel dogs.' It's been estimated the VC carried off at least as many dead as they left behind. The fact they cared for their comrades' corpses is sometimes painted as a mendacious ploy designed to rob the Australians of their rightful body count, but the VC, like any Western army, hated to leave behind their soldiers' remains for their killers to dispose of, or the wild boars to gore.

'The plantation itself was absolutely shredded,' said Doyle. 'It was stark, just like a giant tumultuous thing had decimated the place. We had to go through first and clear it. We took a couple of prisoners, they were treated by our medic.' In the muggy carnage of the morning, the finer distinctions became visible through the mist: the difference between victory and defeat, miracle and massacre – the mourners' consolations.

Sabben remembered 'a crescent of absolutely destroyed trees, and what I can only describe as a slaughterhouse of bodies. And not many of them were full, complete, identifiable bodies either. They were just body parts and pieces of flesh. Up until then, we really had no idea of what damage we had inflicted. Because of the heavy rain, because of the necessity to survive, we hadn't really sat back and taken stock of what was actually happening. And all the assaults that came in on Twelve Platoon's front and Ten Platoon's front, they were just beaten back and we got onto the next thing. We didn't worry about what was out there. And the next morning when we got back, we found what was out there was actually row upon row of bodies, which we hadn't seen first of all for the rain and then for the dark. And the bodies had been churned up by the fact that we had artillery landing twenty-five yards from us for the last ten minutes of the battle, so anything that had already been shot was being churned up by the artillery.'

Sabben described a 'moonscape of stripped trees and bark shed, trunks, pock-holes, artillery shells and bits of bodies all around. We realised then that we had not only been thumped,' he said, 'but we had thumped them even harder. Overnight, we'd counted the casualties and realised one in three of Delta Company had become a casualty: seventeen dead and twenty-five wounded out of 108 soldiers, so we thought we'd been given a hiding. Nothing in our training ever led us to believe we would lose anything like this number of people. Yes, you might have some wounded – you might even have a dead person – but seventeen dead? Thirteen out of one platoon? This was unheard of. Nothing will ever be worth seventeen, but looking out there and seeing hundreds of enemy, that made us feel a lot better.'

The return of D Company to the battlefield turned out to be 'the best thing we could've done,' said Heslewood, 'because they let Eleven Platoon find our own dead. And it was sort of a closing. You picked up your own mates, rather than hearing that somebody else had found so-and-so. Plus, we knew where they were, so we just sort of wrapped them up and put them in APCs to take them back to the heli-base.'

Incredibly, among the corpses and pieces of men, two wounded members of Eleven Platoon were found alive: national servicemen Barry Meller and Jimmy Richmond.

When Sabben reached Eleven Platoon's position, Meller and Richmond were still being treated on the ground, but he saw the dead men of Eleven, Gordon Sharp and the rest, lying in position, one behind each tree, rifles pointing to the enemy, 'and outside the perimeter, heaps of enemy, just like they'd been through a shredder,' said Sabben. Sharp's radio officer was found sitting upright, with static still bristling through the handpiece of his set. When a soldier tried to remove the AK-47 from Sharp's hands, it accidentally discharged, the dead man's final shot.[4] D Company stayed another three days and two nights on the battlefield. 'We had to go through every identifiable piece of body we could find,' said Sabben, 'and see if there was any intelligence on it – paperwork in the pockets, diaries, wallets everything like that. Anything that was ex-human we had to bury. Anything that was metallic we had to put in one spot – all the ammunition, all the weapons, the magazines.'

'We were hunting around,' said Doyle. 'When we'd find a body, we'd use a toggle rope, six- or eight-foot long. We'd tie it around a leg or an arm and pull them over, just in case they were booby-trapped. We buried about a hundred a day, and we just had little pack shovels. They were going to send a bulldozer in, but the Suoi Da Bang River was in flood, it wasn't even possible. We couldn't do a sterling job; no one was given a six-foot-deep grave. Basically, we dug a shell scrape and we buried them the best we could. I found a body, and it was severed through the nipple line. I found the lower part. He looked like he had been cut with a sheet of corrugated iron, like a ripple effect. He must've got a massive blast by a very close 105 Howitzer shell, or something bigger. He was as white as white. Obviously, he had bled out, but also during the night it had rained heavily: there was not a speck of blood anywhere. It was red mud anyway, so there was no trace of it. It's very gloopy, moisturous, it just seemed to wash away. I looked around, searched here, searched there. I thought, The least we can do is bury the bloke and try to put the rest of his body with the other bit. But I never found it.

'Those days there were pretty gruesome,' said Doyle. 'We'd sit down on a log, or sit out in the dirt, and we'd be having a bit of crap Australian twenty-four-hour ration pack food, and there'd be a body here, a body there and a bit of body there. We'd just stop for a feed, or boil up some water and make a tea or a coffee or something.'

They slept on the battlefield – the wool-store clerk, the graphic artist and all the others – unrolling their swags among human remains on the churned-up laterite soil. They had no tents to wall themselves off from the dead. 'Because of the humidity and the heat, things go off real quick over there,' said Doyle. 'The first day wasn't too bad, but by the time we got towards the end of it, the whole thing was getting pretty ripe. We were handling bodies with our bare hands. We didn't have gloves. The only water we had was in our water bottles.'

C Company came out from Nui Dat to help bury the Vietnamese dead. 'We had to contort the bodies into things that would fit,' said Norm Wotherspoon, 'and I realised that these were people who were younger than me – some were older – and this was actually their homeland. And, even though I hadn't been particularly religious, I said little prayers over the ones that I buried, and at the same time I was losing what little faith I had. That was the day that I decided that war was something that, when you'd been to it, you don't actually agree with it. Unless you're a psychopath. It was a dreadful, dreadful day. It changed me from being someone who things happened to and just accepted it. I actually started to think for myself. I was really torn, because I didn't want anything to happen to our fellas, but I really didn't want anything to happen to their fellas either.'

D Company 5RAR went in to the field too. Among them was Colin Poyser, a national serviceman brought up in Bridgewater, half an hour north of Bendigo. 'We were stepping over bodies blown to pieces,' said Poyser, 'and there was one VC, he had his guts opened up, and you could actually see the rice in the stomach. The time we were in there, two or three shots went off, and the message came back "VC escaping", but I don't think that was the case.'

C Company 6RAR's Peter Moore helped clear the area. 'The ARVN were walking around knocking gold out of their teeth,' said Moore. 'They used the back of a bayonet. I think that's where they kept most of their wealth, in their teeth. Our company went out with the APCs to where the APCs first got ambushed on the way in. We found more bodies out there. There was two there that were wounded, but they wouldn't come out. We could see they had weapons.' C Company killed them and buried them in the pits the VC had dug themselves. 'We just pushed them back in there,' said Moore.

When 6RAR returned from their burial party, 'we took all of our clothes off,' said Doyle, 'because we were rotten, and we had all of our clothes – which was only a shirt and a pair of pants, and a pair of boots and socks – put in a big heap, covered in dieseline and burned. We had a cold-water shower: we had a Vietnamese well, and canvas buckets we used to lower into the well – which was full of frogs and shit anyway – and haul it up into a tree, and that was our glorious shower centre. We had a bit of a scrub up and feed.'

When the clean-up was over and D Company returned to Nui Dat, 'There was another whammy,' said Sabben, 'because the Q staff had been through all the dead and wounded who were not returned to us, all of their kit had been collected and put into the Q store. So these soldiers, who were still getting over the loss of their mates, came back to their tents and next to them was an empty bunk where their mate used to live. They had to face that all over again.'

Eighteen diggers were killed, including an APC commander. D Company lost eleven national servicemen: Vic Grice the storeman was dead. Dennis McCormack the labourer was dead. Warren Mitchell the clerk was dead. Douglas Salverton was dead. Colin Whiston the postman was dead. All of them were just twenty-one years old.

Albert McCormack was dead. Kenny Gant was dead. Glenn Drabble was dead. Paul Large was dead. Jack Jewry was dead. Once again, there was confusion around the release of casualty figures. This time, the media was told how many had died before parents knew if their sons were safe, on the instruction of Minister for Defence Allen Fairhall. Radio stations had broadcast reports of what was first described as 'the Baria action' or the 'Battle of Nui Dat'[5] and Fairhall felt the coverage could lead to fears that the Australian loss had been catastrophic, so he gave out the numbers at 8.40 p.m. on Friday 19 August, leaving relatives a night to consider whether their boys were still alive. He admitted to parliament he 'had known that the announcement would precede by some hours notification of the next of kin'.[6]

After the families were informed the next day, Susanne Jewry miscarried, and Jack's child was never born. Everything was 'destroyed in a moment', she said.[7] Jewry's family received letters from him hours after they learned of his death. He told his mum he was glad the platoon had new floorboards for their tents, and finished his note, 'I wish I was at home with you.'[8] Drabble's girlfriend Beverley Pilkington opened his letter asking her to make arrangements for their marriage. 'I should have been so happy,' she said, 'but now this is the saddest day of my life.'[9] Kenny Gant's last letter also arrived home after he was dead. His mother couldn't bear to identify her son's body, so she sent her brother. Due to a mix-up, she hadn't been able to see Gant off when he'd left for Vietnam. She'd never kissed her boy goodbye.

When Barry Vassella returned to D Company from the language course at Vung Tau, none of the his mates would talk about the battle. 'I'd say, "What was it like?" "Yeah." You couldn't push it. You don't ask people, "How many did you kill?"' Vassella desperately wanted to know what had happened to Paul Large. 'And I got two or three different stories about how he died,' he said. 'David Beahan took it very, very badly. They came down to Vung Tau a few days later and we got out to see them and I saw Dave, and he said, "Do you know Largey died?" And he started crying there and then. He said, "I can't believe it. Not Largey." Everyone loved Paul. He said, "The battle was over. It was just a stray bullet at the end, took him straight between the eyes. Didn't know a thing. Dead where he lay." And they kept calling him: "Come on, Paul, get going." And he was just lying there, still with his rifle.

'I wasn't at the battle,' said Vassella, 'and I've suffered all my life because I never went to the battle.'

The empty bunks at Nui Dat were quickly filled with fresh, young soldiers. 'In hindsight, I felt a bit sorry for reinforcements,' said Doyle. 'We really did treat them as outsiders. I could not even tell you the name of one reinforcement. They came there not by choice; they came to replace dead or wounded blokes. I didn't care who they were. I wasn't interested in making friends with them. I didn't shun them, but I wasn't interested in knowing about them. And I think that was pretty universal. So it must've been hard for reinforcements. I couldn't tell you the name of the bloke who took Gordon Sharp's place.'

The wounded were flown to the US 36th Evacuation Hospital in Vung Tau. 'They took you from the chopper, onto a stretcher and into the hospital,' said Robbins, 'and they assessed what was wrong with you, and, of course, you'd got mud and blood all over you and you were probably not recognisable. They had huge scissors and they cut up the laces of your boots and straight up the trouser leg and straight up the shirt and they started washing you down and cleaning you up to take you into the theatre. And all the time, it was just magic, listening to them. They were just so nice to you. It wasn't until the next day, or the day after, that you started to realise who didn't make it.

'When the rest of the company were given leave,' said Robbins, 'they came and saw all of us in hospital and you could see the look on their faces, because we'd been through a hell of a bloody turn-out really, and you could see that they knew we were going home and they weren't. I guess we were happier than they were.

'36th Evac was a sad place,' said Robbins. 'Every day there'd be a tractor go out with a trailerload of bodies, they'd put them on the plane: Yanks going back to the States, and our own. And the Yank generals turning up, pinning all these Purple Hearts on these Yank soldiers. I got to know a lot of Negroes. They found us very entertaining. They used to come with their tape-recorders, and get us to talk, so they could send it home. They'd ask us all sorts of things about kangaroos and koalas, and we'd tell them the greatest lies.'

Robbins lay up in hospital with an arm injury and shrapnel in his hand. 'They sewed the wound up,' he said, 'and then I was on a drip for a good amount of time. Then we decided we were getting better, so why don't we go into town. In our pyjamas. We got into the back of one of those Lambrettas, got the trolley hanging out the back with the bottle swinging away, and away we went. We didn't have any money, but we didn't need it. Because when we got in, the Yanks bought us anything we wanted. They weren't really happy at 36th Evac when we arrived back, when we were all half-sozzled.'

They flew home to Queensland the long way – via Penang, the Cocos Islands, Western Australia and Victoria. In Brisbane, 'people wanted to buy us a drink', said Robbins. He liked to go to the British Empire Hotel with Jimmy Richmond, who was on nil-by-mouth. 'He had a tube and a funnel,' said Robbins. 'He'd put the funnel up to his tube and pour a beer in. And everyone was buying beers to watch it, but they'd buy one for us too. Then all the bubbles would come up, and he'd burp and go on.'

Gordon Sharp was buried in Tamworth, in a full military funeral that stopped the town. His coffin was carried in a gun carriage from St Nicholas Roman Catholic Church to the Lawn Cemetery in Peel Street. It took eighteen minutes for the party to pass. The pall-bearers came from Scheyville, and Scheyville CO Colonel Geddes was in Tamworth to officially represent the minister for the army and the Military Board. The mayor of Tamworth and the president of the NSW Motor Trades Association attended, and Tamworth RSL was represented too.

Sharp's mother and father, Eric and Roma, 'went to pieces' when they heard that Gordon had been killed, said his brother, Tony.[10] The priest who gave the funeral mass talked about Sharp not as a soldier, but as a man. 'He went about doing good,' he said. 'He was generous, humble, reliable, cheerful, genuine and honest – he was good . . . In the midst of this sorrow there is joy – joy that Tamworth has produced a boy of the calibre of Gordon Sharp.'[11]

The funeral of a local boy who'd died in battle was a heart-tearing, street-jamming event, particularly in smaller places, above all for national servicemen, and especially in 1966, before civilian eyes had grown more accustomed to the gun carriage and catafalque party, the coffin shrouded by flag. Young men such as Sharp were publicly mourned by their schoolmates and footy mates, their girlfriends and ex-girlfriends, their aunts and cousins, by strangers who'd grown used to passing them in the street, by neighbours lending sympathy, by all those who felt the death as a loss not just to the family but to the town. Mention of Paul Large's death was made at every church in Coolah before his funeral. The Coolah RSL Club conducted a special service.

Gordon Sharp's former classmate and fellow national service officer O'Halloran returned home in June 1967. 'When I got back to Tamworth, the first port of call was up to see Eric and Roma Sharp,' he said, 'and they asked me to leave the house. I was only one day back from Vietnam, and they said, "No. You wanted to go to Vietnam, Gordon didn't. He got killed."' They told O'Halloran, 'It should've been you.'

12

AFTER LONG TAN

'A lot of our blokes went absolutely crazy after Long Tan,' said 5RAR's Colin Poyser. 'We went on leave to Vung Tau, and there was one guy, we had to hold him down, he wanted to jump out the back of the truck. The same guy, just before we came home, had a few beers and he actually held a cigarette lighter to his hand, burned all the skin off, turned his hand over and did the same to the other side. And there was another two or three blokes went off their head, wanted to fight everybody, wanted to shoot people.'

Both 5RAR and 6RAR still had the best part of a year to serve in Vietnam before O'Halloran could come home and speak to Sharp's parents. The men counted down the days on their pin-up girl calendars, starting in the middle of 1966 with '365 and a wakey' (wake up) and ending in the middle of 1967. For some, the last day in country came sooner. Norm Wotherspoon became more and more depressed in the army. 'The day after a couple of the battalion had been killed or wounded,' said Wotherspoon, 'I think we were doing a whole-battalion operation. A couple of companies were moving along beside a creek, and there was a big open field on the right and there were two enemy walking across an open paddock. So we opened fire, and I remember going over with [an officer] – he wanted to check the bodies out – and one guy was still alive. There was a sergeant from another company who went over to this guy who was just wounded and lying there on the ground, and he put his Armalite right up to his head and said, "They killed some of us last night," and he pulled the trigger. And that just horrified me. I was going to say something to [the officer], but he said, "Good riddance." So I thought there wasn't a lot of point there. But that was a war crime. And I wondered, How often does this stuff happen? I didn't realise we did that.'

Later, Wotherspoon asked to be transferred from company HQ to a rifle platoon and become a signaller again but 'all this stuff was adding up', he said, 'and I was getting very depressed, and I was not holding together all that well, but you put the mask on. We had about a month to go, and we were going to come home. We were guarding some American tanks, and one morning – no danger, no nothing – I had my little nine-millimetre Browning and I just held it against my leg and pulled the trigger. I just had a fit of . . . despair, I think. I missed the bone. I just thought I'd bleed out, but I didn't. I was in enormous pain, writhing around on the ground. The terrain was such that they couldn't get the normal casevac helicopter in, so they brought in a little Bell. They gave me some morphine, put a plastic splint on it, and tied me to the outside of the Bell. They told me to look down, otherwise I wouldn't be able to breathe because of the rotors. Of course, I'm terrified of heights. Just after we took off, the splint went down, my leg was waving all over the place, and the morphine hadn't started to work.

'I got into Vung Tau and they did an operation and by the time I'd recuperated from that, there wasn't any point in sending me back with a wasted leg, so nothing ever happened except I came home. Nobody asked me any questions.'

In October 1966, John O'Halloran and some of his men were sent into the Nui Dinh mountains, southwest of Nui Dat, to search for a VC radio that was supposed to be picking up and relaying signals from the

Task Force. 'You may as well whistle dixie,' said O'Halloran, 'because it's a big mountain range, and in those days it was perfect jungle. We ambushed monkeys there one day. It frightened the living shit out of us. And on the same patrol: a deer jumped out of the bushes and knocked our company 2IC arse over head. That's how much wildlife was up there.'

The patrol was approaching a spur line when it hit the sentry post of an enemy camp. Shots were fired from both sides but nobody was hit, and the VC melted into the hills. 'We swept through the camp and went into harbour,' said O'Halloran. 'While we were sitting there, two of my diggers spotted a wire going through the trees, down a cave. So I said to Mick Birchell and Mickey [Kerry Michael] Rooney, "Have a look what's down there." They went down and they brought out this woman and this great big radio set.'

Battalion HQ sent a helicopter to pick up the prisoner, but the monsoon broke before O'Halloran could reach the landing zone. 'It pissed down with rain,' said O'Halloran. 'I thought, Well, what am I going to do with this sheila? So I tied both of her arms up to one of mine, both of her legs up to one of mine, and then around a tree.' Both O'Halloran and the prisoner, To Thi Nau, were secured to the same tree. 'You had to,' said O'Halloran, 'or else you'd get washed away. It was the monsoon, and we were on a steep slope when it hit us. And the diggers were saying, "Oh yeah, this is lovely, this is. The officers get to sleep with the sheilas and we're out here."

'I let her have a leak,' said O'Halloran. 'I remember feeding her, and I fed her again the next morning with some of our rations. I had an interpreter with me and I said, "Just tell her: if we get hit tonight, by her mob out of the camp, I'm going to have to blow her away. Because I can't try to look after a platoon and drag some [woman] with me."'

The next morning the sky was clear, they reached the landing zone, and O'Halloran called in a chopper. 'We had to blindfold her,' said O'Halloran. 'You used to have white flannel stuff with a red line across it to clean the barrel of your rifle: we tied that around her eyes so she couldn't see, and as the chopper started, she started to spew.'

To Thi Nau had high cheekbones, long black hair, full lips and onyx eyes. She looked more like a princess in mufti than a peasant guerrilla fighter. When the chopper reached Nui Dat and the prisoner was led to interrogation, an Australian photographer took pictures of the composed but frightened woman. To Thi Nau was escorted to a tent, where she was photographed again signing a statement. She was next pictured blindfolded once more, with a cloth that covered her face, a sudden eclipse of her beauty. Then she was driven off in a jeep, to be handed over to the South Vietnamese.

Back in Australia, the tabloid newspapers tittered that a pretty VC 'girl' had been found clinging like a spider to the roof of a cave, but that was all that was publicly known of To Thi Nau until 1968. 'We never heard anything for a while,' said O'Halloran, 'and the rumour went around she had been water tortured, and we said, "Ah, fuck this." The people that were doing the water torture were the Intelligence officers who were inside the wire. If the pogos started to put water torture on prisoners, what's going to happen to us if anything goes wrong? It'd be ten times worse. We were up in arms about it.'

Many years later, decades after the war was over, John O'Halloran returned to Vietnam, tracked down To Thi Nau, and gave her the money to buy a house.

On 2 February 1967, D Company 6RAR was on patrol in the bush east of Dat Do. 'There were lily ponds and things,' said Peter Doyle. 'We were in Indian file around this swamp.' Someone thought he'd heard shooting off to the side, and company HQ called in artillery, which was supposed to fall well back from the Australians and flush out any VC who might be in the area. Six big guns fired one round each, and the next half-dozen rounds were in the air as the first six began to fall.

'You knew if the artillery was going over the top of you, it would whistle,' said John Heslewood, 'but if it was going to land close to you, you could hear it tumble – *bum-bum-bum* – and once you heard it tumbling, you couldn't do anything but put your head in the ground.'

'We were just sitting in the dirt,' said Doyle. 'I listened to the sound and, all of a sudden, I thought, This is going to be close. And then I thought, This is going to be real close.'

'As soon as they started tumbling,' said Heslewood, 'everyone shit themselves. The first six rounds landed, and then they didn't have time to radio in and stop the next lot. You heard the six pops coming, as it was fired from Nui Dat – *pop-pop-pop*, here they come again – and, sure enough, another six rounds landed.'

'The next six were worse than the first six,' said Doyle, 'because we knew quite well where the next six were going to land. What do you do? You just lie there with your hands on your head. Jack Kirby was up and running to help the wounded. The next six landed, and he got a hunk of shrapnel as big as your fist in the chest. Now, here's a bloke who was the archetypal CSM, a big bull of a man. He was a disciplinarian, but he wasn't a butcher. He was a well-respected man, doing what you'd expect a sergeant major to do. He went through Long Tan, didn't get a Band-Aid, and got killed by friendly fire. If he would've been killed at Long Tan, while he would've been sadly missed, everyone would've said, "Well, that's bad luck. He was doing what a sergeant major should do." And it would be accepted. It was not accepted when he was killed by our own side. We just couldn't reconcile to it. And then we got a new CSM. What was his name? I wouldn't have a schmick.'

'We were on a winding track and twelve rounds hit the track,' said Heslewood. 'If they had've tried to do it, they couldn't've done it.' Three other men died as a result of the artillery fire, including national serviceman Douglas Powter, a railway signalman from Parkes, who'd joined D Company as a replacement in December 1966. They were all killed by the New Zealand 161 Battery, the same gunners who'd done so much to save the lives of D Company at Long Tan. No enemy were found in the area.

For about a month afterwards, said Heslewood, 161 Battery would visit the D Company bar with gifts of beer. 'They used to sing and play a guitar,' said Heslewood. 'I think initially they thought we were going to go over there and turn a blue on,' said Doyle. 'Most of them were big frigging Kiwis; you'd want to be good to take them on to start with. We realised that it was an unfortunate accident and, on top of that, the only reason that we were alive was because of what they did for us at Long Tan. And I don't think there was any animosity.'

13

OPERATION BRIBIE

On 17 February 1967, fifteen days after the heart of D Company was torn out by the death of Jack Kirby, B Company 6RAR lost part of its soul on Operation Bribie.

In Australia, well-remembered anti-war demonstrations and much larger, all-but-forgotten outpourings of public support had greeted a visit by Premier Ky in January, and public approval for committing troops to the war was slowly climbing to eventually reach a high of 62 per cent in May 1967. To the Vietnamese, it was the dawning of the Year of the Goat, and the US government had just refused to extend the traditional new-year's truce and resumed bombing North Vietnam. In Phuoc Tuy, the Viet Cong had attacked South Vietnamese forces in the fishing village of Lang Phuoc Hai, south-east of Nui Dat, and pulled back into the scrub. The Australians planned to disrupt their journey to deeper jungle by choppering in three companies of 6RAR to a landing zone north of the village, where they would meet the rest of the battalion in APCs, and confront the enemy.

John O'Halloran's Five Platoon included national serviceman Peter Rumble, born in Griffith, NSW, a reinforcement who had put himself forward vigorously for overseas service in the wake of Long Tan. 'I think I had to volunteer about four times to get there,' he said. Rumble shared a tent with one other national serviceman, Stewie

Mustchin, and two regulars, Gary Chadd and Vic Otway. 'We'd heard that [the regulars] treated national servicemen like a load of shit,' said Rumble, 'but this wasn't the case. They all realised very quickly that when you're in the bush, you're relying on the guy in front of you and the guy behind you to keep you alive. It didn't take long. We all became real good friends.'

On 17 February, B Company were still in helicopters when A Company landed, came under attack, took casualties and pulled back. The landing zone was unprotected because the APCs that were supposed to secure it – and transport C Company into the field – hadn't arrived. Also late were the big guns that were meant to have been flown from Nui Dat, to bring the infantry within artillery range. The helicopters carrying B Company came under fire. 'And all I could hear was *zing*!' said O'Halloran. 'It was like bees or something – but that was fire when you're in the air. I'd never struck that before.'

B Company were told to jump out, because the choppers weren't going to land. The ground was flat and open, and the men had to run to the edge of the scrub to safety, but, said Rumble, the enemy were 'just inside the scrub'. B Company tried to push through, with O'Halloran's Five Platoon on the right flank, Four Platoon on the left, and Six Platoon in reserve, but they were harassed and confounded by enemy fire.

'You couldn't tell where it was coming from,' said Rumble, 'but you knew it was coming straight at you, so we went straight towards it. And as we were attacking going towards the scrub, they were retreating back in, in the hope we would follow them to the main force. But we didn't. We had to wait for the rest of the company to land.

'As we were advancing,' said Rumble, 'we knew there was firing coming from in front of us. We didn't realise that there were enemy tracking us on our right flank, firing into us as well. You couldn't tell where the bullets were coming from. Stewie Mustchin got hit across the top of the scalp. They took him back and put him in with O'Halloran's group, and we kept advancing.'

'You were taught at Scheyville,' said O'Halloran, 'if you start an assault on an enemy position, there's only three reasons you stop: (1) you've reached the objective; (2) you've lost too many casualties; or (3) you're ordered to stop. Four and Five Platoons were up, and we were going through. Four went to ground, and we kept going. And then I got a radio call: "Stop the assault, you're too far ahead and Four Platoon have gone to ground." So we stopped.' O'Halloran was told Six Platoon, the reserve platoon, would move through Four Platoon to meet up with Five Platoon and continue the assault. Six Platoon advanced through Four Platoon, then went to ground themselves. O'Halloran's men were forward of company HQ and the other platoons, both of which had stopped.

'I'm thinking, "Christ almighty, they've lost some blokes,"' said O'Halloran, 'because they haven't reached the objective, they haven't been ordered – because I've got the radio – the company's copped it.'

When the next order came, it was for O'Halloran's platoon to continue the assault alone, and advance towards an enemy machine gun. 'I was only a national service officer,' said O'Halloran. 'And I had twenty-seven blokes – twenty-seven! We were on the ground. I yelled, "Right, this is it! We'll fix bayonets. When I say go, we will get up and run as fast as we can straight at the enemy, yelling as loud as we can." That's what we were trained to do. That's to get your adrenalin going, but to frighten shit out of the enemy. As it worked out, they had three hundred and thirty-odd, dug in with overhead protection. I don't think they were too worried about us twenty-seven running at them. And, on top of that, it helped them, because you can't see in the jungle, and they couldn't see us, but they could hear us, whereas we couldn't see them or hear them. And, on top of that, these three machine guns opened up on our right as we got up there; they hadn't been detected.

'When I yelled out, "Fix bayonets! When I say go, run at them: thirty metres, and that's it!" the corporal on the left hand side – who was killed – yelled back, "Boss, that's no good. There's a machine gun thirty metres straight in front of me. We'll go sixty metres." This is how good my blokes were. So I radioed up, "We're going sixty metres." We got about thirty metres, and the whole of my front two sections were either killed or wounded.'

'The sergeant was wounded,' said O'Halloran, 'one corporal was killed, one [man] turned dog and wouldn't move on me – I should've shot him – and I had so many dead and wounded. The diggers claim I was behind the biggest tree in South Vietnam, but there were five of them trying to get behind my tree. I said, "Piss off, this is my tree!" I was able to get most of the blokes in to where my tree was, so I had most of the wounded, and still one section in reserve. I tried to send some of them around and they were killed anyway, going around.'

'We just kept running,' said Rumble, 'until finally [Corporal Robin] "Spike" Jones said, "That's it, boys, hit the deck. We can't go any further." Then after about thirty minutes of trading fire – once again, we didn't realise there were snipers up in trees, too – Spike asked me to give him some cover so he could try and get back to O'Halloran to get approval to have us withdrawn. So he got up and ran like buggery, and I fired like mad, and he managed to get back. While he was getting that "okay", I happened to hear Vic Otway get shot. He was over to my right. He joined the army to go to Korea, came home and got demobbed. When Malaya came up, he joined the army and went to Malaya, came home and demobbed. So when Vietnam came up, same deal. He used to have dreams in the middle of the night and we used to rag shit out of him, give him heaps. I heard him take the shot and a real deep sigh. I was trying to yell out to tell Spike that Vicky had been hit and there were snipers trying to find where my voice was coming from. So all the sand around my head was jumping up and down and landing in my mouth, and I was spitting the bloody stuff out, still trying to get the message through to Spike.

'We eventually got approval to pull back. We managed to get to where John O'Halloran had his platoon headquarters, and we couldn't get to Vicky Otway. So someone yelled out to him, "Vicky, if you're still there, use your grenades." And we heard a couple of explosions, but didn't know whether that was him or something else, because there was so much happening at the same time.'

'I didn't have a great deal of men left,' said O'Halloran, 'so I sent the sergeant back to company HQ, and he came back with another section, another eight blokes. So I said, "Right, put them over the right side of where the wounded are," because that was where the heavy fire was coming from, and we had no blokes left on the side. By this stage, I had dead and wounded and hardly anybody else, but with this other section coming up, I thought, Well, at least we're compacted. We've got a bit of all-round defence. And they said, "Artillery's arrived." So they started sending artillery out. In jungle, there's no use it falling one hundred metres in front of you. It's got to be fifty metres or less. So I was walking it in with the [forward observer] Captain Jim Ryan. When they were landing about fifty metres in front, you could hear the nogs yelling, and I thought, You beauty, we've got this under control now. Because we were consolidated – although there were wounded and dead, but we were giving them plenty – so they weren't going to hit us. And do you know what happened? Two rounds from the artillery landed on my wounded.'

One round fell 'out in front of us,' said Rumble, 'and one on top of my mate's left leg. He didn't survive. That was Wayne Riley. Brian Waters was beside him, and he didn't survive either. I got wounded. The 105 shell has a killing range of thirty-five metres and can injure people up to sixty metres away. It landed about [three metres] away from me, threw me into the air and I went to my right, but I got most of the damage on my left side, so I must've been tumbling over and over when I was in the air. When I landed, I couldn't see a thing. I thought I was blind, but it turned out it was just the black cordite smoke. A fella beside me spotted the stretcher bearer going from wounded to wounded, and this fella said, "I'll go over to try and protect him, because he won't get down. You try and give us some cover." So I crawled up behind a tree stump and started firing off into the scrub, but I immediately upset a machine gun. It started firing back down my line of tracers. So I'd fire a couple of shots and hug the ground and I kept looking at this stump above me, and it was chipping away, and I thought, Shit, it's not going to last long. So I let go a few more and he seemed to stop. Maybe I got him, I don't know.'

The artillery had 'wounded seven of the eight blokes that'd come up from the other platoon', said O'Halloran, 'killed at least one of mine, and re-wounded those again that had been wounded. So I thought, That's it. We've absolutely had it now. All I've got's more wounded.'

Then the VC hit O'Halloran's tree with a rocket. 'I was looking out one side, and my sergeant was looking out the other,' said O'Halloran. 'It got him down the side of the head and broke his eardrum on the spot, and all I saw was white. I thought, I'm up in heaven here; there's no white in hell.

'As bold as brass, over to my left, I saw the CSM Keith Davidson and the company 2IC Captain Ted Stevenson. I yelled out, "For Christ's sake get down! The cunts are everywhere here!" They said they'd take over,' said O'Halloran, 'because they were higher rank and in charge of casualty evacuation.'

Three APCs finally arrived. 'They sent one forward to the back of where my wounded were,' said O'Halloran. 'They had eleven of the wounded in there, and the company doctor, and a medic they'd brought up from somewhere, and it got hit with three RCLs [recoilless rifle rounds]. Blew the driver's head straight off, wounded the commander, and re-wounded some of my blokes in the back. And that was the third time that day they'd been wounded. We'd walked straight into a horseshoe-type affair. We'd done no reconnaissance on our right-hand flank. And, of course, that's where the three RCLs came from.'

The lead APC 'came screaming up through the little clearing we were in', said Rumble, 'and I had Tony Trevenen with me, who had been wounded. And this APC bloke couldn't see us on the ground. He was roaring straight towards us. So I had to grab Trevenen and roll him out of the road, and the thing pulled up, and I was about to stand up and have a real go at the driver when [an RCL] hit the hatch and blew the engine apart that killed him.'

After Long Tan, Dave Thomas had been issued with an Armalite rifle and made forward scout of Robert 'Jock' Rutherford's section of Six Platoon B Company. Thomas was caught in the APC explosion, too. He'd been told to fix bayonets but 'they didn't issue you with a bayonet on an Armalite in those days', he said. 'It was an American weapon. There's not much you can do about it at that stage. If you're not issued with it, CQMS isn't about to come out there and give you one.'

Thomas could not tell what was in front of him. 'It was only shitty sort of scrub,' he said. 'It was dappled light, shining in through the upper-storey cover. You could basically be right on top of somebody in that sort of country before you see them.' When he went down past Four Platoon, Thomas was told there was an unexploded grenade next to him. 'So I dug a hole around it and basically buried it,' he said. 'But it would've gone off later in the afternoon because the tracer and the artillery set all the leaves on the ground on fire. When I got back to camp a day later, I found all along my forearms and across my stomach I had these little blisters. Sand gets pretty hot with a fire on top of it.'

There was heat closing in on Thomas from every direction. 'We were getting a hell of a lot of fire coming at us from machine guns and so on,' he said, 'plus I got the impression we were getting fire from behind us even, which was high. Then one fella in the section, Joe Nikolajew's got hit. The back of his head and the back of his shirt was on fire.' Nikolajew was an Austrian-born national serviceman. 'Joe's making a bit of a racket,' said Thomas, 'so I've grabbed hold of him, trying to calm him down. I think I may've given him a clip around the ear and told him to shut up, but I remember kneeling over him, putting a shell dressing on him, and Jock said to me to pick my rifle up. I think I told Jock to pick his own bloody rifle up. And I've looked down and you could see these bullets doing a tap dance between us in the sand.' He flicked Rutherford's rifle over to him, then picked up Nikolajew 'like a bag of spuds' under his arm – 'I don't know how he ever got into the army,' said Thomas, 'he's only a little short fella' – and carried him to the aid post at company headquarters. 'He said, "Where's my rifle?" and I said, "You won't need your bloody rifle where you're going." That wasn't very reassuring, I suppose.'

Lance Corporal Don Woolley, a national serviceman from Sydney, was wounded at the time the artillery came in. 'I've tried to pick Don up in sort of a fireman's hold,' said Thomas. 'He was wounded in the legs, so to try and get him out of there, I'd tried to throw him across my shoulders. Well, Don wasn't having any of that. So I've basically had to skull-drag him. I think I got hold of his webbing and I'm pulling him back.'

Another soldier came out to help but, in the confusion, he and Thomas accidentally took one another's Armalites. As they returned from the aid post, 'All hell broke loose again,' said Thomas. 'I've got his rifle, and the bloody thing's jammed. I'm there lying on my back trying to unjam it. I've ended up next door to the APC. Next minute, there's a hell of a gust of hot air and an enormous bloody explosion, and I've thought, What in the name of the Christ is that? and I've gone forward. I've ended up in front of the APC, going back towards the enemy. When I've looked back over my shoulder, here's this dirty great big hole in the front of this APC, and I've thought, Shit, I've gone the wrong way, so I panicked and scurried back the other way to get behind it.

'My right knee was quite sore,' said Rumble, 'that's where I thought I was wounded, but the company 2IC Ted Stevenson crawled up behind me and said, 'Where's your field dressing?' I took it off and gave it to him and he started tearing my trousers on my left leg. I said, "No, no. It's my right leg." He said, "I can see what I'm doing," so he put a bandage on it, just to tie it up. I got to hospital much later in the day and it turned out I was hit by a passing tree, and a splinter off the tree had gone below my kneecap. Shrapnel had skipped through the back of my right leg and into my left leg.'

Rumble continued in spite of his wound. 'I didn't even know I was hit in my left leg, to be honest,' he said. 'You've got to keep fighting.' The grassfire confused the APCs. 'We were sending out smoke for them to find us,' said Rumble, 'and they were saying, "All we can see is fucking smoke everywhere."'

'They had to drag my wounded out of the first APC,' said O'Halloran, 'and put them into another APC, and they set fire to the first one because they couldn't move it and they didn't want the enemy to get any stuff out of it. That was just on dark.'

Stevenson told Rumble to get onto a vehicle too, and he was driven with the rest of the wounded to meet the dustoff helicopters. 'We got on board the chopper,' said Rumble, 'and I had Tony Trevenen next to me, sitting in the side seat, looking out, and he looked across and there was a litter strung across the centre of the helicopter with a body with one half of one leg missing. And I looked at Tony and said, "I think that might be Wayne," and he looked across and he said, "Shit."

'We flew down to Vung Tau to get to hospital,' said Rumble. 'After a while, I got to look around, and there was Gary Chadd, he'd been hit two or three times, Geoff Derby, the guy who was lying beside me and got wounded, he was there. Stewie Mustchin was floating around. We were getting guys from the cavalry regiment who were coming to ask if we knew who the tankie was that had died. I didn't know any of them. It turned out he was a young national serviceman from Victoria.'

The dead man was Trooper Victor Pomroy, a ruckman for Camberwell Thirds, who had bought a flat for his disabled war-veteran father, who was 'living for the day of reunion' with his son. The day Pomroy's death was announced, the flat was shuttered and locked, as his father was in hospital with a stroke.[1]

The day after the fighting, Vic Otway came into the hospital, and was taken straight to the operating theatre. Otway had spent the night on the battlefield. 'During the course of the evening,' said Rumble, 'they put in air assaults, artillery, naval artillery from off the coast, napalm, everything and poor old Vicky was crawling from place to place. He got hit another three or four times through the night. The next morning, A Company were going through clearing the area, finding the bodies, and whatever' and they discovered Otway alive.

O'Halloran's wounded included 'Bluey' Bartsch, who was Mentioned in Dispatches. 'He fired something like eleven hundred rounds out of his machine gun without a stoppage,' said O'Halloran. 'He just kept firing it. He was on loss of pay, and when we were really in the shit, he said, "Hey, boss, I'm not even getting fucking paid for this." I said, "Well, don't shoot at them."'

To Barry Vassella with D Company, Operation Bribie was just 'another bloody shambles . . . a dreadful bloody day'. D Company had been the last to arrive in the field. 'We heard what was going on,' said Vassella, 'and we knew the boys were in trouble. We couldn't get to them, we couldn't see a bloody thing.'

The morning after the fighting, Thomas was told by Jock Rutherford to go back in with O'Halloran as a guide party for D Company. B Company would not be permitted to collect their own dead. 'I think that really upset a lot of the fellas,' said Thomas. 'It upset me, I know. The battle area was torn up a fair bit. We had to identify the bodies for the other fellas. Mick Rooney was basically in a machine-gun pit and they'd cut him to pieces, plus he'd been napalmed that night, which isn't a pretty sight.'

'Delta Company had to assault the enemy position,' said Vassella. 'We were in country where you couldn't see ten feet. It was just thick, high coastal scrub. At that stage, I'd volunteered to be an M79 gunner, so I'd got my M79 and I'd also got my SLR. I didn't like the Armalite, too light, so I went back to the SLR.

'We were pushing forward with the assault, and they said, "We've got all the wounded and dead out. Anything out there, you shoot." I'd gone maybe ten yards and there was this log in front of me. I stepped over the log and there was one of our guys dead on the other side, a Bravo Company guy left from the day before. He'd been shot through the throat, bandaged up, and just left there. I couldn't afford to think about it, had to keep going. What really pissed us off was they'd all got away. There was no VC left. How could that happen? A gap had been left for them. The enemy that caused us the most bloody trouble in the province, we had them nailed, and they just walked through.'

The Australians had entered 'between the bullock horns' of a large enemy force lying in a crescent formation. Neither the APCs nor the artillery had arrived on time, and proper reconnaissance had not been carried out on the area. Eight men were killed in a six-hour battle. This was presented as a victory in the Australian press. In the AAP reports which ran in the big metropolitan papers, the VC were described as members of a 'crack' main force battalion (in fact, the local guerrillas of D445, as ever, perhaps reinforced by NVA) which lost at least seventy dead. Task Force commander Brigadier Stuart Graham said 'a bad psychological defeat' had been inflicted on the enemy, whose fresh graves were seen dotted all over the countryside. Graham insisted the VC had intended to stay in Lang Phuoc Hai, and had boasted that 'no one, not even the Australians, could shift them', but had been 'not only kicked out, but kicked out very badly'[2] – even though they had withdrawn before the Australians had even arrived.

John O'Halloran had lost six killed and twelve wounded, a total of eighteen men. 'And you only ever went bush with about twenty-seven or twenty-eight,' he said, 'so after that, I had all new reinforcements, and I was shitscared, because I didn't know them and they didn't know me. They hadn't been under fire before. But fortunately we never had a big contact after Bribie. Because I don't know how I would've reacted or they would've reacted.'

'Six dead' was a statistic that represented nothing, gave no indication of the scale of personal loss. O'Halloran remembered each man as an individual. There was national serviceman Dave Webster, whose brother had been killed in a car accident while B Company was training at Canungra, and who'd been flown home by the army to attend the funeral – 'They were doing things like that for public relations,' said O'Halloran – and didn't come back to the company. His mates left for Vietnam without him, but he eventually arrived as a reinforcement in August 1966. 'His parents had wanted him to stay at home as the last of a farming family,' said O'Halloran, 'but he said, "I put that much shit on them, eventually they said, 'All right, you can go.'" So he came to Vietnam and got killed with me on Bribie. He lost both of his legs, and part of his arse, and he bled to death. The blokes were trying to help him and they couldn't help him.'

Webster 'was a big fella', said Rumble. 'I used to have a blue with him because we'd go into a night harbour and you'd dig yourself a shell scrape and then you'd have to be as quiet as anything. Dave wore a bloody plastic raincoat to sleep, and he tossed and turned, you could probably hear it nearly three miles away. So I used to keep waking him up.'

Brian Waters, a West Australian national serviceman, 'got it straight through the throat', said O'Halloran. 'The [other soldiers] were sitting him up and holding his head down and he was trying to talk, and he died from loss of blood. We couldn't get him out.'

There was Wayne Riley, a regular, who'd worked in the post office before he'd joined the army. 'After he was killed,' said O'Halloran, 'his parents' letters started off nicely. My commanding officer told me, "You write them a letter, you tell them their son's been killed, you be nice about him and that, but never, ever reply to them after that." And, of course, I did, and [his mother] was writing back saying, "Did he die instantly, or was he in any pain?" And, of course, you'd write back, even if you tell lies: "No, he died immediately." In the finish, his mother used to write to me and more or less say I was a murderer.'

And there was Mick Birchell from Tamworth, the best man at

Cec Bayliss's wedding, who'd played football in the same team as O'Halloran, gone to Kapooka at the same time, and been posted to the same battalion, then the same platoon. 'He was an absolutely lovely bloke,' said O'Halloran. 'From the time I got there to the time he was killed, he never once called me by my surname or my Christian name. It was always "boss" or "skipper" or something. And we'd played football together for three years prior to getting called up.'

When O'Halloran came back home to Tamworth after his national service was over, he visited first Gordon Sharp's parents, then Mick Birchell's, Bub and Jim. Birchell was an only child, and now his parents had nobody, but, said O'Halloran, 'Bub and Jim were just absolutely magnificent: "We're so happy you got home safely." Jim Birchell had served in the Second World War and had been overseas. He knew what happens in war. Not everybody does come home.'

14

THE CHANGING OF THE GUARD

Life for D Company became slower and safer at the end of 6RAR's tour. 'In the last seven or ten days, we just wound down,' said John Heslewood. 'The advance parties of the two battalions that replaced us arrived, so they did all the gun piquets at night-time. We were pretty well finished then.' The HMAS *Sydney* had already brought 7RAR to replace 5RAR at Nui Dat. After the ship had taken 5RAR home, it returned to Vietnam carrying 2RAR (later styled 2RAR/NZ [ANZAC]) a battalion which included first one and then two companies of New Zealand infantry, all of whom were regular soldiers.

On 28 May 1967, when 6RAR's last patrols marched into battalion headquarters in Nui Dat, *The Australian* reported they were greeted with champagne, cheers and what the newspaper described as 'an impromptu jazz band'. 'We did play,' said Bayliss. 'We started when we were about two months from going home. When we were in camp, we used to get our instruments out and I think we learned two marches. We used to march around the battalion area in the red mud.' The hope was they would play for the battalion when they marched through Brisbane.

On 30 May, 6RAR began their two-week journey home on the *Sydney*. 'We got on the boat, and we were not required to do any work whatsoever,' said Doyle (although Bayliss said the band 'practised all the way home'). 'We thought the food was absolutely magnificent,' said Doyle, 'after the crap we'd been eating. We got out in the sun. We just had a pair of shorts on. Everyone had rashes up to their balls.'

When 5RAR marched through Sydney on 12 May 1967 they were met by 'hundreds of thousands of people' in 'one of Sydney's truly splendid occasions' and, according to the *Sydney Morning Herald*, 'it was made all the greater because it was spontaneous, impulsive'. The infantry marched with two hundred men returned from other Task Force units, and a contingent of one hundred from the RAAF, and 'from offices and shops and city building sites men and women came to watch and applaud . . . From the high buildings came showers of floating streamers. The coloured paper caught and twisted in the hats and the rifles of the troops. They marched on, trailing it with them as they passed.'[1]

Nearly one hundred thousand people turned out to cheer 6RAR back to Brisbane on 14 June 1967, and shower the diggers with ticker-tape, streamers and confetti. 'The flags waved, the office girls yelled – and the soldiers marching along Queen Street loved it,' wrote the *Courier-Mail*. 'There were tears in many eyes. And there were quite a few cheers – rare for Brisbane spectators.'[2] The Brisbane *Telegraph* reported, 'Hand-clapping was constant throughout the 20-minute march from the Botanic Gardens.'

There were no protesters at either march, only vast numbers of jubilant supporters, thrilled to see the boys come home alive. At the Botanic Gardens, where 'fathers and sons shook hands, wives and girl friends embraced their men, several mothers shed tears and soldier-fathers hugged the reluctant youngsters who did not know them', Gunner Graeme Cuskelly went down to meet his mates from 101 Field Battery, who were marching with 6RAR and the Aviation troops of 161 Reconnaissance Flight. Cuskelly, a national serviceman, was in a wheelchair, paralysed in both legs after a shrapnel injury. 'He thought his mates mightn't know him,' said his carer, but they crowded around his chair, shaking his hands and shouting, 'How're the nurses treating you?'[3] Bayliss and the battalion band finally marched together 'but, because there wasn't enough of us, they put us in with the navy band', said Bayliss. 'They were real professional musos and we couldn't even read their frigging music, so we just marched and pretended we were playing.'

One of the most enduring myths about Australia's involvement in the Vietnam War holds that the returned men didn't receive a homecoming parade until 1987; another is that their welcome home marches were regularly disrupted by protesters. Some memoirists seem to hold both contradictory ideas simultaneously. But in August 1987, sixty thousand spectators cheered on twenty-five thousand veterans at the Vietnam Forces National Reunion and Welcome Home march in Sydney. Tens of thousands more had lined up twenty years earlier to welcome back a single battalion and associated units – an event reprised over and again through the course of the war. But not every returned soldier saw these huge outbursts of public support. Men who had arrived in Vietnam as reinforcements were often transferred to other units, where they stayed after their mates went home, until their year in country was over. They might return instead on the evening flights back to Sydney, which some came to believe were smuggling them home like thieves in the night, to hide them from demonstrators who were, in truth, probably never expected. The wounded and the sick might precede their units. Other men might disembark the *Sydney* before the ship reached the battalion's home state.[4]

Although the men were welcomed home, there was no fanfare after the parade. 'We went out to Enoggera and handed in our weapons,' said Heslewood, 'and they said, "Go home and come back tomorrow." So I got back to Enoggera at about nine o'clock and I was out of the army by half past ten. I just signed everything that was put in front of me, just to get out of the place.' When Barry Vassella returned to Australia, his nerves were shot. 'In golf,' he said, 'you have to tune out of everything else and just concentrate on one thing. That's not so easy to do when you're listening for twigs cracking, the click of a machine gun. So I became a club pro, rather than a tournament pro, and had a nice career.'

The newspapers were largely keen to paint the shiniest possible gloss on the national service scheme that they had promoted with such ferocious, unquestioning enthusiasm, but were hampered by the puzzling news that hardly any ordinary conscripts from the first intake had chosen to stay on in the regular army. Of the 2145 men who'd served as privates or NCOs, only twenty-seven – less than one in eighty – had signed up for more. However, twenty-three officers who'd come out of Scheyville – more than one in three – had elected to continue their service.

Despite the risible number of men who opted for a military career in the lower ranks, the *Sydney Morning Herald* in 1967 was convinced the experience of the national servicemen had been overwhelmingly positive. For a feature to mark what was essentially the demobilisation of the first intake, 'most of the soldiers interviewed had served some 12 months in Vietnam' and 'readily admitted that their Army service had done them good'. According to the reporter, even though 'all the National Servicemen interviewed said it was "good oh" to be out of the Army', they also said they'd 'learned much'. Unfortunately, the only quotes used were from Lance Corporal Ray Croft of 6RAR, who said, 'looking back it was not too bad, really' and Don Hillier of 5RAR, who was wounded when a mine blew up an APC, killing eight men. Hillier, who'd been hospitalised for six weeks with shrapnel in the arm and spine said, 'National Service is good experience and I have nothing against it, but the Army does make you appreciate civilian life.' In the manner of a man who'd just served a prison sentence, he added, 'You just do your time without giving any trouble – that's about the only thing you can do.'[5]

Despite the official insistence that national servicemen and regular soldiers had the same experiences in the army, between April 1966, when the Task Force went to Vietnam, and April 1967, thirty-three national servicemen and thirty-five regulars had been killed in action or died of their wounds – even though national servicemen made up only slightly more than 25 per cent of the Task Force. In addition, ninety-nine national servicemen and 146 regulars had been wounded in action. The minister for the army, Malcolm Fraser, said, 'Most of the casualties, by quite a large number, are still regulars.' This was true of total casualties, but not of deaths. Although they provided only one-quarter of Australian military personnel in Vietnam during that twelve-month period, they were almost as likely to die as the other three-quarters combined. Fraser explained, 'It is a fact of life that if you have a serviceman for two years there are certain positions for which you can train him and into which you can put him. If you have a man for six years – as a regular – you can put him into jobs which require more training.' This meant, he said, a higher proportion of national servicemen ended up in infantry battalions.[6] The implication was, since the infantry bear the brunt of the fighting, they were more likely to be killed. And since the national servicemen filled the infantry, *they* were more liable to die than men who'd chosen the army as a career.

Malcolm Fraser, who had been too young to fight in the Second World War, and had no military experience beyond cadets at Melbourne Grammar School, did not weep over Vietnam. But Walter Noack did.

PART 2

15

THE UNWILLING

From the beginning, not every anxious young conscript walked willingly into national service, and not every loose-limbed boy who shook himself into a badly fitting set of greens wore the uniform for the full two years. There was always a small number of men with religious or political objections to the army or the war, and a handful of conscripts in every intake who realised in training that they weren't prepared to kill.

And there were others who simply did not want to serve: they just couldn't see the point. Sean Cullip, of the folk duo Sean and Sonja, made the first reported attempt to sidestep national service on non-religious grounds. Cullip was the musician whose record the magistrate had refused to hear in 1965, and he had maintained in court that he shouldn't go into the army because a split with his singing partner, Sonja Tallis, would cause financial hardship, as she depended on him for musical backing. The press fed with dry delight on the idea that his objection was so apparently trivial, and the court was unimpressed. Cullip, who would otherwise have been in the first national service intake, was still in the army months after 5RAR and 6RAR had come home.

Cullip was the son of a fairly prominent Sydney family and had attended Cranbrook, an exclusive private boys' school in Bellevue

Hill. His late father had been a manager of the Australian Hotel, and Lady Nancy Fairfax was his godmother. Cullip and Tallis had formed their act in 1963. They'd met when Cullip was studying advertising at Sydney Tech and quickly recorded three albums and a clutch of EPs and singles for CBS. They sang together beautifully, like choristers, and their audience was growing until 'that dreaded letter arrived', said Cullip. 'We'd had cadets at school, which I'd hated. All this marching around I thought was a useless waste of time. My brother, of course, was RSM [regimental sergeant major] at cadets – my brother was good at everything – so I had to go in as well. We were all given 303s to carry around, and you had to clean your boots and clean your rifle, which I was hopeless at. So, of course, when the national service was announced, I thought, Oh no, please no. Not me. I suppose I was a sort of conscientious objector, but I wasn't going to get up and shake my fist. I was just hopeless at military things.'

The newspaper reports of Cullip's case were less than the sum of his arguments. He had recently lost his father, who'd died at the age of fifty, six months after his elder brother had succumbed to leukaemia. This left only Cullip, his mother and his ten-year-old sister at home. There were more people than Tallis who relied on Cullip, but the magistrate ended his hearing with the acknowledgement that Sean and Sonja might be on the cusp of a successful career, but no finding they would suffer exceptional hardship due to Cullip's military commitments. So Cullip eventually put on uniform in 1966, and found himself in the newest recruit training battalion, 3RTB, in Singleton, NSW, eighty kilometres north-west of Newcastle. The camp, which also housed a training centre for the large number of infantrymen who were to complete their corps training before being posted to battalions, was 'brand new', said Cullip. 'They hadn't even really finished it properly. It was still just dirt, no grass. Up near the gate one day, we had to go and plant a native tree. They said, "The army isn't all about killing people, we plant trees as well." And you had to put a little tag on it with your name and number, and the rumour went around that if you were killed in Vietnam, they chopped your tree down.'

Like many other conscripted musicians, Cullip hoped to get into a military band, but he could only play guitar and piano, and neither were needed in the army. Instead, he was made a clerk in the Royal Australian Army Ordnance Corps and sent to 2BOD, the base ordnance depot in Moorebank, NSW, at the edge of the sprawling Holsworthy military reserve by the side of the Georges River. Tallis found it difficult to perform without him. 'She eventually, at one stage, had a duo with Tony Bonner from *Skippy*,' said Cullip, 'but it just didn't work. There wasn't the chemistry there.'

At 2BOD, Cullip worked in the receiving shed. 'We had a CRS – consignment receipt sheet – in triplicate for everything,' he said. 'One spoon, we got it; one tank, we got it; one set of keys, we got it. After a few weeks of this, I was going spare.' Then he heard there was a shortage of men at the shipping section in Leichhardt. A merchant ship, the MV *Jeparit,* was being loaded with supplies for the Task Force in Vietnam, and 'all the paperwork had to be done for the bills of loading, customs', said Cullip, 'and they desperately needed another clerk, so they sent me up there. There were a lot of civilians out there working, normal people from outside the army. In the office, there was the sergeant, and the typist, Mrs Geoghegan. They were both very intelligent people. We typed furiously. For two weeks, we worked nonstop, didn't even stop for lunch, because all the goods had to be sent out in shipping containers for Vietnam.'

Furious typing was as much a part of the national service experience as jungle warfare. Of the 63 740 men eventually called up, less than a quarter were sent to Vietnam. Others, at various times, went to Malaya, Singapore and Papua New Guinea, but the great majority remained in Australia, filling out forms or fixing cars, or simply training with units not scheduled to go overseas – as every infantry battalion, for example, was given two years between deployments to 1ATF. There were some bloody engagements yet to be fought, but a lot more filing, goods loading, vehicle maintenance, building work, local exercises in the bush, and just fiddling about.

At 2BOD, said Cullip, 'There were no parades, they left us to do our work. The sergeant and I worked out a filing system. At the end of that two weeks, suddenly there was nothing to do, and Mrs Geoghegan said, "Now, I've got six weeks' hiatus, with very little happening, till the *Jeparit* comes back again." I was sent back to Moorebank to the consignment receipt sheets. Every week for the next year, I sent a written request to go back to Leichhardt, and they did send me back for my final six months.' During their regular quiet periods, Mrs Geoghegan taught Cullip how to solve the cryptic crossword in the *Daily Telegraph*.

'At one stage, when I was at Moorebank, they did say, "2BOD is rotating, and will be going to Vietnam. If you don't wish to go, put down your request and we will have a look at it,"' said Cullip. 'My request was, "I don't want to go. Have a look at my rifle-range record." It was two out of one hundred. I was petrified of firearms. In basic training, they wanted us to throw grenades. I said, "I can't. I'll drop it into the pit." So when it was my turn to throw a grenade, they'd just send me to the end of the line. I said, "I don't want to go to Vietnam because I'm useless."'

In 1968, Cullip left the army. He was in Vietnam by Christmas.

In the early years, organised protests against the war tended to be small and mocked, and the demonstrators thought of as Communists, cowards, cranks, or all three. While there was always some public dissent, it was unfocused and divided, with differences between those who opposed all wars, the Vietnam War, or just conscription. In the third quarter of 1966, for instance, while 68 per cent of Australians favoured conscription, only 38 per cent thought national servicemen should be sent to Vietnam, where 61 per cent believed Australia should continue to fight.

Foremost among the early protesters against national service – and the only demonstrators most conscripts would ever encounter – were the women of the Save Our Sons movement, in their hats, gloves and horn-rimmed spectacles, who held regular vigils at army induction centres when 'their' boys were marched in. Members of SOS included Communists and pacifists as well as previously apolitical 'housewives', but most strove to at least look like respectable, conservative, middle-class mothers.

A small number of young people of call-up age joined the Youth Campaign Against Conscription (YCAC) whose initially sober-suited activists staged the first Australian burning of documents they identified as 'draft cards' – probably their national service registration cards – in Sydney in February 1966. But most opponents of conscription and the war simply hoped and campaigned for a Labor victory in the November 1966 general election. But Arthur Calwell's election promise to bring the troops home was spectacularly out of step with public opinion, while Harold Holt's famous pledge to the US president a month earlier, that Australia would be 'all the way with LBJ', was an accurate reading of the public mood. The election was fought specifically around national service and Vietnam, and it ended Calwell's political career. The Coalition emerged with the largest majority in Australian history to that date. Calwell had believed he was a conscience for the nation, and the nation voted him silent. Ten weeks later, his deputy Gough Whitlam became the leader of the Labor Party, out-polling Jim Cairns, the de facto parliamentary leader of the anti-war movement. Australia was more firmly united in support of the conservative parties and the country's role in Vietnam than it had been when the first national servicemen had entered their recruit training battalions. The first act of the new government was to send 940 extra soldiers, as well as additional sailors, planes and airmen, to Vietnam.

As protest was such a marginal and eccentric pastime, many early conscientious objectors had no connection with any anti-war organisation. The first prominent dissenter was William White, who had been called up in the intake of July 1966. His birthdate, like Cullip's, had been drawn in the first ballot, but he'd claimed conscientious-objector status and been refused. He had cited personal rather than religious convictions against war and killing, and both a magistrate and a district judge had ruled he could only be required to perform non-combatant duties – but White didn't want anything to do with the army.

White was a handsome, personable schoolteacher from Gladesville, Sydney, and he continued to teach until July, when he was removed from the classroom and dismissed from his job under the National Service Act. In November, he was dragged from his home by four NSW police and taken into military custody. He steadfastly refused to obey any military order, maintained he was opposed to all wars, and was ultimately – and grudgingly – accepted as a conscientious objector at the end of December. While there was some limited public sympathy for White, an opinion poll in February 1967 found 72 per cent of Australians believed he should have served his time in the army, either as a combatant or a non-combatant.

White's claim received far more publicity than the case of Alwyn Henderson, who went into the army on 28 September 1966. Henderson's father was a dirt farmer in the Dandenongs. During the Second World War, he'd tossed a coin with his brother to decide who should go into the services and who should stay behind to work the land. Henderson's uncle won the toss, went into the army and came out a qualified mechanic. 'It was always thought he had the best of the deal,' said Henderson. 'My father was stuck during the war doing the farming, and finished up being a farmer.'

The family kept firearms and, as a teenager, Henderson had his own shotgun. He went to the local high school, then started a degree in industrial chemistry, studying part-time while testing explosives for ICI in its laboratory at Sunshine. He was called up and sent to Puckapunyal for recruit training where, he said, the worst decision he ever made was to apply for officer training. He ended up at Scheyville where 'there was a lot of stuff about Vietnam, because everyone had to be able to convince their own soldiers that what they were doing was a good thing, so you were expected to be able to mount sensible arguments.' But the indoctrination only raised doubts in Henderson. On a training exercise, he was ranged against soldiers pretending to be the enemy. 'It was very real,' he said, 'there was a lot of machine-gun blank fire and people screaming and carrying on and running around – and it's easy to cross over to the idea that it's actually happening. I can recall noticing one of these guys and taking a bead on him. And I had this sudden very strong feeling that, even though I'd been walking around with a gun almost all my life, it wasn't the right thing for me to be shooting people.'

He had been at Scheyville for seven weeks when he asked to leave, although he was at first willing to stay on in the military. 'They were very unhappy about me deciding I didn't want to be an officer in the Australian Army,' he said. 'They made life quite uncomfortable for the next few days, while they considered what their actions should be. There was more inspection of my personal kit and whether my shoes were brushed in the way they wanted. Someone would get me to march through some mud, then someone would inspect me afterwards and tell me I had mud on my boots.

'The officers were pissed off,' he said. 'They told me the vast amount of money I'd wasted.' He was sent back to recruit training, this time at Kapooka, where his platoon included a large number of regular soldiers. 'The people who signed up as regulars were all a particular sort of person,' he said. 'I didn't warm to any of them. I didn't have a great time at Kapooka. It was as boring as batshit. I can remember spending all night on guard duty with a pick handle.'

On paper, Henderson still looked like a good soldier. 'Despite his comedown from officer training Henderson has shown himself to be very keen,' wrote an officer on his RTB progress record. 'An asset to the platoon.'[1] And, by the time he finally passed out of recruit training, he was extremely fit. 'I was absolutely bloody jumping,' he said. 'I'd had six months of continual physical exercise', but he found himself thinking, 'This is a very bad idea, me becoming a soldier.'

He applied to join the Royal Australian Army Medical Corps, he said, 'so I wouldn't have to shoot people'. RAAMC recruits did their corps training at Healesville, about fifty-two kilometres from Melbourne, camped in tents outside what was once a luxury hotel. Henderson found himself with national servicemen again. 'It was a much more normal group of people,' he said, 'more interested in having a party than anything else.'

After Healesville, he was posted to 3rd Casualty Clearing Station (3CCS) at Wacol, Queensland. 'There were quite a lot of soldiers and medics who'd been to Vietnam working in that unit,' he said, 'who now would be going again and helping train people to go. I developed very strong views about the war, mostly through reading about it, and I started to express these views quite strongly to people, and I think it's fair to say I became regarded as a disruptive influence. A lot of the regular guys were keen to go to Vietnam, and there were a lot of people who couldn't see any great advantage in it. And there were people like me who thought it was a very bad idea to be involved or even attached to the whole thing.

'About this time,' he said, 'I registered as a conscientious objector. I filled out a form and posted it off. I remember waking up one day and saying, "I'm not going to war any more. I'm sorry, I'm staying in bed today." Eventually I was dragged up and brought before the commanding officer. I got from him a pretty fair go. He was a doctor as well as the leader of a unit. He was happy to get rid of me somehow, anyhow. The last thing he wanted was a conscientious objector.

'The problem was there was not really any kind of process within the army to deal with this at all. He said, "Look, I can't have you bloody lying in bed all day. I'll have to throw you in jail." I think I was in a small military jail for a few days at Indooroopilly. The first couple of days were no big deal. I wasn't very popular among the military police, who knew why I was there, but no great harm came to me. And after probably three days I was back in the unit, and an officer said, "Until your court case comes up, you're confined to the library."'

Henderson didn't see much of the other soldiers, but 'a lot of people were sympathetic and said, "Good luck, mate,"' he said. 'At some point in time, I was allowed to live off base. A lot of people did, if they could afford it. I rented a flat with a mate, and I sat in the library nine till five. It seemed reasonable to me. I wasn't actually taking much of a part in the army. Then my court case happened in Brisbane, and I argued my own case, and the magistrate said, "I'm not convinced . . . Go back to the army."'

He was ordered by a Court of Petty Sessions on 28 June 1967 to undertake duties of a non-combatant nature. On 29 June, he wrote, 'I cannot comply with this order because it is against my conscience. The only course of action I can now follow is to cease all military duties and to appeal against the decision.'[2] His second application to become a conscientious objector was refused in August. He said, in a statement printed in the pacifist newspaper *The Peacemaker*, 'When I entered the Army I was generally apathetic to war and the concept of freedom. My beliefs have changed for two reasons. Firstly, for the first time in my life I was confronted with positive knowledge of the horrors, the inhumanities, the insane policies and the desparate [sic], but false rationalisations of war. Secondly, the Army gave me time to think. The Army deprived me of the daily assurances of mass media (a daily newspaper is difficult to obtain in many camps and the TV is usually tuned to the less worthwhile programs), and I was given days and weeks with nothing to occupy my mind but the moral conflict that grew within me. I formed my beliefs after I entered the Army and I formed them by myself.'[3]

Henderson decided if he couldn't be a conscientious objector he'd go AWOL, get court-martialled, and be thrown out of the army that way. In order to merit a court martial, he believed, a soldier had to fail to report for duty for a month. When he was about to abscond, he phoned a journalist at *The Australian* and told him his story 'just in case I disappeared forever', he said. 'It was a very small insurance policy, and he published a very small piece giving my name and what was likely to happen.'

Henderson went on the run in August, and turned up at an anti-war rally in Brisbane where, he said, he met 'people who wanted me to do all kinds of things which I thought were very foolish for my own safety. I knew I'd had a pretty soft ride, and things were likely to get very ugly, but I didn't think it was wise for me to encourage that.' The activists would have liked him to front a campaign. 'I said, "I don't think so,"' said Henderson. 'While I was against the war, the people who were mostly running the anti-war things were Maoists and ratbags of various other kinds. I was never political in that way.' But Henderson returned to Victoria and disappeared into the increasingly radical Monash University student scene. He learned meditation techniques that he thought might be useful in jail, and searched for a way around his predicament. He looked for help and advice wherever he might find it, and called in on Jim Cairns, the Victorian MP who'd emerged as the Labor Party's most prominent opponent of the war. 'I talked to him for a couple of hours,' said Henderson. 'He was very sympathetic and not very helpful. But he didn't suggest that I martyr myself for his cause, in the way that a lot of students would've thought was a good idea.'

Henderson also visited his parents, who thought his absconding 'a very bad thing, generally speaking', and, when his thirty days were up, he turned himself in from the family home. Back in Brisbane on 19 September, rather than facing an immediate court martial, he was given more time in the stockade at Indooroopilly. 'This wasn't what I'd expected at all,' he said. 'So things really got strange.' He refused to follow any orders and was placed in solitary confinement. 'The windows were all closed and it was an especially dark cell.

They said, "From now on, you're on bread and water." I said, "You can forget the bread. I'm on hunger strike, if that's what you want to play." So then I was on hunger strike, and that wasn't really what I'd planned either.'

For the most part, he felt he was treated quite well. 'The only thing they did was they paraded me through the kitchen,' he said, and made him stand in a corner while food was being prepared. On 22 September, a psychiatrist made a report to the army that Henderson 'feels he has been forced into army, he is going to remain on hunger strike until he is given a discharge . . . He is not psychotic or psychoneurotic – he is aware of what he is doing and his motives.' His recommendations were: '(1) He is of doubtful value to the Army. (2) He is not suitable for service. (3) That he be administratively discharged.'[4]

Meanwhile, Henderson stopped having water. 'And that's harder to deal with,' he said. 'I remember waking up in the middle of the night and my throat was all dry and my tongue had swollen up and I had to drink something, and I banged on the door and they said, "Here, you can drink this," and they gave me a cup of milk. That was the only thing I could get. You can starve yourself quite easily, but it's much more difficult to kill yourself by not drinking. And my plan wasn't to actually kill myself. I was basically trying to cause as much inconvenience as possible.'

When he got out of the stockade, he applied for conscientious-objector status again, but this time he hired a lawyer, and won the case in a day. He was discharged from the army on 15 December 1967. He'd been a soldier for one year and thirty-seven days.

As a civilian, he went to live in Carlton, Victoria, where he played a small part in the anti-war movement. 'I went to the big demonstration in Melbourne,' he said, 'and quite a few before that. I didn't join an organisation and I didn't rally the other troops. I decided not to be a joiner.'

The early national-service objectors, such as White and Henderson, tended to be isolated individuals, struggling with personal dilemmas. There was no organisation behind their actions, and no overriding plan, beyond staying out of the army or getting out of it. But while Alwyn Henderson was living clandestinely with students, the Monash University Labor Club had come under the control of group of Maoists. In July 1967, the club set up a student committee to raise money to send to the NLF. It was an action that attracted virtually no public support but a huge amount of publicity. 'That was probably the low point in terms of relationships between the soldiers and students,' said Dave Nadel, president of the Labor Club. But Nadel judged the campaign a tactical success. 'It moved – in society a bit and on campus completely – the whole debate further to the left,' he said. 'I'd spent two years trying to get a motion through the [Student Representative Council] at general meetings, just saying, "This campus opposes the war in Vietnam." I couldn't do it. It was too radical. Once the Labor Club said it was giving aid to the enemy, there was a huge student meeting called to condemn us, but the people who showed up at the meeting were also anti-war. What in fact they got through was the position: "We are opposed to the war, we believe the NLF should be a party to the negotiations" – which was a position the Americans and the Australians opposed – "but, of course, we're also opposed to collecting aid."'

The press wanted to hear from the soldiers, to delight in the drama of this new domestic conflict, but the men who returned from Vietnam in August had been instructed to make no comment. 'We have been ear-bashed by the Army about this. We have been told not to say anything,' one man informed a reporter at Essendon Airport.[5] The government quickly passed the Defence Forces Protection Act, which made it an imprisonable offence to send aid to the NLF, the Government of North Vietnam or the Communist Party of North Vietnam. The Labor Party, including Jim Cairns, voted solidly in favour of the bill.

There had always been men with conscientious objections to war, but the idea that some educated young Australians supported the enemy, and felt able to publicly appeal for funds which might buy them weapons, marked the beginning of something new.

16

THE WILLING

There was nothing of the new about cricketer Doug Walters, nothing threatening and – on the surface – nothing complicated. He came from the bush, which has always excited men from the city. He had big ears, a strong nose and hard eyes, the slow charm of a cockie, the bearing of an Anzac. His mouth didn't move much when he talked.

He had learned the game from his dad, backyard cricket on an anthill wicket on a dairy farm in Marshdale near Dungog, NSW. He was an instinctive, commanding batsman, only sixteen when tradition has it he knocked a six out of the SCG grounds, over Driver Avenue and towards Kippax Lake. When he wasn't away playing cricket, he rose before dawn to help his father milk the cows.

At nineteen, he played England in his first Test match, at Brisbane Cricket Ground. He was only four off a century when the England captain tried to break Walters' concentration by calling for drinks. When play resumed, a dog ran onto the pitch, chasing after birds and pursued by a gang of small boys, followed by a posse of umpires, spectators and fielders. But Walters' composure seemed indestructible, and he went on to make 155, the first Australian to score a century in his first Test since poker-faced Jim Burke in 1951. Two weeks later, Walters hit a second century in his next Test at Melbourne.

There was, inevitably, talk of another Don Bradman. Walters

spoke sparingly, joked languidly. He liked country and western music and, of course, when he was called up at twenty years old in 1966, Doug Walters did his duty. The Sydney *Sun* found him leaning against the fence of his boarding house, the day he went into the army. 'What will he have to gain?' asked the paper. 'A possible bullet by a Vietcong, a hand-grenade splinter, a poisoned spike.' But Walters didn't 'rant or rave about the men who drafted him, the Government which sanctioned conscription, he didn't ask "why" or "what for". He is going quietly without fuss.'[1] Doug Walters was the old style of hero, who just did or died.

He reported to the army depot at Marrickville on 20 April 1966, one national service trainee among five hundred. He turned up on the foggy morning, wearing a cricket jumper, a shirt and tie. On the same day, the HMAS *Sydney* was loading to leave Garden Island for Vung Tau, filling its deck space with trucks, ambulances, jeeps and trailers. Minister for the Army Malcolm Fraser once again denied reports that national servicemen would be given a choice about going to Vietnam.[2] All through the night, demonstrators held a candlelit vigil in Hyde Park against sending the conscripts to war.

Walters told the press, 'I just want to be like all the other fellows going in. If I get to Vietnam, well, I will go – there'll be no trouble.'[3] Like hundreds of national servicemen, he was posted to 1RAR, which had just returned from Vietnam. He joined the battalion at Holsworthy, where he was able to play grade cricket at weekends. He batted in a Melbourne 'Test' to raise money for the bushfire fund, and later told the *Sun*, 'We were on jungle exercises in Queensland at the time. I was acting as a Vietcong when the time came for me to catch a jeep to the airport 60-odd miles away. I radioed for permission to leave and was ordered to get caught. You don't just walk out of a "war". Anyway I detached myself so I wouldn't give our position away, then I ran out into a clearing and started firing until I was out of ammunition. I was grabbed, tied up for some time and then I had to carry another "prisoner" on my shoulder a fair way to the jeep to earn my ride. After all that I got 26 runs in two innings.'[4]

Walters, the batsman, eventually became Walters, the batman, assigned to an officer he described only as 'a second lieutenant'. 'We used to call him "Skip"', he wrote later, 'and he was one of the few officers who would call us by our first names . . . We were supposed to be on parade ground at 7.30 a.m. and Skip would take a stroll through the huts at 7.31 a.m. When he got to my bed, he'd say, "Doug, do you feel like going on parade this morning." I'd roll over and reply, "Not really, Skip." He'd sigh and say, "Well, you'd better make yourself scarce. I've a pair of boots that need polishing and a shirt that needs ironing." He'd do much the same thing when we were going on a route march.'[5]

The officer served by Walters was Scheyville graduate Tim Fischer, who was later to become Australia's deputy prime minister. 'It was bizarre,' said Fischer, 'but he brought me a cup of tea in the Holsworthy officers' mess once, twice – and the third time, I said, "No more. I think this is a bit ridiculous. A farmer from Boree Creek is being brought a cup of tea by the Australian XI."'

Walters saved up enough leave to play Shield and Test cricket in his second year in the army. He captained New South Wales in December 1967 and averaged 127 in two Tests against India. 1RAR returned to Vietnam in April 1968, the month Walters was discharged. Walters has since claimed he was asked to sign on for a further six months by his company commander, Major Anthony Hammett, as it would be better for his image to go to Vietnam with the Australian Army rather than to England with the Australian cricket team. He said he told Hammett he wasn't going to take up his offer as, unlike the cricket board, the army couldn't guarantee him a return ticket.[6]

Tim Fischer extended his national service by nine months to go overseas with the battalion, and almost forfeited his own return ticket at the Battle of Coral.

The conscription of Doug Walters was a victory for the government, the military and the very idea of national service. Not even a sporting hero would be allowed to duck his responsibilities, and not even cricket was more important than building up the army.

While Walters had been carving a name as Bradman reincarnate, Normie Rowe had emerged as an idol of the new kind. In the beginning, the press had loved the man who could apparently drive wild a crowd of pop-crazy teenaged girls but remain, in the words of the Sydney *Daily Mirror*, 'a handsome, stocky, broad-shouldered, well-muscled, mild-mannered, easy-going boy with the good grace to wonder bemusedly how on earth it all started and where on earth it will all end'.[7] Throughout the first half of 1966, the shrieks of Normie-mania grew louder. On 17 June, he was hospitalised after fans mobbed him at Sydney Town Hall. Rowe's manager took a reporter to his bedside, who wrote, 'Rowe was sobbing and writhing and was barely comprehensible when he spoke.'[8]

The Australian king of pop next had to conquer the world, so Rowe signed to Polydor and went to the UK. When he arrived in London, there were only three fans waiting for him. He was an unknown artist from the other side of the world, who'd landed at the tail end of the beat boom, with an act that was already old-fashioned outside Australia – an interpretive singer who didn't write his own hits. 'Everyone was very friendly,' he wrote in September, 'but no one has asked for my autograph.'[9] He had some airplay in England, but his records didn't sell, and he was still in London, searching for success, when he was supposed to register for national service in 1967.

There seemed a dour, processional inevitability to the drafting of Normie Rowe, a destiny set in 1965, when reporters began to ask the eighteen-year-old pop idol questions about the war. It was as if his national service were more the result of a curse cast by journalists than a rune drawn by bureaucrats. By February 1967, his Australian record producer, his international manager, his publicity man and his UK producer had all resigned. Rowe denied he was staying in the UK to dodge the draft. 'Like most young Australians, I don't want to go to Vietnam,' he said, 'but if I have to go, I will not buck anything.'[10] But Rowe had ceased to be a real person to the press. He was no longer a human being who could be hurt. The *Daily Mirror* called him 'the local boy who didn't make good'[11], *People* magazine noted he was playing support to Gene Pitney in Portsmouth, home of the HMS *Victory*, which was 'the nearest he's come to any kind of victory since he came to England'.[12] The Sydney *Sun* said, 'He's only as good as his last pop record – which wasn't good enough.'[13]

Rowe came home in July, and registered for national service at the GPO, after which teenage girls fought for his post office ballpoint. As the ballot had already been completed for men of Rowe's age, he had to go into a subsequent draw, and his birthdate came out of the barrel. 'I don't mind going to Vietnam,' he said, 'but I don't like the idea of being shot at.'[14]

One of the nation's most promising sports stars had been taken into the army, and one of its most popular entertainers was willing to go to war. All that was needed to assure the public that no amount of fame or influence could bring a man special treatment was for a cabinet minister's son to be posted to Vietnam. And, on the same morning as Walters reported to Marrickville Army Depot en route to Kapooka, Allen James Fairhall, the son of the minister for defence, began his recruit training at Singleton.

Allen Fairhall Senior always knew his boy's case might be important to the government. During early cabinet discussions of the national service scheme, he later told a parliamentary interviewer, 'I was conscious of the fact that my only son was coming up to 19 years of age within the period of the call up . . . I can't argue about that [but] I was more conscious of what would be said if he were not to be balloted in, because you know, the public are pretty cynical about these things, and the idea of influence being used, particularly by members of the government in their own favour, is pretty high in the public consciousness.'[15]

The young Fairhall was an announcer on the Newcastle radio station founded by his father and, although Fairhall Senior had not served in the Second World War, his son willingly answered the call. 'I didn't give it a lot of thought,' said Fairhall. 'You get your call-up notice, you're called up. End of story. It's not something I would've done off my own bat, but if Her Majesty required me for a couple of years, I was quite happy to do that.' He said national service wasn't much spoken about at home, and defence 'wasn't the sort of conversation you had around the family dinner table' at the home of the minister for defence. Fairhall was one of the few national servicemen who'd visited Vietnam before he went into the army. He'd travelled to South-East Asia in the early 1960s with his father and they'd stopped in Saigon to do business with President Diem.

When Fairhall was about to board the train for 3RTB Singleton on 20 April 1966, he refused to talk to journalists. 'I've got nothing to say,' he said, 'I don't want any publicity. My father is misquoted in the press so much it is not worth it.' He wouldn't make a statement once he arrived at the base either, and spent most of his time in the army in comfortable anonymity.

Fairhall put down Engineers as his choice of corps. 'I was determined to learn a skill,' he said, 'and being a rifleman and tramping around the jungles wasn't exactly a skill that would be any use to me.' After training at the School of Military Engineering, he was posted to 30 Terminal Squadron, which ran work boats around Sydney Harbour and guaranteed war stores would be loaded for Vietnam. The merchant ships MV *Jeparit* and MV *Boonaroo* had been chartered by the government to transport military supplies to Vung Tau. But while Fairhall was with the terminal squadron in February 1967, the Communist-led Seamen's Union of Australia (SUA) refused to supply further crews for either vessel's journeys to Vietnam. In one of the earliest trade union actions against the war, SUA members walked off the *Jeparit.* However, the seamen had little support within the labour movement. Men from other maritime unions stayed on board, and some SUA members were replaced by sailors from the Royal Australian Navy (RAN). The *Jeparit* subsequently operated with a mixed military/civilian crew, while the *Boonaroo* was actually commissioned into the RAN.

Meanwhile, 30 Terminal Squadron were 'virtually a gang of stevedores that stood over the wharfies', said Fairhall. 'They knew bloody well if they didn't load the ship, we would.' The squadron was not warned for Vietnam. Its soldiers spent much of their time at the Buena Vista Hotel in Mosman. 'We'd assemble inventories of our equipment and we used to all go to the pub down the road after our parade in the mornings,' said Fairhall. 'Some blokes took a taxi. There was nothing to do. We were sitting around doing nothing.'

30 Terminal Squadron was busy only in bursts, and then not for very long. Fairhall had less than a year to serve when he was asked if he would go to Vietnam. 'I was sick and tired of hanging around there doing stuff-all,' he said. 'I wanted to do something useful for a change. There's nothing more boring than a peacetime army.' The son of the minister for defence went off to war on 12 December 1967. Five days later, Prime Minister Harold Holt swam out to sea off Cheviot Beach, near Portsea, Victoria, and never came back in. The government announced his death on 19 December, and John Gorton was sworn in as his successor in January 1968.

17

LOVE, WAR AND POGOS IN VUNG TAU

Like so many other Australian soldiers, Allen Fairhall shored up in Vung Tau, a sand-blown, sleazy beachside town that was once the colonial resort of Cap Saint Jacques. For decades, Saigon's *fonctionnaires* and *hommes d'affaires* had enjoyed weekends in villas overlooking the bay but, by the end of the French time, the town had become a vast, sprawling, irrelevant army camp. The writer Bernard Fall called it France's last 'boondoggle before she left Indochina', built in the vain hope that Diem would allow a French SEATO base to remain in the country. The French, wrote Fall, had 'spent 3 billion francs since 1954 concentrating in this little cape all that an army needed for its upkeep over an indefinite period', but by 1957 it was 'all dead and showing the early signs of tropical decay'.[1]

The 1st Australian Logistics Support Group, established in Vung Tau in 1966, was the backpack for Nui Dat. Like the French, the Australians bloated Vung Tau with their supplies, and the town was the entrepot where all the arms and ammunition, the cigarettes and beer, the machine parts and fuel, arrived and were stored. Including the RAAF personnel at the airbase, there were about eighteen hundred Australians working in Vung Tau. Militarily, it was one of the safest places in South Vietnam, always flooded with fighting troops on leave, Americans and South Koreans as well as Australians. It was not, as many men believed, also a rest centre for the VC. As veteran and historian Lex McAulay has pointed out, a 'general complaint from members of the Viet Cong who were captured or managed to surrender was that they were not allowed rest and recreation away from the unit, or leave to visit home.'[2]

There were ruins of the French fort in Vung Tau when the Australians arrived, the colonial mansions were rotting in the salt air, and the landmark Grand Hotel was 'grand' in name only. Looking out onto the South China Sea, 1ALSG was a castle built on sand dunes, sinking back into swamps. But the press was as expansively approving as it was of all of the army's efforts. 'Vietnam Supply Base: "It's Like The Riviera"' was a headline in the Melbourne *Herald*, for a story that appeared to have no other purpose than to echo this initial comparison: '"This place is rather like a slice of the French Riviera," said 1ALSG CO, Lieutenant Colonel Laurence Chambers. "Almost too much so – sometimes it's hard to keep people up to the mark . . . Why not be comfortable? Any fool can live rough."'[3]

About three hundred and fifty Vietnamese civilians worked at 1ALSG, along with Australian military units including engineers, stores, transport, signals, logistics and provosts. Fairhall belonged to 11 Movement Control Group, which, among other tasks, coordinated the movement of stores to Vietnam, and loaded and unloaded the HMAS *Sydney*. He managed the airport office for Wallaby Airlines, which ran Caribous around the theatre of war. The crews used to fly from Vung Tau to the US mortuary near Tan Son Nhut, sign for the deceased remains of Australian soldiers and bring them back to be loaded onto flights home to Australia.

Scheyville graduate Second Lieutenant David Roubin was also ultimately posted to Vung Tau, with the Royal Australian Army Ordnance Corps (RAAOC), although he had to extend his national service commitment to get to Vietnam and, eventually, take a commission to stay. He arrived in country in October 1967, two years and four months after joining the army, and eventually became a stores officer with 2nd Advanced Ordnance Depot, where life for officers was almost as comfortable as Chambers had promised. 'Our quartermaster was very adept,' said Roubin. 'If you needed anything, he got it. We had a fridge, a bar, comfy chairs and so forth.' They held barbecues at weekends. 'I went to town a lot. I had a couple of girlfriends in town.

'There's a difference in being an officer in a logistics unit and being a soldier in Nui Dat being shot at,' he said. 'I spent a lot of my time trying to convince my soldiers that they weren't fucking rude to fucking nogs. It's all you ever do. The average Australian national serviceman spent six to twelve months there, running around the bush with a rifle, being shot at, shooting – not all the time; there was a lot of waiting and very little action – and the only other Vietnamese they ever met were the bar girls, the prostitutes. So they're not going to have a good experience. Whereas I was working with these Vietnamese all the time, and they were honest, decent, hard-working people, scared for their bloody lives. You come away with a different idea of what it's all about.'

Roubin's posting lasted 505 days, and he might have been the longest-serving national serviceman in Vietnam. 'I was certainly the longest-serving Jewish nasho there,' he said.

Most Australian soldiers saw Vung Tau as a kind of Kings Cross by the sea: a salty, sweaty garrison town of hand-job parlours and blow-job bars, masseuses, brothels, bar girls and the hoons they called 'cowboys'. Most men were given a couple of nights' R&C leave in Vung Tau, to lose their virginity to painted prostitutes with beehive hair, and drink, fistfight and forget. They might return on leave every few months, and buy shot glasses of worthless soft drink – 'Saigon teas' – for the tiny bar girls as if they were courting a sheila back home, paying one or two dollars for cup after cup of sham liquor like it was the drinks, and not the money they paid for them, that would get the women on their backs.

David Cripps, the son of a well-known Sydney real-estate agent, was on an executive traineeship with retailer David Jones when he was called up. Cripps flew over to Vietnam as a reinforcement, on 13 November 1967, on the same flight as another Sydney boy, Michael Evans. Cripps and Evans volunteered for the Defence & Employment (D&E) Platoon in Vung Tau, which was supposed to guard the base, although the base was not actually under any threat.

When Cripps arrived, the Australians were building the Peter Badcoe Club, a recreation centre with bedrooms, bars, and a swimming pool named after Harold Holt. 'Our OC [Officer in Command] was a bit of a thickhead,' said Cripps, 'and about five of us conned him into starting a surf lifesaving club. Because if people were coming down to the Badcoe Club and going to swim in the surf, we reckoned they needed somebody to guard them. I said, "Oh yeah, I've got a bronze medallion," that I didn't have. The boss kept saying, "Where's your medallion?" I said, "I'll get Mum to send it over." It never arrived but when I left, the surf club continued. We had surfboats, surfboards, surf reels, all that.' There was only one problem. 'You couldn't really surf there,' said Cripps. 'You could walk out for bloody miles. We had the chairs, we had the beach umbrella and an esky. We just sat on the beach all day, drinking piss. The OC loved his sports. We had games of football and all that sort of stuff. No patrols. You'd jump the wire every night and go into town, and after about three months we were all turning into alcoholics.'

Everything was for sale in Vung Tau, where cigarette boys trafficked marijuana in Marlboro packs, and opium could be had with a whisper to a Lambretta driver. But the Australians seemed more interested in the military supermarkets such as the Australian Services Canteen Organisation (ASCO) and the giant US Post Exchange (PX), which stocked tax-free alcohol and tobacco. It was 'one long fucking party,' said Evans, 'with booze and broads and bars. I thought, Fuck this, it's not a bad war. The PX'd open, and all the Salem cigarettes and Johnny Walker Black Label would be sold in fifteen seconds flat. No one smoked Salem cigarettes except the Vietnamese, so you'd flog the

Salem cigarettes and you'd have your bottle of Johnny Walker, and the cigarette money would give you money to buy the Coke and ice, and you'd do a job on yourself.'

Vung Tau was made of bodies, not just the bones of the French foreign legionnaires buried in the military cemetery, but young bodies, beautiful bodies, men and women making love and its opposite. Derek Ponting, an Englishman from Liverpool, who had migrated to Adelaide less than a year before being called up – to his surprise – for national service in Australia, told a common massage-parlour story: 'I was lying on the table with only a towel round my middle. A young Vietnamese girl walked through the curtains, she looked about 18 years old, and she was very pretty and had a nice figure too. She started to give me a massage, cracking all my bones. She even stood on my back and cracked my shoulder blades with her feet. Then she told me to lie on my back and as I did my towel slipped to the floor and she could see that I was aroused. Do you want "bum-bum" (intercourse) she said, I nodded, closed my eyes for a few seconds and when I opened them she was gone!

'That's when I got the shock of my life, in walked another girl, stark naked and resembling a sumo wrestler, but not as good looking! She even had pot [sic] marks on her cheeks! Before I could do anything she jumped on top of me and pinned me to the table! At that moment I realised I had two options, fight her or have sex with her, and considering that she weighed about 40lbs more than me, reluctantly I chose the latter!'[4]

But many of the national servicemen had been brought up to be polite and respectful, religious and abstinent, by parents who allowed themselves to worry more that their sons might learn to swear in the ranks than live with the memory of seeing a mate blown to pieces. This wasn't the way sex was supposed to be for a country boy from a church-going family, consummation without courtship, cartoon passion in a parody of the marriage bed, with the smell of other men on the body of the bride. And who ever dreamed their first girl would be Asian?

Buying sex from the bar girls was another stage in the coarsening of the soldiers. They concluded love, for the Vietnamese, was cheap, just like life. If it made it easier to fuck them, it also made it easier to kill them. But the fucking and the fighting brought both sides down and, in the end, it made many of the Australians value themselves less too. But some made the nights in bars mean something, truly believed their girls thought them handsome, that they were the special one, not like the others. A few even found real love in Vung Tau.

For Egyptian-born Lorenzo Montesini and his small group of national servicemen friends, the city wasn't Kings Cross, 'it was Barcelona or Alexandria or Tangiers', he said. 'We were victims of our imaginations. For the three or four of us who always drank together, this was our Spanish Civil War . . . a small, specialised war that was created just for us so we could have our rite of passage, where we could write the big novel, show a bit of heroics, not really get into danger but be observers without losing honour. I cast my life as a sort of aesthetic experience, and this was soldier, warrior-poet, man of action/man of thought.'

Montesini was a handsome, articulate, cultured young polyglot who'd quickly had to learn a new language in the army. In recruit training, he said, 'You start speaking in a different way. And it's baby talk: "fuck this" and "fuck that", "what the Christ". After a while it becomes "fuck fuck fuck fuck"; you don't really try to be mature with your language. The people who were in charge of us were literally sub-literates. The corporal was barely born, he was just a mass of reflexes.'

Montesini and his friends were all posted to the 8th Field Ambulance, to work as medics in the hospital at 1ALSG. They found the ghost of Cap Saint Jacques in Vung Tau, and toasted it with vintage French wine. For Montesini's birthday at the Grand Hotel, they ordered grilled lobster and a bottle of 1954 Gevrey-Chambertin, then found their way to a brothel. 'This was to be my present from my pals,' wrote Montesini in a memoir.

'As if in a dream, I was taken into a little room, a cubicle, really. A small young girl giggled in a bed, the Mama-San, as the procuress was called, rattled to this little creature. I was so drunk that I felt like a spectator, I was outside the action. There was much haggling going on behind us while the girl and I looked at this wobbling person. The haggling done, the bargain struck, it only left the action to be performed. It was as if we were a couple in an ancient ceremony of betrothal, where the entire family and friends pull up to witness the ritual and ensure that the dowry will be passed on. Apparently, I was lowered over this person and, I was told, performed the rite of passage. My friends were of course convinced that this was my first time with a woman. In fact, I had already passed through the mysterious journey we call sex before, quite a few times, with a girlfriend I had at school, but somehow I always gave the impression of virginity.'[5]

Montesini discovered he didn't want to spend time in the hospital, 'so I had to find a way to find an interesting job for myself', he said. He'd been on an army Vietnamese-language course in Sydney, and found his way onto operations famously designed to win the villagers' hearts and minds by building infrastructure and distributing largesse. He was seconded as an interpreter on civic action projects then, he said, attached to Intelligence where he occasionally had to ask questions of a prisoner. 'But it was Mickey Mouse. We had somebody who'd been badly wounded and to me seemed should not have been interrogated but he was. It was pretty fruitless, because I don't think he knew anything: it was as if I was taken prisoner and I was asked questions about movements; I wouldn't know anything.' In Intelligence terms, 'Whatever wins, whatever losses we had, it was purely accidental,' said Montesini.

The base at Vung Tau was also home to a dental unit, which was to have an unexpected impact on Montesini's life. From August 1967, the dentist at the post was national serviceman Colin Twelftree, who'd been the youngest undergraduate in his class when he was called up in 1965, the only twenty-year-old student in third-year dentistry at

Adelaide University. A big, genial man, Twelftree had already been a CMF member of 4 Dental Unit for two and a half years, but was happy to waive his right to sidestep national service and go into the army.

A dental section in the field comprised a dentist, a nurse, a technician and a driver. In the CMF, Twelftree was a driver. He deferred his national service until the end of his degree and, in February 1967, went to Puckapunyal like any other South Australian recruit. 'On day one or two, you file past and they say, "Name? Age? Occupation?"' said Twelftree, 'and I said "Dentist", and that was it. I kept walking. After four days as a recruit, I was sitting in my hut, spit-polishing my boots, and someone came in and said, "Recruit Twelftree, you're wanted in the Q store."' There he was given an officer's uniform. 'I said, "Ah, this is unexpected. And what do I do now?" They said, "Well, sir, you go and collect your gear from the line and your staff car is waiting at the orderly room."' Twelftree had assumed he would eventually serve as a dentist, but there were no established procedures for men in his position. 'If they had thought of planning – which I doubt very much – they weren't expecting a person eligible for direct commission to come in so soon,' he said. 'Because I was a year younger. I started dentistry when I was sixteen. They thought they'd come next year.'

Twelftree was inserted halfway through the first week of the regular army's induction course for undergraduate officers at the School of Army Health. 'At the end of the second week,' he said, 'we all graduated . . . and the army, in their wisdom, posted me back to Puckapunyal, where my fellow recruits were still recruits.' As a married officer, 'I moved into the most prestigious street in Puckapunyal,' he said, 'in this lovely big house in Milne Bay Close. It was the highest street, the grenade range was behind it.'

In August 1967, Twelftree, now the senior national serviceman in the Australian Army, was sent to Vietnam as a captain. All the regular dentists – and most of the regular army – wanted to serve overseas. 'At Puckapunyal,' he said, 'the talk in the sergeants' mess was, "Oh, this bloke's only been in the army for six months and he's going to Vietnam.

I've been here for ten years and I haven't gone yet." They were shitty.'

At Vung Tau, the Dental Unit was next to 8th Field Ambulance. Twelftree said standards were high. 'The army technicians could cast gold inlays in the field. The Americans couldn't believe this.' On Tuesday afternoons, the unit would go out to a village, usually the marketplace at Hoa Long, and offer relief-of-pain dentistry for the villagers – generally tooth extractions under local anaesthetic. Their workrate was 'industrial'. The unit could take out one hundred teeth in an hour. 'Dentistry as a civil aid program was very effective,' said Twelftree, 'because it's immediate. Medicine not so much, because people don't have a medical emergency very often. But lots of people have dental emergencies all the time.' After about six months, the unit stopped travelling to the villages and patients were bussed into 1ALSG instead. Twelftree's was not a hostile war. 'Everyone was fairly pleasant to each other,' he said, 'because the only [Vietnamese] people you came in contact with were either the people you were treating – and you had the responsibility to be compassionate to them – and the people with whom you were doing business, so they had a good reason to be nice to you. Except the taxi drivers.

'I had a wonderful time,' said Twelftree. 'Often, at lunchtime, we'd hop in a Land Rover and go down the beach to have a swim. And it wasn't unheard of to have a beer.' There were certain hardships associated with the posting. For instance, 'you had to take turns being the duty officer', he said, 'which meant not drinking that night.' He relieved the dentists at Nui Dat when they went on leave, and flew to Saigon for four days a fortnight to treat the troops and the embassy staff. He received about the same salary as a dentist in Australia, and a $7000 home loan. By the time he returned home, his wife had bought a unit, where the couple lived for the last six months of Twelftree's national service, which were spent looking after the teeth of troops while they prepared for Vietnam.

For about half of Twelftree's tour of Vietnam, his dental nurse was the dark-haired and handsome Corporal Robert Straub. 'He was a good nurse,' said Twelftree, 'a nice chap. Just one of the normal blokes.' Straub, a housepainter's son from Heidelberg, Victoria, kept the surgery clean, organised the patients, and assisted chair-side.

One night towards the end of Montesini's tour, Straub and Montesini went to a Vung Tau massage parlour together and undressed in parallel booths. 'Only a curtain separated us,' wrote Montesini, 'and I could hear Robert's attendant making all the sounds of interest – an invariable routine. Everything that followed happened predictably and afterwards we found ourselves back out in the street, laughing; we had shared a *crime passionnel*.'[6]

In December 1967, three days before Montesini's departure from Vietnam, 8th Field Ambulance held a party, 'which was loud with glee and drink,' wrote Montesini, 'and someone had the bright idea of organising a game of hide and seek. We ran here and there, falling on empty cans around the outside of the mess . . . At one point, detaching myself, I ran across to a heap of sandbags and Robert followed me. We hid there, breathing hard and laughing after our run . . . I ran to the wire with Rob behind me; we both went under, then over and down the sand tracks and over more wire. We were wobbly and tipsy, there were no lights, the noise behind was muted by the sound of the surf ahead. On the beach at last, boots unbearable and clothes sticky with sweat. Running, I took off all my clothes under the stars, Rob behind me doing the same. I ran into the surf. The water was like champagne, bubbles everywhere; in and out I swam, another dive and out again, then alongside me, under the water, I saw a shape coloured by the vivid phosphorescence of the South China Sea, which made me stop for an instant. The shape grabbed my leg and we fought under, surfaced, a wave caught us and threw us down violently, we ended on the shore, entangled in each other's arms. There was nothing to do but to be. I let myself go for the first time. The boys had been right; I was a virgin. I let myself be possessed, carried off into the dark wood as I felt that tide carrying me into an adult world, a world of terrible dangers . . . '"I love you and I want to live with you forever," Robert had said to me that first night on the beach.'[7]

Lorenzo Montesini and Robert Straub found love in Vung Tau, and remained in love – through many strange adventures that saw their names screamed out in newspaper gossip columns – until Straub died of an AIDS-related illness in 1995.

18

PIGS AND MINES IN THE YEAR OF THE GOAT

Back on the gun-bristled crest of the hill at Nui Dat, 7RAR had replaced 5RAR in April 1967, in time for the early monsoons of the season. That same month, the decision was taken by Task Force HQ to lay the first of 22 592 mines in an eleven-kilometre barrier minefield from the Horseshoe, a caldera looking down upon Dat Do, to the coast near the fishing village of Lang Phuoc Hai. The minefield was supposed to separate the Viet Cong guerrillas from the communities where they might gather supplies and support. It was a fatal error, many times over. Engineers began to plant the mines on 22 April, and men quickly started to die.

A US gunner was killed outside the minefield when another American accidentally detonated a mine inside the wire on 2 May. Two Australian sappers died and several were wounded in a mine-laying accident on 9 May. Terry 'Butch' Renshaw, a Wangaratta cabinet-maker in 1 Field Squadron who had not wanted to go into the army, wrote to his parents that one of the men killed 'had only been up here 2 months, also he had only been married a short time. The fellow that stood on it came up with myself, he is alright, or as well as could be expected, he lost his leg & one hand. I was about 50yds from it when it happened . . . I hope I never see anything like it again.'

Renshaw had two days off, 'as we were working from 7 in the

morning till 6 at night, so we more than earned them', he wrote. It was a week after Mother's Day, and Renshaw hoped his flowers had arrived 'alright & on time, as I didn't get a chance to get into see about them until fairly later in the week'.[1] Two men were killed in a further accident on 20 May. 'All in all, it has been a very expensive kind of a minefield,' Renshaw wrote the next day.[2]

On 30 May, Renshaw and a German-born regular soldier, Sapper Lothar Sempel, were on a party arming the mines. 'Butch heard one of the fuses detonate,' wrote Sempel, 'and he threw himself between myself and the mine. He had more than enough time to hit the deck and possibly save himself but instead he stood in between me and the mine . . . which went off and caused him death.'[3] On 16 June 1967, Malcolm Fraser issued a press statement blaming the sappers for blowing themselves up. The accidents on 9 May and 20 May were due to 'momentary lack of concentration and attention to detail by an individual', he said. As for Renshaw's death, it was 'almost certain that this was also the cause, although the possibility of a malfunction cannot be entirely ruled out'. The engineers had been adequately trained and rehearsed, he insisted, and were carrying out drills as they had been taught. 'The main lesson learnt,' said Fraser, ' . . . is the need for all concerned to maintain complete concentration on the job in hand.'[4]

In 1967, as far as the press was concerned, the mine-laying operation was another success for the army. AAP special correspondent Richard Beckett reported, 'Viet Cong in Phuoc Tuy province were offering "fantastic" prices for rice because of the effectiveness of the Australian Army's 10-mile [sic] wire barrier.'[5]

So 7RAR, who nicknamed themselves 'the Pigs', came to Vietnam in the Year of the Goat, as the mines blew off in the distance and engineers became casualties of war without ever sighting an enemy. 7RAR had been formed at Puckapunyal, and this was its first overseas tour, although its ranks included many regular soldiers who'd previously served in Malaysia. Among 7RAR's large contingent of national servicemen was Jim Booker, a dispatch clerk's son from

Brighton, Victoria, who'd wanted to join the railways when he left school. But, he said, 'My parents were not agreeable to that; my mother was dead against the unions.' So he signed on as an apprentice fitter and turner, then an electrician, with motor-spares supplier Repco. 'That failed and I finished up going to an electrical contractor for about six months,' he said. 'That failed as well. I didn't want to work in a dingy old office, but I finished up doing so.' When he was called up in April 1966, he was a manifesting clerk at Howard Smith Industries. He was against the idea of conscripts being sent to Vietnam, but he just 'accepted things as they happened', and went into the army.

During recruit training, Booker, a softy spoken Congregationalist Christian, was a straggler on the morning runs, and not quite up to scratch in the hut. 'My section was allocated to kitchen duties on one week,' he said, 'and I was busy in the kitchen helping tidy up, and went back to my hut to find out they'd had an inspection by the NCOs, and my bed was untidy. Because of that, the whole building got penalised. So I fronted up, and the next thing I was being grabbed by half-a-dozen guys and carried out and thrown into a bathtub of cold water, clothes and all. I just thought, Okay, because of this stuff-up, I've copped it. I didn't raise "but this shouldn't have happened". I probably should've, but I would've got reprimanded. I just shut up and got back to doing the work.

'I was never a social person. People liked to talk about cars and racing horses. I wasn't interested in those sorts of things, so I just didn't mix.' Booker liked ships and trains, and making models out of Meccano. He applied for officer training. 'I thought, Well, if I can get out of this mire, I'll give it a try. But I didn't succeed. I didn't finish all the questions. I had a go and I failed, and I finished up just being a private infanteer.'

The battle efficiency course at Canungra was 'a confidence course which broke my confidence', he said. A few weeks later, 'the sergeant called me into this tent and said, "Look, I don't think you're gonna make it as an infantryman. How'd you like to transfer to doing hygiene?" Colloquially known as "the Blowfly", the job was to scrub out the kitchen bins after they'd been emptied, to stop the blowflies from hovering around. I thought "Blowfly" was unique to me, but I've found out others were called that too,' said Booker. 'I'm disappointed about that.'

With 7RAR in Vietnam, his duties at Nui Dat involved 'making sure the gutters were free of any bacteria by pouring petrol down and setting fire to it, burning all the bacteria and stopping mosquitoes from nesting; pulling out the sludge from the kitchen grease-traps; scrubbing the bench toilet seats to make them nice and clean for the guys to sit on; the showers had to be scrubbed out, and the posts had to be coated with creosote to stop the dampness and mildew, all those sorts of things. I didn't mind it one bit. I was a whole lot safer in camp than I was going out with the company.

'After one of the battles, the company was still out, but the casualties had been dusted off and taken into Vung Tau – the wounded to be attended to, the dead to be sent home. But the clothing that the guys had was sent back to us, and it was horrific just going through the clothing, sorting out what we could use, what we couldn't use, and creating two different piles – the torn and the greens that were okay to be reused – and knowing that one guy, who had been either killed or wounded, had shit himself.'

In November 1967, Booker asked to be relieved. 'I just felt the work was getting on top of me,' he said. 'As well as doing hygiene, I was waitering in the sergeants' mess. So in the last couple of months, I went out on operations. I was thankful I was with the company HQ section. I heard the fighting in the distance, but I only saw the aftermath. And I had to sleep with the aftermath, and that was bad enough. I saw an NVA enemy lying dead on the ground, in a rice paddy, and I was surprised as to how big he was. He wasn't just an average Vietnamese guy, as thin as a rake. He was very thickset. He was just lying there dead and blue in the face.'

Booker may not have been a great infantryman, but he was

a wonderful blowfly. 'The other guys, when they came back to the camp, they said, "Where's Jim? Oh good." I always had a cheery face for them,' said Booker. He didn't drink much in Vietnam and didn't visit prostitutes, but he didn't go to church either, and he smoked close to a packet of cigarettes a day.

'I still do resent the national service for the two years of our life that we lost,' he said. 'They're the crucial years for a young guy – getting a good career and meeting girls and all that sort of thing – but that was taken away from us.' The saddest time he remembered was 'standing by the signals hut in the company barracks, listening to the guys who were just being killed and wounded, guys who I would never see again – Suoi Chau Pha, 6 August 1967. I was in camp. Barry Heard was out with a company on that operation, and he was phoning in the casualties. And it hurts,' he said. 'Still.'

Barry Heard, a Victorian conscript, born in Melbourne but raised in the High Country, has written an account of the battle at Suoi Chau Pha in his memoir *Well Done, Those Men*, the best book to yet come out of the national service experience. Heard was a radio operator with A Company 7RAR, out on a search-and-destroy mission against VC bases near Hat Dich, about ten kilometres north-east of Nui Dat. A Company crossed the creek called Suoi Chau Pha, killed two enemy on the track then came under sustained and terrifying attack from machine guns, grenades and rockets. Heard wrote: 'The tall, razor-needled jungle bamboo thrashed at our sides, ripped at my shoulder, and tore my legs as the firepower increased and we flung ourselves to the ground. I skidded, nose down, the bloody radio thumping into the back of my head, the antenna and the handset lodging deep into the slimy undergrowth. Pulling my face out of the mud, I noticed I was alone. The incoming fire was very close as I struggled to get the radio off my back. My shoulder throbbed. Carefully, I slid the radio off and stood it upright in front of my head; it wasn't safe to kneel.

In my first quick survey of the area I could just make out the boss only a short distance ahead. It appeared they were very close to the front line . . . shit. I turned up the volume on the radio: no sound, the antenna was almost non-functional, and the handset caked with mud. Great. I normally didn't put on the plastic cover until the rain was about to start, mid afternoon. Now one stuffed handset, bugger it . . . I raised my head and looked around to see what was going on. Shit, that was a bad move; I believe the enemy sensed my movement. I lowered myself hard into the ground and glanced to the side. To my left I saw one of our blokes, dead. The poor bugger had been killed by a direct hit to the head. His blank face stared at me.'[6]

Harold Hayes, a radio operator with 7RAR who was once a junior accountant from North Melbourne, said, 'It was just like the end of the world had come. There was machine guns and rocket launchers, everything, flying in all directions. We were surrounded. We thought there was two people – and another three or four at the most – we didn't expect to maybe be confronted with fifty or one hundred. We don't know how many.

'I'm trying to get help on the radio,' said Hayes, 'because my corporal's up in front of me, he's pinned under a tree, he can't move. I'm pinned under a little sapling. The next thing, they threw a rocket launcher that hit the trees above us, and came straight down. It must've knocked me out when it hit. My sergeant beside me, when I come to, all the left-hand side of him was just an absolute mess. We didn't think the sergeant'd live. I tried to put a bandage around his thigh, and I couldn't get the bandage anywhere near. One of the other boys threw another one to me. I've got a radio on at the same time, trying to get help through.

'I got the help through, anyway. I said to the boys, "For God's sake, keep down. Be careful what you're doing." Next thing, we lost four or five people there. And I had shrapnel everywhere from the top of my head to below my knee on the right-hand side. They're winching us out, and then as they're winching us out – you've got to laugh;

I suppose later you laugh about it – they've had a pot shot at me on the rope going up, and they've actually shot the bloke that was behind the chopper pilot – one of the boys winching us up – through the bloody floor, and hit him through the foot,' said Hayes.

In what was becoming a familiar story, the infantry was saved by the artillery, in this case the guns of 106 Field Battery, firing from a position at Fire Support Base Giraffe. As the VC were massing, the shells tore them apart. After more than two hours of battle, the enemy disengaged, harried by air strikes and leaving behind five Australian dead and twenty-one wounded, one of whom subsequently died. An army press release described Australian casualties as 'moderate', and said a search of the battle area had found five dead Viet Cong, while a further ten were thought to have been dragged away. In time, the estimated number of enemy bodies removed grew to thirty-three, including wounded, then forty, with a further two hundred hit by heavy weapons and bombs.

Hayes had thought it 'totally and absolutely wrong that at twenty years of age you're drawn out of a barrel to go overseas against what you want to do, and ruin your job prospects at the same time'. He deferred while he studied for his accountancy qualification, then joined the army in the third national service intake. 'I applied for armoured corps and the service corps and I did not get them,' said Hayes. 'I wanted clerical work – because of the accountancy background – or a driver's job, but I didn't want to be walking around, sludging and trudging.' He ended up a rifleman in Vietnam.

Hayes remembered his send-off, an event that many men seem to have forgotten. 'The night before we went on the *Sydney*, we had the run of the town,' he said, 'free taxis, free everything, sideshows: if you wanted to go to Sandra Nelson and that, they were all free. We could go to nightclubs and any drinks were on the house.'

Hayes had been in Vietnam for nearly four months when he

was ambushed at Suoi Chau Pha. 'My mother and father, and my grandmother, got the hell shocked out of them,' he said. 'One of the boys killed had the same name, Hayes. And they knocked on our door and told them I was dead. Then they had to come back the next day and tell them sorry, it was a mistake, they were wrong.' Private Harold James Hayes flew home from Vietnam on 14 November 1967. Corporal James Francis Hayes, a regular born in Goulburn, NSW, was buried in St Patrick's Cemetery, Kenmore.

Hayes was due to go home in November 1967. 'And the old sergeant – we used to give him a hell of a bloody time just for a bit of a joke; tell him his smokes were no good – waited until this night. I was in the corner of the canteen, and four guys came in, took me out of the bloody canteen, stripped me bloody starkers, tied me around a tree, and out he's come with four buckets of the iciest water you ever got, which he'd had in his cooler especially for me, and he's decked me in this cold water. And I couldn't do a thing. They had a good old laugh. And the next day we flew out of there.'

Hayes also recalled a different kind of homecoming from Vietnam. 'After I'd been home a month or two,' he said, 'if I went out and there were three or four of us together having a drink, people who knew you were from there would come out and give you a jug of beer: "Thanks, mate." You might have a dinner dance or something like that, and people would come over and say, "Oh, you've been to Vietnam. Here's a jug, mate. Good to have youse back." '

Hayes came from a hardworking family, and grew up in tough suburbs such as Ascot Vale and Flemington. His father was a labourer, and Hayes was one of five children. It was a big step up for him to become an accountant but, after Vietnam, he couldn't go back to it. 'If you'd've said, "I want to go into the army, like a regular, and I want to serve the country for four years or five years," that's fantastic. But if you're drawn out of a barrel and have the hell shocked out of you by the whole thing, how're you gonna feel? It's a lot out of your life. And then you come home and, because you've had that experience, you can't sit behind a desk. Had I got a service corps thing, where I'd've been sitting behind a desk or driving a vehicle, it might've been a different story, instead of trudging around with a radio set. What is a radio operator gonna do when he comes home?'

Hayes' fellow radio operator Barry Heard also found nothing ennobling in national service, and little redemption in soldiering. 'If you go and kill someone,' he said, 'you've got to be a fucking moron. And the general male attributes needed are you've got to be a big tough Aussie that drinks lots of piss, shags himself stupid and watches blue movies. In fact, that's who we were. Subtly the army got us there. By the time I got to Vietnam, the alcohol was the first thing. Very few guys would come out of the jungle and have a shower and read their mail and have a meal – and we'd be bloody starving. Yet we'd drink piss – and, of course, you'd get drunk very quickly.'

But war plagues the warrior returned. 'Once you come out of it and you finally sober up,' said Heard, 'I strongly believe that your spirit and your soul say, "Look, what you did was the worst possible thing you could do to other human beings. You slaughtered them and killed them." For what reason? That's was what affected me, my own moral spirit.'

It shows the small scale of Australia's involvement in Vietnam that Suoi Chau Pha was the largest battle of 7RAR's first tour, and its seven dead the most fatal casualties the battalion suffered in a single encounter. The bulk of the battalion returned to Sydney on 26 April 1968, the morning after Anzac Day, and marched through the city in clouds of confetti. They were cheered on by crowds to the town hall, where six thousand people were packed tight to watch Prime Minister Gorton take their salute. The next day, one thousand anti-war protesters – the largest crowd the movement could raise in the biggest city in Australia – made their way down Market and George streets, jeered by shoppers.

19

CALL UP THE POLICE

Many Australians seemed to favour national service for everyone but themselves. By 1967, groups of schoolteachers, pilots, maintenance engineers and aircraft technicians, merchant marine officers and seamen, agricultural and veterinary scientists, firemen, dental mechanics, railway workers, primary producers, and laymen engaged in church missionary work had all approached the government to ask to be exempted from national service. Every petition was refused.[1]

The National Service Act had been passed to solve the army's manpower problems in a way that spread the burden across white Australian society. There were to be no other considerations. But people struggled to understand this. The Melbourne *Herald*, a loud and energetic supporter of the Act, had no sympathy with men who hoped to avoid conscription, unless they were police officers. There was a shortage of police in Victoria, the newspaper reported, and many youths joined the service at the age of twenty, and might be immediately liable for conscription. Sixteen of twenty recruits pictured by *The Herald* at the St Kilda Road Police Depot in Melbourne in June 1965 were of an age to be drafted. The chief drill officer said, 'I guarantee that those who go into the Army for two years will have forgotten everything they have learnt when they come out.' *The Herald* argued there should be no difficulty about granting total exemption to police. They already have an essential role in the community.'[2] *The Age* agreed: 'Training a policeman is expensive,' wrote the newspaper, and 'selecting suitable recruits is an even more difficult task,'[3] as if the same didn't apply to schoolteachers or scientists.

But there was an audible unspoken message beneath these protests: people could not bring themselves to see national service as a one-way street. It had to benefit both the army and the citizen. And what could police recruits gain, when they were already straight-backed, keen-eyed, firm-jawed and able to stand still for long periods of time without apparently getting bored? Why disturb the careers of orderly, disciplined, clean-shaven youths, uniformed and armed, and devoted to maintaining the peace? In the eyes of many people, the police force was already doing what the army should do – not fighting wars, but making men.

The argument never lost its force. In 1967, Arthur Rylah, then acting premier of Victoria, wrote to Harold Holt in fury: 'Because of the ballot system, long-haired youths remain free to pass and disseminate treasonable resolutions, whilst loyal efficient and spruce young men are conscripted from the Police Force for National Service, where many of them (so I am told) are employed as cooks, painters and in other occupations which are quite purposeless to their permanent careers as Policemen.'[4]

Holt's response to this type of complaint was always similar: if police didn't want to take their chance in the lottery, they could join the CMF. But there was something else that was unsaid and probably unrealised: while the general population might have a one in three chance of failing the army medical, twenty-year-old police officers, who had recently passed the police medical, were almost certain to get through. And while firemen might be Communists and ambulance men could be Quakers (although probably not Jehovah's Witnesses) and schoolteachers could be less than five foot two inches tall, the police force was unlikely to harbour many political radicals, religious pacifists or midgets – or, for that matter, convicted criminals. If a police officer's birthdate came out of the Tattersall's barrel he was perhaps more likely than any other worker in the country to end up in the army. It was another small way in which the balance of men in the national service scheme weighed towards conservative youth with certain occupational backgrounds.

Shortages of labour – skilled and unskilled – throughout Australia were the driving force behind the mass-immigration program that had been in place since the end of the Second World War. In January 1967, after much cabinet debate, most non-British unnaturalised migrants – resident 'aliens' – had lost their blanket exemption from national service, although they couldn't be called up until they had lived in Australia for two years, and were allowed to leave the country rather than enlist. They remained less likely than other Australians to end up in the army, however, as the government recognised it was 'probable that a higher percentage of aliens would fail in the literacy test' (although a handwritten note on an official document prepared for the prime minister advised that the DLNS felt 'this aspect should not be unduly highlighted').[5] So while the odds of being called up had apparently become fairer for everybody, the chances of staying out of the army were still stacked in favour of migrants (and criminals) and against police, which was probably the opposite of what most Australians hoped for and expected.

Ray Wyse, Ron Shaw and Ken Bourke all joined the NSW Police Force on the same day, 10 May 1965. They completed their time as probationary constables on the same day, were called up to the army in the fifth national service intake, began their training on the same day, 14 June 1967, were posted to Brisbane on the same day and subsequently sent to Vietnam on the same day, 20 November 1967. They all served in the same unit, the Royal Australian Army Provost Corps, a military police force. Their class, 101A, included Frank Brown, who was also called up for national service, went to Vietnam a few months after the others, and ended his career as provost marshal of the Australian Army.

Ray Wyse was born in Leeton, NSW, the youngest of seven children. He joined the police at nineteen, and went through training at the Redfern depot with Shaw, once a clerk at the Rural Bank of New South Wales, and Bourke, a former clerk at the Department of Immigration whose father was commissioner of the deliciously named Department of Lunacy. After six weeks' police training, Wyse was transferred to general duties at the police station at Darlinghurst, Shaw to Campsie, and Bourke to Regent Street in the city. 'You went from a nineteen-year-old country kid to a twenty-year-old police officer giving orders,' said Wyse. 'And being obeyed. Because in those days, the uniforms were everything. When you spoke, most people did what you told them. And when you went into the police force, it was a disciplined force. Then, when you went into the army, you'd already had that discipline of obeying the rank structure. So I don't think the army was a worry for blokes who'd been in the police service.'

The three men went to Indooroopilly, Queensland, and later down to South Head to complete their corps training. At South Head, 'The regs didn't like us,' said Wyse. 'We were interlopers. I don't think it was a personal thing, it was more they didn't like nashos. We came in from basic training as corporals. They might've taken four or five years in the infantry; they couldn't go straight into the military police. And a lot of the older senior corporals were bullies.' The NSW police service made up the difference between its members' army pay and their civilian wage, which meant the often younger, better educated and less experienced national servicemen were paid more than their regular counterparts, although this was not widely known in the corps.

Wyse and Shaw were posted to Vung Tau. Their work included night patrols of the bars, where the boys on leave would raise hell among the pickpockets, hoons, cowboys and bar girls, stumbling half-blind through a demimonde which had risen up to drag them down. 'We were like a taxi service,' said Wyse. 'The blokes'd come back from

Nui Dat and they'd get on the piss, get in a bar and cause a bit of trouble, and we'd grab them, put them in the back of a Land Rover, and we could get them back into the camp because the regimental police didn't check military police. We just drove straight through the gates to the barracks and told them to behave themselves. We got a lot though the gates who probably we shouldn't have, but we were nashos and you should be able to get on the piss and have a good time without getting into trouble. And most of the units had slush funds, so if there was any damage done to a bar, you'd say, "Rightio, what's the damage?" and they'd say something and you'd halve it.'

Jim Archbold was a Victorian police officer. His father, Stuart, flew Hurricanes in North Africa in the Second World War, convoy escorts in the Mediterranean, and Kitty Hawks harassing the German retreat. Jim grew up in Mitcham, Victoria. While his 'biggest interest in life was fishing', he loved his father's war stories and shared his enthusiasm for aircraft. Jim joined the Victorian Police Cadets when he turned seventeen, and spent eighteen months with duties such as manning school crossings, before he was sworn in as a police officer at the age of nineteen. He had twenty weeks in the police training centre, learning the law and mastering a policeman's ponderous two-finger typing, before he was let out on the beat in Melbourne, with no radio or firearm, just a short stick and handcuffs. Archbold was a hunter. He knew how to stalk and shoot. But he didn't get to use his bush skills until he went to Vietnam.

He started his national service training in 1967, then chose the provosts. 'Usually, you'd do your corps training and a little bit of corps work,' he said, 'then you'd get called into the office and they'd say, "Look, you've been picked for Vietnam." The story was we were all supposed to have volunteered, but sometimes I don't think it was even brought up. Obviously, if you said, "Yeah, all right," you must've volunteered.'

Archbold was perhaps the only Australian soldier to be taken to war by his father. Stuart Archbold flew his son as far as Singapore, on a Qantas charter, and returned twice to visit him during his year overseas. In Vietnam, Jim was sent briefly to Vung Tau, then posted on to Nui Dat, where there was a small prisoner-of-war compound. It was part of the provosts' job to look after the POWs who were brought in from the bush. 'We'd get them back to our area, and our Intelligence would have a good talk to them,' said Archbold. 'A lot of them were just peasants who were too close to the wire – they weren't supposed to be there, but they were there looking for plants or whatever. Who would know? They were called "detainees" and usually we'd end up with them in the back of the Land Rover, and we'd have to take them back to Hoa Long. Anyone they figured was Viet Cong would be classified as suspect prisoners of war, and then from there they'd be choppered to Long Binh.

'There were a few occasions where it was women, especially in the detainee category, because they'd be wandering in trying to get seeds or tucker close to the wire, the infantry would grab them and want to know why they were there.

'I never struck a problem,' he said. 'They didn't want any trouble. I guess it's pretty daunting when everyone's armed, and the Viet Cong were probably half your height. Occasionally, it was too late at night to do anything, and we'd have to do a night piquet on them. We had a little two-storey setup we could sit in, and we'd have had a shotgun, and we'd guard them and make sure they didn't try to disappear. But I never saw any instances of them going, because where were they going to go to in the middle of the camp?'

Archbold sent regular letters home from Vietnam, sometimes describing his fishing trips. 'Two of us headed out to a spot near a checkpoint to cut some bamboo,' he wrote. 'We brought it back to camp and instructed the VC prisoners to make some fishing poles.'[6] He could go wherever he chose with his mates and their poles. 'No one ever says to a military police vehicle or the people in it, "What're you doing today?"' he said.

20

TET

In the days before the feast of the First Morning of the First Day, the women of the south crowded their streets and markets to buy rice and beans, pickled cabbage, candied fruits and watermelon, to prepare the special foods eaten over the holiday to celebrate the lunar new year the Vietnamese call Tet Nguyen Dan. At home, they laid custard apple and papaya, coconut and mango on the family altars, sweet offerings for the spirits.

Tet, which fell between January and February, was a time for families to come together, and for children to return to the places where they were born and their ancestors were buried. But the children of the south were spread widely now, in the jungles and the bunkers, the tunnels and the caves, and some even to the north. At the end of 1967, as every other year, old faces were seen again in the cities and towns. Brothers, sisters and cousins came home to their mothers and uncles. And behind them arrived the strangers.

The Communists had proclaimed a truce for Tet. The Free World Forces had some idea an offensive might be imminent, but people who believed nothing else said by the Communists at least expected they would observe a break in the fighting to honour the traditions that had belonged to all Vietnamese before the war, to parade masked in the streets, and dance hidden in the bellies of dragon-lions.

The North Vietnamese had switched time zones in August 1967, so the First Morning of 1968 fell on different days for north and south. But history remembers the beginning of Tet 1968 as 30 January, when the VC and the NVA launched their campaign to slice through the knot of the war, and drive an axe between the South Vietnamese and their US allies. Some 70 000 soldiers and guerrillas throughout the south attacked more than one hundred cities and towns, and ravaged Saigon.

Just as the Emperor Quang Trung had driven the Chinese out of Hanoi and sealed the unification and independence of Vietnam under cover of Tet in 1789, the Communists would calligraph a country with their own blood. They stormed coastal cities and highland towns, and they stood and died in provincial capitals, led to their targets by local cadres and then driven away from them by US and ARVN troops. The Communists took ground easily, but they couldn't hold it. They hoped for a general civilian uprising to welcome them as liberators, but the people largely hid themselves away, as if this wasn't their revolution.

It was masting time for Saigon's ancient, towering hardwood trees, and their brownish fruits littered the roads like spent ammunition. In the early hours of 31 January 1968, four thousand VC and NVA poured into the capital, the heart and head of the southern regime, and the seat of US and South Vietnamese military commands, both of which were attacked. Everywhere the VC rose like sweat to the surface of the skin of the city. According to tradition, the first visitor to any home on the First Morning will determine the luck of the household in the year to come. The first callers on the US embassy were a team of VC commandos, and their suicidal assault was seen on television screens throughout America and the world – and first-hand by a national serviceman from Leeton, NSW.

Provost Ray Wyse had been posted to Saigon, where the Australian military police (MPs) worked twelve-hour shifts, patrolling the Commonwealth embassies. Just after midnight on 31 January 1968,

Wyse was out in the Land Rover with a partner. 'We'd come across town,' said Wyse, 'and there was a call from the American embassy that they were under attack. One car said, "We're attending," and there was just a shot and that was it.' The two American MPs in the first vehicle had been killed. We answered and said, "Ten-four, we're only two minutes away,"' said Wyse. 'Then another American said, "We're just around the corner. We'll be there," and they got shot up. One was killed. We were driving up the road and the bullets started flying. The VC had got the M60 off the first jeep and it was firing at us. So we bailed out of there, where the second lot had been shot up.'

The Australian MPs threw themselves on the ground outside Notre Dame Cathedral, a basilica built with red bricks from Marseille on the site of a ruined pagoda, a symbol of piety and conquest. An American jeep pulled up, and an officer asked the Australians to guard the effort to secure the US embassy compound. The VC had penetrated the grounds, but not the embassy itself. 'So I went on duty at the cathedral,' said Wyse, 'at a bloody big intersection, and [my partner] just disappeared. I didn't see him again. [The VC] had machine guns firing, so the jeeps couldn't get past where I was really. I only had a nine-mil pistol with one magazine, thirteen rounds – that was my full armament. The Americans were leaving their jeeps, and the MPs were running past me. As they were running past, I asked them for their pistols – because they had their Armalites. So they were dropping their pistols, and I ended up with five or six .45s and they had two and three magazines in, so I put my pistol back in and I was just using the .45s.'

There was US TV news film shot of Wyse, standing six foot two inches tall at the intersection, as US military police charged by, armoured in flak jackets and tin hats, carrying Armalites and side-arms. Wyse had only his soft Australian hat, designed to protect him from the sun. He stayed in position for nearly twelve hours, a big exposed target, shouting, 'Get back! Get back!' and almost begging to be hit.

'I would've fired two or three hundred shots off out of the pistol that day,' he said, 'just warning shots in the air. I kept them back a good two hundred metres away from me. I must admit, I did fire a bit close to a couple who wanted to come forward on their motorbikes – they knew I meant business. I don't know where the bullets went, to be honest.'

The US MPs were the Americans' main fighting force in Saigon and twenty-two were killed that day. When the battle at the embassy came to an end, the US ambassador was safe and all nineteen guerrillas inside the grounds were dead, but war still raged through the city and the rest of the south. Wyse returned to the Australian base, where the provosts asked for better weapons. 'The Australian Army wouldn't give us anything,' he said, 'so we went to the Americans and they supplied us with M60 machine guns, grenade launchers, grenades, tin hats, flak jackets and Armalite rifles. And we didn't have to sign anything: "Where do we sign?" "Just go away and kill gooks."'

For the next days, with the city in flames, Wyse rode with US and sometimes South Vietnamese MPs on armed escorts for convoys speeding from one side of Saigon to the other, stopping for nothing. The fighting in Saigon lasted until the middle of February. Cholon, Saigon's Chinatown on the northern bank of the Thi Nghe Canal, was virtually destroyed by its own defenders. 'They just bombed the shit out of one complete suburb,' said Wyse. 'The main bridge got blown in half – there was only half of it open – and when we first went up there the next day there were fifty or sixty VC bodies still on the bridge.

'At the back gate to the airport, there would have been two or three hundred VC. There were bodies everywhere. You didn't know if they were booby-trapped or not. And the explosives ordnance blokes, wherever they went, we had to escort them. We were the fighting force. We had a platoon's worth of ammunition in one jeep, plus a radio system.'

There were more Australian troops in Vietnam during and immediately after the Tet Offensive than at any other time previously. A third battalion of infantry, 3RAR, had arrived at Nui Dat in December 1967, to be followed by a squadron of tanks in February 1968. Some Australian forces had been sent north-east of Saigon to help defend the vast US base at Long Binh, and men from 3RAR were dispatched from Nui Dat to repel attacks on Phuoc Tuy's provincial capital Ba Ria, and then the village of Long Dien, to Ba Ria's east. Rifleman Doug English, formerly a proofreader with the *Sydney Morning Herald*, had just arrived in country and was waiting to be posted to a battalion. He watched the night fighting over Ba Ria from Nui Dat, when the Americans brought in the Douglas AC-47 gunships known variously as 'Spooky', 'Snoopy' and 'Puff the Magic Dragon', each a bird of prey loaded with half a dozen mini-guns. 'When it fired,' said English, 'you heard the engines rev up to take the recoil from all these things going off at once. There was a lot of tracer, and that's why they called it Puff the Magic Dragon, because you'd hear this roar from the bullets, and you'd see this flame channelling down to the ground, like fire. I saw that and I thought, Fuck me, don't tell me it's going to be like this every day.'

One of 3RAR's platoon commanders was Twelve Platoon D Company's Second Lieutenant Norm Peatling, a former junior clerk in a stockbroking firm. Peatling was an outstanding officer who finished second in his class at Scheyville and won the OTU athletics prize, even though he was only five foot four. Although the Australian military command had some warning of the possibility of a VC attack, 'Tet, down at company-platoon level, was a bloody big surprise,' said Peatling. He knew nothing until A Company 3RAR went into Ba Ria, drove the VC out of town and released a group of US advisers who'd been held under siege. Peatling's friend, Second Lieutenant Peter Fraser, came back from the fighting 'flashing a .45 pistol he'd got off a VC who'd been killed by his group. He was agitated and excited to a point I'd never seen anyone before,' said Peatling, 'and he went through what he had gone through. We were then aware something big was happening.'

D Company were loaded into APCs and dropped off outside Long Dien, a village in the middle of a rice plain, where they'd been told the ARVN's 2nd/52nd Rangers were under pressure in the village marketplace. Peatling's men were left 'in a pretty stupid place', he said, 'a very open paddy field area, two to three hundred metres from the beginning of the houses. I fanned the platoon out into some sort of arrowhead-type formation and, something like one hundred and fifty metres away, we came under fire for the first time.' But the homes of Long Dien were shuttered, each as still and expressionless as its neighbour. 'You just couldn't pick where the fire was coming from,' said Peatling.

The paddy fields were dry and dusty in February, grazing ground for buffalo, soccer fields for children. They were easy to cross on foot, and D Company withdrew for the night and camped outside the village, to attack the next morning from a different angle. Once again, they came under sniper fire. Eleven Platoon lost its first digger, national serviceman Robert Caston from Adelaide, and Peatling's Twelve Platoon took its first wounded, national serviceman Lance Corporal Brian Temby, whose 'arm was pretty damn shattered', said Peatling. 'To see him for the first time, as a young man, with the bones and the blood, and him looking up at me, I felt pretty damn pissed off and sad for him. We then got caught in quite a big firefight, and we got into houses. We could see the enemy across open paddies and so on, so we laid down a lot of fire. I stuffed up badly there. I was yelling at one of my blokes to get the M79 underway, and he couldn't get it working so I took the bloody thing off him, broke the breach, stuck another round in, pulled the breach shut and fired a round between my feet. And they were looking at me and I felt I'd better do something, so I did it again, and fired a round through a bloody roof. I threw it back, mentioning something about "pretty shitty trigger mechanism". It wasn't a very auspicious piece of leadership.'

The fighting was nerve-racking and desperate, but the Australians had to search every home to flush out snipers who might be hiding inside. The men of 3RAR had never been trained in urban warfare, and had to adapt what they knew about jungle fighting to fit the situation. 'All of a sudden, the worst possible scenario was placed in front of Delta Company,' said Peatling. 'We'd been practising jungle fire drills and open-air fire drills, because they were the two areas we expected to be caught. And the first contact we had, we were moving from house to house. There were so many areas where [the enemy] could fire from. We had to yell out to each other, "Where do you see the fire?" and then have a go at that area – remembering this is a civilian-occupied village. So you were also wary of what seemed to be civilians trying to get out of the way.

'But we managed to put enough pressure on them to clear our way into the marketplace,' said Peatling. 'But the people we came in to help, the 2nd/52nd Ranger Battalion, were looting as they were leaving. We took over and they just pissed off . . . I was always particularly wary of being around the ARVN from then on.'

Of the thousands of images of conflict and destruction at Tet, the best remembered pictures are photographs and television film of the street execution of a VC suspect by General Nguyen Ngoc Loan, chief of South Vietnam's national police. Loan shot the bound prisoner though the head at point-blank range with his revolver. The dead man was photographed with his skull caving before the bullet, and in the film his legs buckled, his body fell and his blood puddled in the road. Much about the pictures was contested, from the character of the killer to the role of his victim. They didn't tell the whole story, but they seemed to show a regime not worth fighting for, an insupportable barbarism, the murder of the helpless.

Many in the government, the military and even the media blamed the pictures of Tet for turning Americans against the war. An

Australian legend also grew – transplanted from US lore, as surely as the Roman myths owed their origins to the Greeks – that inaccurate reporting transformed the military defeat of the Viet Cong into a propaganda victory. In fact, after a stunned response to the first night of the offensive, the Australian press tended to portray the fighting over Tet as a series of victories for the US, the South Vietnamese government and, most of all, the Australian Army.

On 2 February, *The Age*'s banner, 'Viet Cong Build Up Offensive' headed a story with the subhead 'Allies Kill 5800 Reds', and an attack on Nui Dat was presented, on balance, as a victory for the Australians, since the diggers took no casualties, while an Australian patrol of nearby Hoa Long had killed at least one VC.[1] The next day, when *The Age* ran the photographs of Loan killing his suspect, the newspaper led with 'Red Attacks Smashed: "Total Defeat" Claim'. Loan's victim was described as a 'Viet Cong officer' – although his role has never been satisfactorily established – and the picture was printed next to another showing the bodies of two American soldiers lying dead in front of their jeep after a VC ambush. The caption quoted Loan after the shooting: 'They killed many Americans and many of my people.' A third picture framed the bound man's corpse.[2]

The Australian, the most consistent Vietnam sceptic among the press, presented 3RAR's retaking of Ba Ria as a heroic episode in which 'Diggers rescue Americans in savage battle'.[3] Although newspaper editorials expressed exasperation at the capacity of the enemy to launch such heavy attacks, and a weary distrust of claims they could be vanquished, a selective reader of the front pages might assume the Tet Offensive was an enormous VC attack aimed largely at Australian forces who heroically repelled them while taking no significant casualties.

But the American and Australian public had already been told the enemy was exhausted, its support had waned, its military capabilities were mangled, its plans in disarray. The Tet Offensive seemed to show the VC could move among the people like a current in the water,

PHOTO CREDIT: James Evan Jones

The fourteenth intake of national servicemen practise grenade-throwing at Puckapunyal, Victoria, 1968.

PHOTO CREDIT: James Evan Jones

The passing-out parade after infantry corps training, Singleton, NSW, 23 March 1969.

PHOTO CREDIT: James Evan Jones

The fourteenth intake of nationa[l] servicemen on a twenty-mile route march at Puckapunyal, Victoria, in early December 1968.

PHOTO CREDIT: James Evan Jones

National servicemen Mick Coulter and Daryl Golding of the fourteenth intake at Puckapunyal, Victoria, 1968. All soldiers were rostered on for mess duties, scrubbing pots and pans, dish washing and operating the legendary potato-peeling machine.

PHOTO CREDIT: Australian War Memorial

Errol Noack, the first national serviceman to be killed in Vietnam, on his last leave in Port Lincoln, South Australia. Noack died on 24 May 1966, just ten days after he arrived in the country.

PHOTO CREDIT: Australian War Memorial

L-R: Second Lieutenant Gordon Sharp, officer commanding Eleven Platoon D Company 6RAR; Company 2IC Captain Iain McLean-Williams; Company Commanding Officer Major Harry Smith; and Second Lieutenant Geoff Kendall. Sharp was the only Australian officer killed during the Battle of Long Tan on 18 August 1966.

The day after the Battle of Long Tan, the men of D Company 6RAR return to the battlefield. L-R: Lance Corporal Gordon Crowther, national serviceman Private Peter Doyle and Corporal William ('Bluey') Moore with captured Viet Cong weapor

PHOTO CREDIT: Australian War Memorial

PHOTO CREDIT: Australian War Memorial

Second Lieutenant Dave Sabben, officer commanding Twelve Platoon D Company 6RAR, advances slowly through the rubber plantation on 19 August 1966, the day after the Battle of Long Tan.

PHOTO CREDIT: Australian War Memorial

The 1st Australian Logistic Support Group, built on the sand dunes of the seaside resort of Vung Tau.

PHOTO CREDIT: Jim Archbold

Corporal Pieter Versluys with national servicemen Corporal Jim Archbold and Corporal Graham Birthisel in Singapore, February 1968, en route to Vietnam. Archbold's father, Qantas captain Stuart Archbold, piloted the plane that took his son as far as Singapore. All Australian troops were required to wear civilian clothes during the layover.

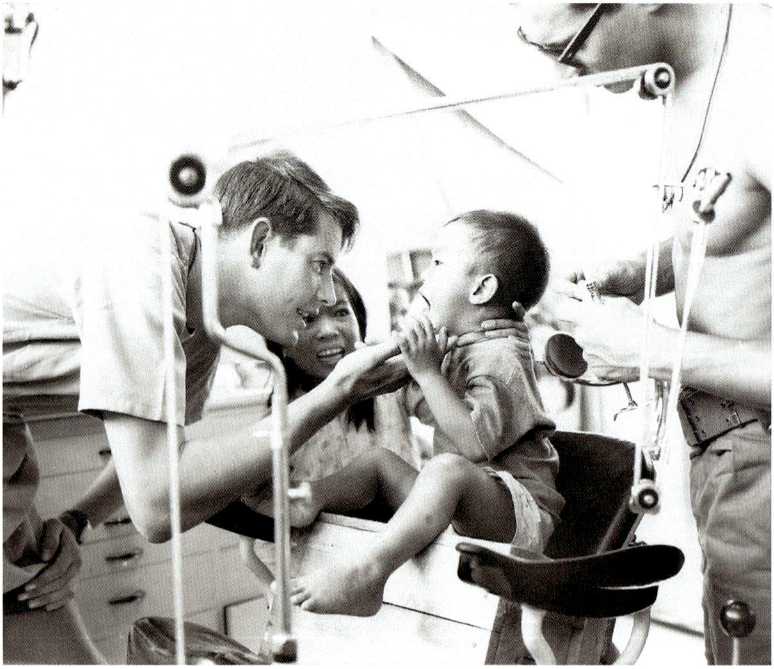

PHOTO CREDIT: Australian War Memorial

Captain Colin Twelftree of the 33rd Dental Unit examines the teeth of a South Vietnamese child, December 1967, Vung Tau. The child's sister looks on with interest.

PHOTO CREDIT: Australian War Memorial

Military policeman Corporal Ray Wyse gives directions to an Australian soldier on R&C leave in Vung Tau, December 1967.

PHOTO CREDIT: Brian Harold Stanley Mayfield

The aftermath of the Tet Offensive of early 1968 at Cholon, in the west of Saigon. The suburb was heavily bombed in the defence of the capital.

Second Lieutenant Norm Peatling of 3RAR takes a break in Phuoc Tuy province, April 1968.

PHOTO CREDIT: Australian War Memorial

PHOTO CREDIT: Australian War Memorial

The sign marking the entrance to the prisoner of war compound at Nui Dat, August 1971.

The men of 5RAR on HMAS *Sydney* docked at Fremantle, WA, 5 March 1970.

PHOTO CREDIT: James Evan Jones

Military policeman Corporal Jim Archbold's quarters and provisions at Fire Support Base Cor Bien Hoa province, Sout Vietnam, May 1968.

PHOTO CREDIT: Jim Archbold

Lance Bombardier Larry Davenport of 12th Field Artillery Regiment with his M60 machine gun at Fire Support Base Coral, Bien Hoa province, May 1968.

Lance Corporal Ken Myers and Private Malcolm Deveson, national servicemen of 3RAR, inspect an enemy RPG-7 and light machine gun, captured after the battle at Fire Support Base Balmoral, Bien Hoa province, May 1968.

PHOTO CREDIT: Australian War Memorial

BELOW: The Long Dien village marketplace, Phuoc Tuy province. During the Tet Offensive, D Company 3RAR went through Long Dien house by house in an attempt to flush out the enemy.

PHOTO CREDIT: Australian War Memorial

PHOTO CREDIT: Shaun Denis Gibbons

Pop star Normie Rowe arrives in Vietnam to start his tour of duty as a member of 3rd Cavalry Regiment, Royal Australian Armoured Corps, on 14 January 1969.

PHOTO CREDIT: Australian War Memorial

The Peter Badcoe Club at 1st Australian Logistic Support Group, Vung Tau. The club was an important R&C centre for Australian troops, with facilities including the Harold Holt Memorial Swimming Pool, the Kevin Wheatley Gymnasium and a bar.

Captain Neil Weekes, platoon commander of 1RAR, with his wife, Lyn, and parents, John and Edna. The family shares a congratulatory drink at Government House NSW on 23 September 1971 after Weekes received the Military Cross for his actions as a national service officer at Fire Support Base Coral.

PHOTO CREDIT: Australian War Memorial

PHOTO CREDIT: Australian War Memorial

Folk duo Sean Cullip and Sonja Tallis sing for the troops in Saigon on 19 November 1971.

PHOTO CREDIT: Australian War Memorial

L-R: Singer and dancer Beth McDonald, national serviceman Private John McGovern, singer Lorrae Desmond, national serviceman Lance Corporal Frank Bernhardt and singer Sonja Tallis, of the duo Sean and Sonja, at 1st Australian Logistic Support Base in Vung Tau. The performers toured as part of a concert party to Vietnam in November 1971.

PHOTO CREDIT: Australian War Memorial

Private Evan Jones, 5RAR, on stage at Luscombe Bowl, 1st Australian Task Force, Nui Dat, in 1970. Jones was a well-known performer in Adelaide before his national service and, along with his brother Idris, wrote the number-one hit 'The Pushbike Song'.

PHOTO CREDIT: Copyright unknown, in the collection of Jim Archbold

Under the watchful eye of a military policeman, Australian troops board a Boeing 707 to return home from Tan Son Nhut airport in 1968. At the time Tan Son Nhut was one of the busiest airports in the world.

Cheering crowds on George Street, Sydney, welcome the men of 5RAR home on 10 March 1970 with a ticker-tape parade. Many returning troops received similar welcomes, contrary to popular opinion.

PHOTO CREDIT: Frank Burke/Fairfax Syndication

that they could be invisible in vast numbers and strike everywhere at once. And if they were beaten or driven out – as they were, from every town and city – it was by technologically superior but morally inferior forces, who were neither for nor of the people, nor deserving of the backing of the outside world.

There was always an irony in Vietnam, forever a further contradiction to mock those who hoped to tame the lion-dragon. The irony after Tet was much of the enemy was exhausted, its support had waned, its military capabilities were mangled and its plans in disarray. The southern-raised VC had borne the brunt of the fighting and suffered devastating casualties. Its cadres were out in the open, its secret networks suddenly known. The Communists had massacred thousands of civilians during their occupation of the former imperial capital of Hue, and the people of the south had not risen en masse to help expel the Americans and overthrow the regime of Ky's recent successor as premier, President Nguyen Van Thieu. But few in the West cared to hear that in 1968, because a war, like a life, can only be lost once, and even if the VC had really been defeated, history showed they would return.

On 7 February, while the fighting raged on from the Mekong Delta to Khe Sanh, *The Age*, still the most sober of broadsheets, devoted the most prominent section of its front page to a young pop star's grooming. Normie Rowe had been inducted into the army at Puckapunyal and had a haircut. According to the Melbourne *Herald*, 'About 20 girls turned up to weep and kiss him. Rowe, 21, arrived in a black Rolls-Royce taxi with his parents and sister . . . Then Normie, pop king of Australia, visited the barber for the first time in six years.'[4] The *Herald* piece was written by cadet reporter Michael Frazer. Two years later, Frazer himself was in the army in Vietnam. According to the Sydney *Daily Telegraph*, Rowe's 'shorn curls' would be 'sent for safekeeping to the pop star's fan club'.[5] The stories were pure PR for the army. When asked about the food at Puckapunyal, Rowe replied it was better than he had tasted in most motels. At a special army press day a fortnight into recruit training, he said, 'I'm feeling the best I've ever felt in my life. You make good friends . . . It's a good thing for people to learn to get on together.' However, he did not seem a particularly convinced militarist. 'If more people could learn to live happily with others,' he said, 'there wouldn't be any more need for armies.'[6]

While Rowe's service – and even his haircut – gave the army a boost in the press, the sad reprise of the story of To Thi Nau had the opposite effect. Nau, the young VC whom John O'Halloran and his men had captured in the Warburtons in October 1966, re-emerged unexpectedly as a public character in Australia's Vietnam drama in March 1968. She was a rare female addition to the cast, beautiful, poised and wronged, and even acquired a *nom de guerre*, 'the water torture girl'. After O'Halloran had left her at Nui Dat, Nau had been taken for interrogation by Australian troops, one of whom had tried to make her talk by forcing water down her throat. The story that a female prisoner had been tortured by the Australians appeared in a book by former US Marine Martin Russ, published in the US in 1968. He wrote about the episode as one he was sorry to have missed, which had involved 'forcing water into her until she talked freely'.[7] Unusually, there were photographs of the victim taken immediately before and after the incident, by an Australian photographer at the invitation of Major Ross Smith of army PR. The pictures showed her being led from a helicopter into the tent where she was questioned; signing a statement at the end of her interrogation; then blindfolded and placed in the back of a jeep, to be driven out of Nui Dat and handed over to the ARVN.

When Russ's allegation became known in Australia, Minister for the Army Phillip Lynch claimed there was 'not one scintilla of evidence' to support it, but an Australian correspondent, John Sorell, came forward to confirm the torture had occurred. Sorell claimed to have seen, from outside the tent, a warrant officer 'pour water down the struggling girl's throat' for half an hour while 'another soldier prised open the girl's mouth'. He was asked to move away, he wrote, 'as the girl started to scream'.[8]

Sorell hadn't written the story in 1966 because he hadn't felt it important, but published his account eighteen months later to support his friend Russ. Lynch eventually conceded Nau's Australian interrogator had 'held her nose, and when she opened her mouth attempted to pour water into it using some four or five tins cups of water at intervals'. There was much unpleasant public debate about how much water constituted torture, when the Australian people would have preferred to think their troops didn't ill treat women in any way. And it may have seemed unlikely to some that, if one prisoner could be tortured while the press watched, she would be the only captive abused like this. Nor was it particularly reassuring when Sorell and the photographer said they had ignored the story at the time because there were so many worse things going on.

Ross Smith, who had remained outside the tent, later said he doubted there had been any water torture. In 2010, a former regular soldier, Peter Barham, told a reporter from the *Fraser Coast Chronicle* that he had been present at the incident and 'two soldier cowboys bound her wrists behind her back, placed a wet towel across her face and as she breathed in the towel went in and they poured water down her . . . They weren't that good at it but it went on for at least half an hour and I felt sick but couldn't leave the tent because I was the interpreter and had to relay what she said during her torture. She was distressed and this was after the soldiers asked me to tell her in Vietnamese that they would pull her nails out, stick objects up her orifices and do to her just about anything else very painful that you could imagine.'[9]

Whatever the extent of Nau's ordeal, it was titillating for press and public, and sold tens of thousands of newspapers in 1968, as the various rebuttals, accounts and denials rolled out. Author and Long Tan veteran Terry Burstall, a former regular soldier with 6RAR, discovered Nau in Hoa Long in 1989. She confirmed O'Halloran had treated her well, but also that the Australians at the base had fed her water until she'd choked and fainted. In the hands of the ARVN, she said, she was subsequently tortured and 'sexually abused using electricity',[10] then regularly beaten for a year.

A long time after Burstall's visit, John O'Halloran and a group of mates flew to Vietnam, found To Thi Nau still alive, and gave her the money to buy a house.

21

THE RIPPLES OF TET

There was to be no peace in South Vietnam in the Year of the Monkey. Enemy attacks simmered on through the early months of 1968 and there was fighting in Phuoc Tuy when Second Lieutenant Neil Weekes arrived, fresh from Australia, in March.

Weekes had been a primary school teacher in Clermont, south-west of Mackay, Queensland, but he'd grown up on a cattle farm. 'I was a very, very good shot,' he said, and 'became a professional kangaroo shooter when I was home on holidays to earn my keep. My old man taught me how to track. My brother and I used to go out and live off the land. We wouldn't go out with any food or water, we'd go and shoot pigeons, or shoot the fish and cook them in coals or mud.'

Weekes graduated from Scheyville, was posted to 1RAR, and left for Vietnam with the battalion's advance party on 17 March. 'We landed at Tan Son Nhut while it was under attack,' he said. 'There was smoke billowing up, and mortar rounds landing around the airport. As we landed, we were issued our weapons, because they were all in the hull. We grabbed our weapons and ammunition and took shelter in the bunkers where the jet fighters normally were. Then we were very quickly put onto a Caribou, and flew down to Nui Dat.'

He was with the Task Force by four p.m. on 18 March, and in

Ba Ria with A Company 7RAR by four-thirty p.m. the next day. Ba Ria was under attack again in the slipstream of Tet and at seven forty-five p.m., 7RAR was hit by about two hundred Viet Cong. 'That was my welcome to Vietnam,' said Weekes. 'The company commander, Jake O'Donnell, called me in and said, "Right, you are now the platoon commander of Three Platoon, A Company, 7RAR. The platoon commander has been badly wounded a couple of days ago and medevaced to Australia; the platoon sergeant has gone back to Australia with our advance party, on the same plane you arrived in." So I went down to the platoon, and I was sitting on the bunker overlooking this paddy field and river, having a brew with the corporal, when we were hit. I jumped down the pit and I said, "What do I do now?" And the corporal, the most experienced man in the platoon, said, "If I were you, sir, I'd keep my head down and we'll get on with it."

'The next night, I took out an ambush into an old graveyard,' he said. 'It was a moonlit night, and the guy that was in the lead of this group – including a couple of women, we think – saw [our] Claymore mine shining in the moonlight, and bent down to have a look at it.' It was a command-detonated mine, and the corporal set it off. The blast killed the lead VC and blew the leg off the man behind him. They were Weekes' first enemy casualties. 'I remember getting in trouble with Jake O'Donnell because I claimed them for the 1st Battalion,' said Weekes, 'and he told me to go and get lost. I was part of Seven.'

Other Australians found war with the Americans. In April 1968, Jim Archbold was with a group of provosts escorting a convoy to the US base Bear Cat, home of brigades of the 9th Infantry Division, where they were told there was space for one man to join a fact-finding mission to the Mekong Delta with the military police. 'About four of us said, "We'll be in that," and drew straws,' said Archbold. He won the draw, and travelled with the American colonel. 'We headed through Saigon and down into the delta,' he said, 'and went to a base called Dong Tan, right down on the rivers. I was sitting in the escort vehicle with a couple of blokes, having a bit of a yack, and they seemed like good guys. For some reason, I got back into the colonel's jeep, and we headed back up this horrible dirt road with bush right up to the edge, and we ran straight into an ambush.' The two men in the escort jeep were shot. 'One bloke was killed – the guy who survived was shot five times. But they were thrown out of the vehicle and their vehicle ran off the road. We were probably forty, fifty foot behind, eating their dust.

'I tried to help the guy on the road,' said Archbold. 'There was still a bit of shooting going on, and I didn't really know whether he'd just become unconscious. Obviously, he was hurt bad and I couldn't move him, so I thought I'd try and get some rounds back. I was lying across in front of him. It's very hard to tell where rounds are coming from. They're popping in the distance. I got some rounds off down the road.' The enemy fire stopped.

'I didn't know where anyone was,' said Archbold, 'or what was going on, or anything, so I got back in the scrub for a little while, and then American infantry came through. My biggest worry was the American infantry, because people with cocked and loaded M16s are a problem. So I waited until [a soldier] crawled across virtually in front of me – I'd been hunting since I was eighteen, and so I was real good at keeping quiet and watching what was going on – and I just introduced myself, and he nearly fell over backwards. I joined them, and they did sweeps, and they captured a few Viet Cong.

'We put some rounds at one that was fleeing,' said Archbold, 'and he got shot. And I got to guard one fella that we grabbed out of the scrub for a couple of minutes. He could've been a farmer. He was just dressed in old, ragged stuff. You wouldn't know if he was a civilian or a Viet Cong or who he was.'

Afterwards, Archbold was less concerned about the fighting than 'worried about what the army was going to do', he said. 'I was a million miles away from where I was supposed to be.' He was eventually awarded the Military Medal for his actions on the day.

In May 1968, peace talks opened in Paris, and the Communist leaders, true to their strategy of fighting while talking, unleashed another attack on the south, this time spearheaded by fifty thousand NVA who'd struggled down the rugged Ho Chi Minh trail through Laos and Cambodia to replace the casualties of Tet. At last, the claims of the American and Australian governments were true, and the main enemy fighting force in the south was regular soldiers infiltrated from the north, but informed citizens of the West had heard this said many times before, and now some turned away.

On 4 May, the Communists sprung out of the hills and poured down towards the cities and towns, although this time many were halted and routed before they reached their targets. But thirteen divisions made it through to Saigon and, once again, the capital was shown to be vulnerable, even fragile, as the great city burned.

When the May Offensive hit, 'everyone was prepared, battle-trained, you knew what to expect,' said Ray Wyse. His mate Ron Shaw was transferred to Saigon, where the curfew was back in force. 'The only people allowed on the streets at curfew, six p.m. to six a.m., were the Australian and American military police, the Quan Canh Vietnamese military police, and the ARVN,' said Shaw. 'Even the American infantry weren't there until a bit later. There was no streetlights. It was as black as black can be, and that's pretty terrifying. And you know there's Viet Cong in the area. They know where they're going. And we lived in Cholon, in the St George Hotel. There was contact there, on patrol, shots fired, snipers. A lot of the Viet Cong had relatives in Saigon, and they'd stay with them and they'd snipe from windows. It's pitch-black, so you wouldn't know where it comes from. You've got to get on the radio, try and pinpoint the position and have the ARVN come in.'

Bernard Clancy, a journalist on the *Gippsland Times* who had been drafted into the Service Corps, worked as an assistant to the Commander Australian Force Vietnam, Major General Arthur MacDonald. Clancy was living in Cholon's Hotel Canberra when 'we woke up one morning to this bloody firefight', he said. 'They had machine guns and rockets in a building probably two hundred metres away. We were up on the roof, saying, "Huh, a real war . . . " We were evacuated from there and went into the headquarters for probably a fortnight, and lived and worked there.

'Saigon, the whole city, was just a battlefield. Everywhere we went – and we didn't go out much – there were bodies. And when we went back to our hotel, there'd been a pretty major firefight in the streets around the hotel. You see things that stick in your mind, like dogs walking down the streets, walking up to these bodies, sniffing them and pissing on them. You realise you're not a human being any more, just meat – meat in a gutter.'

The casualties of what became known as Mini-Tet included three Australian reporters and an English colleague, who were executed by a VC commander while the journalists were trying to get into Cholon. One of the Australians, the young AAP correspondent Michael Birch, was cut down on 5 May as he called out '*Bao Chi!*', the Vietnamese term for journalist. The image-conscious NLF called a press conference in Moscow to deny responsibility for the shooting. It feared a reaction in the West, but the murders of the four journalists provoked surprisingly little comment. The Australian government appeared barely concerned. Although the media had been largely supine, patriotic and incurious, Prime Minister John Gorton said he would not investigate the NLF's claims of innocence, since they came from a press coverage in Vietnam which 'if anything, does not support, as it might, the efforts of Australians and others in that area'.

He blamed the journalists for the war.

22

THE BATTLE OF CORAL

The arrival of a third infantry battalion lent Australian forces the numbers to operate outside of Phuoc Tuy province, far from the shadow of the guns of Nui Dat. But when troops moved out of the Task Force's artillery range, fire support bases (FSBs) had to be set up to provide them cover in the bush. An FSB was a fortress without walls, an artillery battery in a circle pocked with gun pits and ringed with barbed wire and Claymore mines. Other troops, including MPs, medics, engineers and Intelligence corpsmen were also based within the camp, and armoured vehicles were the cavalry's covered wagons.

A field battery was the artillery's equivalent of an infantry battalion, and a lance bombardier held equal rank to a lance corporal. Lance Bombardier Larry Davenport was born at Victor Harbor, SA, eighty kilometres south of Adelaide, where once there were whaling stations. He left school, tried teacher training but didn't last a year, then became a stock-and-station agent in Lameroo, near the Victorian border. When he was called up, he was happy to become an artilleryman, specialising in signals, and was eager to go to Vietnam.

By the time Davenport arrived in country to join the 4th Field Regiment in November 1967, they had less than six months of their tour remaining. He could have returned to Australia with them in

April 1968, but chose to stay in Vietnam and transfer to the 12th Field Regiment. 'I didn't want to go home to polish rocks for nine months,' he said. 'As a national serviceman, once you'd finished in Vietnam and were back in Australia, they really had nothing for you to do.'

On 12 May 1968, in the heat of Mini-Tet, units of 1RAR and 3RAR, including 1RAR's mortar platoon, travelled to a point eighty kilometres north-west of Nui Dat in Bien Hoa province to establish Fire Support Base Coral. The first to arrive were D Company 3RAR and the New Zealand 161 Field Battery. The guns of 12th Field Regiment's 102 Battery and 1RAR's support company – its mortars, anti-tank platoon and assault pioneers – were expected to join them, but their advance party mistakenly set up about a kilometre away. Three companies of 3RAR were to the west of the base, and 1RAR's rifle companies to the east, as planned. Intelligence reports had indicated that NVA and Viet Cong troops were in disarray and withdrawing towards the area of the new FSB. They were supposed to be low on ammunition and demoralised, heading north with their wounded on their backs.

'Coral started out as a shambles,' said Neil Weekes, who was now with 1RAR. 'We were going to kill all these bastards who were on the run from Saigon. They didn't realise there was going to be another raid on Saigon. We got these orders that we were flying in there to have a turkey shoot, and all these helicopters were allocated to us. But during the morning, everything started to go astray. The helicopters were taken off us.' The reconnaissance party hadn't been able to properly identify the terrain on the landing zone 'because the pilot, an American, refused to go too low because there were big contacts down there. The Big Red One, the 1st Infantry Division of the American army, was just a couple of kilometres away from where we were going to land and they were in deep shit. 199 Brigade was over there and they were in deep shit. So our whole landing pattern was put back. We were supposed to land, secure a fire support base, leave an infantry company there to secure it, and then go out away from the fire support where the guns would be located, put in these ambushes and shoot all these bastards coming back. Kill them all.

'We should have been there by midday. The fly-in got delayed. When some of our companies first landed, they found all the signs of battle. They could hear the Big Red One, bloody bombs going off, artillery. They found dead NVA with brand-new AK-47s, in uniform, sitting under trees. They saw groups of forty enemy moving around. We didn't get into our location until half past five in the afternoon.' The plan had been for the rifle companies to harbour up as far as three kilometres away from the FSB, and begin patrolling for enemy at dawn. 'We should've consolidated around the fire support base,' said Weekes, 'then worked out what we were going to do the next day. The enemy saw what was happening, and launched a regimental-style attack on the fire support base that night.' Instead of blocking the exhausted ragtag remnants of a defeated army fleeing back to its bases, Coral had got in the way of a fresh, disciplined force of North Vietnamese regulars advancing to Saigon.

A former high-school classmate of Weekes, John Quane, was a national servicemen with 1RAR's anti-tank platoon. Quane was a visual tracker and cover man for a dog handler and his labrador Justin, one of the two Australian tracker dogs at Coral. Justin was 'a feisty dog', said Quane. The other dog, Tiber, was later described as 'a shell-shocked Digger who will be in Vietnam until he dies' by the Melbourne *Herald*.[1] 'The dogs didn't bark,' said Quane. 'They were purely a tracking dog. In training, they'd take them down to a range when there was firing going on, and if they reacted adversely to that sort of noise, they didn't stay in the program.'

Davenport's birthday was 13 May 1968 and, 'a little after midnight, the first rockets and mortars started coming in,' he said, 'and following them, we got the first frontal attack, human attack, on Coral. We had very little in the way of defences done, because people had got in late, it wasn't in the right place, fortifications weren't prepared. A lot of the guys didn't have fighting pits, all they had was scrapes, and the attack came to HQ battery and to the guns.

'There was a lot of small-arms fighting,' said Davenport. 'The 1RAR mortar platoon, which was just in front of where we were, beside the guns, were almost wiped out. The guy who was sent out of the command post when I arrived on the radio, he was killed. He had no time to dig a scrape. The enemy overran one of our artillery pieces. The gunners fought back and retook it. They overran it again, we retook it. It was very close quarters. At times, it'd be like being in the front stalls of a symphony orchestra when all the drums and the cymbals are going.'

'Justin survived okay,' said Quane. 'He just huddled down with the dog handler. The three of us had two small scrapes down – that's all we had time to do – both of us probably wouldn't have been more than two inches at a scrape down. We just lay on top of that with the dog in between us.'

Lance Corporal Alan 'Jack' Parr was a schoolteacher born on a fruit farm near Rockhampton. Since teachers were permitted – and expected – to defer until they had completed their tertiary studies and served one year in the job, there were virtually no teachers in the first year of national service, few in the second, and then, by 1967, a deluge. There was one intake of national servicemen every three months, but the teachers tended to march in to recruit training only in January, once the previous school year was over. So not only did all the teachers arrive in the same years, the majority came in at the same time. The military in Vietnam could rarely use them as teachers, so they ended up scattered throughout the army. Scores of 'chalkies' found themselves in New Guinea, training the Pacific Islands Regiment, but there were at least four with 1RAR at Coral, including Parr's teachers'-college classmate Ross Coulter, a signaller with D Company. Parr himself was radio operator for the mortar platoon, which set up north-east of the guns, just outside their perimeter.

'Digging in was fine,' said Parr, 'not difficult as [Second Lieutenant]

Tony Jensen and I had ditched our "tools entrenching", and I now carried a small pick and he had a small shovel. We dug a double slit for the mortar command post and a combined one for our sleeping pit, down to about ten to twelve inches with the spoil mounded around the edges . . . a shell scrape. We erected a fly over our sleeping pit and a canvas cover over the command post. Mortar pits were down about the same. After all we didn't arrive until after 1600.'

He felt no more or less vulnerable that at any other time in Vietnam. 'As a digger,' he said, 'I had no idea where we were, except that we were north in Bien Hoa province and I had no idea what the enemy situation was in the area.' In fact, they were less than ten kilometres from the headquarters of the NVA's 7th Division. 'The usual standard operational practice is that mortars have perimeter protection with an infantry platoon and the guns have an infantry company,' said Parr. 'That was non-existent, so the guns, mortars and elements of 12 Field HQ set up a makeshift perimeter. We had one M60, which was set up covering a track, and firing arcs coordinated with the artillery machine guns (two, I think). We had no standard perimeter defences like Claymore mines, trip flares or wire.'

The men of the mortar platoon were close, Parr said, particularly 'those who lived together at Holsworthy, which the sixth and seventh nasho intakes did. I especially knew Errol Bailey very well as he had been at Singleton with us.' Bailey was a coal miner's son from the Hunter Valley, NSW, who'd won a teachers' scholarship, an all-round athlete who'd been dating his girlfriend, Julie, since high school. Once Bailey qualified as a teacher, he got a job at Rosehill Primary School in Sydney, where he coached the soccer team. He was not happy to be called up. He and Julie married in January 1967, just before he went into the army. By the time he was posted to Vietnam, they had a baby son. 'Bailey was very well liked and respected amongst the diggers,' said Parr.

Nobody at Coral realised the enemy had been hiding in the scrub, watching the Australians set up, delighted by their vulnerability. 'We had an incursion around midnight,' said Parr. 'Just a probe to see where we were. A group of them just came up the track. I wasn't on duty, but I soon woke up. I remember getting my gear and heading up to where the gun was, if they needed me. Someone else was on the radio. So I scampered up there but it was all over in about ten seconds.' Then, at about two-thirty a.m., came 'a mortar barrage followed by a rocket attack then a human wave assault by several hundred.

'I was on radio piquet at the time,' said Parr. 'We were quickly overrun, enemy all around us. And they were very good. They managed to creep right up to our position, about twenty or thirty metres, before we knew they were there. And, all of a sudden, they hit us with a barrage of mortars and then followed by rockets and then a ground assault. And that all happened in a few minutes. We couldn't fire our own mortars – that was out of the question – so we just had to use our own personal weapons to protect ourselves. It was impossible to form up any sort of a concentrated defence.

'My sleeping pit took direct rocket fire and was obliterated. It was about five metres from where I was on the radio. It was a visible structure, a target. All that structure disappeared, and it ended up just a hole in the ground. Later on, we got some of the wounded and we settled them down there for a bit of protection.' The kit in Parr's pack 'just got blown apart'.

'Jock Whitton – he was one of our corporals – was out of his pit and he was wounded,' said Parr, 'and Graham Stevens went out to drag him back into the pit, and that's when they both got hit with a rocket. I can still see Jock taking the full blast of an RPG. My shell scrape saved me. All the small arms and everything went over the top. I had a little mound of dirt on the edge of it, and that was enough to get under cover. Two grenades went off about two metres from our pit – Tony Jensen was beside me. All the time, we were exchanging bits and pieces of what was going on, and one stage he just yelled out, "Grenade!" So I made myself half an inch thick and this grenade went off just above my pit.'

Parr believes Jensen's vigilance saved his life. 'A little bit later, he yelled out, "Another grenade!" and that went off,' he said. 'I saved his life too. There was an enemy group with a machine gun that I spotted, and his attention was elsewhere. He was between me and the enemy group, and I had to fire over the top of him to get rid of the enemy. There was three of them. They were silhouetted and I engaged them. They were only about ten or fifteen metres away, so they didn't stand a chance.

'On the radio, I called for all the fire support I could get – remember, it was dark and we could only see by the light from the explosions; later Spooky dropped flares.' The artillery battery, Parr said, 'actually depressed their barrels and fired directly into our position with anti-personnel rounds, in order to neutralise the enemy. So that was being fired over the top of us, and at the same time we were calling in our own friendly mortar fire from 3RAR, as well as helicopter gunships and the Spooky gunship. So they were firing into and around our position all morning. And this was in the dark. We could only see by the flash of the fire what was happening.

'I was in contact with the gunships and the 3RAR mortars and our battalion headquarters,' said Parr. 'Spooky was tremendous. I directed his fire into very close proximity.' But best of all for Parr were the tens of thousands of darts of splintex that whirled out of Australian shells and into the enemy, blasting bodies into pincushions. Parr felt 'absolutely bloody scared. That's the only way you could feel. I didn't feel excited or exhilarated or anything like that. It was just survival.

'I couldn't hear a thing the next day. And ever since. The ears were bad, really bad.' But he could still operate the radio. 'It's amazing,' he said, 'when you put a handset right into your ear, you can hear it, even though your ears are ringing and then feel flat.'

Brian McInneny, a former railway clerk, by then with the mortar platoon, said, 'I was at the far extremity of the assault and I could hear rockets, firearms and could see flares lighting all around. Figures came toward us and every time I fired toward them a rocket came back. A short time later John O'Brien crawled up to me; he had had to withdraw from his mortar after being overrun and was looking for the command post. I pointed to where it was and John crawled away. He was KIA [killed in action] shortly after.' O'Brien, a national serviceman and spray-painter, 'died right next to me', said Parr. 'We were overrun in the dark in the first ten minutes and it was every man for himself. It was the fire support that saved us, otherwise there would have been all eighteen of the mortar platoon KIA.'

The mortar platoon lost five men dead and eight wounded. 'I was still at my shell scrape,' remembered McInneny, 'and all of a sudden I heard a loud blast and my left arm was blown off my rifle. My whole left arm was numb and I lay there trying to feel where I had been hit. I looked up and saw an enemy soldier standing above me, he had his rifle pointed at me and let go a short burst of automatic fire. I felt the rounds hitting the ground near my feet. I could not turn my rifle toward him and was waiting for the next rounds as he aimed again. I heard a blast of fire but it was not at me: Tony Jensen had seen what was happening and he shot the enemy soldier before he could fire at me again. I found later that I had been hit by a piece of shrapnel from a rocket and was wounded in the left wrist. Luckiest man alive, I believe.

'Shortly after this,' said McInneny, 'another one of the guys crawled up to me.' It was Brian Buzzard, a schoolteacher from Northam, WA. 'He had been hit twice. He asked me to treat his worst wound with his one shell dressing. I saw that he had been hit by shrapnel of some sort in the rear of his left thigh, this was not bleeding at this stage but appeared to be a fairly deep hole. He had been hit in the lower jaw and was in a lot of pain and bleeding quite heavily. I bandaged his jaw and he crawled away.'

Ken Bourke, the Sydney police officer who'd joined up with Wyse and Shaw, had arrived in Coral as a provost the afternoon before the attack, and had only partly dug in by nightfall. He was on duty in a command tent, with a candle for a light, when the enemy mortars began to land. 'I just blew out the light,' he said. 'Where I dug my position was probably forty or fifty metres away, and I wasn't going to go that far under fire, so I jumped into the nearest trench. In doing so, I injured my back slightly – and landed on another fella. For three hours, it was hell on earth. But because we weren't on the perimeter, we couldn't use any firearms – we had guys in front of us.'

The attack was finally repelled in the early hours of the morning. 'The sky lit up and the Yanks came in with planes,' said Bourke. 'It was just like Guy Fawkes. And you lie there and just hope you're not the one that's going to die.' A Douglas AC-47 gunship soared in and 'just chewed up the whole front', said Davenport. When the American bombers joined in the fight, he remembered, 'watching the afterburners, a red-purple cone of fire' and noise like 'sitting next to a railway track while a freight train goes past'.

'Once morning came,' said Quane, 'we did a sweep out and around the front of the artillery position, and in front of the mortars. A couple of us were then assigned to move the bodies of our blokes back into an area where they could be airlifted out. Another fella and myself moved a couple of the mortar blokes who'd been killed during the course of the evening. That was not an easy job to do. One bloke, particularly, I knew reasonably well, Errol Bailey.' The teacher from the Hunter Valley was dead, all his education wasted.

'I was emotionally and physically exhausted,' said Parr. 'The clearing patrol could not believe the stark looks on our faces . . . The battlefield was a complete mess, utter devastation, there were over fifty bodies and body parts, like a complete intact human brain on the ground. There was blood everywhere soaked into the ground; it had a characteristic odour – stunk – combined with the smell of cordite.

'The clearing patrol with the doc attended to the wounded, [who] were dusted off; the KIA were then taken out. Any ratshit equipment was dumped into my sleeping pit and burned. All the rest of the platoon was returned to Nui Dat except for Tony and myself. A section of 3RAR mortars in APCs were brought in under our command and we set up adjacent to the original baseplate. The following day we got our remaining section from Nui Dat as well as a new section of reinforcements. So we became operational again in a slightly different position, this time with perimeter defence.'

National serviceman Leigh Boneham, formerly 'a suited-up bank johnny', was among the reinforcements. 'Where we landed, there were bloody bodies,' he said, 'a lot of movement, people moving back. We moved back a few hundred yards from where the original contacts were. We took our mortar barrels out with us; I think most of the stuff they had there, they tossed it out. It was a hell of a mess, the place itself. I reckon we were fairly fortunate that they never attacked again until the next day.'

The events of 13 May were feted in the Australian press as another unqualified military victory, and recorded in the *Sydney Morning Herald* under the headline 'Aust. troops kill 46 Reds'. An army spokesman said Australian casualties had been 'light'.[2] The next day, when it emerged nine men (later revised to eleven) were dead and many more wounded, the newspaper felt bound to explain, 'U.S. Army rules adopted by the Australian Army in Vietnam define casualties as light when a unit is able to carry on after a clash with the enemy.'[3]

Jim Archbold had returned to Nui Dat after Bear Cat, and was sent on to Coral. 'We got up there right on dusk,' said Archbold. 'I got out of the helicopter and they heaved out all the supplies, and as I looked around I thought to myself, This is not a good place. You could feel it in the air and no one was smiling, there was no welcome, nothing. And I had no idea where my little unit was. There was someone there, and I said, "Where do you reckon?" and he said, "If I were you, I'd get into that hole."

'So I dived into this big hole, and I lay on the bottom trying to get some sleep, which was impossible because there were rockets coming in, a bit of mortaring, then there was our stuff putting artillery around the edge, then there was the allied aircraft flying around. I had no idea what was going on.'

The next night, the tracking dog Tiber broke away from his handler and ran towards the front line. They found him in the morning, unharmed, but 'after that, he was no good for tracking', said Quane. 'The noise had got to him.'

The rifle companies of 1RAR had pulled back to the FSB. Once they reached Coral, wrote Weekes, who was commanding Three Platoon, A Company, 'We quickly occupied an all round defence posture and sent out patrols to dominate "No man's land". Unfortunately there was no coordination of the defensive position and there was a huge gap, of approximately 100 m, between my left pit and the first pit of C Company.' Weekes feared the enemy could walk straight through the gap, so he lined up guns to cover it, and moved forward all his men except platoon HQ, until they reached a position where there was one big tree on their left, near Seven Section.

On 15 May, Weekes later wrote, 'Just on dusk, Shorty Thirkell, the section commander of 7 Section, and his second-in-command, Frank Matons, were going from pit to pit telling the soldiers what time they were on machine gun piquet. Suddenly a heavy machine gun opened fire and both were hit. Shorty was hit in the left arm and although his arm was almost blown off, he survived. Matons was hit in the left thigh. Both were evacuated by helicopter and sent back to Australia. To this day I do not know who fired those machine guns. I believe it may have been our own APCs to our rear.'[4]

At two o'clock the next morning, the enemy attacked Coral a second time, storming towards A Company. 'And they hit us with mortar fire, recoilless rifles, satchels and Bangalore torpedos,' said Weekes. 'We had no wire up, nothing.'

Weekes had put his entire platoon on the front perimeter because he had to cover such a huge area. 'Normally, you have some depth in case the enemy penetrate,' he said, 'But I couldn't, I had to put all my sections up, which goes against all the teachings you have at Scheyville. And the noise! They hit my platoon with mortars and 75 mm RCLs and 57 mm RCLs, and we didn't even *know* they were firing at us, because of the cacophony of war.'

The enemy assaulted Weekes' position from the left, where he now had a private soldier, Ron James, running Seven Section. 'Private James came back and said, "They're all dead. The whole section's dead." So I actually had to crawl down, and I came to the first pit and Johnny Wallis and [Alexander] Young were both dead. There were flares going off and I could see that they were dead. I went down to the next pit, where James was, and he had [Rodney] Clarke as his mate there, and Clarke wasn't there, but there was blood all in the pit. I thought, Oh Christ, the enemy's got Clarke. Or Clarke's somewhere out there in the weeds, lost. I went down to the furthest pit, and found Andy Anderson and [Graham] Manteit still alive, but not aware of what was going on. So I moved them back to platoon headquarters, and then James and I went out searching for young Clarkey. And the enemy were all around us. And thank God, we found him. In the grass, he'd been badly wounded, shot through the guts. He lost his spleen, part of his liver. He survived.'

Weekes and his acting platoon sergeant Bruno Flematti took turns in carrying Clarke back to platoon headquarters, in a fireman's lift. 'The enemy was all around us at this time,' wrote Weekes, 'and we shot several at point blank range. They didn't seem to be worrying about us as they were concentrating on the artillery guns that were behind my position.

'On arrival at Headquarters I was blasted by the Company Commander for leaving my platoon but I responded that someone had to bring the wounded back, that I had no depth to my platoon as all three sections were in the forward line and that we needed more ammunition. The Company Second in Command, Captain Bill

Raggatt, got out of his pit and directed us to the ammunition bunker where we grabbed some machine gun and rifle ammunition and a box of grenades . . . I had implemented an "above ground" policy as I left. This meant that anything seen above ground was suspected of being enemy and was to be shot,' wrote Weekes.[5]

'We came down right along the front line issuing ammunition,' he said, 'yelling out, screaming our guts out that we were friendly and we were coming up with ammunition. The jets were coming in, and we got pieces of hexamine and put them between our legs and our shell scrapes so the jets could see the line of lights but the enemy couldn't. And they were dropping bombs just down in front of us, and strafing, and then they dropped napalm. There were flares everywhere, artillery going off everywhere.' The enemy had set up a heavy machine gun in the pits they had taken, and it was firing at Weekes but the shots were going over his position and slamming into battalion HQ. 'Battalion CO came up on the platoon radio and asked me what I was going to do about it,' wrote Weekes. 'I told him that I would launch a counter-attack but I would need mortar support. He asked me if I was aware that this would necessitate calling mortar fire down onto my own positions and was I prepared to accept friendly casualties.'[6] Weekes agreed that he was. 'So I called mortars down,' he said, 'and I wounded a couple of my own soldiers.

'To get orders to my front troops, I had to send Private Scholtz, my runner, down, or I had to go down in the grass,' he said. Weekes was directing artillery from the tree 'and a big piece of burning red-hot shrapnel hit that tree, and the zing of it going above my head scared the living hell out of me. So I knelt down, and I was bringing in the mortar fire on my own pit and the artillery, which was right in front of us, I was bringing in closer and closer and closer, until Bob Sutton, the platoon commander on my right, said, "Ay, Neil, that's getting pretty close. Can you move it out of here?" Because these were eight-inch guns, leaving huge craters.

'And then the enemy came through, and thank God Bruno Flematti and I, when we got back to our pit we found we had this heavy box of grenades we'd forgotten to give to the troops, so we sat there all night throwing grenades around, to stop the enemy getting to us.'

When the mortars began to fall, Weekes had given the order to 'Fix bayonets'. Corporal James Moyle was in command of Eight Section. 'To this day,' wrote Weekes, 'even through the noise of battle, I can still hear Moyle curse his disbelief.'

Weekes gave covering fire and yelled out for Moyle and his men to move forward, but they didn't seem to make any progress. 'Jimmy Moyle explained to me, in very loud tones, that every time I ordered him to move the enemy would engage his section with the heavy machine gun,' wrote Weekes. 'But we managed to silence the enemy long enough for us to do a counter attack,' he said, 'just my platoon headquarters, Private Anderson and Private Manteit, with a machine gun, and managed to kick the enemy out. I think there were 27 enemy bodies around our platoon headquarters.'[7]

Private Alan 'John' Wallis and signalman Alexander Young, the two soldiers who'd died in the same trench, were national servicemen. They had only been in country since March. 'I had my fellas,' said Weekes. 'I got to know them very well. Wallis, I went to his bloody wedding around about 2 March. He was killed on the night of 15 May. I had to write letters to his wife.'

But that second attack on Coral was 'when the mortar platoon really shined and came of age,' said Jack Parr. 'There was all this shit coming in, with Tony out there in the open calling fire orders to the base plate, and Leigh Boneham doing the plotting with no cover from incoming.'

Boneham said, 'My rifle was there but I don't think I ever picked it up on that night. There was people waiting to get fire missions – and Jack Parr managed all that. It just went from one mission to the next mission, and it was absolutely flat strap. It was bloody chaotic. One mission might only be a few hundred metres, and another would be one thousand metres. They were dropping very close to the troops. I was doing the plotting, and all I had was a bloody little torch, and in the scheme of things, the dot of a lead pencil is about ten metres. It's my understanding that we never dropped anything short, so we never knocked any of our own people over.'

'Then there were the two guys who commandeered a Land Rover,' said Parr, 'to get resupplies of mortar ammo several times whilst under fire . . . disobeying the orders of an officer who was going to charge them until Tony told him where to go. We fired more rounds in those couple of hours that morning than our yearly allocation, buggered two barrels in the process. The barrels were actually glowing red and you could see the cold round as it went into the tube. The feeling after this action was elation.' Boneham said, 'We were pretty happy that we were all still there, to be honest. And the damage inflicted on the North Vietnamese was massive compared to what previously Australians had experienced. It was bloody horrendous.'

One of the casualties of the second night at Coral was Second Lieutenant Tim Fischer, now a transport officer with 1RAR, who was hutchied up with his signalman, national serviceman Bob Edelman, when the mortars and rockets began to rain. They jumped into their shell scrape, but Fischer put his head up to see what was going on, and was hit by shrapnel on his right shoulder, chest and forehead. 'He was a little dazed,' said Edelman, 'and there was blood streaming down his face . . . I told him to pull his head in before he got it shot off.'[8] The next morning, Fischer was evacuated to Bien Hoa.

The *Sydney Morning Herald*, once bitten, reported the second attack with more caution than the first. The enemy had pierced the defences of the FSB and been repulsed for the second time in four days. Although Australian casualties of the four and a half-hour battle had again been described as 'light', the newspaper was bound to remind its readers of the new definition of 'light'. A day later, when casualties from the two combined attacks totalled nineteen dead and fifty-four wounded, the *Sydney Morning Herald* conceded these were 'the heaviest casualties, in terms of numbers, that Australia has suffered in the Vietnam War'.[9] Statistics, however, could be deceiving, and the paper was quick to reassure readers that the wounded of Coral were not, broadly speaking, as badly wounded as those at Long Tan, as they had largely been hit by shrapnel, not bullets, and a number of them were still on duty.

Archbold wrote home from his pit, 'At nights we are wringing wet with perspiration.'[10] 'On one night, the mortars walked right through our area,' he said, 'and one missed our hole by four or five feet. All the tents were ripped, full of holes, and we had rubber trees around us, leaking rubber everywhere: that gives an idea of the amount of shrapnel that rips across anything above ground level with mortars.' When the aircraft came in with their mini-guns blazing, 'They sounded just like if you walked up to a long corrugated-iron fence and got a stick and ripped it down the fence,' said Archbold. 'And at night, you've got red fingers poking around – and there's a tracer every five.'

During the day, the infantry took out probing patrols, and regularly came back with prisoners, who became the provosts' responsibility. A POW cage was built from barbed wire, and the men of Coral hung their blankets and clothes out on its teeth to dry. Archbold choppered in and out of the base several times, carrying captured enemy soldiers to the US base at Long Binh.

'They had quite a few POWs,' said Boneham. 'They put them in a compound near where mortar platoon was. I wouldn't've liked to be in their shoes. They got a bit of a rough trot. Some of them were on stretchers and all sorts of bloody things. It was a mess. But the interpreters were trying to get information out of them; it was pretty bloody savage.'

On 23 May, Centurion tanks rolled into Coral. 'The opposition didn't want much to do with that,' said Boneham, 'so the Australians were able to move out and track down where they had some of their tunnels and so forth.'

But skirmishes and mortar attacks around FSB Coral didn't end until three weeks were out. Surrounded by the memory of death, in ground fecund with enemy corpses, Archbold wrote to his mother and, in traditional Australian fashion, talked only about the weather: 'It was really hot and sticky up there and when the rain did eventually come, everyone stood under and showered . . . Our underground bunkers filled with water, so we had to sleep in the mud.'[11]

23

THE MEN OF BALMORAL

In their summer shorts and sunhats, David Cripps and Michael Evans guarded the beach at Vung Tau, through high tide and low, until April 1968, when they decided they'd had enough. 'The blokes that had been with the D&E Platoon at the time had been there the whole year,' said Evans, 'and they'd never went into the front line up in the battalion, and they'd no spark in them. After a while: "Ah, we're going into town," and they'd say, "Stuff it, I'm going to read a book," and we'd be chafing to get in there.'

Evans, as a boy, had never dreamed of going to war. 'I just wanted to be independent,' he said, 'be myself, find happiness somewhere.' He didn't want to shoot anyone and he didn't want to be in Vietnam, but he found himself volunteering for battalion duties anyway. Cripps left Vung Tau first, on 16 April 1968, to join B Company 3RAR. 'I went straight out to Balmoral and Coral,' he said. 'That was my introduction to real infantry stuff. I thought, Shit, what am I doing here? I should be back at the beach.'

On 24 May, 3RAR moved to FSB Balmoral, 4.5 kilometres north of Coral, where Cripps was joined by Doug English, who'd been posted to 3RAR on 27 February. English had been a copy boy at the *Sydney Morning Herald* before he'd graduated to the reading room, but he was also fantastically fit. He trained with weights at the gym at a time when only boxers, wrestlers and bodybuilders sweated over dumbbells; he ran long-distance, bodysurfed at weekends, and had never drunk alcohol until he went into the army. He could pump out eighty push-ups with one arm.

He had no desire to fight in Vietnam, and his father, once a commando in Borneo, was angry his son had been chosen by a lottery. 'I took a lot of aggression to Vietnam,' said English, 'because I didn't want to be there. I was always number two on the machine gun. I carried a lot of bullets: my whole idea was if I'm gonna go, I don't want to go without bullets; I want to kill as many of these bastards as I can. And it wasn't because they instilled the rage into me about these people: I had the rage that they'd sent me there.

'When someone's shooting at you, it doesn't make you frightened,' he said, 'it makes you very, very cranky: "How dare you shoot at me?" '

Balmoral was to be a fire support base without guns, put in place to invite the enemy to attack. Additional artillery was flown instead to Coral, to cover Balmoral. But the new FSB would also harness the power of the recently arrived Centurion tanks.

The Australians were determined not to repeat the chaos of the fly-in at Coral, so D Company 3RAR were sent in first, on foot, to the area where the base was to be built. Early in the morning of 24 May, said Norm Peatling, commanding Twelve Platoon, 'We tied pull-through cloth to the back of each man, walked in single file in the darkest, dirtiest, blackest night of all on a compass reading to the area we were supposed to go to. It was like walking up Bourke Street. There were Charlie everywhere. I reckon we had eight contacts, but we certainly had six contacts before light. As light came across, we ran into a bunker system.' They cleared some of the bunkers but they couldn't do much because they had to get to Balmoral.

Ken Myers, a machine-gun number two with Twelve Platoon, was a plumber from Dromana, Victoria. 'When we pulled up,' he said, 'there was this huge bloody clearing in front of us, like a massive football oval. And there was two big B-52 craters, one out in front of Eleven Platoon, who were hidden in the trees. Ten Platoon were in a bit of cover, but Twelve Platoon were stuck out in this bloody flattened area, because my gun pit – our fighting pit – was right next door to a huge B-52 crater. But right out to our right flank, a fair way from the wire, there was a bomb crater that had water in it – they'd hit a spring – and when we were setting up the star pickets and putting up all the concertina wire, we were having dips in the bloody water.'

B Company arrived a little after D Company. Peatling dug in and watched the rest of the battalion carried in by US helicopters. They were dropped in the open area the men remembered as 'the football oval', and the aircraft 'showed us a massive amount of American firepower', said Peatling. 'They came in with gunships, firstly using all their mini-guns, all the rockets, all the M79 automatic launchers, and they dropped a massive white smokescreen in front of that vegetation, and the battalion was virtually on the ground before the smoke cleared.'

Peatling was worried Twelve Platoon was too exposed. He knew the lines had been breached at Coral, so he tried to get his defences in place as quickly as possible. 'I got at least triple concertina wire out and maybe a bit of apron before night fell,' he said, 'but I concentrated on barbed wire because I hated my position.'

Myers at the machine gun dug in deep. 'The pit was probably up to our chest,' he said. 'I was a plumber, I could dig. I had that pit dug before anyone else. The next day we dug overhead cover, our shell scrapes became like a grave, and we put star pickets and sandbags over the top, so we had about a two-foot-square hole. You'd go down and you'd lie in there and look up at the stars.'

Peatling was surrounded by old friends at Balmoral. He had two high-school classmates, including his closest schoolmate, in other platoons of D Company, and his best friend in civilian life was Peter Clark, his radio operator. He'd met Clark at work. 'We were the closest mates you could imagine before we went into the army,' said Peatling. 'He did the same job as me. We were good drinking buddies, we chased the sheilas together. We got called up on the same day, went to Puckapunyal; I never saw him again for six months.' Peatling had known Clark was in 3RAR when he was posted to the battalion, but had no idea he might graduate from a signallers course into Twelve Platoon. 'And he walked a pace behind me for nine months,' said Peatling, 'and I had to show absolutely no level of favouritism at all to him, the poor bastard.'

A platoon favourite was Johnny Desnoy – 'a terrific little bloke', said Peatling. 'He was no taller than me, he had a six-pack stomach and he looked like a little body builder. He was just a lovely fella. He had a wispy little moustache – and he loved motorbikes.'

On the morning of 26 May, 'Most of the blokes were lying on top of the ground because it was a very hot night,' said Peatling. 'I actually was lying on top of the ground myself for comfort. At about quarter to four, I heard *pop-pop-pop-pop-pop*. As I sat up, I saw a whole line of white light across the other side of the "football field". My initial thought was, That's not good, but what the fuck is it? Soon I found out that they were the primaries of the mortars they were firing at us.

'As a young man who'd never been mortared before,' said Peatling, 'your first inclination is to get into your pit quickly as you can and curl yourself up into a ball and hope one doesn't land in the pit with you. That was the frightening part to me. You were just lying there, exposed and playing roulette with your life. Is one going to land in yours, or is one going to land next to you, or is it going to go to some poor other bugger, or are we going to all be lucky?' The poor bugger turned out to be Johnny Desnoy. A mortar entered his pit and killed him instantly. After the mortars came 'a massive amount of firepower', said Peatling, 'RPGs, RPG-7s, heavy machine guns, light machine guns, small-arms fire . . . That machine gun at the front was under massive pressure.'

'They were just coming at us from bloody everywhere,' said Myers, in the gun pit with his number one, national serviceman Mal Deveson. 'They were right on the wire, and the wire would've been thirty metres from our gun pit. But we had Claymores in front of the wire, and the Claymores didn't work, because the mortars had hit the Claymores. So your first defence had gone.'

The M60 loosed more than five thousand rounds from its two barrels, 'because these pricks were trying to knock us out of this gun pit, firing rockets at us and Christ knows what', said Myers. A live round jammed in one of the machine-gun barrels, then the second barrel malfunctioned and had to be fixed. 'The ammunition, after three weeks out in the bush, gets a bit bloody dirty, so it stuffs it up. We got new ammo brought down by our staff sergeant and sergeant and our medic – fair dinkum, they were bloody heroes.'

Dave Hodder, another national serviceman, was in the gun pit too, and he'd modified his SLR to fire on automatic, so while the machine gunners tried to repair their M60, they had Hodder's rifle firing like a machine gun, and they pulled M60 rounds off the machine-gun links to feed the SLR.

The US gunships came in, and the artillery fire from Coral, and the NVA eventually broke off their attack. 'My knees knocked so much, the next morning I could hardly frigging walk,' said Myers. But the NVA 'got a decent whacking, because the next morning when we did the clearing patrol there was a foot sticking out of a hole, or an arm, and drag marks everywhere.'

On 27 May, a bulldozer was flown in from Coral to build bunds of earth in front of the tanks' night position, to give them added protection. When the NVA attacked again the next night, 'They opened mortars from the same position,' said Peatling, 'and they opened fire on Delta Company from the same position, but this time they went around to the north-east and attacked Eleven Platoon. On both occasions when they opened the ground attack, they created a diversion or feint towards the south, against Alpha Company. I think on one occasion they broke their wire but didn't exploit it. They also mortared Coral, to try to keep their artillery silent in support of us.'

'Twelve Platoon was sitting right out at the front,' said Myers. 'We were switched on, with clean ammo. I was still shitting myself, but my knees weren't rattling.' The tanks opened up from the start of battle, using white phosphorous tips on their fifty-calibre shells, setting enemy soldiers alight on impact. 'These poor bastards, if they got hit, they were running into what water was left,' said Myers, 'because they would be on fire.'

Doug English had a fighting pit with Dave Cripps. 'The tanks were using high explosives,' said English. The four Centurions fired canister shells, each of which contained 800 ball bearings with the capacity to clear out jungle to a distance of 100 metres. 'That really slowed them down,' said Cripps.

'We were in our slit trenches,' said English, 'firing at ground level, just at flashes out in the darkness. That was all you could do. You couldn't see anybody.' The enemy 'got close to one perimeter. They got on the wire, and the machine gunners around there shot them off the wire, killed them all, and we couldn't see anything at all.' The tanks breached the wire first, and again exchanged fire with the NVA, before silencing the battlefield with machine guns, personal weapons and canister shells. Then, said English, 'They volunteered five people – I was one of them – to go and see who was out there. That's when you get a bit twitchy. I had to walk out of our area and walk around and come in another area. When you go out and see what I saw, it'd blow your mind: not only bits and pieces of bodies, but they'd got bodies and they'd piled them up, like a wall.'

'We had some of the most grotesque and horrendous sights in front of us,' said Peatling. 'There were forty-two bodies there, but there were bits and pieces of human beings, and human steaks and heads and things all over the place.'

'They got in the engineers,' said English, 'and they had this little bulldozer we'd choppered in before the battle. It got all the bodies and pushed them over into a massive B-52 bomber strike hole, and filled it to the top.'

Five Australians were killed and many more wounded at Balmoral. Up to three hundred enemy were thought to have been slaughtered. Judged by the yardsticks of ball games, the battles were victories, but every Australian soldier was glad to leave the FSB in the first week of June. 'We were one of the last platoons out,' said Peatling. 'The Chinook came down and dropped its ramp and twenty-six or twenty-seven blokes never hit the ramp so quickly in their lives. They were pretty bloody keen to get out of there.'

Peatling came home in August. Within a month of his return, he and Clark visited Desnoy's family in Elsternwick. 'They were absolutely devastated,' said Peatling. 'It was the most uncomfortable hour. It's very hard for a young man of twenty-two years of age to know what to say to a mother and father and siblings. The fact is that he was dead and he died quickly, but that didn't really help matters much. He wouldn't have known what hit him. We tried to at least put in front of his family that he was a highly valued and loved person in the company, in the battalion, and in our platoon particularly. And hopefully we got the message across – but who knows?'

When Doug English returned to Nui Dat, he shared a tent with Cripps and Evans. On the base, the battalion kept memento mori harvested from the killing fields. 'They'd got some skulls from Long Tan,' said English. 'They went through the area of Long Tan, and the skulls had come out of the ground. When you're in a war zone like this, you've got to find some very strange senses of humour, otherwise you'd go fucking nuts, so they brought two skulls back and we had one as a night-light. It's a skull in a little box, and we put a signal battery behind him and got someone to get a ping-pong ball and we cut it in half and stuck them in his eyes and put veins in the eyes and little lights behind his eyes. And he used to have the old KB gold can with him there too, and he was our night-light to the boozer. You could look along this dirt road and you could see his little light glowing way down the end, late at night when there was no moon. And the barber had [another skull] with a toupee painted on the top of it. I've got one of the skulls with crazy-looking eyes tattooed on my arm, and it says "Bony Fide Members of 4 Platoon". Everyone else was going to get one. I'm the only sucker with one.'

After Balmoral, 3RAR reverted to a war of patrols, trying to find the enemy in order to fight them. English spent the rest of 1968 marinating in sweat, chopping through strange country in search of men who knew every cave and clearing, every hill and stream. On patrol, said English, 'We worked guerrilla tactics. If we saw a trail, we'd ambush it at night-time, but we wouldn't walk up a bloody trail and get ourselves blown up or trip-wired, or come into a gun pit. We'd cut across trails, and the forward scout would use a pair of secateurs to cut holes through the bamboo so he didn't make any noise. Sometimes we'd do a mile from sun-up to sundown, dragging ourselves through bamboo.'

In the areas English patrolled, 'everything was meat', he said. 'In other words, it was a kill zone. We didn't go in where there was civvies, you weren't around a town – unless you did a cordon and search – and we never killed anybody that didn't have a weapon. And we never said, "Hello, can you put your hands up?"

'You'd see a couple of people sitting over there, and very quietly you'd say, "Okay, bring the first platoon up." And the first platoon would line up, with the machine gunner there, and the machine gunner would say "fire" on the gun, everyone would sight up on these people, and as soon as the machine gun would start firing, every [man] and his dog would shoot them. A lot of the time, you saw nobody, and it was very boring, very mundane and very frustrating, because you were pumped up. Adrenalin's the biggest drug in the world and when you come back home to civvy street, you can't get that high any more. And that high is just staying alive. I can understand why a lot of people either neck themselves or get on the juice or on drugs, trying to find that high again.'

Most of 3RAR went back to Australia in early November 1968, but English and others stayed in country until their replacement company arrived. 'We were holding fort,' he said. 'We didn't have to go out in the bush if we didn't want to. I still had a bit of time to go, so I was there to basically show the company that took over how everything worked. They sent over a small force to start with, and we had these guys really stuffed in the end, because we were so slack, because we'd finished our time, and they wanted us to go out and show them what goes on in the bush. 'I said, "No, I'm not going out again, that's it. I don't have to go out and I'm not." '

Another member of the 3RAR rear party, Lance Corporal Anthony Quigley, a national serviceman from Adelaide, went out for a night recce on 5 November, sleeping outside the wire. 'He had ten days to go home,' said English, 'and they killed him. They shot him out the front.'

24

OBJECTION OVERRULED

From the start, the government had refused to allow a man to conscientiously object to a single war. While it accepted he could be a pacifist who would not bear arms against another person, it couldn't accede to a citizen the right to decide who he was prepared to fight. If a man was willing to defend Australia, then he must also be ready to go to Vietnam. Within the logic of government policy, Australia was actually fighting a defensive war in Vietnam, preventing the southward spread of Communism which, unchecked, would reach Australia. And even if this argument were rejected, the simple act of keeping the US in South-East Asia would help make Australia secure. To the government, it wasn't a conscientious act to oppose the war in Vietnam; it was, at best, second-guessing the defence policy of a democratically elected administration and, at worst, making a hateful moral judgement on ministers who were all honourable men. It was a blood libel, a slander against a just war.

Dennis O'Donnell was among the first national servicemen to say he would defend Australia if his country were attacked – but he was not willing to play any part in an army that was at war in Vietnam. O'Donnell, the son of a tax agent, grew up in Brunswick, Victoria, and was schooled by the Christian Brothers. 'Boys who'd been to the Christian Brothers handled the army very easily,' he said, 'because the Christian Brothers were much tougher than the army. And less predictable.' He left school early to get away from 'all the crazy, violent brothers', had 'one wonderful year' at a normal high school, then joined the tax office. 'There was actually no work in the taxation office then,' he said. 'You had five people doing the job of one person.' So he and a group of friends sat around a table for a couple of years doing their matriculation together, as if they were being paid to study. 'It was sort of like being on a scholarship,' he said.

His birthday was drawn from the barrel, and he went into the army in Puckapunyal in February 1967. He had misgivings about Vietnam – 'I kind of knew it was rubbish,' he said – but was ready to play along with soldiering. He thought it would just be like another two years of Christian Brothers. O'Donnell was fit, a distance cyclist, and he'd been in school cadets, so the work didn't bother him, although he heard other boys in the barracks crying at night. He put in for officer training, primarily to get out of the grinding Puckapunyal routine, but failed to get into Scheyville. 'I don't think I had leadership qualities,' he said. 'I've always been more of a subversive influence, a bit of a malcontent.'

O'Donnell said most recruits believed service in Vietnam was more or less voluntary unless they went into a combat arm, so he put in for the Australian Army Catering Corps, and completed his training in Broadmeadows, just north of Melbourne. He enjoyed it, and lived at home most of the time. But O'Donnell was part of a group of young people who were fascinated by rock'n'roll and everything American, and he came across radical ideas about the Vietnam War in imported US magazines bought from a Collins Street bookstore. It was an edition of the Californian publication *Ramparts* which changed O'Donnell's life. *Ramparts* was a militant, campaigning journal with Catholic roots, whose January 1967 edition featured a long, heavily illustrated and horrible story entitled 'The Children of Vietnam', which talked of village infants melted by the American weapons of napalm petroleum jelly and white phosphorous. 'Torn flesh, splintered bones, screaming agony are bad enough,' wrote correspondent William Pepper. 'But perhaps most heart-rending of all are the tiny faces and bodies scorched and seared by fire . . . The initial urge to reach out and soothe the hurt was restrained by the fear that the ash-like skin would crumble in my fingers.'[1]

Much of the story also described terrible conditions in South Vietnamese hospitals, and at least one of the pictures apparently showed victims of a Viet Cong attack rather than a napalm shower, allowing BA Santamaria's pro-war National Civic Council to brand the idea of children burned by sticky fire as 'the napalm hoax'. For O'Donnell, however, the words were enough, and he resolved to have no part in this war, where the victims seemed mainly civilians and the civilians largely women and children.

'I was just in an agitated state,' he said. 'I didn't know what to do. And my girlfriend saw an ad in the paper that said "Conscientious Objectors (Non-Pacifist)". There was a meeting on. She said, "That sounds like you." So I went, and it was almost like a recruitment meeting where, I realised later, they were looking for someone who was going to be the person who was going to be the cause. And I got the job.'

In the room was Jean McLean, convener of the Save Our Sons movement, along with several other SOS supporters. Much of the opposition to the war 'was really organised and run by women', said O'Donnell. 'Even the person who organised me was my girlfriend.'

O'Donnell met a 'very bright young lawyer', John Little, whom he believed was a member of the Communist Party of Australia (Marxist–Leninist), the pro-China faction that had split from the more Soviet-oriented CPA. O'Donnell felt Little was 'in many ways too clever by half for a lot of magistrates and judges; he was always putting radical, unacceptable positions to the judges. 'He'd say things like, "Of course, Dennis, you do realise you're going to be tortured, don't you?" That was all I needed.'

Little helped O'Donnell prepare an application for conscientious-objector status. There would have to be a court case and the verdict Conscientious Objectors (Non-Pacifist) wanted would exempt a non-pacifist from serving in the army based on an objection to a particular war. Only a judge could rule on this, but O'Donnell had to first face a magistrate. 'The thing I didn't really know was, basically the idea was: I was not to win my first case,' said O'Donnell. 'I realised later – I felt a bit used, later – that they knew it was useless for me to win a case with a magistrate.'

When O'Donnell's brother, a priest, heard he planned to be a conscientious objector, he suggested he first speak to his friend, Santamaria of the NCC. 'Bob Santamaria was the kind of person I actually liked watching on TV,' said O'Donnell, 'a fantastic presenter and very clever; I always liked him, even though he was really right-wing; he was just so good, the way he did it. Out of curiosity, I went and met him, and we had a long conversation about causation. It was an old Catholic argument that relates to how they treat abortion: that it's okay if the baby or the foetus dies if your aim is to save the mother's life; similarly, in war, if your aim is to free some people and other people get killed, that's permissible too. We talked about the idea of a just war, and Santamaria was incredibly charming and wonderful . . . I came away from it almost convinced.'

After corps training, O'Donnell had been posted to the hospital at the army base at Watsonia, Victoria. Instead of going to the catering office, he went in to see the staff sergeant, and handed him a declaration that he was a conscientious objector and would no longer work in the army. The sergeant was baffled. O'Donnell, in Watsonia, was objecting to the war in Vietnam, in which he wasn't being asked to fight. O'Donnell next went in front of the commanding officer at Watsonia. 'The army kept saying, "As far as we're concerned, you're a non-combatant anyway,"' said O'Donnell. "All you've got to do is cook in the hospital; what's your problem?" He was told he wouldn't have to serve in Vietnam. 'I said, "I don't care if I don't have to go,"' said O'Donnell, '"I'm not working in the army any more."' The CO asked O'Donnell if he objected to helping people in hospital. 'Straight from that moment,' said O'Donnell, 'my every action was questioned morally [but] I'd already become part of a collective movement, rather than a fairly confused individual.'

O'Donnell went AWOL while his application for exemption was lodged, but turned up at the City Court, Melbourne, on 7 September, represented by John Winneke, a lawyer unearthed by Conscientious Objectors (Non-Pacifist). 'I was set up really terribly,' said O'Donnell. 'The day before my hearing, I didn't even have a barrister, and I was absolutely shitting myself. I actually fronted up to court having not even met [Winneke], and he stood up in the courtroom and introduced me by saying, "Your Honour, my client is a deserter from the Australian Army."'

O'Donnell told the court that as long as he was a national serviceman, he felt he was a symbol of the government's policy in Vietnam. 'The N.L.F. and the North Vietnamese people have justice on their side in the Vietnam War. If Australia and America were going to interfere in the war they should have intervened on the side of the N.L.F.'[2] The magistrate dismissed O'Donnell's application. And in November, O'Donnell lost his appeal to the County Count. The judge conceded it was possible to be a conscientious objector to a particular war, and that O'Donnell fell into that category, but that didn't entitle him to exemption under the National Service Act, so O'Donnell went AWOL again, on 23 November 1967.

He moved from house to house in Melbourne, and met Alwyn Henderson and radical students from Monash and Melbourne universities. 'I was really scared,' he said, 'because we were alienated and isolated. We were a very small minority with mainly Communist Party people, really, supporting us. As far as I was concerned, good on 'em. I'd be quite happy to be described as a "fellow traveller". I probably would've joined one day but I never did.' He met people who showed him another way to think and live. 'I'm really grateful for all that happening,' he said, 'in one way. Although the school of hard knocks is possibly not the best school. But it transformed my life, so that decision to object I've never, ever had second thoughts about it.

'For a while,' said O'Donnell, 'the government had a strategy of not touching me. Then they decided to pick me up, and I wasn't taking precautions by that stage, because I thought they wouldn't be looking for me. But they arrested me in Collins Street, right outside that bookshop where I bought the copy of *Ramparts*. I was dropping my girlfriend off. They dragged me out of my car.'

O'Donnell was arrested by military police on 26 March 1968. He was detained at Puckapunyal, where he encountered Desmond Phillipson, a former clerk with the Department of Army, who'd been called up for national service in February and applied for exemption a few weeks into recruit training. O'Donnell became aware of Phillipson when he was carried past O'Donnell's cell, ignoring his guards' orders to march. The two men talked through the cell walls. 'And Des felt I was almost complicit in the war,' said O'Donnell, 'because I wasn't lying down and refusing to move. He had a very extreme position.'

On Thursday 28 March, O'Donnell wrote home from his cell, 'I am being treated like a pig, not by direct action but by a systematic psychological brain scrambling exercise. On Tuesday I was wisked [sic] straight to Puckapunyal and placed in a base cell without a light. My shoes were taken from me and I was simply left alone and isolated, except for the sounds of a Nasho in a cell next to me sobbing from the effects of his confinement and a hunger strike which he had sustained for 4 days . . . Occasionally a guard came out and hurled the vilest abuse at him for not co-operating.'

Later in the day, he wrote another letter, saying, 'I have come closer to ramming my head against a wall than ever before . . . The corporal in charge posted a guard with a bayonet at the back door, one just inside and one near my window. He pushed a plate of mashed potato, hot mince and tomatoes under the bars and said, "sorry no utensils". I went hysterical . . . I want to record this moment before the intense bitterness of it is forgotten.'[3]

At the court martial on 4 April, O'Donnell was represented by John Little. He pleaded not guilty to the charge of going AWOL, as he felt a judge had agreed he was a genuine conscientious objector, and therefore he wasn't legitimately in the army. The army, finding no evidence O'Donnell had been discharged, proceeded with the prosecution anyway, and sentenced him to forty-eight days' detention at the Military Corrective Establishment at Holsworthy. O'Donnell lost his appeal for a writ of habeas corpus before the High Court of Australia, and finally had his appeal against the rejection of his application for exemption from military service dismissed by the Privy Council in London, which was then the highest court of appeal available to an Australian citizen, and which ordered costs against him. 'Losing the case was really bad,' said O'Donnell, 'because that meant a precedent was created whereby you *couldn't* get exemption.

'Holsworthy was pretty tough,' he said, 'but, again, not as bad as Christian Brothers. You had to run everywhere, all the time. Even when you were talking to the staff, you had to run on the spot with your hands on your chest. It was humiliating, mainly. They beat up a lot of people there, but by that time I was all over the newspapers so I was protected, to an extent. I probably could've done whatever I liked.

'I saw them do something terrible to Des Phillipson. His initiation, if you like, into Holsworthy, because he was non-complier, was to be taken to this compound and it was explained that he hadn't had a bath or a shower for three weeks, and this is how we clean people who needed a bath. So they turned a fire hose on him and hosed him across the compound while we watched.'

Students held a round-the-clock vigil for O'Donnell in Post Office Place, Melbourne, and twenty-one people were arrested at a demonstration outside Holsworthy calling for his release. On 10 May, he was let out of jail early and posted to Canungra, as a cook, 'which was the most provocative thing that could've happened', he said, 'sending me to work at the main training camp for Vietnam. So I went AWOL immediately again. I hitched a ride to Melbourne with some guys who were on leave – of course, not realising ASIO were watching me all the time.' But the army wasn't trying to provoke O'Donnell. It had always intended to send him to Canungra after Watsonia, and was carrying on as if the matter had been settled.

O'Donnell didn't know what to do now that every line of appeal had failed. He spoke with a number of people, including Jim Cairns, while he tried to decide how to proceed. But while O'Donnell was driving back up from Victoria to Queensland, Cairns told parliament a transcript of a conversation he'd had with O'Donnell in Holsworthy had been handed to him by a member of the Liberal government. When the attorney-general denied O'Donnell was being watched and bugged, Cairns said the only other person who could've prepared the transcript was O'Donnell himself. This led to speculation O'Donnell might be a spy for ASIO. 'Suddenly, I was a suspect,' said O'Donnell. 'So I had a really bad breakdown. Everything just went completely wrong. I was really paranoid and really upset with Cairns, and I was being interviewed by a whole lot of officers, and I just broke down and started crying.' O'Donnell asked Cairns who had provided the transcript, but Cairns wouldn't say. 'That annoyed me about Cairns too,' said O'Donnell. 'You're pretending we're in this together but you won't tell me your source, as though I'm a bloody newspaper reporter.'

A couple of weeks after O'Donnell's breakdown, Colonel Edwin Griff of the army's Northern Command called him to ask if he could do anything to help. 'This guy had a real charisma,' said O'Donnell. 'Even though I could do something that was radically individualistic, I was a sucker for a mentor and a guide. And I liked this guy. I believed he genuinely wanted to look after me.' Griff offered O'Donnell a posting that was still in the army but essentially working for the

Department of Defence in family welfare. 'I gave in, I guess, at that point,' said O'Donnell. 'A couple of days later, he called me and said, "I'm really sorry, but the CO in charge of that section won't have you. A lot of people won't have you. I've found one bloke, Colonel Wilson, the only bloke in the Northern Command meeting who'd have you in his unit – the school cadets."'

So O'Donnell saw out his national service in 1 Cadet Brigade in Brisbane. He didn't have to wear a uniform. 'I played darts all day,' he said. 'They would enter me into the inter-unit darts competition, which they were keen on.' He was allowed to take part in political activities and demonstrations, but told he couldn't be a leader. Instead, he helped to plan and organise protests, and collect bail money for arrested demonstrators. He spent a year nominally working for the cadets in Queensland, although his commanding officer allowed him to enrol at La Trobe University and begin a degree course in Victoria. But he had to make up all the time he had spent AWOL, so he didn't get out of the army until the middle of 1969.

O'Donnell's case received heavy media coverage. Although he never believed he was wrong to protest the war, 'I felt constantly that pressure that I'd let down the team,' he said, 'and I wasn't part of the group of young blokes [in the army] who were – temporarily at least – my friends. They didn't make it hard for me, though, because no one ever called me out on it. But I did still feel that there were people actually fighting in Vietnam and they were reading about people like me, and it must've been bad for their morale, and I actually hated that. I would've loved to have somehow made it a process they didn't have to read about. Because it was never about opposition to those guys.'

Des Phillipson also had his application for conscientious-objector status and his subsequent appeal dismissed, but was medically discharged before his second application was heard in December 1968. He alleged he had been mistreated in Holsworthy: dragged seventy-five yards along a road when he refused to march, had his hair pulled, his arms twisted, and a pin stuck into his shoulder when he was lying on the ground. The pin and how it had been used became a subject of much debate, with an army investigation finding 'no evidence that pins had been stuck into Phillipson but a pin had been held between Phillipson and a wall' and 'Phillipson had been slouching back on to the wall'.[4]

It's impossible to gauge what effect a single incident might have had on public opinion. But in October 1968, after the Tet Offensive, the water-torture reports, the battles of Coral and Balmoral, and the cases of O'Donnell and Phillipson and other high-profile objectors – such as journalist Simon Townsend, who refused to answer his call-up notice, and postman John Zarb, who became the first man imprisoned in a civilian jail for non-compliance – some people at home were growing weary of the war. When, for the first time in seventeen months, a Gallup poll asked if 'we should continue to fight in Vietnam', only 54 per cent of respondents said yes, down from 62 per cent in May 1967. When the question was posed again in December, the numbers in favour fell below 50 per cent for the first time. But the 49 per cent who wanted to keep fighting still strongly outnumbered the 37 per cent who hoped to bring the troops home; 14 per cent of the Australian people remained undecided.[5]

Demonstrations against conscription and the war, although still small, were growing in size and militancy. But the general tone of popular press coverage of national service remained jaunty, even celebratory. On 29 January 1969, the Melbourne *Herald* published a large photograph of a young man sitting on the shoulders of his friends while drinking champagne. Under the headline 'Beer, tucker, then off to Pucka' was a story which began, 'It was like Melbourne Cup Day outside the Swan St. Army barracks in Richmond today. Champagne corks popped and chickens were carved and eaten on the lawns and sports grounds opposite. The 15th National Service intake was a whale of a party.'[6] At seven a.m., the Hawthorn Rowing Club drank breakfast champagne with cornflakes soaked in beer to farewell rower Philip Murphy, a commerce graduate. When the gates opened, they carried Murphy into the army, feet first like a corpse. Other men turned up with their mates, swinging packs of stubbies or cans of beer. It was all a bit of a lark, really.

The media reflected the public mood. Refusal to serve was far less popular than the fighting in Vietnam. The next day came the results of a Gallup poll showing only 28 per cent of those surveyed believed a young man should be exempted from military service on the grounds of objection to a particular war. The results were the same among men and women and in every age group, from those in their twenties to the over-seventies.

A feeling has grown up in the years since the Vietnam War that most ordinary Australians held a deeply felt opinion on the conflict, or cared at all. There is an idea that there was a starkly delineated ideological divide, and people had to choose one side or the other. In fact, many were entirely unaffected – personally, emotionally or intellectually – by the war and even those national servicemen who deplored being in the army did not necessarily reject everything about it.

When reluctant conscript Sean Cullip finished his national service in 1968, it took more than a year for Sean and Sonja to find their first club gig. Finally, said Cullip, 'Noeleen Batley went sick', leaving a gap at the Dapto Leagues Club in New South Wales. Once they began to play again, they signed with a new agent and re-established themselves as a live act. 'We did television shows,' said Cullip. 'We ended up on *Bandstand* again. But folk music had died out.' The duo's time had come and gone, while Cullip had been working on consignment receipt sheets, or filling in the cryptic crossword with Mrs Geoghegan. But during the long, dry period before their Dapto Leagues comeback, Sean and Sonja had been approached by the Australian Forces Overseas Fund (AFOF) about going to Vietnam to entertain the troops. The people from the AFOF knew Cullip had been in the army, 'and they thought it would be good for me to see it first hand', he said, 'albeit being protected by the army rather than protecting somebody else'.

His first response was, '*Ergh*. But then I thought, It's not as if I have to carry a rifle,' he said. 'So I said, "Okay."' Sean and Sonja travelled to Vietnam in December 1968, as part of a small concert party, with comedian Johnny Holmes as compere. They toured for sixteen days, playing a circuit of Australian and US bases. On Christmas Day, they performed at Nui Dat, with the diggers pressing to the front of the stage to get a view of Tallis's legs.

'She had a very good body – a tiny waist, good hips, very well presented in the breasts – and this skin-tight mini-dress,' said Cullip. 'And she looked absolutely fabulous. And, of course, all these guys were going ape over her. To hell with me. You'd do a show at ten o'clock in the morning, and these guys would come up with a beer and say, "Have a beer with us," and you couldn't refuse. And then they'd take Sonja off with them somewhere. And she'd come back and say, "I didn't want to drink that bloody beer." While Sean and Sonja had lost much of their audience in Australia, 'these guys wanted to see us', said Cullip. 'They wanted to talk to us. They wanted to share a beer. Albeit at ten o'clock in the morning. What we heard most of all was, "Thank you for coming."'

In the end, even Cullip, who feared and disliked the army so much he'd gone to court to try to avoid it, had few burning convictions, and the exclusion from history of lightly committed Australians who just wanted to get on with their lives has contributed to a distorted picture of a polarised nation. Cullip didn't feel that entertaining the troops was endorsing the war. 'I never thought about that,' he said. He didn't even follow the progress of the war 'because it was happening to other people elsewhere', he said. 'I think my main concern was how we were doing with our work in Australia. Were we singing the right songs? Where would we get the next job? How much would we be paid?

25

THE INTELLIGENCE TEST

Although the majority of national servicemen were posted to infantry battalions, there was always a scattering of conscripts in the army's more rarefied corps, some of whose functions were a mystery even to long-serving regular soldiers. The most enigmatic of all was the Australian Army Intelligence Corps. Many national servicemen mistook the name of the corps for a description of its manpower requirements, and asked for a posting to Intelligence because they believed themselves clever. Few were chosen, particularly in the early years. But those who found their way in tended to have a singular time in a corps which, in the words of national serviceman Jeremy Packington, 'attracted an unusual selection of people' even before the conscripts came.

Packington, Brian Timberlake and Michael Phoenix were all posted to Intelligence after their recruit training in 1967, and all served in South Vietnam between 1968 and 1969. Packington was a British-born law student who lived in Perth and had failed the third year of his degree and lost his deferment. Timberlake had left school in Victoria at seventeen years old, to work for a pharmaceuticals wholesaler. Phoenix was a South Australian butcher's son who had dropped out of an Arts/Law degree. They all went to corps training at the Army Intelligence Centre at Middle Head – 'a magic old place', said Timberlake, where nineteenth-century fortifications and gun pits looked out between the lush pincers of the heads of Sydney Harbour.

The national servicemen were made to feel 'like part of a little family', said Packington. They were amazed to be personally welcomed by the officer commanding and chief instructor of the School of Army Intelligence, EJ 'Ted' Mulholland, whom Phoenix remembered as 'one of nature's true gentleman . . . sitting on the corner of his desk, puffing his pipe'. Timberlake said, 'The people in the hierarchy were fairly attuned to the fact that they were dealing with people who may not even want to be there, and perhaps didn't put the pressure on that you might've got in other corps.'

'A lot of their old training aids were hopeless,' said Phoenix, 'MI5 stuff from 1938.' Packington said, 'We spent a lot of time looking at aerial photographs through stereographs; we spent a lot of time trying to learn to type.'

In November 1967, everyone at the centre was required to help run one of the periodic Code of Conduct exercises held within the ruined fortifications to the east of the intelligence centre, on the headland where canons once ranged out to sea. 'It was like Colditz,' said Phoenix. 'You'd go down all these steps and it was just cold concrete. There'd be blocks of sandstone dripping water and mould everywhere. You'd have to be careful which door you'd open because there'd be one step, then there used to be a rope ladder or something leading down. One false step and you'd end up on the rocks.' Code of Conduct was counter-interrogation training for SAS troopers, fighter pilots and others who might fall into enemy hands. Servicemen were given no warning of what was going to happen. They were told they would be taking part in an Intelligence course and simply invited for a chat with the commanding officer. 'We'd be in a lecture room with double barn doors on one side and one at the back,' said Phoenix. 'Dear old Ted would be sitting at the corner of his table and say, "Oh, gentlemen, just be prepared for what's going on." And these doors would fly open and there were people with balaclavas and smoke grenades going inside: we were the staff, all dressed up in these grey uniforms.' The surprised course members were taken prisoner, 'hooded and bundled out, driven all around Mosman at one hundred miles an hour, called "capitalist running dogs" then returned to the place where they'd started, and locked in tiny cells in the Middle Head fort', said Phoenix. They were regularly given mock interrogations. 'Every time they got out, it'd be, "Put your hoods on. Get out of your little cage, and stand there!" "Before you go anywhere, comrade, can you remember the third principle of Communism?" '

'A bit of bastardry went on,' said Timberlake, 'because we knew they were officers. It was made to look realistic, which it wasn't. They were fed a bit of shitty soup and, outside some guy's cell, someone would fill the ladle up and say to someone else, "I feel like a piss," and they tip the soup out of the ladle like they were pissing in his soup before they fed him.'

'They'd take them to a little ammunition hut,' said Phoenix, 'and then hit them with loud music for ten minutes or so. Then they'd be taken out down to the interrogation room, where there was a bank of photographic lights, and the guys already had old army battledress on, so it was steamy. After a couple of days: Phwoar!'

The men on the course were supposed to hold out for three days. Some tried to escape, but none succeeded. Packington said, 'The idea was for the people undergoing the course to give some information to prevent themselves getting killed or really badly injured, but as little information as possible. So they were all interrogated repeatedly, and if they weren't forthcoming with some sort of information, they were awarded notional broken arms or legs.' After a while, said Phoenix, 'Everybody got into the fact that it wasn't real. Once they realised that your punishment is just a little card saying, "Prisoner 123 has had both hands broken," they realised it was an exercise.'

Although the corps may have been a bit rough on paper with its 'captives', it treated its own troops with unmilitary affection. Phoenix turned twenty-one during the Code of Conduct course at Middle Head. 'I was escorting a prisoner and was told, "Comrade, Comrade Wust wants to see you. Come back to the main headquarters." I walked into this bare bunker room, and there were all my comrades dressed in grey uniforms with a star on, and a bloody birthday cake. Captain Wust had come from Germany after the war. He had a strong German accent: "Good morning, Corporal Phoenix! Happy birthday!"

'In the last part of 1967, we were tied up with our training,' said Phoenix. 'After that, they let us loose. I ended up in the graphics section, where they kept all the maps.' Photocopying, which was to become a theme of Phoenix's service, was rudimentary. 'There might've been one [Thermo-Fax] photocopier in the whole unit,' he said. 'You'd put the original on top of a piece of paper and you'd hope that when flames came down, your original wasn't burned.'

Around Christmas, the Army Intelligence Centre moved to Woodside, SA, which was 'a desolate army camp, much like Puckapunyal', said Timberlake. At Middle Head, there had been 'a whole lot of strange people who weren't soldiers', said Packington, 'who were civilian workers attached to the mess, I think – cleaners and things – single, older men, and they all enjoyed a drink, and they all got taken off to Woodside. Obviously the colonel regarded them as part of the establishment, and they sort of lived in.' Max, the unit's Alsatian mascot, moved with them too.

The tone of preparations changed as the national servicemen came closer to deployment. 'By the time we were ready to go to Vietnam,' said Phoenix, 'there were warrant officers coming back saying, "Hey, fellas, we're training people for a cloak-and-dagger war in Europe in 1939, where this is a very, very different war. You get Thompson's book and read that. This is what it's all about."' British Army officer Robert Thompson's *Defeating Communist Insurgency: Experiences from Malaya and Vietnam* set out a detailed, methodical response to guerrilla warfare, emphasising the need to win the support of the people. His principles were often honoured in Vietnam, if only in the breach.

Phoenix was the first of the three national-service mates to leave Australia, posted to 1st Division Intelligence Unit in Nui Dat, in July 1968. There were other Intelligence people in Vung Tau and Saigon. They tried to work in rotation because at 1ALSG, Phoenix said, 'all they were doing was security checks on Vietnamese local labourers . . . We'd swap with people in Saigon, who were just handling paperwork and typing out reports and things like that.'

His first CO in the camp was Captain Geoff Boscoe. 'Geoff was a very cautious man,' said Phoenix. 'He said, "We've got to be careful out there, and keep our contacts out there." So we weren't aggressive and didn't go out and look for trouble, and do active searches and stir the possum. So morale was pretty low.'

In August, Major Jack L'Epagniol took over, and ordered them to change tactics. They started Acorn operations, in which they were expected to snatch and detain targeted Viet Cong suspects in the villages, then take them to the CIA's Provisional Interrogation Centre in Ba Ria which, said Phoenix, 'looked like a motel, with a pebble garden outside'. Acorn operations were aimed at the so-called Viet Cong Infrastructure (VCI), the political workers who organised local logistics and support for the guerrillas, and often acted as a shadow government – or the only government – in the villages.

The Australians did not generally question their prisoners. 'Our unit was tied to the water-torture incident,' said Phoenix. 'Until then, people used to be brought back to the Task Force, handed over to the Australian military police, who'd arrest them as a prisoner, then some of our blokes would go down and interrogate them. After [To Thi Nau], anybody you got out on the road, you didn't bring them near the Task Force.' But any intelligence was fed back to the Australians by the CIA.

'It was interesting,' said Phoenix, 'the interrogation reports saying, "The suspect was averse to giving information at the start. However, having been apprised of his situation" – in other words, when we put an electrode here and an electrode there – "he provided the following information . . . " ' Phoenix said the process continued until he returned home in June 1969. 'Our unit was more and more and more working for the CIA,' he said. When the Australians came across intelligence, 'it was a matter of, "Shall we tell Task Force headquarters?" "Yeah, all right." The CIA finally got us in, to drag us a little bit closer, because we couldn't get resources from Australia for our photocopier. To photocopy things in realistic quality, with this crappy bloody Thermo-Fax, you put an original through, and it'd likely have a burnout and have to be sent back to Australia.' The Americans offered to help. 'And we saw one of the first self-feed things,' said Phoenix, 'a massive great thing. It was state-of-the-art. If you had a stable sort of document, you could feed it through. But others would come out of the jungle in shreds, and we'd just have to lay it on a plate and photocopy it like that. A guy came from the Philippines and spent about a week with us, firing this thing up. The Task Force electrician didn't like us. We'd photocopy something and then suddenly the lights would go out in the Task Force – because the wiring was like a bloody twenty-first birthday party, with lights going in here and a bulb there; you'd go in the tents and there'd be a light bulb, and a double adaptor for three stereos and a fan.' The Americans were happy to share technology with their allies. 'They said, "No strings attached, buddy, but just get us a copy of everything you copy." It was a gradual shift. The photocopier was just part of it. Next thing, we'd be sending mounds of photocopied documents to the CIA. Somebody would be down the CIA mansion in the backstreets of Ba Ria every day. "Who're we working for? Them?"'

'I came to a love of the people and a love of the country,' said Phoenix. 'We'd be invited down to people's places – the local policemen and so on – for a little meal. It's spectacularly beautiful. You sit and look out at the green fields with the blue mountains in the background. The sadness was, you'd be dealing with somebody one day and you'd find out somebody'd come into the village and shot up their family at night. You'd deal with it unofficially.'

Phoenix felt fortunate he'd served in the field during his time in the army. 'I met one of the guys I went through jungle training with at

Canungra,' he said, 'and he was carrying drinks around on a tray for the officers' club at Vung Tau. It could be a dangerous job. You could get stabbed by a little umbrella.'

Packington and Timberlake received their Vietnam postings later in 1968. By then, they were aware of the anti-war movement back home, but the demonstrators were 'just ratbag uni students, as far as we were concerned', said Timberlake. 'The rest of the world seemed to be with us.' Both men began by working at Battle Intelligence at Nui Dat, collating information and marking maps, recording the points where enemy mines, ammunition caches and bunkers were found. They later went out to the various FSBs, where they performed similar roles, receiving information from Australian and allied units in contact with the enemy, and logging numbers, locations and casualties. The Intelligence officer would use their data in briefings to Task Force headquarters.

Timberlake remembered replacing Packington at the first fire-support base – probably FSB Julia – where one night 'the outer perimeter opened fire and we actually killed a child. I say "we"; I didn't fire a shot – there was a kid out in the swampland with people who shouldn't have been there. The next morning a patrol went out and there was this dead kid that they'd left. There were blood trails but no one else found. And I didn't quite understand at that time the concern that our linguist sergeant and the New Zealand captain had. I thought they were either enemy or they shouldn't have been there anyway.'

A party from the FSB went out to see the boy's family. 'They got in touch through the village chief,' said Timberlake, 'to try to say sorry, I guess, and suss out what the bloody hell they were doing there and whether they were up to no good. The linguist sergeant and the New Zealand captain came back a little bit affected that we'd killed a kid, and the effect on the family. It wasn't until many years later I looked at my own daughter, about fifteen . . . and that started to haunt me a little, that I didn't feel as I perhaps should have at that time, over the death of someone.'

26

NORMIE GOES TO WAR, MANY DON'T

For the Australian Army, the most significant event in the first half of 1969 was the Battle of Binh Ba. For the tabloid press, it was the fact that, on 14 January, Normie Rowe finally made it to Vietnam as a trooper with the 3rd Cavalry Regiment. Rowe's service record contains effusive training reports. He topped the driving, gunnery and signals courses. His signals instructor wrote, 'Tpr Rowe has consistently given his utmost during this course. His very keenness and enthusiasm were infectious not only amongst his own crew but amongst the course as a whole.'[1]

'I was incredibly diligent with learning as much as I possibly could about everything,' said Rowe. 'I just couldn't think of surviving myself if I'd caused somebody else to die.' As it turned out, in Vietnam, 'There was nothing I did that caused anybody else – perhaps even the enemy – any injury.'

Through training and beyond, the media were always in the background, tapping Rowe on the shoulder, whispering questions in his ear, treating him as a curio rather a person, with the most impudent of queries, things a reporter would never ask another soldier, such as how he felt about his chance of coming back alive. 'I wouldn't be game to go if I thought I was going to die,' replied Rowe, with his customary congenial optimism.[2] His remarkable propensity for being honest while struggling to say the right thing emerged again. 'I really enjoy the Army,' he said, 'and I think it's a great thing if you've got nothing better to do.' Even though he was an enthusiastic soldier, he admitted, 'I love entertaining and the entertainment business more . . . For a while there, I was getting to the stage of not knowing what to do – go AWL [sic] or quit show business completely. When I was in Pucka, I'd get just enough time to do one or two shows and get the taste of it and that was awful. Going AWL would be silly so I thought, Well, Vietnam is the only thing for me. I can get experience at something and finish it completely, which is something I've never done before.'[3]

On the eve of his departure for Vietnam, the *Daily Telegraph* published a piece entitled 'Normie Has His Doubts' in which Rowe revealed, 'I don't know whether to be frightened or not to care less . . . In the carriers it is not so much the bullets but the mines I will be afraid of.'[4] He told another journalist, 'At first I felt butterflies in my stomach and didn't really want to go. Then the excitement built up inside me and now all I'm doing is looking forward to arriving.' With resigned cheer, he said, 'I feel it is always good for an artist to get away from his audience for a while.' By now, Trooper Rowe was an APC driver-signaller. He knew he would be attached to the Task Force, and saw his job as being virtually 'a taxi, just to be on hand to help the infantry'.[5]

Rowe went out on his first operation the day after he reached Nui Dat. 'I was on a resupply at six o'clock into Fire Support Base Julia,' he said, 'into the [armoured] car and driving that afternoon, and we went out to this ambush site. I knew there were going to be dead bodies. I knew there were going to be some pretty shithouse periods of time. But to arrive in country the day after I was in civilian clothes and go out into the field and have to more or less clean up the results of a very successful ambush that had been executed on the Viet Cong . . . I don't think anybody can really be prepared for a thing like that. I'd seen dead animals, drowned dogs and cats in the local creek, kangaroos out in the bush, but I'd never seen human beings. They looked to me like dead animals. My respect for any human being who's just lost their life is incredibly high, but it might as well have been a leaf that had fallen off the tree.'

Rowe's unit was divided into three sabre troops and a headquarter troop. For most of his tour, each troop was allotted to one of the infantry battalions. There would be two troops out in the bush and the third left behind in Nui Dat to carry out local operations and small ambushes, minor repairs and maintenance. 'But 3 Cav was stretched thin,' said Rowe. 'The preponderance of time was spent operating out of fire support bases.'

By April 1969, Rowe had found a cause in Vietnam. Surprisingly, it was freedom of religion. He wrote 'from the battlefield' to Yvonne Corless at the *Sun*, 'I don't think Australians realise that the [Vietnamese] generally are a very devoted people, especially when it comes to religion . . . ' Maybe without war 'this country might be slightly happier', he wrote, but were the US and others to withdraw, the Communists would take over and 'would not allow religious practices'. Rowe had to admit, 'I am not the most religious person in the world, but I can understand when a person has to believe in something and I feel it is everyone's right to pray to their God, and this is my justification for being here.'[6]

In August, Rowe was promoted to lance corporal and given command of an APC. Home on R&R in September, he told the press, 'It seems nothing happens when I'm around – my company always misses the Vietcong. Not everyone is so lucky – I've lost two good mates who were killed by a VC mine.'[7] But Rowe was later injured in the field. 'We had a new troop leader,' he said. 'You couldn't work an armoured column in Vietnam the way you would in the open-range warfare that hitherto was the norm. So you wouldn't have formation attacks, and he was hell-bent on having his troop do a two-up formation attack. We'd practised those sort of things on the range at Puckapunyal, but the terrain just didn't lend itself to it. The topography was way too dangerous.' The APCs were sweeping through open savannah, where elephant grass grew as high as the vehicles, when Rowe hit a crater gouged out of the ground by a five-hundred-pound bomb. 'If you can't see that because of the grass,' he said, 'and you're travelling at twenty-five or even thirty kilometres per hour, when you hit it with an armoured vehicle, you're in trouble. We hit this thing, and I had this big tow-frame in front of my vehicle, which stopped the vehicle from actually rolling forward and squashing both the driver and myself, but my right leg got caught between the machine guns and I was left dangling upside down out of the carrier turret. They flew me in, the medic put some – I don't know – Vicks VapoRub or something on it, put a bandage around it and sent me back into the field.'

Rowe came home on 19 December 1969. He told journalists, 'The army has been a great experience. There's not one bit of it I haven't enjoyed, apart from being near a couple of stoushes with "Charlie."'[8] Rowe's two years in the army were often held to have killed off his career as a teen idol, but Rowe said he'd realised it was over by the time he'd marched into Puckapunyal. 'I'd looked at most people who'd been successful artists, and most people have a notoriety on the way up, and all of a sudden they have this big spike then they come back down,' he said. 'And that lasts five years. And I'd had my five years, and I thought, This can be a soft landing. At least I don't have to bury myself in despair that my success is finished.'

He played his first show back home on 1 February 1970 and 'died on my arse', he said, 'then went down and languished on the beach at Torquay in Victoria and thought, My life's over. I don't know what to do. I know two things: the entertainment game and the army. Perhaps I'll go back in the army. I'd lost my management, I'd lost my band, even my close show-business friends had moved on to doing other things, and I was really, really lost and confused for a long time. I had six months of a real struggle. I looked at it, and I said, "I don't even like what the business stands for. It stands for self-flagellation, self-aggrandisement. It stands for being patted on the back for doing something that didn't seem to mean much compared to a young woman whose husband has been killed – by either side – and she's got two or three kids, and she's trying to grow enough rice just to have the family survive."' After the army, 'Show business to me just didn't seem to have any value whatsoever,' he said. 'The only thing I was ever really good at, I couldn't find a reason to believe in any more.'

Not every public figure went into the army with the enthusiasm of Normie Rowe, nor served his time as stoically. At nineteen years old, in his first senior VFL season, Richmond centre half-forward Royce Hart already looked like one of the most astonishing players of his generation. He could jump his own height with preternatural poise. In Richmond's 1967 grand final win against Geelong, he flew above his mark, Peter Walker, perching for a moment with one leg on Walker's shoulder while he stole the ball from the air. Hart kicked fifty-five goals that season, and won recruit of the year. He was called up in 1968, but apparently failed three medicals because of a thigh injury, which also kept him out of the first five games of the new season. In an autobiography published perhaps prematurely at the age of twenty-two, Hart said he was accepted on the fourth medical and joined the army on 29 January 1969. He seemed unimpressed by everything military and concerned only that he could somehow keep up his football training. At Puckapunyal, he was able to run with Brenton Miels, a South Australian national serviceman who had played football for Sturt. After recruit training, Hart asked for the ordnance corps but was posted to the School of Artillery at North Head, Sydney. Since the artillery at that time provided all the army's PT instructors, Hart hoped to become a PTI, but somehow failed the entrance tests. He flew from Sydney to Melbourne every weekend of the 1969 football season to play for Richmond, and believed he was earmarked for Vietnam until he was transferred to the 16th Light Anti Aircraft Regiment at Woodside, SA. As Hart pointed out in his autobiography, there was no desperate need for anti-aircraft guns in Vietnam, since the Viet Cong conspicuously lacked an air force (although some men from his regiment served with other Task Force units during the war).

Hart much later said he was able to avoid going overseas – even though the artillery wanted to send him to Vietnam and he'd been told by his CO, 'You can't get out of it' – by the intervention of Richmond secretary Alan Schwab. According to Hart, Schwab called a politician, whom Hart declined to name even forty-three years after the event, with the result that Hart was posted instead to Woodside.[9] Hart offered no evidence to support his claim.

He didn't like Woodside at all, calling it 'gloomy' and 'miserable', but was at least able to go to Adelaide and train with Glenelg. When he came back from football training at ten p.m., he would find his hut mates asleep and snoring and, by his own account, 'used to have to wake them all up before I could get off to sleep myself'. It's possible Hart was not the most popular man in the hut, and he described those nights as the worst of his life. He was elected honorary captain-coach of the army Australian Rules football team but 'tried not to play'. On an exercise in the bush, he told a warrant officer to 'go away and play your war somewhere else'.

Hart also claimed to have paid another man $100 to take his place on an exercise that clashed with the 1969 VFL grand final, allowing Hart to fly back to Melbourne and help Richmond along to victory against Carlton. The Richmond team that afternoon included another national serviceman, Kevin Sheedy, who was stationed at Puckapunyal with 21 Construction Company, and a third team member, Rex Hunt, who went into the army the following year. None of them ever found their way to Vietnam. Hunt later said he 'filled in time until the day I got out because all I did was drive the colonel around'.[10] Sheedy became a more active coach of the army football team than Hart.

The indomitable Hart also represented Glenelg in the SANFL grand final against Sturt, one week after Richmond took the flag. At the end of the 1969 season, Hart won best and fairest for Richmond and was made All-Australian. He was still a national serviceman when his autobiography was written in 1970. 'I don't think Army life is of any benefit to a footballer,' he wrote. 'A chap who works for a bank or the public service has his position held for him until he gets out. It's guaranteed by law and they can't take it away from him. Being a footballer – or an entertainer – is a day by day proposition. A player may not be able to reach the peak he was at before National Service; someone may have come along better than him; the club may have found a new star to fill his place. There is no reimbursement for him.'[11]

The cases of Hart and the brilliant league player Bob Fulton, who also saw out the war in Australia, fed public scepticism that footballers would not be sent overseas. But random draws throw up statistical improbabilities, and one VFL club, Essendon, had six of its players posted to Vietnam as national servicemen: Keith Gent of 7RAR, Ian Anderson of 8RAR, Lindsay McGie of 6RAR then 2RAR, provost Ian Payne, signaller Greg Perry, and Bill Thompson, who served with the ordnance corps.

The first to go had been McGie, who returned home unscathed to resume his career in August 1967. He'd kept his skills up in Nui Dat training with half-forward Gent, who'd won the under-19s best and fairest in 1964 but only played seven games in the 1965–66 season.

Essendon had sent a football for Gent to 7RAR's battalion HQ. It went mildewed and flat in the tropics, but the men were able to reinflate it with a bicycle pump supposedly left behind by the VC. The three footballers kicked goals between the rubber trees when they could, but Gent was eager to get back to Windy Hill. He wrote to Essendon to tell the club he was 'bursting' to return. He'd dropped a stone in weight and was worried his skills had rusted, 'but I'm hoping that when I get back I'll put the weight back', he said in June.[12]

In January 1968, days before the Tet Offensive, Gent was deployed with D Company 7RAR to help defend the approach to the US base at Long Binh. Gent was on patrol north-west of Bien Hoa when, he said later, 'We just stumbled on this unit of Vietnamese who were dug in at the top of a ravine. We walked straight into them and they opened fire, taking out our forward scout and medical officer. We all fanned out and got behind trees to return fire. They were firing little mortar bombs and hitting trees above us. That's how I got hit. The shrapnel sprayed down and hit me in both legs and an arm. I crawled behind a rock and just waited and hoped.' The Australians called in air strikes and, when the fighting cooled, Gent was choppered out and hospitalised. 'I remember the surgeon saying to me before my operation, "If you can get out of this, be thankful." I got out of it.'[13] But Gent's sciatic nerve had been severed, and he was left without feeling in his right side for fifteen months. He returned to Australia in February, but his playing career never recovered. He played for Essendon Reserves in 1969, then joined Preston, Brunswick and Reservoir, a journeyman in the lower reaches of the game.

Less feted than footballers, but well known to Melbourne's sporting fraternity, were identical twin amateur boxing champions Henry and Leon Nissen. The Nissen brothers were born in a refugee camp near the site of Bergen-Belsen in Germany in January 1948. Their Polish-Jewish father and Russian-Jewish mother had moved to the camp after the Second World War, trying to find relatives. 'Both came from big families,' said Leon, 'but they were now virtually all dead. The family received immigration papers from Australia and left Germany when we were three months old. My parents suffered tremendously trying to survive in Australia. When we were about three years old, my mother had a nervous breakdown. Henry and I were sent out to homes or families for a year at a time. My mother never fully recovered. She was sick for more than fifty years – she heard voices . . . When she was normal, she was a very loving and caring person. When she was sick, she was as hard as nails – emotionless. Henry and I craved the affection we were deprived of, so when we grew up, we were very affectionate to everybody. Because we had suffered, we didn't want anybody else to suffer. As youngsters, they took us both into a special class and gave us extra gymnastics, because our bodies weren't developing properly and we needed the extra training to help us become normal kids. We were small, and we had experienced situations where we were picked on. At primary school we had a significant number of fights – there were always underlying feelings of anti-Semitism – and we realised we couldn't go through life without some knowledge of self-defence, so we took up boxing.'[14]

'When I was about fourteen,' said Henry, 'I was standing in the school canteen queue waiting to buy my two cream buns for lunch, and the fellow behind me just started punching me. The best I could do was cry. I felt, I can't go through life getting belted up all the time. I'd heard of an ex-fighter, Peter Read, who was living in our street. I started learning, and I didn't want to tell Leon; I wanted to know something he didn't know. But the bugger followed me one day; I thought I'd escaped him but I led him to the boxing gym.'[15]

The Nissens grew into tough, gifted boxers, and between them had gathered a number of state and national amateur titles before they marched into Kapooka together in August 1969. Their father, Sam – who, said Henry, was 'Communistic in his philosophy and his beliefs' – was a regular anti-war marcher who had earlier been to a demonstration at Pentridge Prison in support of the conscientious objector John Zarb. 'I am opposed to my boys going in the army, perhaps to war and to be shot,' Sam told a reporter. 'But the boys are too inexperienced to heed me.' Leon said, 'I like this guy Zarb's view and if I had any guts I would probably do the same.' Henry, always the brawler of the pair, disagreed. He said, 'I reckon national service does every young fellow the world of good.'[16]

Leon, an aircraft mechanic, joined the Royal Australian Electrical and Mechanical Engineers and was posted to 1 Aviation Regiment at Amberley Airbase in Queensland, where he won the Queensland amateur flyweight belt. Despite his Queensland title, he was selected to represent Victoria in the amateur championships, so the army allowed him to transfer back to Melbourne, where Henry also ended up – as a PTI in Watsonia. The job was not onerous. There was one other PTI at the camp, and, 'We didn't need to both be there together,' said Henry. 'Either he'd work the first two days of the week and I'd work the next two days or whatever. So we'd give each other plenty of time to do what we needed to do.' Henry lived off base, continued his boxing training with Peter Read, helped run the family clothing business, and turned professional as a fighter. 'Life was very, very busy,' said Henry, 'and the army bent over backwards to keep me happy and help me do what I wanted to do because, obviously they got a lot of good publicity from my boxing and me.'

On 12 September 1970, Henry fought the Aboriginal boxer Harry Hayes at Earls Court, Victoria. Although he caught a black eye, a bruised fist, a cut cheek, a cut head and a bloodied nose, he kept Hayes on the back foot through fifteen three-minute rounds and, in only his third professional fight, Henry won the Australian flyweight championship. By this time, Leon already held the national amateur title in the same division.

When Henry had about six months left in the army, 'I actually applied to go to Vietnam,' he said. 'I thought, Well, if I go to Vietnam, I'm going to be just keeping the troops fit, not going to the front line fighting. I can handle that, and then I'll get the war service pension or whatever is.' But he was told he'd have to give a full year's service, and he didn't feel he could neglect his business or his boxing for twelve months. On the whole, said Henry, he had a 'thoroughly wonderful time' in the army. 'For me, it was just a picnic, doing whatever I wanted to do as long as I was working within the rules, and fitting in my own life around it. It didn't put me out at all.'

27

THE BATTLE OF BINH BA

The village of Binh Ba, six kilometres north of Nui Dat, had always sided with the Viet Cong. The Australians had tried to win over the people with medcaps and dentcaps, and to uproot the Viet Cong infrastructure with cordon and searches, but in truth the village itself was Viet Cong infrastructure and never going to be swayed by tooth extractions or the internment of its sons. Binh Ba was a neat, clean village of brick houses, built by the French for workers on the adjacent rubber plantation.

According to press agency reports, by the time the Task Force had arrived in South Vietnam, the VC were firmly in control of the village, and the two French plantation managers had chosen to carry on under 'Communist rule', despite having once been stripped, beaten and humiliated in front of the villagers and forced to work as rubber tappers.

But as early as 1966, Australian newspaper readers had been assured Binh Ba had been 'taken' by Australian troops, the VC operatives all captured, the VC tax collectors had made 'their last tour of the village', as time 'finally ran out for the Communists',[1] who'd fled into the jungle only hours before the arrival of 5RAR at their doors. However, on the evening of 5 June 1969, in what looked like a show of force, Binh Ba was occupied by perhaps a battalion of NVA troops together with local VC. An Australian tank and an armoured recovery vehicle passing by the village were fired upon the next morning, and troops from the same 5th Battalion that had supposedly driven out the VC three years earlier were sent from Nui Dat to assist South Vietnamese forces in routing them again.

In February, 5RAR had relieved 1RAR, the first battalion to return for a second tour. On 5 June D Company had just come off operations when its men were told to climb into APCs and head for Binh Ba. Ray Knapp was a corporal with Twelve Platoon and number two on the machine gun. His father ran the Beechwood Hotel just outside Wauchope, NSW, and hoped his son would one day take it over. But when Knapp left school he'd gone to work at the Bank of NSW. 'I wanted to be a jockey,' he said, 'but I got too big. Then I thought I'd join the mounted police, but I was too small. So the next best thing was a bank johnny.'

Although the Australians knew there were enemy troops in Binh Ba, they had no idea how many. Twelve Platoon's machine gun had gone into the armoury after their last operation, so Knapp had to take out one of Eleven Platoon's guns. The infantry rolled up the road in APCs, with four Centurion tanks out in front, and ARVN forces moving to block the enemy's exit. Outside the village, the convoy stopped for an hour. 'Someone said the armoured corps wanted the infantry to go in front and they would back them up,' said Knapp. 'That sort of thing was flying around.' While they waited, the Australians came under attack from men with RPGs. 'The tanks opened fire on a couple of houses where these people had jumped into,' said Twelve Platoon's Arnoldus Vanhulst, a bakery worker. 'We shot at a couple in the field to the left of us, then went into the outskirts of Binh Ba. Ten Platoon, Eleven Platoon were dismounted; they were going to go through by foot. We stayed on the APCs.'

Inside the village, the red-roofed, white-walled houses seemed to turn on them. Bullets flew from buildings and the gaps between them, and the Australians returned fire from the APCs. 'I ended up with my head above the top of the APC,' said Knapp, 'firing away, and then my bloody gun jammed. So I got in and pulled it apart, got back up, and it still wouldn't go. And I could see half-a-dozen North Vietnamese at the corner of this shop, and they'd got a mini-gun or something on a set of pram wheels. I was tapping the APC gunner saying, "Hit that! Hit that!" And *he* misfired; it jammed as well. And next thing, you see them walking off in front of us. And we couldn't do anything about it.'

They began to realise they might be facing a large enemy force. 'Once you see heavy weapons,' said Vanhulst, 'it's never indicated a small group of people. When somebody's dragging a 50 cal on wheels, it was never going to be a small argument. Tanks levelled out a couple of houses. We were still taking fire.' Helicopter gunships and artillery from nearby FSB Virginia fired in support of the Australians, and many local people were led to the plantation rubber sheds for safety. 'We had villagers trying to get out,' said Vanhulst, 'and we actually got them out in behind the APCs, so they didn't get hit or shot. I took photos. I put my weapon down and started photographing bits and pieces of the helicopter gunships coming in and whatnot. How stupid was I, sitting in the back of an APC, taking photos and not shooting?' Many years after the war was over, when Australian troops in Binh Ba were accused of massacring civilians in the village, Vanhulst produced his pictures of the evacuation.

D Company pulled out, and Knapp was given the company headquarters' machine gun to go back in and do a second sweep. 'And it lasted to that evening, and then it jammed up, so I spent until dark trying to get it going again, and then I got permission to do a test fire the next morning. I got in front of where the APCs had formed up, tried to fire again and it wouldn't go, and I looked up and saw all these blokes coming down through the bloody rubber. I jumped up and ran like hell. I was going to the tankies, "Let me in!"'

B Company had arrived after D Company the previous day, and gone into harbour at the edge of the rubber plantation. In the morning, 'I was pretty relaxed,' said Bill O'Mara, a national serviceman from Sydney. 'I even took my boots off. I'd never done that before, and I certainly didn't do it again.' Early in the morning, an Australian on piquet spotted a lead enemy soldier in the rubber. 'Our sentry waved to the guy,' said O'Mara, 'because he thought it was some of our blokes. And they, in fact, waved back. I think our guy came to his senses before they did, but they had fired an RPG at us. From very, very close range.' The rocket went over their heads, and the Australians turned all their firepower on the enemy. 'I went through two magazines,' said O'Mara. 'I walked up to where they had fired from, with my laces still undone. We expected there would've been two or three of them dead by the time we'd finished, but there was not a sign, no blood trails, nothing.'

The Australians went back into Binh Ba to clear the area. 'Twelve Platoon was then put in as a blocker at the back of the village,' said Vanhulst, 'while the rest of the platoons swept from house to house. You didn't go through the door. You'd smash the window – which was only wood, anyway – and normally inside of the hut was a hole, and in the hole was a tunnel that went underneath. It was like a bunker. And the VC/NVA had the villagers in there with them: you had to knock them, so you threw the grenades in, and you were clearing each house that way. We did about eight houses. We just used to open doors, throw a grenade into the bunker, then come back out. We knew that by that time the villagers should've – and would've – been out. There were a lot more VC and NVA killed than anybody else.'

'You never had a clue what you were walking into,' said Knapp. 'You had to treat each place as individual, a different area. Because the yards were different, the sheds might've had animals around them.' When he reached a house, 'I'd give it a spray with a few rounds, basically to give them warning we were coming, to get out. If we were taking fire from there, someone would come up and throw a grenade in, but nine times out of ten they were trying to get out when they heard that we were coming. They were trying to go from house to house, to sneak out around the back of the houses, to edge their way out of the village – and running into us at the same time. At one stage, an old grandfather and his young fella were pushed out from one of the doors. They were so lucky. I nearly wiped them out, the poor buggers. But the other fella that was in there with them went out through the back. We weren't trained to do house to house; we just trained to shoot the enemy. We had one bloke – I don't know how many bullets he had in him – and he came up and said, "Me no VC! Me no VC!" And he pulled out a wallet with his wife and kids' photos, and we got him to lie down and got one of the medics to have a look at him and calm him down, then they handed him over to the South Vietnamese.'

In the confusion of battle, there was an army film crew. When B Company reached the village, 'Somebody on top of the APCs, one of the photographers from the film unit, wanted us to throw some grenades into the houses,' said O'Mara. 'We just told him to piss off. They were never around when we were doing anything in the jungle. As we conducted searches in each house, there was nobody alive. And each house was pretty badly destroyed. There was a lot of dead people. When I considered it to be all over, a lot of the villagers came out of the schoolhouse. They'd been put in the schoolhouse for their protection, and some of the Viet Cong had infiltrated the civilians and put civilian clothes over their uniforms.'

When the fighting had finished, the village was in ruins. 'There was bugger-all left,' said Knapp. 'We recovered the bodies, brought them into the town square, and I believe they brought a dozer in and did a mass burial.' The battle had spilled into the adjoining hamlet of Duc Trang where, said O'Mara, 'I ended up with another guy burying six Viet Cong that our platoon had killed, and the Viet Cong were pretty badly mutilated and shot up. It took two attempts. The first grave was too shallow, so we had to take the bodies out and dig a lot deeper. All we had was the little entrenching tools.'

Binh Ba was a victory for the Australians, a successful collaboration between infantry and armour, with artillery firing support and aircraft overhead. One Australian died, 5RAR national serviceman Wayne Teeling from Clovelly, NSW, who had been in the country less than a month, while the enemy lost more than one hundred. But Australian press agency reporter Robin Strathdee, who walked through the village the day after the fighting, betrayed the kind of doubts that were increasingly becoming felt. 'Binh Ba was an attractive village with plots of lush banana trees, well grassed and clean,' he wrote, but now it was ' . . . a village of the dead – and their conquerors . . . Scarcely a house has escaped the attention of shells, rockets, grenades or bullets.' The bodies of civilians who'd been unable to flee were found lying in their homes and the bunkers beneath them. As the villagers trickled back from the rubber sheds, most were stopped before they reached their homes. 'Just one man was let through,' wrote Strathdee. 'His two children had not been seen since Friday. The man found them in his home – both dead, one with his head off, caught in the crossfire.' But Strathdee's melancholy reflections, as printed in the *Sydney Morning Herald*, were offset by a larger and unrelated photograph of CMF commandoes rappelling down the northern pylon of Sydney Harbour Bridge in a recruiting exercise which was also a fundraiser for the NSW Quadriplegic Association.[2]

Australian civic action teams and engineers rebuilt Binh Ba, in an exercise some believed won hearts and minds.

The same battle is experienced in a hundred different ways by a hundred different people. Sydney-born Dave Sturmer, an engineer with 1 Field Squadron, saw Binh Ba from behind the turret of a Centurion tank. Sturmer was a bright, stocky, amiable, fit young bloke. His father, an army engineer in the Second World War, had died when Dave was twelve years old. 'I didn't get to know him well,' said Sturmer, 'but I loved him dearly. He didn't mind a beer and he didn't mind a cigarette, but he worked really hard.' Sturmer's mother 'struggled all the way through', and ended up working as a cashier at

Ashfield swimming pool, in Sydney's inner west. Sturmer failed 'pretty well everything at school', he said. He would've loved to play league, like the immortal, unstoppable Big Artie Beetson or the feinting, striding Graeme Langlands, a ghost crab to catch. By 1968 he was playing B-grade, second-division union for Canterbury on Saturdays and B-grade league for Lakemba on Sundays. He was light on his feet, but also lightly set. 'At about two stone wringing wet, I was never gonna be any good,' he said. 'The mind was willing but the body was never big enough. You weren't called Chicken Legs for nothing.'

Sturmer had left an apprenticeship as a commercial artist to become a builder's labourer when he went into the army with the thirteenth national service intake in 1968. 'I really wanted to go,' he said. 'I had no idea where Vietnam was. I had no idea what conscription was about. I had no idea what Communism was about. I had no idea what the yellow peril was about, or the Domino Theory. It was just that there was a war on. I thought I had to do my bit. And my family was proud. I felt like to follow in my father's footsteps was the honourable thing to do.' And he joined the engineers, like his dad.

The *Sun-Herald* ran a syndicated US comic strip called *Prince Valiant*, an elegant Arthurian saga of bloodless medieval heroics, illustrated with lines as fine as sword cuts. There were no speech bubbles, only painstakingly lettered captions. It was almost an illuminated manuscript. 'To help me to learn to read better, I'd read the comics to my dad on Sunday morning,' said Sturmer. 'Prince Valiant was a legend. He was always there to save the day. And I thought, That's my task in Vietnam: I'm going over to save the day; I'm the white knight. I was naive as buggery going into it, and it was probably, in a sense, the best thing. I would've rather that way than someone saying, "Well, you're gonna get your balls blown off, mate, and it's gonna hurt when it hits you."'

The army messed up his papers and, although his only training had been the ten-week course at the army's School of Military Engineering, he was sent first to the workshops at 1ALSG, with the qualified tradesmen at Vung Tau. They used him to sweep out the warehouses. 'I was very good at that,' he says. 'I was very good at darts, and having a beer at the boozer, and that was about the size of it.' He made his first trip into the town of Vung Tau with a laundry truck from the unit. 'They'd teed it up with some of the girls on the street,' he said. '"This is the new cherry boy," and they're all, "Cherry boy! Love you long time!" I probably wouldn't've changed that for anything. That part of the adventure was amazing.'

Eventually, he was transferred to 1 Field Squadron, where 'the world changed dramatically'. He was instructed to forget most of what he'd learned at the SME and was retrained for the realities of mine warfare. Sturmer was sent to FSB Virginia, where he was drawn into the Battle of Binh Ba. He and a mate, Sapper Ron Smillie, were assigned as engineers to the cavalry. They followed the convoy's lead APC in a vehicle with a crane attachment, and were told to fetch ammunition for a tank that had broken down close to the village. Helicopters were dropping resupplies down the road, and Sturmer and Smillie worked behind the tank, harvesting the shells and feeding them up to the tank crew. 'Every now and then we got spotted,' he said, 'and the VC would have a crack at us, but when you've got a tank of fifty-seven tonnes or so in front of you, you feel pretty safe.' While the infantry fought house to house, 'the Red Cross brought in sandwiches and cold drinks and stuff', said Sturmer, 'and Smillie and I managed to get a hot cup of tea. It was raining and the fans were going in the tank, and we just sat behind the turret, and it was like grandstand seats. We didn't hurt anybody, and every now and then Charlie would have a pot shot at us, just to let us know he was still in there. Then they rolled the tanks. The last guy standing, they obliterated him. They had trouble getting him out of where he was, so they just rolled the tank up and got rid of the house and him.

'Right in the middle of all that,' said Sturmer, 'when we first arrived, I was standing on the safe side of the APC, and I kept peering around, wanting to get into the fight. I wasn't scared at all. I had my war face on. And the driver and the crew commander were just laughing, looking down on me going, "You're an idiot." I was standing there and this bloke came up to me and said, "Is your name Dave? I went to Ashfield Tech with you." And then he vanished. And I thought, It's a pretty small world.'

28

THE DAY MANKIND KICKED THE MOON

If the Battle of Long Tan has become the stone of statues, it's been left to the mine incident of 21 July 1969 to provide the stuff of song: a ballad of tragedy written by a radical singer and adopted by the post-war veterans' movement. The single 'A Walk in the Light Green (I Was Only Nineteen)' was recorded by the Australian folk group Redgum in 1983. Like many of the veterans themselves, it was punchy, bitter and full of questions, lashing out every which way. It had been composed by Redgum songwriter John Schumann based on the national service experiences of his brother-in-law, 6RAR forward scout Mick Storen. 'A Walk in the Light Green', named for a strip of scrub and sparse forest south-east of Dat Do, was an anti-war song adopted by old warriors. In part, it was embraced because it spoke of the commonly recognised symptoms of post-traumatic stress disorder, and alluded darkly to Agent Orange. But more than that, it put into popular verse a vocabulary that had previously belonged to the veterans alone: from the passing-out parade at Puckapunyal to the exercises at Shoalwater, from 'contact' to 'dustoff' to the Grand Hotel in Vung Tau. The ballad was played by Schumann at the Vietnam veterans' welcome-home parade in Sydney in 1987, and veteran Frankie Hunt, who in the song 'kicked a mine', joined the singer on stage.

Just as 'A Walk in the Light Green' drew originally from the words of the veterans, in their later years it has come to colour their language. They are the only group in society likely to refer to the Apollo 11 landing as the day 'mankind kicked the moon'. The song also helped popularise the misbelief that many national serviceman in Vietnam were 'only nineteen' whereas, probably, none were. Nor was nineteen-year-old Frankie Hunt, a regular soldier, going home in June (he'd only got to Vietnam in May) but a song has no brief to stick to the facts. And since there were no Australian sappers at Khe Sanh, 'A Walk in the Light Green' is more or less all the veterans have.

Schumann's song shows the mine incident through the eyes of Storen, and places Hunt at its centre. But the story of 21 July 1969 also belongs to many other men, including Dave Sturmer and Phil Baxter. A field engineer in Vietnam belonged to a two-man so-called 'splinter' team. He spent the first part of his tour as a number two in the team. In July 1969, Sturmer had only been in Vietnam five and half months, and his number one was twenty-four-year-old Baxter, a well-respected man in the unit, older than most national servicemen, and a qualified engineer. Baxter, who had been in country since September 1968, was Sturmer's mentor and guide. His name had been pulled out of the barrel for the first intake, but he deferred to finish his qualifications and didn't go in until the eleventh. After he'd sat for the Leaving Certificate, Baxter had planned to bum around on the beach. 'I loved surfing,' he said, 'and I had some mates, we were just going to get in a car and go up the coast. My dad said, "No, you get a trade and then you can go and do your surfing" – which never eventuated because the number came out.' Baxter saw military service as a responsibility, a part of growing up. 'I wasn't even old enough to vote when the first ballot was around,' he said, 'so it was other people that voted me, and you felt that if that's what other people wanted you to do, you don't object.'

As an adventure, Vietnam replaced the surfing trip.

On 20 July 1969, Baxter and Sturmer were a splinter team, patrolling south-east of Dat Do with 6RAR/NZ, searching for the enemy, their tunnels, their weapons and rice. The battalion, which included a company of New Zealand infantry, had arrived in Vietnam in May. Although the engineers moved with the riflemen of Three Platoon, A Company, their task was primarily to clear mines and other booby traps.

When the patrol found a bunker system, 'I was having my first hot food, I think, for four or five days,' said Sturmer. 'I was really enjoying a cup of tea or coffee and, all of a sudden, I heard these rounds, contact to our left, and it was one of the other platoons from A Company.' Three VC had walked into an ambush, come out the other side unscathed, then blundered straight into Sturmer's section. The gun group shot one, and two other VC dived into a bunker.

'They tried to fight their way out of it,' said Sturmer, 'but the noose closed in on them. These guys were stumped. All they could do was put their rifles out and *duh-duh-duh*, hold them over their heads. They'd made their own grave by getting into the bunker. If they'd've stayed on top and moved, they may have been able to get past, but the Australians got on top of the bunker, threw a couple of hand grenades in, and finished Charlie off.'

When the fighting was over, Baxter and another digger approached Sturmer, 'and I couldn't get up', he said. 'It was like I was welded to the ground. In the morning I was still flippant and joking with Phil – who, I must say, had great tolerance – and all of a sudden, all the bravado, all the carefree flippantness, just went down the gurgler. They helped me up, I started to walk and my knees buckled, but they seemed to understand that. I'm quite sure they'd all been through a similar thing.' The next day, he said, 'I acted entirely differently. I acted with purpose, knowing we were in trouble.'

The platoon was travelling east to west, crossing a path, when the men stopped and brewed up, and watched US air strikes on the Long Hai hills, like a war film projected into the sky for their entertainment. Second Lieutenant Peter Hines, a regular officer with 6RAR/NZ, sent men to guard the perimeter and ordered the engineers to put together their mine detector and clear a track. But the engineers wore steel plates in their boots to protect them from panji stakes, and the detector sometimes took positive readings from the soles. Sturmer said, 'What I was getting – and this is where I believe I stuffed up big-time – was a reading off the mine as well. There was so much shrapnel on the ground, every time we made a sweep, we'd get another ping. So we stepped over our gear and started clearing the track, and Lieutenant Hines came up and he was talking to Phil, and I turned around. We'd just passed the gunner to our left, and the louie took my headphones off, and said, "The Yanks are on the moon." I didn't even know they were up there; I don't think anyone did.'

The space race wasn't so much about the moon as what was happening on earth. Fuelled by military technology and patriotic ambition, it had come to symbolise the ideological war between US capitalism and Soviet Communism, as if whichever system conquered the skies would gain the moral authority to rule on the ground. The Soviets had won the initial skirmish, when cosmonaut Yuri Gagarin became the first man in space, but the US triumphed overall when Neil Armstrong – who'd seen action against the Communists as a navy pilot in Korea – 'kicked the moon'.

After he'd told Sturmer the Americans had landed, Hines let go of Sturmer's headphones, which snapped back onto his ears, then the lieutenant stepped over the engineers' gear and walked straight onto a buried M16 mine, which sprang out of the ground. 'And it came up under his bum,' said Sturmer, 'and cut him in half. His whole bottom part of his torso had just been blown away. It was like a surgeon had got in there with a scalpel and laid everything out.

'There was people in front of him screaming,' said Sturmer. 'The medic had been hit, the sergeant had been hit. Everybody was basically immobilised. The people on the eastern side of the track were still relatively intact, but the majority on the western side copped a bit. The radio operator especially copped lots of it.' Sturmer hadn't heard the mine go off, because he'd been wearing the detector headphones. 'I hadn't felt the shrapnel hit me,' he said. 'Phil pulled me to the ground and said, "You're bleeding from the back of the legs." I just looked at him, and he was really not looking well. He said, "I think I've been hit." I checked him out, and he did have heaps of [shrapnel] up his back and legs. He wore the main brunt of what I probably would've worn.'

'I got hit down the back,' said Baxter, 'because I was standing behind Dave. I thought that a bomb had dropped short somewhere, but after about thirty seconds, we realised what had gone wrong. It was a jumping-jack mine, with a plunger out the top and three little prongs in it. So when he steps on the prongs, the plunger goes on, sets off a small charge which blows it out of the ground, and when it gets to about waist high, the main charge goes, and it throws out the shrapnel, or whatever's in it, three hundred and sixty degrees. And bearing in mind a lot of people were sitting down and having a brew at this time, there were eighteen people injured, some very bad.

'You don't even bleed a lot,' said Baxter. 'You didn't feel it. It goes in, it's white hot and, as it goes through, it seals the entry wound. Where there was blood, we fixed one another up. The main thing was to get everyone to keep still, to not move. It was hard not to run to a mate who's been wounded, but the Vietnamese were known for putting other mines near mines, hoping to get people rushing to them.'

The engineers had to be meticulous, methodical and calm, although they were wounded themselves and surrounded by yelling, bleeding, shattered men. They didn't know how many other mines waited for them beneath the soil, but they had to find a way through them. They rescued their machine gunner, who had shrapnel lodged in one of his grenades and feared it might explode. They cleared the grenade, but missed the 'very large piece of shrapnel' lodged in the machine gunner's back. 'We virtually said, "You're okay, mate,"' said Sturmer, 'and moved on to the next one. Phil was really quite white and pale, so I sat him down. Where I sat him was only metres from where the second mine was. And I kept looking at Lieutenant Hines, who was on the western side of the track, and his right foot was facing his face, sort of looking at him. Phil said, "Get a safe lane to Hines," which I did. [Hines] was an amazingly brave man. He took control of the platoon, and issued commands as I worked my way to him. He went through the chain of command to find pretty well everyone was down, except the guys on the eastern side of the track, where Corporal Needs was, and he passed command onto Corporal Needs. Needs then had to work out where people had travelled and not trodden on anything, so the track marks became safe lanes.

'By that stage,' said Sturmer, 'I'd reached Lieutenant Hines, and we chatted, and he just passed away. His blood just ran out. I said a prayer for him, and from there Phil had managed to get himself quite well together, and started moving up the track again to help find a landing zone for the dustoff helicopter.'

Baxter and Sturmer could not by themselves clear lanes to all the wounded and cut a landing zone for the chopper. They had to radio for a combat engineer team: seven more men, a corporal and three pairs of 'numbers'. So Sturmer made his way to the radio operator, Frankie Hunt. 'Frank was in terrible trouble,' he said. 'His left thigh, the back of his leg, had been blown off. We carried bandages, and I just packed those into the hole and strapped that up. He had a lot of spinal injuries, and to try and reassure him, I remember patting him on the head saying, "You'll be okay, mate." I think he went into a coma at that time, but before that he'd handed me the radio and said, "You talk to the helicopter coming in." So he handed me the phone, and I had no idea what to say. So I said, "Hi, helicopter," to which the helicopter pilot replied, "Who the eff is this?" With that, Frank took the radio back. From there it was just moving through everybody until the engineer combat team arrived.'

It had been Lieutenant Hines, not 'Frankie', who'd kicked the mine, but the detail was changed in the song, to save the feelings of the lieutenant's family.

Lieutenant Colonel David Butler, the commanding officer of 6RAR, came in on a helicopter with the regimental medical officer, Robert Anderson. 'They couldn't land,' said Sturmer, 'and they didn't want to land, because they didn't know how many more mines were there, so they winched them down – and as they winched them down, they'd winch another casualty up to the chopper.'

Sturmer was among the wounded who had to be evacuated. 'When I was finally taken up, Phil was on the same chopper,' he said. 'There were five or six of us, including myself, a door gunner and a medic. We were very dirty, and people were on the verge of crying. We got airlifted to the hospital at Vung Tau. There was so many people wounded, it was like a line going up the hall into the operating theatre. While we were there, we received the information that the medical officer had trodden on the second mine, killing Corporal Needs instantaneously.

'The medical officer had seen a sign that said there was a mine. He stepped off the safe lane, which had been laid, walked over to it, to take it off the tree, and the mine was at the base of the tree. Then the poor buggers on the ground had to go through the whole thing again – those that hadn't been hit – so you really have to wonder about their mental state.' They must have been 'amazingly strong people to just stay there', said Sturmer.

'A small piece of shrapnel went through [Needs'] heart and that was all, so he wouldn't even have known what hit him. And the MO: the mine, instead of jumping up off the ground, went off under his feet – it went straight up and stripped him of his front. The last I saw of him was that night after we came out of our anaesthetic. They wheeled him through the ward and he was just like a plaster cast. He lived. He was blind. He survived, but Needs didn't.

'Reinforcements came in to rebuild the platoon,' Sturmer said, 'then they pushed south at night, getting out of the area but looking for more Charlie. I went to sleep while I was in the hospital waiting for my surgery. I remember waking up and there was an elderly nurse and a skylight and it hit the back of her grey hair and I thought she was an angel. I'm in heaven.'

The corporal in charge of the engineers' combat team called in to support Sturmer and Baxter was Dave Wright, a sheet metalworker born in Preston, Victoria. Wright's father, who'd worked for the PMG, died when Wright was thirteen. Wright had a brother, Jeffrey, two years older, in the first national service intake, posted to 1 Field Squadron. 'I never talked to him much about it,' says Wright, 'or he never talked to me much. All's I knew he was in the army, all's I knew he went to Vietnam. When he did his march-out parade at Puckapunyal, we went up and watched him. After that, he went to Vietnam, and the only thing he told me about it was he was there for the Battle of Long Tan and, being an engineer, one of his duties was to put all the coffins of the men who'd died in action there onto the Hercules to fly them home. He was in headquarters troop. He virtually never went out on operations.'

Wright wanted to go to Vietnam, but he deferred his national service for a year to finish his apprenticeship, and he ended up in 1 Field Squadron, like his brother. 'During the last six months of my tour, I spent more time in the minefield than anywhere else,' he said. 'I had about a month to go in country, and my section were given the job of clearing a minefield around the Dinh Co Monastery. We'd been given a mud map done by the VC, which showed where the mines were. We had the infantry support so we could do our job without being shot at. We spent five days there, and there was six of us. It was pretty hard work, because we had earphones on, flak jackets on, steel helmets, and it was bloody hot. We only found one mine in five days. Where they said they were on the map, they weren't. When you'd find a mine, you'd search around it with your bayonet, clear the area. We'd very rarely pull them, because we weren't sure whether they were booby-trapped. We'd blow them in situ.

'After five days, our troop sergeant said, "You guys are being relieved. There's another combat team from 1 Troop coming in to give you a break." Which we really needed, because we were physically and mentally knackered. The next morning, we were told at about nine o'clock there was going to be a B-52 strike on the Long Hais. Right on nine o'clock, the mountain started erupting with explosions. And at about nine-thirty, we were having a smoke, and our troop sergeant came running up to us: "There's been a mine incident out in the Light Green. Get your packs together and away you go. You're going to get picked up by a chopper in the next ten minutes." All we knew was that an infantry troop had walked into the middle of a minefield.

'As soon as we landed, we walked up to where Phil Baxter was and I said, "What's happening? What've you done?" and he said, "I've cleared this, this and there." When we cleared an area, we used to put plastic strips, so we knew where we were walking and it was safe to do so. So I gave orders to my sappers, "Right, boys, you go out to there, there and there. Make it safe for those infantry to come back in." And that's what they started doing. Myself and another two sappers walked fifty metres up the track, we got a lot of charges out and blew the whole area, so the choppers could come in. A couple of choppers had actually winched out some of the more severely wounded just before we got there. We were working quite feverishly to clear the LZ [landing zone], to get out to the other diggers who were out in the bush. In the meantime, while we were clearing the bush, the medical officer of 6RAR was choppered in. He was wandering around, tending to the wounded, and I made an announcement: "No one walk off the strips!"

'I got called down the other end of the track,' said Wright, 'because when my boys were clearing the track they looked up a tree and there was a sign.' The VC would often leave an indication of where they had laid a mine, so as not to endanger local people. 'Unfortunately, my platoon walked in from the other way, so they couldn't see it. We were talking about what we were going to do about it, and – *bang!* – another one went off. The doctor had actually stepped off the track, because he'd found another sign – which we hadn't seen – high in a tree. I came running back, straight after the explosion, and the doctor was standing there, and he looked like someone had got a bucket of blood and poured it right over the top of him. It was an amazing sight. There was two of my guys – John Fleming and Bill Wilcox – very badly wounded. They'd copped most of the blast. Bill Wilcox was read his last rites on the way to Vung Tau hospital, and when he got back they read him his last rites again.

'At this stage,' said Wright, 'the platoon was down to probably about twelve of us. I was off with the fairies because of all that'd happened, the intensity of it. I was on another planet, more or less, physically and mentally fucked. Anyway, we got our orders. What was left of my combat team, we were to stay with the platoon. There were five of us, and we stayed for the next three or four days, and we just kept doing our job. After all that.'

Baxter recovered in hospital at Vung Tau, came out and served the last few weeks of his year in Vietnam, then flew home. 'I was posted back to 6ESR out of Penrith,' he said, 'an engineers' stores and workshop. Nothing happened out there. I'd drive all the way from Belmore of a morning, go to the roll call, jump back into the car and disappear to a boozer. If you stayed out there because it was wet or something, they'd just tell you to go to the bedding store where all the mattresses were, and you'd climb on top of the mattress and read a book or something. A few people got posted to Victoria Barracks, and they were used in honour guards when bodies were brought back and they had a military service.'

Baxter's surf trip was postponed forever. 'I never did get back to surfboard-riding once I came home,' he said.

Bill Wilcox, who twice was read the last rites, was a fitter and turner from Oberon, NSW, a farming and timber town in the central tablelands. He'd played league for the Oberon Tigers, and had a trial game with Souths in Sydney just before he went away. He was invited back, but never made it after the war.

The Wilcox family kept show horses. At one stage, they had twelve ponies, which they exhibited all around the tablelands and his sister had been killed on a show horse a couple of years before Wilcox went into the army. His father was a Second World War veteran. 'He didn't talk a real lot about it, but he was quite happy that I went in,' said Wilcox. 'Mum wasn't, naturally.' However, 'Dad wasn't really happy when I was told I was going to Vietnam,' said Wilcox. 'I had a cousin from Bathurst going in. We were just silly young kids. My cousin, Harold Hurst, ended up getting killed over there a couple of weeks before he was coming home. He was an engineer, the same as me.

'Demolitions really intrigued me,' said Wilcox. 'As a kid, we always used to have the old tuppenny bungers. It wasn't just cracker nights, we had them all the time. You'd be blowing tins up and different things.' At the School of Military Engineering, 'I was up in the top of the class all the time in all our courses – weapons handling, demolition and things like that. I was like a kid with a new toy every time I got something new.'

He went to Vietnam in June 1969. On 21 July, Wilcox was with Dave Wright, 'a terrific bloke'. 'They were doing a B-52 strike on the Long Hais,' said Wilcox, 'and we were sitting in Fire Support Base Rush waiting for the enemy to come down after they were bombed. They'd come down bleeding from their ears and noses, we were there to do the mop-up. And that's when we got the call that 6RAR had walked into the minefield over in the Light Green. They had to drop us in by winch because there was no landing zone cut. I was with my number one, Johnny Fleming. He did get wounded, but not really bad, when I got hit. I copped most of the shrapnel up the side that would've got Johnny higher up.

'We cleared through it,' said Wilcox, 'and we found a mine. The nogs had put in a warning for themselves, a three-pronged stick in a tree, a sign that there was three mines in that area: the one that got Dave, the one that we found and made safe, and then the one that got us. So we found all three of them. Unluckily. The one that got Dave and them and the one that got us were only metres apart. We came in from behind them. They were heading back towards where the big minefield was. We were clearing up to where Frankie Hunt was, and the lieutenant who'd stood on the mine. All the wounded were still on the ground. We'd found the other mine about thirty metres away, further up the track. We cleared around where they were, went ahead, hit the track, and found another one.

'We were laying the safe lanes, and we taped to all the wounded, and went up the track to where there was another guy and he wasn't wounded, but we cleared up to him, found the mine just not far from him and went back down to clear back in to where one of the other guys were. And that's where the medical officer came in from the chopper and stepped out of the safe lane and on the bloody mine. I was right beside him.

'I told them: as soon as they were coming through, "Do not step out of this line!" He just took one step, that's all it would've been. His one foot would have gone out of the safe lane and his other back in. And we were standing there. I suppose we were in the way and he wanted to push through past us, like officers do.

'This mine was a jumping jack,' said Wilcox, 'and if they've got a faulty powder bag underneath the jumping part, they won't jump out of the ground. And this one exploded underground, and we were standing right on top of it. It got me in the calf, probably a foot up from the ground at the lowest spot, then right into the base of the chest. I've got probably fifty scars up the side of me. I was hot, just hot, that's all it was. I was conscious right through the whole thing, right until I got to the hospital. I put my hand to my knee, I couldn't feel my knee, and I looked up at my hand, which was covered in blood. I thought, Oh, my leg's gone. I wasn't game to look at it. But what it was, was my hand was all smashed up too, and the blood was coming from it, and from the knee as well. All up the left side I copped it, right through.

'They hooked me up to the outside, to the runners on the chopper, in a makeshift stretcher, and flew me back that way, because I was too bad to leave for the next chopper and they'd loaded this one. I was flying over and all I could see were the tops of rubber trees, zooming along underneath me. They took me back to the American hospital, and I spent a week or so in it, then they took me to the Australian hospital for a week, and they sent me home. I spent six months all up when I couldn't go back to a unit. I couldn't walk for three months. I ended up back at Penrith, at what they called "the old man's home". I could've got straight out, but I still had six months left, so I said, "No, I'll stay in." I ended up doing a lot of truck driving, running down to Melbourne and different places. I enjoyed the last six months.'

On 21 July 1969, the largest headline on the front page of the *Sydney Morning Herald*, stretching across all ten decks of the broadsheet, was 'Men On Moon'. The lead editorial comment addressed the more parochial issue of rising water rates. But it was dwarfed on page two by a commentary by 'The Editor' entitled 'A Case for Conscription', which took up a similar amount of space to the moon-landing story. The editor noted the tenth registration for national service began that day, and called opposition to the scheme 'naïve in the extreme'. The *Sydney Morning Herald*'s support for national service had not shifted a step over the previous five years.

The next morning, when news of the mine incident had come in, it shared the front page with the moon walk. A press agency report described two platoons as having been 'scythed down' by flying shrapnel. It noted 'Australian officers said they believed Vietcong had taken the mines from a minefield laid in Phuoc Tuy Province two years ago' and that 'more than 20 Australian and Vietnamese soldiers working with them have been killed and about 100 wounded by mines near Nui Dat in the last two months'.[1] A bullet point at the foot of the story directed the reader to 'Saturday casualties' on the results page of the sport, finance and classified sections. Here, the dead and wounded from Australian operations in Phuoc Tuy on 19 July were listed along with the rugby league scores, as if war were just another game to be followed by men at the breakfast table, or in the carriage on the train to work.

29

THE MYTH OF THE SIXTIES

The world changed the year mankind kicked the moon, but the late 1960s in Australia are, in part, a myth. 'People think everyone in the swinging sixties was walking around with flowers and feathers in their hair. They weren't,' said Broderick Smith, the British-born singer of Melbourne's Adderley Smith Blues Band. 'If you lived in the suburbs and you walked around like that, you'd get bashed. The sixties was rockers and jazzers. There were guys in duffle coats and little chin beards, and they'd ride on Vespas, or maybe in Volkswagens, and the rockers were normally about four or five in a car, with cigarettes stuffed up the sleeves of their terry-towelling shirts. If you were involved in a group, or music, you were regarded as being a poofter. All the young Australian boys wanted to be Richie Benaud, or Ron Barassi. When I look back on the sixties, all I can think of is the sun shining, blond boys with a neat parting in their hair, white shirt with an open collar, neatly pressed, great Fletcher Jones pants and ropey, ripple-soled shoes, playing cricket in a spare lot somewhere.'

On 20 January 1969, Richard Nixon had replaced Lyndon Johnson as US president, promising 'peace with honour' in Vietnam. In the same month, Broderick Smith, a twenty-year-old white boy with the blues voice of a forty-year-old Southern Delta black man, marched into the Singleton Infantry Training Centre from 2RTB.

Smith arrived in the same intake as another musician, Broken Hill–born Evan Jones, who played with his brother Idris in the Gingerbread Men, who'd had a small Adelaide hit with 'Let the Little Girl Dance'. Evan and Idris had already written 'The Pushbike Song' when Evan was called up. They'd performed it on the TV show *Uptight*, had some interest from record companies, but not yet made a recording.

Jones, a tall man, handsome like a prince, with a faint distance in his boyish eyes, was quite willing to go into the army. 'I'd seen what it was doing to Normie,' Jones said, 'and obviously that was the end of the real Elvis Presley, but it wasn't too big a deal for me. I'm a bit of fatalist, and whatever turns up in life you do your best at and you go along with it.'

Broderick Smith 'naturally liked America,' he said, 'because we lived in an American time, and I was making money at the weekend playing their music. I was kind of socially conscious, but I was exposed to information more because I worked in the folk and jazz scene. I'd listen to older people, like artists and folk musicians – and some of it I wouldn't agree with, because I could see they were, like, professional socialists, and I was a bit wary of them. I still liked to hang out with rough heads and all that.' His influences, he said, were 'nothing like what the average Australian young guy would be exposed to . . . Robert Menzies was not a good word in our house. I thought he was a dull and boring, smug sort of thug.' Smith's family was opposed to the Vietnam War, and his father, a fitter and turner, offered to send Smith to his brother in Canada to escape the call-up. But Smith felt, 'We all like it here in Australia, we're grateful for being here, so if they want me, I should go in the army.' He was, however, determined not to go to Vietnam.

Glenelg footballer Graham Cornes marched into 2RTB on the same day as Smith and Jones, and knew both men at Puckapunyal. Cornes was smart, funny, mouthy and rebellious. His career in football had just begun, and he had already won the best and fairest first-year medal. He'd been able to defer his national service until the end of the

1968 season. The day he'd received his call-up papers Glenelg had lost to Sturt by a point. 'It was my man who kicked the point,' he said.

Cornes' parents had 'a really acrimonious divorce', and, as children, Cornes and his younger brother were placed in the custody of their father. 'He didn't know how to look after us,' said Cornes, 'so he took a second job and put me as a boarder at Ivanhoe Grammar School [in Melbourne]. I was seven years of age, and he was working two jobs to pay the fees.'[1] Boarding was 'horrible' for a seven-year-old boy alone, said Cornes, 'and I remember writing letters to my mother saying, "Look, I want to go out, I want to leave this place. Please come and get me." I don't know how she did it, but she broke into the dormitory in the middle of the night and struck a match in my face, and I knew straightaway it was her, and she picked me up, and I don't know what they thought the next morning, when I was gone.'[2] Then they were 'on the run', he said, 'my mother and I, all over Victoria, trying to get away from my father and the authorities who were trying to find us.'[3] But his mother, too, struggled to raise him. 'After six months of threatening to send me back to my father every time I was naughty, she just came out and said one day, "Well, look, I just can't look after you."'[4] Cornes first went to live with his grandmother, then he and his brother were put in a children's home near Heidelberg. 'We were only there briefly,' said Cornes. 'Dad rocked up in the Studebaker and we piled in the car and we drove to Adelaide.'[5] He didn't see his mother again for forty years. 'I used to think of her a lot, and in the early days wrote letters,' said Cornes, 'but then the letters didn't come back.'[6]

At 2RTB, Cornes was chosen for Scheyville. Jones did not put in for officer training, believing 'foolishly or gullibly' he would go into the band corps. 'I applied as soon as I could,' he said, 'to be a trumpet player or whatever, and they said, "Oh yeah, that's infantry. Do a bit more training and you'll get siphoned off into music." Well, it didn't work like that. Next thing I know, I went up to infantry corps training in Singleton.' Cornes was marched out of Scheyville a week before graduation. 'I was pretty immature and didn't take it that seriously,' he said. 'I got lost on a navigation exercise.' At Scheyville, Cornes had listed his preferred posting as 4 Base Ordnance Depot at Keswick 'so I could come back and play football if I graduated as a second lieutenant', he said. Since he didn't pass, he and a couple of mates decided to put themselves forward for the next battalion going to Vietnam. 'You didn't pay tax, you got a combat allowance and you qualified for a war service loan,' said Cornes. 'We didn't contemplate there was a fucking war on. It was just another great adventure.'

He joined 7RAR in March 1969, just as the football season was starting. 'So when I got weekend leave, they were flying me home to play footy,' he said. 'That really annoyed the other regular soldiers and the NCOs.' Unlike most men who'd gone through Scheyville, he wasn't given a lance corporal's rank. 'Any qualifications I had were just smashed,' he said. 'They hated me. I wasn't promoted – in fact, I was constantly being charged.'

Outside of the army, Australian public opinion, a noise more heard than heeded, was shifting against the conflict. By March, opposition to conscription had grown louder and angrier as students were arrested for distributing pamphlets inciting men to defy the National Service Act. Demonstrators in Sydney clashed with police, whom, the *Sun* noted – 'resorted to force – fists included – to control them'. A protester in Melbourne was assaulted by a soldier, who tried to snatch from him a Viet Cong flag. The accompanying picture showed the student with 'his ankle trodden on' by police.[7] The families of dead national servicemen occasionally spoke out. Grantley Scales from Adelaide was accidentally killed by a fellow soldier in Bien Hoa. Scales, who'd worked in the family business before he was called up, had strayed outside his unit's perimeter, and been shot by a sentry on 3 March. Even before he knew the details of his son's death, Scales's devastated father said, 'What other country in the world pulls boys' names out of a barrel and sends them to fight in a war in a foreign country? . . . Grantley was a good boy . . . He hated it in the Army . . . I want to appeal to all mothers to try to put an end to this vile war.'[8]

A lingering suspicion that national servicemen were doing the work of civilians, for lower wages and with poorer conditions, was confirmed in April, when the minister for the army, Phillip Lynch, admitted a 'small number' of conscripts were filling skilled technical civilian positions at the Army Design Establishment in Maribyrnong, Victoria. Lynch said the men were 'not being used for this work on the basis that they formed a cheap source of labour, but in accordance with the aim of the National Service Act', which was 'to provide manpower to allow the Army to meet defence obligations and commitments'.[9]

None of this simmering discontent had any notable effect on public affection for those who were called up and went to serve in Vietnam. On 30 May, 4RAR, who had been in Vietnam since June 1968, came home to Brisbane to what the *Courier-Mail* described as 'a most spectacular "ticker tape" reception . . . Offices and shops emptied and work virtually came to a standstill.' Lieutenant Colonel Lee Greville, the battalion's CO, was quoted as saying, 'The boys have been through a lot, and they appreciated every cheer and wave. When I took my shirt off later it was full of confetti, a bit different from Vietnam.' Although there were no demonstrators reported at the parade – nor at any parade in Queensland ever – the paper claimed, inscrutably, 'Protest leaders decided not to proceed with any demonstration because Brisbane gave the troops one of the warmest welcomes since World War II.'[10] On the same day, the government announced extra benefits, in the form of training and loans, for national servicemen who agreed to stay on in the army for an extra three months.

Far more significant than anything that happened in Australia was a meeting in Saigon in June at which Nixon declared twenty-five thousand US troops would be withdrawn from Vietnam by the end of August, their roles to be taken by ARVN soldiers. 'Vietnamization' was the new catchcry. The South Vietnamese would be helped and taught to fight for themselves. Later in the month, Nixon said he hoped 250 000 further US troops would be withdrawn before the end of the following year. A US opinion poll showed 42 per cent of respondents thought the president's withdrawal plan was too slow.

While the future of the war was being decided in the White House, Broderick Smith, like Graham Cornes, had been posted to 7RAR. 'I'd already made it known vocally that I didn't believe in Vietnam,' he said, but he was willing to serve anywhere else. 'They spread the rumour we were going to Malaya,' said Smith. 'So I started training and I ended up being, for a few weeks, an acting corporal in the bush with a little squad. I just loved wandering around, playing cowboys and Indians, basically. At one point in 7RAR, I was in the bush five days a week for four or five months. At a weekend I'd wander up to the Cross, or go to Surry Hills and play with the Foreday Riders blues band.' He stayed with friends from the cast of the antiwar musical *Hair*, including the actor John Waters. 'They were funny,' said Smith, 'because they'd kind of take care of me. I was the token nasho. At that time, people that were more student types would like to have a token nasho boy that they were helping.' In July, the *Sydney Morning Herald* refused to publish an advertisement by the Committee in Defiance of the National Service Act expressing support for men who did not register for conscription. Although the paper reported the text of the 'statement of defiance' it judged it 'wrong in principle' to encourage people to break the law.[11]

Evan Jones went to Vietnam as a reinforcement on 16 July, and soon joined 5RAR as an Intelligence dutyman. At first, he worked at battalion HQ inside Nui Dat but, he said, he managed to persuade his boss, the magnificently named Captain Battle, that his time would be better spent taking photographs of troops on operations. 'I'd said to Captain Battle, "This is Australian history here and nobody's understanding the importance of the situation. We should be recording this for posterity." A couple of days later, he handed me the camera and said, "You're on the next chopper."'

Jones flew out to join different units at fire support bases, patrolling with them and photographing what he could of prisoners and captured goods. He kept a diary, recording day-to-day life in the jungle: 'Some lads sleep in hammocks if there's a handy spot. Others on "blow ups" on the ground, some don't even use "blow ups". Machetes are used to clear bed spaces if the undergrowth is thick. I use a mosquito net as I'm allergic to bites more so than others, but not everyone uses a net. Some guys put up hutchies, others don't worry. The Resupp arrives every three or four days, with rations, fruit, water, clean greens, goffers [cans of soft drink], cigars, lollies, cigarettes, toothbrushes and other essentials. A lot of work to sort it all out evenly round the Company . . . Lying in the sack at night it's eerie to hear the artillery rounds flying overhead then landing with a shattering explosion a thousand or two metres away. The buzzing, chirruping insects are silenced only for a second though. Early morning is rifle and gun cleaning time. No one wants to get caught with an inoperable weapon.'[12]

Sometimes a patrol encountered the enemy. 'Everything would go quiet,' he said. 'Maybe the creatures around you in the bush go quiet, because they aren't used to people on a path. The hairs all over your body start to go, and – *boom!* – a Claymore mine, or just a bit of shouting, and the forward scout would start firing down the track. Because I was behind, there was no way I could fire, so I just had to try and put my head as flat to the ground as possible – a bit like a cartoon character – and hope nothing got past the trees or bushes. In the morning, very early daylight, the guys would make sure it was clear, and they'd go out and check the bodies. I remember having to photograph a Viet Cong body, and I don't know whether they had done it, or we had done it, but the ears had been cut off, and I was aware of the ants crawling up the side of the head, into the ears. And I photographed it and I realised, "That guy's gone. There's just a hunk of meat there now." And I remember thinking, Where's *he* gone? Where's his soul gone? That could be me tomorrow. If I get out of here, what should I be doing with my life? What's life about? You're watching the chaplain say a prayer to the guys before they go out on patrol, or giving little services when he flies out to a fire support base, and I'm going, Well, just over the hill, the Viet Cong guy, the Buddhist, is saying the same thing to them. It's all the same. Go and kill them and be safe yourself? That didn't add up to me.'

A Gallup poll taken in August 1969 showed a majority of Australians were now in favour of bringing the troops home. Only 40 per cent thought the Task Force and its national servicemen should stay in Vietnam, while 55 per cent were opposed. That same month, it was revealed ninety qualified doctors had seen their final deferment lapse and were liable to serve – although only fifty-one had passed the medical. (The general pass rate for the medical had fallen alarmingly from 1965, when only 37.7 per cent of men failed, to 1970, when 51.2 per cent of men examined were found unfit for military service. This is often held to be partly due to collusion between reluctant youths and sympathetic GPs.) The junior doctors protested their own call up 'as a serious disruption to their essential medical training' which 'would set them back for years, and could alter the course of their careers'. The army admitted not all of them could work as doctors in the medical corps, but the remainder would 'be employed so that their medical knowledge and training' was 'used to the best advantage'.[13]

There had already been a smattering of doctors and dentists, such as Colin Twelftree, called up for national service, but these were the first to arrive in numbers, and appeared largely unenthusiastic. However, the doctors' draft signalled an important social change. The earliest national service intakes were largely made up of unqualified men, then came those who'd completed their apprenticeships, the first of the graduates, the teachers, and now the medical and other professionals. It wasn't until 1970 that the national service cohort came close to mirroring white Australian society, and only towards the end of the year might this have been evident in Vietnam. But by then Australia's war was already drawing to a close.

While Broderick Smith and Evan Jones served their time in the army, musicians in the US were calling on crowds to resist the Vietnam War. August 15 was the first day of the huge Woodstock festival of 'peace and music' at a farm in New York State. Many of the greatest acts of the sixties – from the Creedence Clearwater Revival to Jimi Hendrix to Melanie Safka – sang out for the cause of love not war. They were the artists who recorded some of the songs for which the era is best remembered – Creedence's 'Fortunate Son', Hendrix's 'Machine Gun', Melanie's 'Lay Down (Candles in the Rain)' – each of them a howl of anger and pain at the killing in Vietnam. In the US, a new musical culture was being built around the antiwar movement. In Australia, Johnny Farnham was singing about Mr Whippy. There was a small local political folk scene, in which small local acts played to small local crowds, but the US made the music that mattered. On 18 August, the last day of Woodstock, Country Joe and the Fish played the 'I-Feel-Like-I'm-Fixin'-to-Die Rag', the most famous of all the anti–Vietnam War songs, with its three count and chorus asking what we were fighting for. That same day, the men of 6RAR erected a cross in the Phuoc Tuy rubber plantation that was the site of the Battle of Long Tan. They were an ocean, a continent and a generation away from Woodstock.

On 2 September 1969, Ho Chi Minh died of heart failure in Hanoi. In Adelaide that same month, a masked gang threw buckets of red liquid 'believed to be animals' blood' over furniture and at files at the Adelaide offices of the DLNS, in one of a handful of events that have perhaps been misremembered as involving blood poured over soldiers. Nevertheless, the uncompromising militancy of the act pointed to lost patience and desperation. In Canberra, Robert Wilton, twenty-two, burned his 'draft card' outside Parliament House. Robert was the son of General Sir John Wilton, chairman of the Joint Chiefs of Staff Committee. 'Failure to register for conscription is a more effective way to combat the National Service Act than conscientious objection,' he said, an opinion that was increasingly shared. But the government had never been looking for trouble at home, and whenever possible seemed inclined to leave dissidents alone, rather than martyr them, particularly when it came to bringing prosecutions for inciting defiance of the Act. In search of publicity, the anti-conscriptionists resolved therefore to prosecute each other. A Canberra magistrate wearily dismissed charges against ten people, mainly academics and students, who had been summonsed by another sympathetic student for encouraging men not to register for national service. Later in the year, the prominent draft resister Simon Townsend successfully prosecuted thirty-seven people for the same offence.

On 3 October, Broderick Smith's battalion, 7RAR, was formally warned for Vietnam. 'I was getting despondent,' said Smith. 'I seemed to be losing energy. And I couldn't do bayonet practice. I remember the others were joking when they were doing it, ramming it into the sack and that, but I was seeing it for real, and I looked at them and I started crying. I was crying for them, because they were innocent and they had no real thought about what all this meant. I started jacking up from that point. I'd do stupid things, like I'd grow a moustache, and it wasn't allowed to go below the lips or out the sides, so I curled it up like Salvador Dali. Then they told me to get rid of that, so I turned it into a Hitler moustache, and parted my hair the same as Hitler, and that drove them nuts, because that was legal. Then I shaved half of it off and only had half a moustache.

'I was on a bush exercise near Wollongong, on guard duty one night, and I had nobody relieve me, and it was pouring rain. I'd been out there about four hours and I was frozen and soaked. I started to think, How can I get out of going to Vietnam without affecting any of the other guys? I went through a trauma, and this voice in a tree just said, "Go." It was a very nice, friendly voice too: kind of like a mature Australian documentary narrator. "Go!" I went, "Shit, okay." So I put all my gear into my hutchie, and I went to the corporal's tent and I said, "I'm going." And he woke up and said, "Ah, you stupid bastard, go back to sleep." I said, "No, I'll see you." When the morning came,

I wasn't there. I walked straight through the bush – didn't know where I was going – I followed a star or something. It was white sandy ground with scrub. I saw this white dog, out of nowhere, soundlessly run towards me and straight through my left leg. I've got some dear Koori friends who said that what I saw was a ghost dog. Some of the elders have seen it when they're out in the bush. I followed the way the dog was running from and there was no sound or anything. This was *not a real dog*. I just hit the freeway, I had my army waterproof jacket on, and I was hitching. This van came along, and these people said, "What're you doing?" I said, "I'm trying to get back to Holsworthy army camp. I'm on this initiative course where they dropped a bunch of us off in the bush and the first one that gets back to the camp, by any means, gets the weekend off." So they drove me all the way to the camp.

'I went straight back to camp, went into my room, took my clothes off, slept, got up in the morning and went on parade. I remember the captain coming up and saying, "What're you doing here?" and I said, "I came back." And he said, "*Why*?" And I said, "Because I'm a civilian." They put me back out in the bush, and I said, "I'm a civilian." They didn't know what to do with me. At first, they made me a Viet Cong, and they used to beat me and knock me around, but that wasn't really bothering me. So they made me like a UN observer.

'They put me on a trial after that,' said Smith. 'I kind of had to lie, because they were kind of asking me to lie. I said, "I don't believe in Vietnam and I need to have a cause. I'm a civilian and I can't go to war to fight people that I kind of like." Then they asked me, "If your family was threatened by a guy with a gun, what would you do?" I looked them in the eyes and I could see what game they were playing, and I said, "Nothing," which is what they wanted me to say. They gave me a $10 fine, posted me out of the battalion.'

While Smith was assigned to non-combatant duties, Graham Cornes – who felt Smith was the bravest man in the battalion for making his stand – was preparing to go to Vietnam. But Cornes' scheduled battle efficiency course at Canungra clashed with the

SANFL grand final in Adelaide on 4 October. 'I'd applied for leave to come home for the grand final,' said Cornes. 'I got it knocked back because we were doing jungle training. Our club president wrote to our CO, Lieutenant Colonel Grey, with this impassioned plea about letting me come back to Adelaide to play, because three hundred thousand people depended on it. It was just a stupid letter really, but the CO was impressed by it and he pulled me out of the course, and got me a driver down to Surfers Paradise. I flew home for the grand final and we lost.'

Glenelg faced Sturt at Adelaide Oval, in front of a crowd of 56 000 people. The Sturt team included Royce Hart, in his only outing for the club. Although Hart was taken out early, Sturt won. 'I was on a charge while I was away for my rifle being rusty,' said Cornes. 'I was supposed to go back that night but our club doctor, who was also medical officer for Central Area Command, said he thought I had concussion, so he gave me a chit for two days so I could celebrate or otherwise. I went back to another charge.'

A general election was scheduled for October. Neither conscription nor the war were particularly big issues in the campaign, but the government mooted that national service could perhaps be reduced in length, although never abandoned. Minister for Labour and National Service Leslie Bury said while national servicemen made up more than one-third of the strength of the regular army, they accounted for more than half of those 'actively fighting' in Vietnam. 'If we stop National Service it would be equivalent to starting to disband the Army,' he said.[14] In a rare case of public dissent, a group of national servicemen in Townsville confronted Prime Minister Gorton and 'complained that they were spending up to 18 months of their time at minor desk jobs'. Significantly, the soldiers were protesting not about being sent to war but about having nothing to do.[15] On 25 October, Gorton's Coalition won the election with a reduced majority, and only retained government on the strength of DLP preferences. On the same day, three Australian soldiers died in Vietnam, including one national serviceman, West

Australian Sapper Alan Duncuff, killed by a mine. Two more national servicemen died in the next two days. On 2 November, Evan Jones was moving through the jungle with A Company 5RAR, who were trying, with armoured support, to force a group of enemy out of their bunkers and into an ambush. The tanks got bogged, and the Australians called in an air strike on the bunkers, and bombarded them with mortars from tubes mounted on APCs. Jones, with company HQ, followed the previous day's tank tracks and found a wounded VC. 'No interpreters,' he wrote in his diary, 'so I had to try and talk to him. Got a few facts out of him . . . his lower left leg very badly smashed by shrapnel. Medics did all they could. I took as many photos as I could on slow speed due to darkness. Later I helped put him on [the] winch of "Dust Off" chopper. Quite exhilarating to see him safely up the winch and into the chopper with all the noise and wind etc.'[16]

'The guys from our unit were all saying, "Is he all right?"' said Jones. '"Does he want some water? Does he want a fag?" They were treating him like one of ours. They really cared for him. He was on the other team. He got shot, like he got damaged on the football field, maybe, but he was just one of us. Whatever he told me – I didn't know if it was the truth – I passed on.'

On 15 November, a huge demonstration was held in Washington DC, calling for a moratorium – or cessation – of the war in Vietnam. Half a million people gathered outside the White House and listened to radical folk singer Pete Seeger perform John Lennon's 'Give Peace a Chance'. The same day, an unclear picture began to emerge of a US massacre of South Vietnamese civilians which had taken place in March 1968 in the hamlet of My Lai, several hundred kilometres north-east of Saigon. The full details of the incident only became known in the years to follow, but at first it appeared that at least one hundred elderly people, women and children had been rounded up and shot by GIs, their village burned and livestock slaughtered. During the course of courts martial and investigations, it was later revealed there had been no enemy fighters in My Lai, and the people had offered no resistance when the US troops came, but between 347 and 504 non-combatants were murdered. Many women were gang-raped and sodomised. Bodies were mutilated. A baby was used for target practice. The killers' defence, as articulated by Second Lieutenant William Calley, whose platoon had carried out the massacre, was that they were only following orders. His words conveyed a certain frozen-hearted logic in Vietnam, but made no sense in Australia, where the government had always insisted the war in Vietnam was not a civil conflict but a battle between north and south. The civilians of My Lai were supposed to be on the same side as the US. What could be made of a war in which US troops tortured and killed their own allies? What was the point of it? And what if Australian troops, out there in the jungle where nobody could see them, were receiving the same orders? The reports of the trial helped stir the ALP and trade unions into action. The executive of the ACTU called for the repeal of the National Service Act and the return of all Australian troops from Vietnam and, famously, Sydney wharfies refused to load the *Jeparit*. In Vietnam, an informal campaign grew up among the diggers to 'wallop a wharfie' on their return home.

Dave Sturmer, the engineer blown up on the day mankind kicked the moon, had been promoted to corporal, and on 8 December 1969 he was in the May Tao mountains, at the north-eastern point of Phuoc Tuy province, as his patrol moved south-west from the huge FSB Picton to FSB Discovery. 'The Australian Army had a bridge-layer,' said Sturmer, 'and you had to use it, because this dinosaur piece of equipment had nothing else to do except find something to make a bridge of. As we were going out, we came across a dry creek bed and the armoured officer said, "Bring the bridge-layer in and put it across there." I was standing on one bank of this dry creek bed, and I said, "There's no need. There's nothing there. I'll show you." And I walked down and across and up and back again. "No, no. We have to use it," So they brought up the bridge layer, and over the two big spans went, and you had to drive over the two spans, which were really not very long at all, they'd just gone from one bank to the other. And we stopped on the other side.'

John Greene, a clerk from Paddington, NSW, was Sturmer's number two. 'Johnny Greene said, "Retract the bridge," ' said Sturmer, 'and, as it did, the two big spans gave way. They collapsed, crisscrossed each other, back onto the body of the bridge layer, and I couldn't do anything but laugh. So that held up a lot of the column that was heading south.' Sturmer and Greene were riding the lead APC when they hit the first of three anti-tank mines placed across the track. The mine went off under the driver, a regular trooper named Vivian Albert French. 'It lifted the carrier up,' said Sturmer, 'and that's eleven-and-half tonnes – and all I saw was this flash go up in front of me, and it was straight under Frenchy's arse.' Sturmer said the explosion blew French out of the driver's hatch – 'and as he came out, from where his hands were on the sticks, the lip of the driver's hatch severed his hands' – and sat him on the ground.

'Johnny had started to fall,' said Sturmer, 'and we landed on the second, much bigger mine, and that catapulted me up the track. It's funny what you think about: while I was in the air – and I knew something was gravely wrong – at Enfield swimming pool, we'd go off the high board, and tuck into a ball to make a bomb, and I figured that was about the safest way. Where I was going to come down, whatever I hit, I was better off being in a ball than going splat on all fours. Greeney had been blown straight up from falling onto the second mine, and the percussion would've caved in all his vital organs. So there wasn't much – I did see his body on the way back but he was just very still, dead as. And Frenchy had died not long after. But because I'd been blown up forward of everybody else, all my clothes had been blown off, except we carried a map pocket on our pants. That part of my trousers was still intact, with the belt.

'I thought, I've got to touch this. I don't know what's there and what's not there. There was a lot of smoke, so I couldn't see a lot, and it's funny: you always go for your balls first. I don't know why blokes do that, but they do. So when the shooting stopped and one of the Cav guys took his weapon and raced off into the bush, I was starting to work out that I could move a little bit, and I think it was just the adrenalin happening. The guy in charge of the combat engineering troop that was our backup on the ground had sent a young bloke up. He was totally inexperienced, and he walked up on Greeney's side of the damaged track and started to come up in a very unsafe area, and I remember ripping the shit out of him and told him to fuck off back and get this guy called Jon Fuller to come up.'

Sturmer made his own way to safety, climbing from carrier to carrier, avoiding the ground. He felt he was finally secure when he looked up and saw Fuller heading towards a helicopter. The rear rotor propeller of the chopper set off the third mine, blowing off the aircraft's tail. 'I guess, for me, at that point, the world ended,' said Sturmer. 'I was a shattered mess. All the strength I'd had to get myself back came to a sudden stop, and I guess the shock stepped in. The only thing I really remember was the pilot and the crew had brought out their life raft in the middle of the bush. It was quite a funny event, really, I guess. It was a really bright colour. And they asked if I wanted an Australian biscuit, or some Australian water in a tin can they had. Er, no.

'The dustoff chopper took me back to Vung Tau hospital again, and once I'd been attended to in triage I was put back in the bed and obviously given something to relax me, and I remember the young doctor who'd looked after me the very first time, he was standing at the edge of the bed and he said, "You're back. I think you might be going home this time." And I was really relieved to hear those words.

'So from there it was just wait to be discharged from that hospital onto the transport Hercules to bring me home. They flew us into Butterworth, we were there for quite a while. My eardrums had been perforated. Butterworth is a beautiful place, magic, but they'd put this stuff in my ears and it burned like hell, because the eardrum was very tender, raw. It was like someone poking you right in the middle of the head. I had superficial burns on my arms and things, blast burns.

Whereas the crew commander, Roger Locke, being half out of the turret, he was quite crisped, but he lived. During hospital, I remember his beard was growing back through the facial burns, and he was standing in front of the mirror in the ablution block and shaving, and he had tears rolling down his face. I said, "I don't know whether you should be doing that." He said, "Mate, it's driving me nuts." He wanted to rip his face off. The nurse said it was probably one of the best things he could've done at the time. It exposed all the new skin that was there, that was trying to heal.

'We were brought back from Butterworth to Richmond air force base. I was in hospital there for about a week. I was burned both arms, I'm not sure what had happened to my eye, but something had happened badly there. My reflexes had got a round away off my rifle, another round was rammed up behind the one in the spout, and didn't discharge, luckily, but the white cutting heat of the blast had cut the barrel off the rifle. How lucky am I?'

On 9 December, the day after Sturmer was blown up for the second time, there was an attempt by about twenty people to stage a rally at a welcome-home parade for 9RAR in Adelaide. The battalion had been in Vietnam since November 1968. The parade attracted the usual large crowds of wellwishers, and young women tossed rice as confetti into the ranks of marching men, but when the troops reached the town hall, they passed twenty silent demonstrators wearing black armbands and carrying banners reading 'Withdraw Them All Now' and 'Peace Now' (rather than the folkloric 'Babykillers'). As 9RAR marched past them, the demonstrators formed two columns and joined the end of the parade. On Waymouth Street, the demonstrators were attacked, initially by 'several elderly men', who ran up and tried to grab the banners. According to the Adelaide *Advertiser*, one man shouted, 'We can't let you scruffy lot of b------s spoil Adelaide's honoring fine lads back from Vietnam.' Others called the demonstrators pigs and dogs, and cried, 'Why aren't you over there?' and 'Why don't you get your hair cut?' The newspapers noted 'elbows were freely used in the melee'. The demonstrators – identified as 'an anarchist group' along with members of the Women's International League for Peace and Freedom, and including politics lecturer Brian Abbey and draft resister Bob Hall – were cordoned by the crowd, and police confiscated their torn banners. Hall said they had chosen the 'least emotional' slogans they could find, and only at the last moment decided to fall in behind the march.[17]

Like so much else that happened in the closing years of the war, the march is remembered far differently to the rather comprehensive way it was reported – and photographed – at the time. Some soldiers, showered with rice by wellwishers, recalled instead being pelted with vegetables by demonstrators. The silence of the protesters became a cacophony of abuse. The troops' supporters melted into insignificance. One 9RAR national serviceman recounted only 'boos, taunts . . . vegetables, abuse, name calling, it was so humiliating . . . so embarrassing . . . so disgusting. We thought we would've been welcomed home and we were rejected by our own Australians.'[18]

Although there were occasionally very small protests at battalion welcome-home parades and send-offs, these events were not generally a focus for confrontation. While some veterans may be haunted by the ghost of Nadine Jensen, arms outstretched, a bride of blood, there were no similar apparitions on any comparable occasions. But after My Lai, the rhetoric of parts of the anti-war movement became more revolutionary, the anger of the protesters more real. On 15 December, a meeting of two hundred Victorian shop stewards passed a resolution encouraging 'all those young men already conscripted to refuse to accept orders against their conscience and those now in Vietnam to lay down their arms in mutiny at the heinous barbarism committed in our name upon innocent aged men, women and children.' Jim Cairns and fellow Labor MP Tom Uren, a survivor of the Thai–Burma Railway, joined a fifty-car 'freedom ride' from Melbourne University to Sale Prison, where another conscientious objector, Brian Ross, had been jailed. Outside the prison, Cairns said that if My Lai was a war crime then it was a war crime for President Nixon to support action in Vietnam.

Along the route of the ride, a man stood in the rain at Yallourn, hurling abuse at the cars; there was a small counter-demonstration at Traralgon, where about a dozen youths 'booed and screamed protests against the demonstration'; police on the highway swooped on the convoy and wrote more than a dozen tickets for speeding, unroadworthiness, and, in one case, having a Viet Cong flag out of the window; and even in Sale the local RSL slipped into the procession with a float showing members of the armed forces. But real counter-protests such as these have been forgotten while other apparently imagined demonstrations are recalled. Many years after the war was over, tales began to be told about demonstrations that supposedly met returning men at Sydney Airport, usually in 1969 or 1970. The most spectacular of these appeared in an official publication of the Department of Veterans' Affairs, which quoted 'Mike' from Perth, a national serviceman who served in the artillery, and came home, relieved, in January 1970: 'At Mascot, the relief turned to anger,' said Mike. 'We were pelted with tomatoes and spat on. But we got our satisfaction afterwards – 150 toey, angry lads from Vietnam versus 400 demonstrators – they didn't stand a chance.'[19]

An airport riot involving five hundred and fifty people would have been one of the worst incidences of political violence in Australia since the 1940s, and the biggest clash to that date around the Vietnam War. But there were no anti-war demonstrations at Sydney Airport reported in 1970 in any Sydney newspaper, or *The Australian*, or the NCC's *News-Weekly*, which delighted in chronicling the smallest impertinence of the anti-war movement. There is no evidence of the organisation of airport protests in the radical press, where other small demonstrations were built through advertising and propaganda, and no debate about their effectiveness as a strategy in the often furiously sectarian media of the Maoist, Trotskyist and anarchist groups. Even the smallest demonstrations leave traces. There are photographs, for instance, of a three-person Australian Nazi protest at Brisbane Airport in 1971, against the arrival of child psychologist Benjamin Spock, an opponent of the Vietnam War.[20] A clash between a handful of Australian Nazis and perhaps sixty anti-apartheid protesters, assembled at Mascot Airport to object to the arrival of the all-white South African surf-lifesaving team, featured on page two of the *Sydney Morning Herald*.[21] In the earlier years of the Vietnam War, it was not unknown for small groups of demonstrators to stage obscure protests at airports during daylight hours. When Sydney's Anglican archbishop, Hugh Gough, flew to Vietnam to visit Australian troops on 8 November 1965, six members of the Women's International League for Peace and Freedom picketed his departure, an event reported on the front page of the *Sydney Morning Herald* the next day. There are no published photographs of airport demonstrations against returning soldiers – as opposed to politicians – in Australia.

The flights carrying troops back to Sydney from Saigon returned late at night, which many veterans have come to believe was an attempt to shield them from demonstrators. But there were operational reasons for the Qantas military charters to arrive at Mascot at eleven p.m., the extreme end of the airport curfew (they did not deliberately land any later). The more flying hours a plane averages in a year, the more profitable it is for its owner. When a Qantas flight reached Sydney at eleven p.m., ground staff had to remove the economy-class seats from the front of the cabin and replace them with first-class, and take the cargo beds out of the back, a process that might take a couple of hours. The plane would then be ready to fly commercially the next day and could even complete a return commercial flight to Christchurch before arriving back at Mascot at five p.m., at which time – if necessary – it could have been reconverted to a military charter ready to take off for the night flight to Saigon via Singapore. The plane would have been in commercial use for eighteen hours of a twenty-four-hour period, prime yield for an airline. The possible presence of demonstrators was not a consideration when scheduling the late-arriving flights. The airport-demonstration stories ignore a number of practical factors, from the difficulty of organising a protest outside the city after dark to the presence at the arrival of each flight of armed military police to escort the troops to the airport's makeshift army pay office. Nor is it clear why any group might repeatedly hold demonstrations last thing at night, when there would be only soldiers and airport workers around to see them. Nor does it make sense that the government might smuggle in troops by air at night, but welcome home those who arrived by sea with huge public parades. It would seem the parades need to be forgotten for the protests to be recalled.

There were, however, also Pan Am flights coming into Mascot from Tan Son Nhut carrying, among others, US and Australian troops taking R&R in Australia. These charters ran on a different schedule to the Qantas planes, and perhaps they sometimes met hostile comments from other passengers at the baggage carousel.

There are no dead certainties in Australia's Vietnam War – it's always prudent to lay a bet both ways.

30

THE MYTH OF THE MORATORIUM

The stories of airport pickets probably cluster around the turn of the decade because 1970 was the setting of the first and largest Australian moratorium demonstrations. In memory, the Year of the Dog has become one long procession of bearded men and Nadine Jensens, waving NLF flags, 'Baby-killer' banners, and chanting the name of Ho Chi Minh.

Evan Jones returned to Sydney with 5RAR on 3 March, two weeks after Graham Cornes had arrived in Vietnam with 7RAR. The HMAS *Sydney* carrying 5RAR docked at Garden Island, where the battalion's mascot a Sumatran tiger was brought over in a cage from Taronga Zoo to greet them, and the wharf was packed with friends and relatives carrying welcome-home signs. Five hundred and twenty troops from 5RAR marched through the city to Sydney Town Hall, accompanied by about the same number of returned men from other corps and the RAAF. Four marching bands played, and ticker tape clouded the sky like a snowstorm in the mountains. A cheering crowd of tens of thousands stood up to fourteen deep. Minister for the Army Andrew Peacock took the salute, then the entire event disappeared from folk memory, to be replaced by a tableau of sneering, spitting students, and a nation united behind marchers of a different kind.

When Jones disembarked the HMAS *Sydney*, he went home to

Adelaide for a week, then travelled back through Victoria to New South Wales. He stopped in Melbourne on the way, and listened to a recording of 'The Pushbike Song' made by his brother's new band, the Mixtures.

The first time Cornes went outside the wire at Nui Dat, it was as part of a cavalry unit, with a tank, and the mortars mounted on two APCs. 'We stayed out overnight,' he said. 'We harboured up, and we were petrified because we were out in the jungle. I'd done my piquet duty by the machine gun, and just after midnight I went and draped my mosquito net over me, and lay back on my pack right beside the Centurion tank.' He was dozing off when he heard 'this huge explosion. I sat bolt upright, got tangled in the mosquito net, and I was trying to get my rifle and cock it. There was machine guns firing *ch-ch-ch-ch-ch*, tracer bullets going everywhere. What the f–! You had no idea what was happening.

'I was right alongside the track of the Centurion, and it let go one of its rounds and the thing lifted off the ground. *Bang!* And it crashed down in front.' It might have been over in a minute, but 'sixty seconds is a long time in a contact', said Cornes. 'They said they heard people chattering on the radio. So they opened fire, and let the Claymore mine off. They'd taped plastic explosives to the Claymore, and that was the big explosion.' There were no human casualties in the incident. 'They think it was a herd of pigs,' said Cornes. 'There was all these pigs that were shot up.'

After weeks on operation, Cornes returned to Nui Dat. His section was on duty in the camp, which meant they had to be in the lines in case they were ordered out on a fire mission. Each member had to man the radio and do a two-hour piquet. Cornes went to see a movie while he was waiting his turn. He told the lance corporal he could be back in ten seconds if required. The lance corporal was doubtful, but didn't order him to stay behind. 'But when I came back after the movies,' said Cornes, 'the platoon commander, in some sort of pique, had come through the lines tipping guys out of bed. He said to the corporal, "Where's Cornes?" "He's gone to the movies, sir." "Did you tell him not to go?" "Yes, I did." "Well, charge him."

'So as this charge was being heard by the company commander, and subsequently the battalion commander, I was just thinking, Oh well, it's another charge.' said Cornes. 'I didn't mount my case. I didn't defend myself at all. And then when the commander said, "Seven days in the detention barracks. March him out," I thought, Fuck, this is serious. It was too late then. I was put in the military prison for seven days at Vung Tau in a cell that was virtually a cage. There were no real hardened criminals in there. One guy had fallen asleep and missed his bus. Another guy was on piquet and was following a jeep with his rifle, and it accidentally discharged. It didn't kill anyone. But the military policemen were Kiwis and they were real bastards. It was the first time I'd ever kept my mouth shut and done everything. We were up at five. You had to parade. You had to prepare all your jungle green webbing, every little hole Brasso'd and everything beautifully black. And they worked you really hard during the day. We were on the sand hills, laying barbed wire and putting stuff up. There wasn't much respite.' But, he said, 'It was much easier than being in the scrub.'

After he'd served his seven days, he returned to his platoon. 'And within two weeks I was charged again with disobeying,' he said. 'A corporal told me to pick up some cigarette butts; I said I didn't smoke. He said, "Pick 'em up," and I said no. Then I was before the CO again. He was a bit more annoyed that I'd come before him again so he said, "I'm transferring you out to a rifle company to make better use of your temperament."' It was the end of April 1970. 'Within half an hour,' said Cornes, 'I'd packed up and I was in this chopper, dropped in a landing zone and joined Five Platoon, B Company.' Six platoon commander Second Lieutenant Peter Winter, a first-intake national serviceman who'd joined the regular army, reacted to Cornes' arrival in solid army style: 'He will certainly be useful when it comes to the inter-company sports day,' he wrote to his wife.[1] He told her Cornes was a 'beaut bloke' who 'used to be in the Mortar Platoon but didn't like the idea of being in base for too long, so he played up a bit'.[2]

On patrol, said Cornes, 'Your section was always under-strength. There should be ten guys, but six or seven was the norm, so you've got six or seven guys doing the work of ten men, with watches and things like that, so you're constantly sleep-deprived, and always tired, always hungry, mostly thirsty, filthy dirty.' He experienced only three contacts, 'none of which', he said, 'posed any real serious threat. I felt we were always in control. At the moment it's so exhilarating and exciting – and we didn't get any casualties. It was bad enough dealing with enemy casualties: some young guy lying there, he's got little pockmarks out of his skin but he doesn't even look like he's been severely injured.'

When an inter-company football match was scheduled at the end of July, B Company beat C Company: 9.4 to 2.3. 'Private Cornes, our Glenelg star, was in the ruck,' wrote Winter to his wife, 'and his talents, although a bit rusty, were the main reason for our success.'[3]

Although he later changed his mind about the war, while Cornes was in Vietnam, he felt confident he was doing the right thing. 'You're totally indoctrinated,' he said. 'You're totally committed because you could see the atrocities committed on the ground by the Viet Cong. You could see that you were making a difference. So any resistance to the war, we regarded as treasonous. We kept getting stories about the protests; it was infuriating, because we really thought we were doing a good job.'

The major Australian moratorium rallies were held on 10 May. The latest Gallup poll examining Australian attitudes to the war had been conducted in October 1969, prior to the first My Lai revelations. Only 39 per cent of Australians believed the troops should stay in Vietnam; 51 per cent thought they should come home. This was the lowest figure ever polled in support of the commitment (the highest was 62 per cent in May 1967). Opinion about both conscription and the war had shifted not just in the arts faculties of metropolitan universities, but also in the shorter-haired, more clean-shaven corners of Australian society. In February 1970, even the Young Liberal movement had condemned national service, and called on the government to 'rapidly phase out' the scheme and instead improve pay and conditions in the regular army.

In the US, the Nixon-appointed Gates Commission on an All-Volunteer Armed Force reported on how the US Army could survive without conscription. The commission, whose members included the economist Milton Friedman, arrived at the conclusion that better pay and conditions along with a vigorous recruitment campaign might attract more men to a military career. The commissioners had considered the Australian experience which, noted their report, some people had cited as evidence that an all-volunteer force would be unfeasible in the US. They rejected this idea, and found that, prior to introducing national service, Australia had made no 'concerted effort' to attract volunteers, and once the decision had been taken to use conscripts, 'no serious effort was made to increase voluntary enlistments either by raising pay or redoubling recruiting efforts'.[4]

But all this was inconsequential in comparison with the fact that on 20 April, Nixon announced the withdrawal from Vietnam of one hundred and fifty thousand more US troops. Gorton had little choice but to foreshadow Australian cutbacks. Two days later, he said the Task Force would revert to two battalions: 8RAR would not be replaced in Nui Dat. All these decisions were made weeks before the first mass demonstrations. The beginning of the Australian departure from Vietnam had nothing to do with protesters in Australia, just as Nixon's 1969 announcements of the first huge US withdrawals had preceded the first huge US demonstrations. But moratorium protests were held in every Australia capital city in May 1970, with about seventy thousand people marching in Melbourne alone, and perhaps two hundred thousand across Australia. Subsequent rallies were smaller and more prone to violence between demonstrators and police, but in May they passed peacefully except, once more, in Adelaide

On 8 May, two days before the big, official demonstration, 1000–1500 students left a teach-in on the Barr Smith Lawns at Adelaide University to begin a 'march against imperialism'. At the corner of North Terrace and King William Street, they were met by soldiers from Woodside-based 3RAR, all dressed in civilian clothes. The soldiers first jeered the marchers, then charged at them. According to the Adelaide *Advertiser*, a newspaper with no discernible sympathy for student radicals, the soldiers 'kept up a running battle with 1,000 peaceful Moratorium marchers', attacking them 'at least 20 times'.[5] The soldiers grabbed NLF flags and tore them to pieces, or set them alight and threw them back into the crowd. A nineteen-year-old woman, Margaret Barry of Murray Bridge, was punched unconscious. In Pirie Street, a spectator joined in, and hurled two large ice-creams at the marchers.

Outside the Ruthven Mansions in Pulteney Street, the soldiers linked arms and spread across the street to block the passage of the march, but were quickly dispersed by police. When the marchers tried to return to the university, the soldiers ran ahead of them and slammed the gates. Later that evening, there were further clashes outside Parliament House. Officers from Woodside came down and persuaded the men to leave, but they returned half an hour later, chanting 'We'll kill the Communists' and staged a sit-down opposite the building.

The Adelaide incident – the only large confrontation between demonstrators and soldiers ever recorded, rather than imagined – tends to be either ignored or misunderstood. *The Official History of Australia's Involvement in Southeast Asian Conflicts 1948–1975* said the men from 3RAR had 'recently returned . . . from service in South Vietnam',[6] echoing a claim made by the *Advertiser* at the time. In fact, 3RAR's tour of Vietnam had ended a year and a half earlier, in November 1968. The *Advertiser* quoted a 3RAR soldier named 'A Wait' as saying he'd 'been overseas'[7], but nobody by that name went to Vietnam with 3RAR. Certainly none of the national servicemen involved could have yet been to war. Some of the 3RAR counter-protesters wrote a privately published account of the day, which began with a 'sizeable group of soldiers' drinking in hotels when word reached them that there were Viet Cong flags coming down King William Street: 'The diggers were into the crowd of demonstrators like bandicoots through a blackberry bush. North Vietnamese flags were soon burning up and down the footpaths. One digger even set one alight from the roof of a fruit cart. Speaking of fruit carts, those that were in the vicinity sold out of tomatoes like lightning – and a hail of vegies ended up in the crowd of protesters a split second later. It was huge fun.' In the streets of Adelaide it was protesters, not soldiers, who were pelted with food. Two junior officers, John Wheeler and Bob Lewis, were described as 'conspicuous by their leadership' of the attack, but it's possible Wheeler did not take part.[8] Neither officer was a veteran on the day, but Wheeler, a Duntroon graduate, was killed when the battalion returned to Vietnam in 1971, and Lewis, a national serviceman, was Commended for Distinguished Service during that same tour.

Five members of the battalion were arrested at the demonstration, and charges of civil disturbance against twenty-one men were heard at Woodside. Sixteen were immediately found guilty and fined. Seven were fined $40 and confined to barracks for seven days. The Victorian Liberal MP Sir Wilfrid Kent Hughes, a former Fascist sympathiser and POW of the Japanese, said he was willing to pay half the men's fines. An army public relations officer said there had been a number of similar offers from the public, although the army could not accept them. All the sentences were later quashed anyway.

The student theoreticians of the anti-war movement did not blame the soldiers for attacking them. In the eyes of South Australian radicals whose reports appeared in *Revolution* newspaper, 'The only confrontation that actually occurred was between victims of the same oppressive system. Radicals who wanted to smash the Nashos were simply no longer thinking in terms of their own analysis. The situation was counter-productive: to feel anger at the pitiable indoctrinated soldiers, whose only claim to having ever done anything right is to have killed in Vietnam, is to deflect the direction of criticism away from the real source of oppression, the government and the military-industrial complex.'[9]

On the last day of the moratorium in Melbourne, a pop concert billed as 'The Wake' was held in Treasury Gardens. The big draw was Ronnie Burns, who had recently had a national number-two hit with 'Smiley', a song written by Johnny Young about a happy young man who goes off to fight an Asian war and whose laughter won't be heard again. Years later, Young revealed the ballad had been inspired by Normie Rowe.

In some veterans' minds, the size of the moratorium demonstrations has come to obscure, rather than highlight, the differences among the protesters. The moratoriums were not massive pro-VC rallies. As *The Bulletin* reported, while Melbourne Maoists marched under NLF flags, 'Dr Stephen Murray Smith wore a white carnation in his buttonhole and carried a placard WOT A MOTHER'S DAY. Wizard Ian Channell from the University of New South Wales was dressed in khaki shorts, a union jack shirt and a fireman's helmet decorated with flowers. He had a sign around his neck "Handle Me With Care in Case I Break up Easily."'[10] The slogans on other banners seem to have rearranged themselves in memory. Words directed against the US government have seen their meaning changed to become accusations aimed at Australian soldiers. A sign filmed by TV cameras asking 'if you were being raped would you ask for negotiations or immediate withdrawal' – a reference to peace talks – has become 'Rapists!' (In the same way, a poster showing a dead child after My Lai, and demanding young men take sides with either the 'the Vietnamese kid with his guts blown out . . . Or the soldier who pulled the trigger' has seen its text reimagined as 'Baby-killers!')[11] There was a picture of a naked child on one of the larger, more prominent Melbourne moratorium banners. Its stomach was distended. It seemed to be starving.

Coincidentally, the men of 6RAR/NZ, whose tour ended in May, were unable to come home on the HMAS *Sydney* as the ship was in the docks for a refit. Instead, they flew back to Australia, company by company, over several weeks. There was no welcome-home parade for these soldiers, and to some it must have seemed that the moratorium was their real public reception, the spit in the face so often cited, perhaps emblematically, as evidence of the way they felt they were treated.

Towards the end of his two years, a man's military service often seemed to simply fade away. Broderick Smith, who stayed behind in Australia, was made batman to Brigadier Donald Dunstan, who was later appointed governor of South Australia. 'He and I got on very well, and I had a lot of respect for him,' said Smith. 'He called me "Killer". He became a great man.' Evan Jones was posted as an Intelligence dutyman in Holsworthy. 'There was not a lot happening,' he said. 'It was pretty bloody boring, just waiting out my time, so I got permission to sing again. I started doing Brian Henderson's *Bandstand*; I won the grand final of *Search for a Star* on Channel 10.' In September 1970, Jones' brother Idris and the Mixtures had a number-one hit in Australia with a cover of UK band Mungo Jerry's rollicking, relaxed 'In the Summertime'. Mungo Jerry's original was at the top of the charts when it was denied airplay by a local radio boycott of major-label UK and US releases, and the Mixtures' version simply slipped into its place.

In order to come up with a follow-up hit, the Mixtures 'changed the rhythm of "The Pushbike Song" to echo, or match "In the Summertime"', said Jones, taking it 'away from its original Beach Boys sort of style. It had a rolling faster rhythm, they changed it to "*uh-choo, uh-choo*".' It turned out the whole world wanted a reprise of 'In the Summertime', and 'The Pushbike Song' reached the Billboard Top 100 in the US and number two in the UK.

Graham Cornes left Vietnam on a charter flight on 20 August 1970. 'We were in Nui Dat that morning,' he said, 'got off the plane in Sydney, kissed the tarmac and went straight to the Cross. I was really lucky. I came home to the Glenelg Football Club, and the Glenelg Football Club provided me with the discipline, the infrastructure and support that a lot of other soldiers didn't get. I was in Vietnam on Thursday morning, then playing for Glenelg Reserves on the Saturday, then playing for their senior team the following week in finals.'

Cornes got to play for Glenelg against Sturt in the SANFL grand final for the third time in three years. Sturt won, for the third time in three years.

Although the great mass of Australian people never turned against their soldiers, they were not necessarily in favour of sending them to war, and many doubted the justice of putting conscientious objectors in jail. In May, the government had decided that convicted evaders might instead be sent to work on infrastructure projects in the outback for two years, but the idea was soon dismissed as unworkable and contrary to the requirements of the United Nations' International Labor Organization. In July, Malcolm Fraser accused politicians, ministers of religion and schoolteachers who advocated defying the National Service Act of having 'taken to themselves a peculiar type of arrogance – an arrogance of mind which they believe gives them the right to determine the conscience of 20-year-olds'.[12] But the changed mood of the nation was evident even in the dour theatre of the magistrates court, where a Melbourne magistrate told an anti-conscription protester that he too had misgivings about the Vietnam War – before sentencing him to one month's jail for inciting others to fill in false national service forms (a charge which, in this case, had been brought by the Commonwealth police). The day after conscientious objector Brian Ross was released from Sale Prison in September, he appeared on the TV show *This Day Tonight* and called upon all twenty-year-olds to do their 'darndest' against the National Service Act. Then, extraordinarily, Gough Whitlam, the leader of the opposition, advised national servicemen who objected to the war to give written advice that they would not obey an order to serve in Vietnam. The next day, he said NSW police officers who had returned from Vietnam were bringing discredit on the force because they'd been 'corrupted'. The *Sydney Morning Herald* judged, 'The latter piece of idiocy no doubt has less serious national implications than the incitement to mutiny.'[13] The mercurial, pragmatic Whitlam had never seemed overly committed to his party's policy of withdrawal from Vietnam, but now appeared to have taken a stand alongside the most militant members of the ALP.

On 28 September, the national service ballot was drawn in public for the first time. Major General Robert Risson CB CBE DSO, the executive director of the Melbourne Transport Committee, plucked the first marble while the minister for labour and national service, Billy Snedden, looked on. Snedden, who had not seen the draw before, described it as 'awesome'. He said the government had decided to publish the results because they were 'of great importance to the young men involved', as if the question had never been raised previously and the answer was obvious for all to see. He said the media had been admitted to show that 'everything is absolutely fair'. The birthdates drawn were published in the daily papers, as naturally as the results of the official state jackpot lotteries.[14]

As to the moratoriums, their effect on public opinion seems to have been misunderstood. They called for the end of the war and the return of the troops, and the war subsequently ended and the troops came home – but there was not necessarily a causal connection. There is no evidence the government altered the timing of Australian troop withdrawals in response to the protesters, rather than the actions of the US, nor that the protests won over public opinion, rather than reflecting changed sentiment. The first Australian moratorium had been followed by a second large national mobilisation in September. In the wake of both demonstrations, and almost a year of revelations about the US massacre in My Lai, the Australian population had become more stridently pro-war. By October 1970, 42 per cent of people agreed Australian troops should stay in Vietnam (the highest number since August 1969) while only 50 per cent wanted them home (down 5 per cent since August 1969). If the moratoriums and the massacre had any effect on people's thinking, it was to turn the uncommitted against the anti-war movement.

Nor did the demonstrations necessarily affect the way the public treated Australian soldiers. Jim Conley of Carlton, Victoria, a national serviceman who in mid-1970 was waiting in Camden, NSW, for a posting to Vietnam, said, 'It was quite an honour to be in the army at that time. If I got a long weekend, I could walk out on the road with my slouch hat on and put my thumb out, and every single car would stop. No one would drive past you. And some of them could and did drive two hundred miles out of their way to get me to the next whatever. I felt quite proud.'

Another moratorium-era myth is that most Australian journalists were somehow political radicals. There had been national-service journalists in the army since at least the second intake, when Chris Black from the *Dubbo Liberal* marched into 2RTB and later Saigon. The journalists had every kind of political viewpoint and – just as often – none. Michael Frazer from the Melbourne *Herald*, who had reported on Normie Rowe's haircut at the height of the Tet Offensive, arrived in Vietnam in April 1970, working in public relations as part of the Royal Australian Army Education Corps, based in the capital.

Frazer, author of the 1984 novel *Nasho*, had no particular concern with the Vietnam War 'other than it was a story, interesting from a journalist's point of view'. At Puckapunyal, he'd struggled to be a good a soldier. He had problems firing a rifle, as he normally wore spectacles for distance, but couldn't use them with gun-sights. 'I was hopeless,' he said. 'The training sergeant said, "If you feel you're not handling things, put on the safety catch and just stand up and stand to attention." But I didn't do that, because I wanted to be successful. It was really hard, because I was a journo and a drinker before I went in.'

Frazer was posted to army PR. During his corps training in Canberra, he learned 'nothing, nil'. 'They wanted us to write press releases, basically. It was very strictly military, to do with reverence and the appreciation of the rank of people.' Frazer worked as a writer and subeditor on the *Army Newspaper*, which he described as 'a public-relations sheet controlled by Bruce White, a secretary of the Department of the Army, and all copy for the paper had to go up through him.' Frazer was confounded by the news values of the publication. The civilian media carried human-interest stories about men killed in Vietnam, which Frazer felt might have been appreciated by those who'd served with them, 'but the army press totally, totally ignored reality', he said. '"Don't mention the war" sort of thing. It was like a media release for all soldiers to read, to do with what the management of the army wanted soldiers to know.' Casualties were briefly noted under the heading 'Passing Parade', 'down the back of the paper, before the sports section'.

Throughout his time in Australia, Frazer was agitating to be posted to Vietnam. 'There was no point in spending two years in the army sitting in Canberra,' he said. When his chance came, he was sent to the battle efficiency course at Canungra, where he found he could use an Owen Machine Carbine, despite his vision problems. In Vietnam, the PR unit was based in Cholon, where his job was 'tapping out press releases of the most innocuous kind, run up on the Gestetner. In army PR, you're not there to break stories about what goes wrong. Plus every day we had to read an Australian news service on AFVN, the American Forces Vietnam Network.'

Frazer served with national serviceman Reg Henry, a Brisbane journalist born in Singapore, where his father was the Reuters news manager. Henry had been a cadet reporter on the Brisbane *Courier-Mail*. He marched in before completing his cadetship. Rather than put off his military service, he deferred his evening university studies – 'partly because they weren't going very well', he said. 'They bored the hell out of me.' Even though he was a child of an industry that supposedly denigrated the idea of the war, Henry 'went to the army as a deliberate choice'. Unlike Frazer, in corps training, he said, 'I didn't learn nothing. I saw snow for the first time, and I got drunk twice in a day. That's something, I think.' On Russell Hill in Canberra, he wrote press releases while Frazer worked on the *Army Newspaper*, and he combed Australian newspapers looking for stories to rewrite and send to the radio announcer in Vietnam whom he eventually replaced. 'I did not volunteer as such for Vietnam,' he said, 'but I certainly didn't complain when they sent me. I thought, This'll be fun.' He was, of course, going to write the great Australian war novel 'and I made attempts to do it', he said, 'with no success'.

Although newsreading was his main job in Saigon, he also occasionally went out to do stories with the diggers. 'I drank a lot of beer with Mike Frazer and a few others,' he said. 'I remember the most successful thing Frazer and I ever cooked up: he was given a story that some digger in Saigon had tried to get meat pies to Saigon. We didn't have meat pies, and he'd bought two boxes full. And they got lost in transit. Frazer said, "This is bloody awful," but I thought that it could actually be pretty good. Think about this: "Somewhere between Saigon, South Vietnam and Sydney, Australia lies the riddle of the missing pie . . ." He said, "That's great!" So he wrote it up in tabloid style and it took off like nobody's business. The press in Australia loved it, and soon we were bombarded by pies from people. I probably achieved more in influencing Frazer to write that story than from anything else I did out there – and we got good meat pies to boot. We were army journalists, but it's an oxymoron in a sense, because we weren't going to be uncovering war crimes. Our thing was happy news that would keep people interested. But in terms of investigative reporting, the Great Pie Mystery was probably the closest thing I did.'

They also had to host Australian reporters visiting Vietnam, which led to 'a bit of tension', said Henry, 'because we thought some of them were complete dickheads. If we liked them, we cooperated with them. The people who went as correspondents weren't necessarily the top notch. There were a lot who were just adventurers, who went to the sounds of the guns and wanted to be Ernest Hemingway.' The acclaimed Tasmanian combat cameraman Neil Davis was unpopular with the army, he said.

At night, for entertainment, the PR men would drop water bombs from the roof of their hotel onto local people walking on the pavement. 'We would hold five-cent nights,' said Frazer, 'where the barbecue would be put on about four storeys up, on the top of the Canberra Hotel, and cans of beer or slugs of any grog you liked would be five cents. That was sort of at dinnertime, which was about six o'clock. So by the time nine o'clock came along – which was about time to go to bed, because we were always woken up at about five or six in the morning to be at work at seven – a fair bit of drink had been consumed. So the other thing that was always available down the front – amazingly, in a blue box that was, in fact, an ammunition box painted medical blue – were frangers, condoms. After lots of drink, they would finish up on top of the building, filled with water and dropped overboard.' Henry said, 'I was suitably appalled but laughing at the same time.'

Henry, like Frazer, served throughout 1970, while the moratorium demonstrations closed down the streets in every Australian state capital. He was a journalist and part-time student in the army in a period where journalist, students and the army are now often held to have been on different sides, and yet, 'We didn't really have strong opinions about the war,' he said. 'I had a great time. It was a blast.' To his chagrin, he was sent home a few weeks before his tour was due to end, on 16 November 1970. 'We were playing rugby against the Cercle Sportif,' he said. 'There weren't any goalposts, but I leaped over the line, hands outstretched, and scored the try, but I popped my shoulder out. It was really, really painful and they took me to the US Army Field Hospital at Tan Son Nhut. The Americans repaired my shoulder, then they sent me to Vung Tau, and that was an experience too: every day the orderlies came around with a cart carrying two Victoria Bitters, if you weren't dead. I went home in this Hercules plane with all these guys who'd stood on mines and things. And there was me with my rugby injury.'

31

2RAR'S WORDS OF WAR

In May 1970, at the start of the rainy season, when the paddies flooded and the orchids blossomed, the men of 2RAR arrived in Vietnam to replace 6RAR/NZ. Their battalion was once again designated 2RAR/NZ (ANZAC), as its four Australian companies were joined by two companies of New Zealand infantry. They landed in Vietnam less than a week after the first big moratorium demonstrations, and between two Gallup polls that showed domestic support for Australia's war hovering around 40 per cent (although a majority continued to favour national service). The moratorium rallies had included bands of Maoists and their fellow travellers waving NLF flags and, from a distance, it could look like all two hundred thousand Australians were calling for victory to the Viet Cong, rather than the safe return of the troops. In fact, the protesters were no more of one voice than the national servicemen were of one mind.

The journalist Robert Coleman had cleverly noted civilians looked more like soldiers when they put on army uniforms. Whether they marched in step, boots and buckles shining, or crept through jungle, smeared in sweat and cam cream, from a distance it seemed they were components of a great, efficient, single-minded whole. It was as if they had the same thoughts and feelings, the same hopes and anxieties, but if there were 15381 national servicemen who went to

Vietnam, then there were 15 381 different stories.

2RAR was destined for a fairly quiet tour of pacification operations and patrols in a largely subdued Phuoc Tuy province, where the enemy were perhaps simply waiting for the Australians to leave. But like every battalion, it brought together national servicemen with wildly different ideas and experiences, men far beyond the beer-drinking, whore-fucking, fist-fighting, sun-squinting lockstep knockabouts of Anzac lore. In the ranks of the battalion was a pretty young gay Christian from Melbourne, who regularly slipped out of his greens under the banyan trees of Townsville, where 2RAR was based; a socialist schoolteacher from northern New South Wales; and a Catholic farmworker from Queensland, who did not want to kill.

David Collyer, a survey draftsman with the Department of Crown Lands and Services in Victoria, came from a Liberal-voting family with a military tradition. His grandfather had been at Gallipoli, his great-uncle Hector was killed in Belgium, and his uncle Cam served as a lance bombardier at El Alamein. His father never talked about the Second World War, which he had seen out in the Atherton Tablelands. 'Because he didn't go overseas, I think he felt he hadn't done enough,' said Collyer.

Collyer realised he was attracted to men in his mid-teens. 'I was lucky I had a very accommodating boy next door for a number of years,' he said. 'I didn't hit the scene in Melbourne until just about the time I turned eighteen, when I started work.' He was both actively gay and actively Christian 'so there was a lot of conflict'. He could have used his homosexuality as a way of avoiding national service, but he felt like he was in a rut at work and he wanted to join the army. 'I was a little bit concerned about the physical side of it – whether I'd be able to pass the phys-ed side of things – but as it happened that was no issue at all.'

Collyer published a short memoir, in which he recalled the day in recruit training where he had to strip his rifle blindfolded and was told to love it 'more than a woman'. 'Well, that bit wasn't too hard for me,' he wrote.[1] His corps training took place inside 2RAR, at Lavarack Barracks in Townsville. He found no gay men in the army. 'Who's going to tell anyone?' he said. 'Mind you, I did make full use of the uniform – only when I was off duty.'

'The others probably thought I was off to a Prayer Meeting or Bible Study,' he wrote. 'And sometimes I was. But more often than not, I'd get dolled up in my finest and head off down to the Strand in Townsville and simply take my choice of the passing parade of meat . . . No-one back at Lavarack ever knew that one of my pairs of trousers had the bottom neatly cut out of the pockets. This made things very simple for someone I fancied to simply slip his hand in my pocket to sample what was on offer. Then it was a very short walk either down onto the beach or in among the aerial roots of the banyan trees to get down to real business. Others were always welcome to join in too if they wished.'[2]

Also in the battalion was Des Sloman, whose family had a sheep property in Dundee, north of Glen Innes, NSW. Sloman went to a one-teacher school, then the local high school, then on to teacher training in Armidale. It was only a two-year course, and Sloman was living in a pub and teaching full-time in the bush at nineteen years old. He had to stay at the school to pay back his two-year bond to the education department, but was happy enough to leave when he was called up, even though he was strongly opposed to Australia's involvement in the Vietnam War.

'If I were going to make a choice in it all,' he said, 'it would be more likely that I'd be fighting on the other side. My sympathies would certainly have been with the Vietnamese. Those people who did national service in '70 were very different from the people who did national service in 1965. They were a very different generation, moulded by that different pop culture. The people of the seventies had all that Bob Dylan, all that folk influence and hippie influence and that sort of liberating that was going on. I was very anti-establishment, and I disliked the church. I didn't like the sight of those priests and padres coming out of the bush looking for confessions. So it was a bit of an odd thing, going into it with that mindset.

'I was probably taking the course of least resistance,' he said, 'just going along for the ride, and jumping through the hoops and not causing any disturbance, and living my own life. I certainly had strong political opinions, but once you got to a battalion and a platoon you could discuss your ideas on the war pretty freely amongst your mates, perhaps even the corporals. It was only in recruit training that was tantamount to some sort of betrayal.'

On 2 May, Sloman wrote in his diary, 'I do not think it is worth sacrificing 400 Australians, 47,000 Americans, 675,000 Vietnamese troops and 390,000 Vietnamese civilians, as well as hundreds of thousands of injuries in order to secure military dictatorship in South Vietnam. For the sake of hundreds of Australian families and lives ruined because of the effects of the war I condemn Australian involvement in Vietnam.'[3]

Frank Donohoe, a friend of Sloman's in the battalion, came out of a beef cattle stud on the Darling Downs, Queensland. He had a twin brother who was exempted from national service because of a bad knee. As his brother could help his father on the land, Donohoe decided to go quietly into the army. Donohoe was a devout Catholic and was distressed at the low church attendance at recruit training. 'One time I was the only one there for the Sunday Mass,' he said. 'And that was quite disturbing. I remember crying in the church that day.'

Donohoe began his tour of Vietnam as batman to one of the lieutenants, but he found it boring and ended up as number two on a machine gun. Sloman was 'one of the best mates I've ever had,' said Donohoe. 'I liked his philosophy, his attitude, his way of thinking. He seemed to be able to see a bit more right from wrong. Everybody in the platoon kind of respected Des. We didn't really understand the history of Vietnam. We didn't know who or what we were fighting, what they were fighting for, or even really what we were fighting for

I think Des asked questions a bit more and understood more of what he was doing – and what we were doing.'

On 12 May, Donohoe, Sloman and Collyer were shown to 2RAR's lines in Nui Dat. Living conditions on the base had become more comfortable since 1965. 'The lodgings do have floors,' Sloman wrote, 'boards a few inches off the ground. Tables, bookcases etc. are also featured in the tents. They are the handiwork of soldiers who have come to this place in other years . . . Each Coy. has its own canteen. There are several base entertainment centres . . . including cinemas, billiards, volleyball, TV rooms etc. The TV here has 8 channels – all American of course.'[4]

There was a feeling the war might be winding down, with the enemy quelled and peace being negotiated far away. 'A runner came round to say that most of the Yanks in Nui Dat will be leaving soon and we will be moved down to Vung Tau,' wrote Sloman in his diary. 'The possibility of such an event occurring is minute but something to hope for. There's nothing like a good rumour to brighten the attitudes of soldiers. We thrive on sanguine expectation.'[5]

He described his first piquet: 'The gun post is a feature situated near the wire – and removed somewhat from the lines. This gives it a solitary look – grey, dark, unearthly. The construction consists of a pit around which and over top of which are sandbags. On top of this covered pit is a platform of sandbags on which there is the machine gun and two chairs. The sentry sits back on one of the chairs and keeps watch on the area to his front. At night one looks to his front and this is what he sees . . . Directly to my front was the perimeter wire – a tangled mass of barbed wire and steel pickets in which lay dead shrubbery, mines and flares. It would be virtually impossible for an enemy to probe through the wire without making a noise and thus alerting the sentry. This foreground makes a startling silhouette against the iron grey and dark shadows of the midground. The rubber trees, the barbed wire, the dead craving arms of the sprawling vegetation and the steel pickets appear with amazing sharpness and clarity – black, disorganised, rough, cruel and hard. The mid-ground is the cleared area around Nui Dat. This gives the impression of vague, enigmatic, eerie, unknown danger. One can gaze at this blankness and allow thoughts to flow through the mind. The silhouettes in the foreground help to make these thoughts usually unpleasant – hidden enemy, danger. The background consists of the hills and flats of rubber – a dark horizon at night.'[6]

Sloman was a rifleman with A Company for about six months. Whereas other platoons lost men to mines, Sloman's sergeant, a veteran, 'kept his officer under control and kept us off all the tracks', he said. 'We avoided the mines, largely because of him.' On patrol, said Sloman, 'You'd start out a bit vigilant, looking for things, but really you'd just plod. Behind the person in front of you. It's an odd thing but even in those situations where there could be an ambush, if it doesn't happen, I can remember switching off. I'm sure all of us switched off, except perhaps the scout up the front. So there was just that plodding through this hard landscape and setting ambushes at night. When you think of it, that's all people were doing. There were these little groups of thirty-odd men in each platoon on our side, and smaller groups on their side, and they were all setting ambushes for each other. We're setting an ambush for someone, and perhaps they've got one for us, even further up the same track. It was all a very weird scenario.'

One of Sloman's platoon's ambushes was triggered on 19 June 1970. 'It was a typical ambush situation,' he wrote, '2 guns being manned by 4 diggers, and there was little expectation of contacting enemy. It came as a surprise to Ian and myself therefore, to hear footsteps beating the shrubbery . . . Ian and I were on the gun at 9 talking quietly and tactically smoking (not tactical) our minds far from the activities of war . . . we peered above the knee high grass to see what was coming. We saw a small group of V.C. moving across our front in single file and 2 yards apart . . . Ian had taken control of the gun – I, of the Claymores. We watched the sharp silhouettes move to what we thought was perfect for the first impact of fire power. We watched quietly observing every detail of our first sight of the enemy – 7 figures, backs slightly curved, heads bent forward, black against a thick grey light. Another silent second and Ian gave a nod. Practically instantaneously the Claymores and gun blasted their lead towards the silhouettes . . . I moved to Ian's right and fired a flare. Brian bounded from his tent to support us in our fire. He took over the gun and sprayed the area. I supported him with our S.L.R.s. A slight pause in fire. We waited, listening for any evidence of enemy movement. A sudden sound interrupted us. A V.C. dashing madly away from the fire zone brought another burst of fire from us. Another pause – move movement – slower this time – crawling – another burst – then silence . . . We waited until we were sure that the enemy were either dead or had fled. Ian and I had seen two drop on the initial burst from the guns and Claymores. We had assumed that these two had been killed but we were a bit doubtful as to whether they had been shot down or purposely dropped to the ground to avoid fire.'[7] At dawn, they swept the area and found nothing but footprints and a pair of sandals. Sloman believed the enemy escaped unharmed.

His diaries were detailed and frank, but he chose not to record 'the exhilaration of it, and some sense of victory', he said. 'I would've been concerned about it being found, and your parents reading bits about how there was this enormous thrill from killing someone.'

In August, the platoon opened fire on a group of VC early in the morning. Although once again they discovered no evidence of enemy casualties, a couple of days' later, they came across a lone guerrilla propped up against a tree. 'The V.C. was wounded and did not appear to be carrying a weapon,' wrote Sloman. 'We called to him to halt (Dung lai). "Don't move or we'll shoot!" Getting him to lie down, he was searched. It was arranged to take him back to C.H.Q. He looked half starved and was covered by leeches. About 35–40, we assumed him to be a V.C. rather than N.V.A. It was assumed that he had been wounded in the contact we had 2 days before. Several vociferous members claimed to have shot him and yelled: "Shoot him. Shoot him. Why take him back. He's only trouble." We did however take him back and it was a surprise to many that he had not been wounded in our contact at all. He had been wounded at Hoa Long in an Ambush in which 9 V.C. were killed and 4 captured.

'He was being carried back to the V.C. H.Q. in this area when we contacted them. His friends had abandoned him and fled. He also informed us that they were also carrying another wounded soldier (V.C.) whom they also abandoned.'[8]

David Collyer had a shorter, less dramatic time in Vietnam where 'he was certainly a bit of an oddity', said his friend Sloman, 'because he was different, and he certainly had some gay mannerisms'. Collyer was an Intelligence man with company HQ, and sent a letter to his parents in June 1970, after witnessing his first shots fired in anger. 'I've just found out how I react under fire,' he wrote, ' . . . the bullets were ricoquetting [sic] off the huge boulders all around me. Some of the rounds came very close and I'm still a bit shakey [sic] as I write this.'

He had been cooking tea on operation, harboured up with a couple of infantry platoons, when the shooting started. 'My heart was immediately like a bass drum,' he wrote. 'I grabbed my webbing containing my 140 rounds and dived behind the nearest rock. As soon as I was there I realised I had my webbing on inside out! I must say I was really terrified as I had to secretly slip it off and put it on the right way. It didn't help either when the Major seemed to go to pieces and the old C.S.M. took over.' Collyer said later, 'This major was going off his head, yelling and screaming orders that didn't make sense, and that old company sergeant major was overriding him and keeping us all calm.'

In his letter, Collyer admitted, 'After some time I thought, "I don't even know if I'm on the right side of this rock!" So I made myself as small as possible and sang hymns (inside of course). I . . . only hope it doesn't get too much worse – it really was terrifying!!'[9] After about an hour, the men were told to stand down as the contact was over. 'I think in the long run that turned out to be friendly fire,' said Collyer.

On 23 July, Collyer was sent back to Australia after an accident. Sloman stayed in country until December 1970. Only Donohoe served a full year, returning to Australia on 1 June 1971. When he'd arrived in country, he said. 'I basically lay in the tent, sick for a week, in Nui Dat. I was so scared about Vietnam. But after a while, you become used to it. I'm a country person: the jungle has its own beauty. There were peacocks and there were wild pigs. There were lizards and there were plenty of insects to look at. There's lots to learn about in the jungle. I didn't mind the jungle. I wasn't afraid in the jungle.'

Donohoe's platoon made two fatal mistakes, accidentally killing an ARVN soldier and wounding two others in one incident, and killing two civilian woodcutters in another. On 14 January 1971, Donohoe's platoon was harboured up in a rubber plantation and set up a night ambush with Claymore mines on the track leading from the nearest village, a few kilometres away. 'During the night we can see these lights getting around and about in the plantation,' he said, 'and hear a few shots. The flashlights were coming closer and eventually they came into the area, the Claymore mines were off and everything started firing like crazy. One guy was apparently down in a bit of a ditch and he was wounded, and he was screaming and crying and everybody was firing at him. Eventually, the officer got on the radio and found out it was a few ARVN soldiers hunting rabbits.'

On 20 February, the Australians were patrolling in a free-fire zone near a village when, said Donohoe, 'The shooting all started and we advanced. It didn't last very long. We did a sweep forward and, when we got there, there was just an oxen cart and some dead woodcutters on the ground. They saw us coming and they ran, and the forward scout and the corporal opened up on them. They got killed mostly because they started running towards the ox cart. The forward scout wouldn't have seen the ox cart. The villagers all came and surrounded us, and we had to fix bayonets and lie down on the ground and get ready to take the whole bloody village on. They were pretty aggressive, they had a few machetes.'

Other troops were choppered in, and 'we just moved away from the village and left them with the bodies,' said Donohue.

Donohue mentioned the first incident briefly in a letter to Sloman in February 1971. The note, from one soldier to another, shows a difference in tone and content from the correspondence national servicemen customarily sent to their mothers and girlfriends, and hides the sadness Donohoe felt about the killings. It also put lie to the myth that Australians, unlike Americans, did not measure success in terms of body count.

Donohoe had just come back from R&R. He wrote: 'I did my arse in Hong Kong, spent $500, and only came back with a watch and some cloths. But I had a real ball and aren't really sorry about it. Yes I had a bird, and I'll agree with you about having to separate sex from marriage . . .

'Stretch killed 3 [sic] ARVN, they were out shooting game and ran into our ambush. Of course Stretch doesn't care who they were, he counts them as kills. Any how they shouldn't have been there, teach them a lesson.

'2 PL. got 3 kills up near F.S.B. Lynch. We have just finished an op. up along the Song Rai river . . .

'C. Coy has got up 20 kills . . . and only got one of their own wounded. A. Coy went up yesterday and took over from them. I've had to stay back on rear details . . .

'We went to Vungers on the 30th, had a real ball, and as usual half the Coy. is facing charges. I've been smoking a fair bit of grass lately, it's just crazy. I even have it back here at the Dat, but no-one knows about it. It's a pity you couldn't have tried more. They aught [sic] to legalise it in Aust., we'd be able to have a ball. I'd like to bring some back but the risk is too great.'[10]

'Going through Vietnam,' said Donohoe, 'I never did want to kill anybody. With all the firepower that was going on, I fired a few shots – I didn't fire much – and I fired a bit high. I wasn't against wars or anything, and I don't want people to think I was a coward. I just didn't want to have the blood of another man on my hands. Because we had to bury one guy one time. I lifted him by the feet and another guy lifted him by the hands, and we had to bury him in the grave, and I was surprised how heavy he was for such a small guy. But he had photos of his children on him. It's so disturbing when you realise that these people have got family.'

Donohoe didn't like drinking and preferred to wind down with a joint on R&C. Although he shared the odd smoke with Sloman and others, 'I thought I was pretty much out on my own,' he said. 'I wanted to keep it quiet, because I was scared to hell.'

2RAR came home as a battalion on 1 June 1971, at the end of the rainy season in Phuoc Tuy. It was winter in Townsville, the driest time of the year, when only XXXX on ice could quench a man's thirst. That same month saw the last of the big moratorium demonstrations in Australia, when tens of thousands once again took to the streets to call for an end to the fighting.

None of the actions of Collyer, Sloman or Donohoe had any effect on the course of the war in Vietnam. The schoolteacher, farm labourer and survey clerk fought in no battles, and probably killed nobody. 2RAR left Phuoc Tuy pretty much as they had found it when they handed over the province to 4RAR at the end of May. Their casualties had been light – the battalion had lost only eight men, of whom five were conscripts – but the significance of 2RAR's stories is no less for that. They show the lines in Australian society were not drawn nearly as neatly – or as thickly – as they are remembered. There were socialists who believed in the Viet Cong cause, but nonetheless ambushed them on the trails; there were Christians who went willingly to war, but shot over the heads of the enemy; and there were middle-class gay men who marched with the army rather than the anti-war movement. It's too simplistic to see the soldiers on one side and the protesters on the other, when the divisions in society could be mirrored in one man's actions. Within 15381 national servicemen, there were 15381 battles between morality and expediency, obedience and rebellion, patriotism and universalism, bravery and its opposite.

Only their uniforms made them look the same.

32

REBELS IN THE RANKS

The Australian Army suffered few of the disciplinary problems that bedevilled US forces in Vietnam. Race was barely an issue: the DLNS could never be nudged into finding an administrative solution to the legal problems around calling up most Aboriginal men; non-naturalised immigrants weren't conscripted until 1967; and non-English-speaking migrants would have been unable to reach the army's minimal educational requirements. Although there were a few Asian Australians, a number of Aboriginal regulars and some Aboriginal national servicemen in Vietnam (Graham Cornes and Broderick Smith remember with awe the Indigenous boxer Alan Aldenhoven, a corporal with 7RAR) the army generally was as white as Arthur Calwell's immigration policy. Australian soldiers rarely took drugs, and there were few instances of 'fragging', in which officers or NCOs were attacked by their own men. Nor was there any organised dissent among national servicemen. Acts of rebellion tended to be isolated and individual, the work of men searching for solutions to their own moral dilemmas. There were a few options open to a soldier who opposed the war: he could accept non-combatant duties; he could refuse to obey orders and try to leave the army; or he could continue his military training with the aim of one day turning his guns on his officers. The latter course of action was the rarest: in fact, it may only have been taken up by one man.

The common compromise was to agree to a non-combatant role, but this could come with its own ironies. The journalist Michael Frazer believed his platoon at 2RTB – One Platoon of A Company, sixteenth intake – was a 'misfits' platoon' – largely made up of men who wouldn't fit in anywhere else. 'We were not up to standard,' he said. 'We had people like me, who were just hopeless. And Costello.'

Max Costello was a schoolteacher from Camberwell, Victoria, whose birthdate had been drawn in the first ballot. He'd been able to defer while he was studying for his arts/teaching degree, but had nonetheless written to the DLNS in April 1968 stating he didn't believe Australia should be a party to the Vietnam War 'and since national service may entail fighting in Vietnam I cannot in conscience undergo National Service'.[1] Then Costello failed a subject and his deferral expired. By this time, Dennis O'Donnell had lost his bid to be recognised as a conscientious objector to a particular war and John Zarb had been jailed. Costello was concerned that if he refused to go into the army and ended up in prison, he would never be allowed to return to teaching in state schools. He rang an official at the DLNS and asked if someone who had applied for conscientious-objector status would be sent to Vietnam. He said the answer he was given was, 'No, but I haven't told you that, have I?'

His DLNS personal data sheet described him as a 'tall, well-build [sic] intelligent young man. Speaks well – not too keen to do Nat. Service'. His religion was marked as 'refuses to state'.[2] Confident he would not be sent to Vietnam, Costello marched into recruit training, where the army offered its Character Training Program, moral and religious instruction taught by clergy. 'Being an atheist, I asked to be excused,' said Costello. 'They had this grand parade, and the sergeant who was running the parade must have been required to asked if there were any troops who were exempted, and his way of doing that was to yell out, "Who hates God? Do you hate God, Costello?" Since then, I've thought of a thousand smart-arse answers, but it took me so much by surprise I just said, "No, sergeant."' Costello took the course.

Costello said he found military training 'a source of amusement'. He had no interest in being in the army. 'It was known by the trainers that I was an objector to Vietnam,' he said, 'so they were naturally hostile to me, and if there was any error in marching or any other drill activity, if I made a mistake – there may well have been others making a mistake – it was always, "Costello!" But I understood that was how they felt, so I didn't take it personally at all.' He had no curiosity about weapons and was not used to learning by rote. He was 'well and truly the last bloke' at 2RTB to put his rifle together. The instructors looked at Costello as if to ask, '"What the fuck are you doing here?"' said Frazer. 'Because some of these blokes had been to Vietnam. They had a job to do, and they didn't need people like him.'

Costello ended up posted to the Australian Army Psychology Corps in Melbourne, where his commanding officer was a clinical psychologist and former actor from Western Australia – 'sort of a showman', said Costello. In Melbourne, Costello the soldier shared a house with two unmarried radical couples. One of his housemates was on the Student Representative Council at Monash University. They invited the CO around for dinner. 'He was very entertaining,' said Costello. 'He didn't have any trouble with my politics.'

Costello joined and campaigned for the ALP, but he did not take part in anti-war activities while in the army. At one of the moratorium marches, he said, 'The only thing I did was walk along the footpath wearing military uniform. I was in the demonstration, in a way, because I was walking alongside, but not right out in the streets.' His job in the psychology corps was to mark and record the results of basic intelligence, maths and English tests conducted to assess the suitability of potential soldiers for the regular army. The conscientious objector worked in army recruitment.

Only a small number of Australian families had experience of the great political passions which had divided Europe, Communism and

Fascism. But there were exiles from Hitler, Mussolini and the Greek dictator Metaxas, and postwar arrivals of displaced people included Jews and other refugees from Soviet-occupied Eastern Europe, many of whom carried with them blood debts to Nazis or Communists. Their children were men such as John Karajas, who was born in Perth, the son of Macedonian Communists who had fled the Metaxas dictatorship before the Second World War. 'All the Karajases were Communists in Macedonia,' said Karajas. 'One of my uncles died fighting for Communism in the Greek Civil War.' So when Karajas was called up to fight Communism, 'It troubled me immensely,' he said. 'At the same time, I was a patriotic Australian bloke and, with the weight of authority pressing down on me, I thought, I'll cooperate. My parents did not like that at all, but I went along with it.'

He had graduated with a degree in geology in April 1970, marched into Kapooka the next week, and was selected for Scheyville. 'I hated the place,' he said, although the other soldiers were 'a really nice bunch of guys. The humour was superb.' He lasted thirteen weeks, long enough to become a senior cadet, but it became 'just untenable. Everything about the place was totally against what I was about. I felt so alienated. We were there to prevent Communism spreading through the whole of South-East Asia. With my family background, I knew that people turned Communist not because they were influenced by this great big politburo in the Kremlin, or Mao's henchmen in Beijing. It was people who were oppressed. The reason why people turned Communist is to seek a better life. I thought the people in South Vietnam were fighting for independence and a better lifestyle. In retrospect, you could say they were mistaken, but it was genuine. So I was sympathetic to the Viet Cong. But I love Australia, and I'm deeply upset I had to take this position during 1970. Even now. It was awful. It was hard, really hard. I was a very troubled young man, and at the same time I was extremely irritated with the way the army carries on.'

He resigned from Scheyville and was posted to the School of Military Engineering, where he applied for conscientious-objector status. He was given two months' leave without pay to prepare his case but realised, to his horror, that he was due to go to court on Remembrance Day. 'I got very concerned about this,' he said. He wrote to an acquaintance who passed on his letter to the Communist newspaper *Tribune,* which published a front-page story claiming Karajas was 'waging the struggle against the Gorton Government's war and conscription policies inside the heart of the war machine itself' and 'actively engaged in encouraging draft resistance and especially in urging conscripts inside the armed forces to get out without delay'.[3] In fact, he wasn't doing anything but fighting his own case. Karajas's court appearance was deferred and the army lost interest in retaining him. He was granted an administrative discharge later in November. He was approached to join the Communist Party but declined.

Karajas was followed at Scheyville by Aarne Neeme, a twenty-six-year-old theatre-company director from an Estonian family. Neeme's father had fought the Russians as a partisan in the Second World War, worked as a policeman under German occupation and then fled when the Russians returned. Neeme spent the first five years of his life in a displaced people's camp and was raised in the tight and insular Estonian community of Oakleigh, Victoria. 'We were virtually living in Estonia,' he said, 'except for five hours every weekday when I went to an Australian school. When I went home, I spoke Estonian. We belonged to Estonian Boy Scouts, our social life was purely Estonian. It wasn't until I left school at the age of eighteen that I went into the workforce and sort of entered Australia fully.'

He'd been called up in the first ballot, but managed to defer for more than five years of tertiary study and postgraduate work, during which time he marched in several student demonstrations and directed a show at the week-long Arts Vietnam festival against the war in 1968. He was married with a baby and, he said, 'really torn between my feelings about war – particularly this war – and my sense of responsibility to my family and to the community'. So when he could defer no further, he agreed to go into Puckapunyal, then

Scheyville. But at officer training, he felt manipulated, conditioned and desperately unhappy. After about a month he decided he couldn't be in the army, and didn't want to go to 'somebody else's country, carrying a gun and not having the choice of whether to use it or not'. He 'decided to make a stand', he said. 'I basically just took my uniform off. Having made that decision, what a weight it was off my mind! After years of inner debate, to have that clarity! I thought, I don't now care what happens to me. I was quite prepared to go to prison for two years. It was saying, "I've made my mind up. There's no more bullshit. This is what is right *for me.*"

'For two days, I kept in my cubicle, so for two days they said, "No Queen's uniform, no Queen's rations." The other guys were terrific. People smuggled things in from the mess. It certainly didn't feel like I was being ostracised, there was nobody saying "you weak prick". I got that from some of the officers, but not from the recruits.'

He claimed conscientious-objector status and won his case at a court of petty sessions. The anti-war movement didn't give him aid. 'I never sought it,' he said, 'and it was never offered.' Nor did he attend any more demonstrations. 'It was probably selfish of me,' he said, 'but I just felt it was me against them, and that was finished. In a funny way, I'm not proud of getting out, and I honour the people who decided to do their duty – if that was a conscious decision, rather than just being herded into that situation.' Neeme was ostracised by the Estonian community, but said, 'My father – whom I feared most in terms of his anger, his disapproval, his disappointment – was so forgiving. He said, "I never wanted you to go through what I had to go through."'

Errol Heldzingen was perhaps the only radical who chose the hardest path of all – to join the army and subvert it from within. It's unclear if this was part of an abortive Communist Party strategy, floated and then forgotten, or speculation taken seriously, and acted upon by a man desperate to do something useful.

Heldzingen had always felt different, like he didn't fit in. His father had been blown up at Tobruk and he'd come home to Australia to marry Errol's mother but was never well again. 'The relationship with my mother wasn't very good, and he was in the repatriation hospital,' said Heldzingen. 'Consequently, I'd been put into an orphanage. I got out of the orphanage when I was four years old. I think it was a condition of the divorce settlement. My father went up to the hospital in Brisbane, and I lived a squalid sort of existence in Melbourne with my mother. My mother had eleven children, ten surviving.

'I had a Catholic primary school education,' said Heldzingen, 'and I went on the road when I was thirteen and tried to survive, mostly around the Murray River, the Murray–Goulburn Valley and the Riverina of New South Wales. I spent about a year traipsing all over the place, picking fruit or whatever I could. When I was fourteen, I went back to Melbourne and got a job in a factory. I did factory work for about three years and became a builder's labourer in 1964.'

Heldzingen was a little guy but tough. He knew how to fight and he wasn't afraid of much. 'I wasn't a good reader,' said Heldzingen, 'but I used to read from time to time, especially in the country, where it's pretty boring. As a builder's labourer, there was a lot of political activity and discussion on the job. I was seventeen then, and probably a bit of a drunkard. I started to become something of a socialist, I suppose. I saw a demonstration one day coming home from work, where people were demonstrating against the war in Vietnam outside the Victoria Barracks on St Kilda Road. I jumped off the tram and went over to see what was going on, and I got some pamphlets and spoke to a few people, and got some information about the Eureka Youth League. I became involved and learned some stuff. I had to learn things. I wasn't very good at anything. I needed leadership. I needed people to point out how to do things, because I really didn't know.

'I've always had a feeling about authority,' he said, 'a rebellious feeling about the forces of oppression. Ned Kelly was a bit of a model for what I thought about Australia and the world. I eventually developed an understanding of imperialism, of colonialism, of capitalism. I'd started to understand where I stood in relation to struggles that other people were going on with. I thought, This war in Vietnam, if I was going to be involved in that, I'd be on the other side. Not a lot of people agreed with me, of course.'

He joined the Eureka Youth League, read *The Quiet American*, *Catch-22*, the works of Frantz Fanon, and the great Russian novelists. 'I was hoping to educate myself through some sort of osmosis or something,' he said. 'It didn't really work.' When his time came to register for national service, he was working as a locomotive fireman with the Victorian Railways. 'I thought I might've found my vocation,' he said. 'I thought, I'll become a train driver, and that'll be my life. I was quite happy with that.' He openly refused to register for national service, because he felt that was the right thing – not to cower or hide, or hope he wouldn't get chosen. 'In the Left parties, there were no policies about what you should do,' said Heldzingen. 'The Communist Party didn't have a policy. If there was a position, it was that you register, you obey the government's rule; if you missed out on the number being pulled out of the ballot, well and good. If you didn't and you got called up, you would either become a pacifist or you only then oppose it. My position was that you oppose it from the outset, that I thought it was criminal what they were doing to those people. I didn't know what those Vietnamese were when I was twenty years old. They were just peasants, people who ate worms or something. I didn't know what they did, but you don't go and kill them.'

He looked for backing from his union, the Australian Federated Union of Locomotive Enginemen. 'There was a bit of half-hearted support,' he said, 'and a bit of opposition.' As it was illegal to continue to employ a man who hadn't registered – and as Heldzingen was actually paid by the Victorian government – the railways were obliged to fire him. The secretary of the union was Frank Carey, an ALP veteran who'd been in the repatriation hospital with Heldzingen's father and said he could make Heldzingen's problem go away.

Heldzingen didn't want it to go away – he was determined to fight – but the union threatened industrial action if he was sacked, so his employers did not touch him. 'I think they didn't know themselves what to do,' he said, 'both those who had to enforce these rules and those who made the rules. It just didn't occur to them that somebody would reject their view of the world.'

He said he faced some harassment and spying, 'became more and more paranoid and less and less secure, and I felt like I had to get on the road again'. He disappeared for a while. 'I was just sort of hanging around, really,' he said. The Eureka Youth League had become the Young Socialist League, there'd been some publicity about GIs 'fragging' their officers in Vietnam, and there was talk among Communists about setting up cells inside the Australian Army. Heldzingen had heard about Algeria, where the French Young Communist movement had turned entire units to mutiny. He said leading Communist Party members, including full-time organiser Paddy George, spoke to him about the idea. 'I think they said, "You can now join the army. That'd be a good thing, because you can be a white-anter. You'll meet other people, other cadres in the army who'll make the connections, and you'll work underground." I thought, Well, that seems all right. I can do that. Of course, I never met anybody else, but that was the plan. I went in there and that was it, basically. I was on my own again. But I'd been used to being on my own.'

He was told to give up resisting the draft and fall into police hands. So he returned to Melbourne and began turning up at demonstrations where, he said, he was quickly noticed by the Victorian Special Branch. He was arrested at a May Day rally in Melbourne on 2 May 1971, when he was 'bashed up', he said, 'thrown into the paddy wagon, taken to the police cells and bashed up again, and I consequently had to go to court – they wouldn't bail me out – and explain why the police bashed me up and why I hadn't registered, and I was sent to Pentridge jail. When I came out the Commonwealth police were waiting outside, and they gave me my call-up papers there.'

He reported to Watsonia, passed his medical, and went to Kapooka and into the army. He planned to keep a low profile and fit in as best he could. 'I thought what I'd do was probably integrate with these other soldiers,' he said, 'and see how it goes. I can't be influential in any way if I'm antagonistic or opposed to the other soldiers.' He was put in a platoon made up entirely of regulars. 'I didn't meet national servicemen until I was sent to the battalion,' he said. He didn't much like recruit training. 'If I'd've been fighting for the Viet Cong, I would've gone gung-ho,' he said. 'It was like playing cowboys and Indians. You get some sort of camaraderie. Some of the blokes are funny, some of them are kind. Some of them are psychopaths: they don't give a fuck ideologically, they just want to kill people.'

He asked to go the catering corps, he said, 'So they put me in the infantry. I wouldn't expect anything else.' He completed his infantry training – 'You rush like crazy, then you get to a place and you do nothing, then you moved on. It was a bit silly' – then went to 8RAR in Brisbane where he was made a steward in the officers' mess. He was dismissed, he said, when he drunkenly poured wine over a major in dress uniform. He trained as a radio operator and 'there were times when I didn't mind it', he said, although 'marching up and down didn't thrill me. I was interested to learn how to operate a radio. I was interested to learn how armies work. I was interested to know how to read a map. When it comes to guerrilla warfare, I want to know how they operate and how I should operate, if I were a guerrilla.'

Nobody in the army ever asked him outright about his years as a draft resister but he believed the sergeants searched his locker for propaganda. 'There were various people I assumed, in my paranoia, to have been there to tail me or befriend me,' he said. 'I never had any evidence for it. There'd be people coming up to me telling me how much they liked Lenin. I'd go, "I thought he was one of the Beatles." They were always trying to set me up somehow or other and, as a paranoid, I didn't bite.'

Since Heldzingen was undercover, there was not much room for him to propagandise. 'You had individual conversations with people,' he said, 'and you'd get drunk and philosophise. People want to talk about some deep and meaningful things sometimes but mostly I was just another digger. I didn't do anything that made any difference to the world. Never have.'

He found almost no political awareness in the ranks. 'They didn't have a clue. You'd talk to people and they'd say, "What's going on in Vietnam? Is that the Communists?" What does that mean? "Oh, they want to kill you, they want to rape you. They're evil." What, you reckon the bloody peasants over there are sitting around discussing dialectical materialism? "What's that?" They're probably wondering about surplus value. Most of the time, there was no point arguing. You could have a discussion sometimes with some people, but mostly it was just nonsense. They don't know what a Bolshevik is. They just think that's an enemy.'

In April 1972, Heldzingen went to visit a friend in Brisbane, Pekka, who ran the Maoist bookshop East Wind, which was threatened by a group of Queensland Nazis led by the notorious Gary Mangan. Pekka was often alone in the shop and Heldzingen worried for his safety. 9RAR 'had been ordered out on an exercise,' said Heldzingen, 'and, the night before, they issued us with our guns. They normally don't do that. The armourer wanted to have the morning off, so he issued the guns. In order to leave the barracks, you've got to have a leave pass. I didn't have a leave pass. But I had a gun. But I didn't have any bullets. I had a trench coat, so I put the trench coat on and the gun, and I went to see Pekka. These Nazis came around, and I was standing behind the stacks in the shadows, so I pulled the gun out and cocked it, threatened them. They shit themselves and they bolted, but I had to go on exercise in the morning and while I was away they shot up the bookshop.' On the night of 19 April, the Communist Party's Brisbane office was bombed with sixteen sticks of gelignite, and three bullets were pumped through the window of East Wind.

Eventually Heldzingen became mentally and emotionally exhausted, and went AWOL to Sydney, 'just got my head back together'. He returned to the army determined to still follow his plan, but was sent to the military prison at Holsworthy for forty-two days.

When he was released, he was posted to Watsons Bay, then marched into 7RAR. But he posed no danger to the battalion. 'They had me tamed,' said Heldzingen. 'They didn't have to worry. I think they were still suspicious about what I might be up to, but they couldn't prove anything, they didn't have any evidence. They didn't have a [Communist] cell in the army. They didn't know about it anyway. And I didn't know about it either.'

33

SAS: THE NASHOS' CADRE

The men of the Special Air Service (SAS) regiment were expected to disappear like mist into the jungle and return like rainfall, swollen with whispers about enemy movements beneath the forest canopy. They crept like vines, pressed fast against trees, and padded silently off tracks, to observe and ambush, keep count and kill.

Ever since the first national servicemen had completed corps training and Errol Noack put himself forward for selection, the SAS had quietly taken the cream of the conscripts, tested them to the peak of their capabilities, and offered them a posting to the best trained regiment in the Australian Army – provided they immediately signed on as regular soldiers. Peter France of Launceston, Tasmania, was one of a handful of conscripts who got through SAS selection in 1966. The regiment was divided into company-sized squadrons, and the four national servicemen who survived France's 'cadre' were offered places in 1SAS, a 'sabre' squadron which was to fly to Vietnam the following year. Before they were posted, they were marched in to see the CO and, France said, told 'something like, "You've got one choice – you can either sign up and stay here, or get out and go back to your previous unit."'

But as the VC fought on, the regiment changed its policy to allow the best of the national servicemen to join a squadron without enlisting in the regular army, and by early 1971 conscripts made up about a quarter of the strength of 2SAS in Vietnam. Once again, among the tough guys and adventurers were accountants, bank clerks and schoolteachers, professionals who had planned to live their working lives at desks, among books.

Many of 2SAS's national servicemen had come into the squadron through the so-called 'nashos' cadre' of Easter 1970, when officers from Swanbourne, WA, had chosen from the infantry training centre at Singleton about forty conscripts, along with about twenty-five regular soldiers, to travel across to Perth and try out for the regiment. National servicemen on the cadre included Rolf Kling, the German-born son of a man who had fought in the Waffen SS. 'My father was from a broken home,' said Kling. 'He joined the Hitler Youth, and that basically became his parenting.' Kling had come to Adelaide at three years old and grown up hunting and fishing in the hills. As a teenager, he was a crack shot. He said he could hit a rabbit in the eye. Kling had studied to become a schoolteacher, but failed his second year. 'I'd come from an all-boys' school,' he said, 'to a teachers' college where the girls chased you. It was just girls, girls, girls, so hang the study.' Rather than retake the subjects he had neglected, he headed west and found work in the oil fields of Barrow Island, off the north coast of WA. He had been there nearly a year – 'I didn't think anyone would know where I was,' he said – when he received a form letter instructing him to report for national service. Kling was an accomplished athlete, the former captain of the school swimming team. Even on the rigs, he would run in the mornings, sweat through nine hours' physical work, then surf in the evenings. Like many of the men in the SAS at the time, Kling was part-racehorse, part packhorse. He was not particularly tall but had great upper-body strength and could carry heavy loads over long distances.

All the men of the nashos' cadre found soldiering easy, but few seemed especially suited to infantry life. They often resented the discipline, despised being drilled and abused by weaker, duller men, and despaired at all the shouting. They were leaders who didn't want to be officers, who thought critically and acted independently, and felt they did not belong in the same army as the sweet boys from Christian homes who still played with their Meccano sets, and the overgrown children who cried themselves to sleep in the barracks. At Singleton, said Kling, 'I thought, I'm going to Vietnam with these guys who I wouldn't trust walking behind me with a loaded weapon. You'd see guys get out on the live firing range, and they couldn't hit a man-sized target at ten paces with a submachine gun with a magazine full of ammunition. I was terrified that I was not only going to be shot at from the front, but also from the back.'

Kling heard that those who passed the cadre would be trained for a year before being sent to Vietnam, and thought the SAS might be the safest place for him. If he was going to war, he wanted to go with the best. But he wasn't a bloodthirsty man. Gus Howard, a national serviceman who knew Kling at Singleton, described him as 'a very sweet guy, kind of like a sooky Alsatian'.

Also selected for the cadre was Mike Crane, a design draftsman from Fairfield, NSW, a trade unionist who'd hated school cadets and disliked the army from the beginning. He had passed his matriculation and could have tried out for Scheyville but 'I wasn't a true believer', he said. 'I use that term in a general way, for people who think this is all great and wonderful, freedom and democracy – all those terms that I don't know what they mean and people can't tell me.' He was 'in a way, definitely' a sympathiser with the VC, he said. 'We were invaders, there was no doubt about that, and people don't like being invaded. And they do this "hearts and minds" – what a load of rubbish – you come, you've got a gun, you take over.' The cadre was joined by Denis Bird, a bank officer whose father worked as a linesman for the PMG. Bird grew up in a housing commission home and went to a state school, played first-grade football in Gympie, Queensland, played hockey and swam.

The men travelled, by bus and train, from Singleton to the SAS base in Swanbourne, via Sydney, Melbourne, Port Augusta and Kalgoorlie. 'That was a bit of bonding in itself,' said Barry Jones, a volunteer national serviceman from Victoria. They reached Perth on Good Friday 1970 and, from the regulars in the SAS, 'There was some animosity initially, I suppose,' said Jones, '"How could blokes straight out of civvy street possibly fill our shoes?" But for the rest of it, we were one and the same.'

'The only time I ever heard anything derogatory was when Sergeant "Dinger" Bell picked us up at the station,' said Bruce Wilson, a red-haired accountant inevitably nicknamed 'Bluey', who had played seconds for Essendon. 'We went and unloaded our gear down at Swanbourne, and he was showing us around. He took us up to the boozer, and I heard, "Here's Dinger and his little nasho mates." Once the cadre started, though, apart from one or two, the regs dropped out bang-bang-bang. A lot of them were gone after the first two weeks. But we had a very high rate of getting through. I don't think any of us dropped out, and we broke the record for the twenty-mile run as well, by miles.'

The cadre was a famously gruelling three-week test of strength, endurance and mental focus, held in Swanbourne, and on Rottnest and Garden islands. There was 'a lot of running, climbing, a lot of shoulders, a lot of rope work, a lot of up and down cliffs, running barefoot places', said Jones, 'and a lot of people came down with injuries, couldn't go any further, physical exhaustion. Some broke down through just the stress of the tiredness, and the stress placed on you to do one thing after another nonstop. At various stages, we'd have a break for a day and they would cull some people. One guy was probably the best long-distance runner in our group, we were out in the scrub doing some sort of course and he was carrying the radio. They said, "Boycey, do a radio check." He picked it up and looked at it and said, "It looks all right to me." He was off. We never saw his face again. Others got right to the very end, got through all the different steps, the physical side and everything, and they were told, "Listen, sport, you've done a good job but..." I remember thinking, What did they do wrong? It must've been pretty heartbreaking for them.'

The men who passed cadre went on to parachute training at Williamtown, NSW. 'I hadn't been in a plane before,' said Crane, 'so the first time I was in a plane, I had to jump out.' SAS training, 'up to that stage, was the best thing I'd done', said Crane. 'It was just fantastic, a boys' own adventure, something I could never've afforded.'

Once they had their wings, the men were awarded their berets and became members of the squadron. Kling loved life in the lines. 'I really felt that I'd found the right place in the army,' he said. Nobody ever shouted, there was no mechanical saluting, and rank was not the sole measure of a man's worth. 'I just revelled in it,' said Kling. 'I was busting out of my skin. The regiment seemed just like a big party. You had your training to do, but it wasn't a twenty-four-hour-a-day thing.'

The regiment held a month-long reconnaissance and commando course in Collie, south of Perth, when Kling was captured, bound, blindfolded and thrown in a creek up to his neck. After a while his captors pulled him out and let him dry by their campfire. 'That's the sort of thing they did with guys who fitted in,' said Kling. 'If you were an outsider or not part of what they considered the group, they could kill you.' At the end of their training in Australia, each man had to be chosen individually by a patrol commander to become a member of a five-man team that would stay together throughout their time in Vietnam. The patrols were then taken up to New Guinea for jungle training, where they were dropped by helicopter into the bush and had to walk about one hundred and sixty kilometres out of the highlands to the coast. When they returned, they were ready to go to war, and the squadron held an assembly. 'They said, "Look, we've got 123 trained for a squadron strength of 120,"' said Kling. '"Anyone who doesn't want to go, now's the time to put your hand up." Up until that point, I was prepared to go, and I was going with good guys. I was confident. I'd sat around the campfire listening to regs' stories about what they'd done. And it didn't particularly enthuse me because, as much as I could do what I had to do, I still had in the back of my mind that I was going there to kill people, and the one thing I did recognise was the SAS guys kill more people than the troops.' In ambushes, 'inadvertently, you knock over women and children. And I didn't really see myself wanting to do that. And I saw myself as different to the regs who were in the SAS. As much as they were friends of mine, I saw them as dogs of war. They wanted to go there and they wanted to do that. I was there because I had to be there.' Kling chose to stay behind. 'I had to go and see the CO, and the CO said to me, "Klingy, I'm very disappointed. You've done everything we asked of you. You knew we were going to send you to Vietnam. Why don't you want to go?" I said, "If you tell me I have to go, or you don't give me a choice, I'll go and I'll do everything I need to do. But if you give me a choice, six months from now, I'm due for discharge. I've got a job waiting for me and I'll choose not to go. I know you can't understand that because you're a professional soldier, but I'm not." '

2SAS left for Vietnam on 17 February 1971. 'I went to Perth Airport to see the guys fly out,' said Kling. 'It was the most emotional farewell I've ever been to. And I thought, A lot of these guys, I'll never see again. And that haunted me in my quiet moments for the next forty years. Because I felt I'd abandoned them – for the right reasons, I know – I felt the lesser for it.'

It was towards the end of the dry season when 2SAS arrived at Tan Son Nhut. 'We were watching body bags on the tarmac get loaded onto American planes,' said Wilson. There were already national servicemen attached to the SAS in Nui Dat, including Signaller Bill Gray, a journalist who'd interrupted his cadetship with the *Border Mail* in Albury NSW to answer the call-up. Gray had grown up on a farm in Rutherglen, on the Victorian side of the border. 'We used to shoot foxes,' said Gray, 'that was part of growing up. But I just had a military bent. I used to read all the Boys' Own annuals and collect

Commando War Stories comics. So it all sort of fell into place.' He 'didn't disagree' with the anti-war movement, he said, 'but this was just too big an opportunity for a young journo. It was a big story. Even though I was a bit left-wing, I saw this as an experience I wanted to have.' Although he had been through a later cadre than the others, Gray had by then completed his specialist training as a signaller, and been sent to Vietnam the previous September.

At Nui Dat, the men were based on SAS Hill, overlooking the Luscombe airstrip and the Kangaroo helipad. 'The sigs' primary job was to keep the comms centre operating and the equipment maintained,' said Gray. 'We really had it quite good, and there was an element of resentment from the grunts because they were doing it hard all the time but we had an air-conditioned comms centre. But then, whenever we could, we would go out on patrol. From time to time, there'd be a need for Sigs, because their signaller would be crook or something.

'The sigs were on the highest point of SAS Hill. Up on the pinnacle was a very small American signals base – only two men – and they were high the whole time. But, being signalmen, they had the whole place rigged, so if anyone ventured near, alarms went off and they were able to shake their heads and look as if they'd been busy. They were relay stations, so it wasn't critical, they just had to keep the equipment serviceable.'

A little below the Australian signals base sat the tents for the sabre squadron. At the start of Gray's tour, those tents were occupied by 1SAS, replaced by 2SAS in February. 'The whole SAS area was off limits to everyone else,' said Gray. 'The only guys who came up were the drivers with the booze. And [the RAAF's] 9 Squadron. The 9 Squadron helicopter guys were integral to our operation. We were really close to those guys. There were two bars. One was the officers' and sergeants' mess, which was as boring as batshit. The other was the ORs', which was where all the fun happened. Our beer allocation was two stubbies, but with the patrols constantly out, you'd have their beers.'

'It was nonstop,' said Jones. 'We'd go on patrol for a minimum of a week. If you'd completed your task, or got into a big shitfight, you'd come out. If you'd looked at the area and cleared it, or if you'd called in the battalion and there was nothing more for you to do, you wouldn't want to stay there when there was a battalion coming through, not knowing, shooting everything up. Other times you might go out for a given period, then it would be extended, and you'd have to be resupplied, which was bloody hairy because they'd have to bring out extra tucker for you, and helicopters coming anywhere near you just gives you away. You become so used to being quiet, covert, and nobody knowing you're there, the extremely stressful periods are going in and going out – going in, particularly. You're compromised by a helicopter hanging over you.'

'When they put us in,' said Wilson, 'they'd have a chopper that us five blokes would be in, but they'd have two other choppers, and we used to get guarded in by a couple of gunships and stuff like that. They used to all come down to the same spot in different areas.' The enemy would not know which aircraft was carrying the troops. 'I had a love-hate relationship with choppers,' said Wilson. 'I hated them when they were taking me in, but I loved them when they were taking me out.'

The patrols were watchers, white eyes in the darkness. 'You'd be sneaking around, and you'd stop and you'd listen,' said Bird. 'You'd be surprised how hard it is to see something when it doesn't move. Because you're cammed up, you look like you're a tree, and if they're looking straight at you, they won't see.'

'You had your scout out the front,' said Gray, 'and he would usually alternate with someone else in the patrol. Then you'd have your patrol commander. He had to be in a position to keep the scout in sight. Then you had the sig. He was protected, he was in the middle, he had the comms, so he was in the safest position – again, the sigs win. Then you had your medic–rifleman, and he would often interchange with the scout. Behind the rifleman you had your 2IC tail-end charlie. He was usually a corporal. Your patrol commander was usually a sergeant or an officer. And they would stay together. They became very tight with each other. They were matched on their temperament. They had to almost read each other's minds, and after months and months of patrolling, the whole patrol had to operate like that.'

'I had a sheep counter on my pistol grip,' said Wilson. 'My job in the patrol was to judge whenever we'd done a metre. And some days you'd only do 300–400 metres, if the jungle was really thick. Especially in the dry season, before you put your foot down you'd have to move the leaves and sticks and that, and then you'd have to do the same with the next.'

They lived like native animals, like vegetation. Bank clerks became bark, accountants melted into leaves. They communicated among themselves only with hand signals. 'Sometimes we'd be out in the scrub for fourteen days and never say a word,' said Wilson, 'and when you'd get back on the chopper and start talking again, your voice sounded funny.' But a troupe of monkeys in the jungle made the noise of a battalion, and a patrol would creep beneath a shower of animal droppings while the apes danced and sang in the tree canopy above. 'You'd be surprised what animals are in the bush, if you sit still,' said Bird. He once watched an eel travelling between mud puddles.

The business of the squadron was to gather intelligence. 'We'd ambush different enemy groups to see what they were carrying,' said Jones. 'If we needed to bring in air strikes or artillery or battalion, we could do that, but our major defence was being covert, nobody knowing we were there.' With an ambush, said Bird, there were 'endless hours of waiting. You just can't appreciate how bloody boring it is. What usually happened was the enemy would come along and you'd knock them over and grab their packs.'

'Sometimes we'd come across woodcutters and people who shouldn't be out there,' said Jones, 'and no doubt a lot of them got hit.' But the SAS patrols did not generally attack. 'You'd let them walk past you a lot of the time,' said Wilson. 'You'd see all the weapons they were carrying. You did something wrong if you were compromised.'

Crane's patrol had a few contacts, 'but other people went out and didn't see anyone for six months,' he said, 'then they stopped carrying as much ammunition.' The men Crane labelled 'true believers', who knew the war was over and this would be their last chance to fight, 'started walking on tracks', said Crane, in the hope of getting into a skirmish.

Crane's patrol leader was Second Lieutenant Brian Russell, the first national serviceman to become an officer in the SAS. 'The group found a bunker system,' said Crane, 'and the majority decided they were going to attack the bunker system, but they needed a backup. So instead of five guys, they wanted ten, and went to land in close – which was totally unusual at this time – so,' said Crane sardonically, '*they didn't know we were coming*. I shouldn't make light of it. Well, I can. I'm the one that got injured. We stood up. Here we were, most of the time, hiding, and we stood up and did an infantry push through the bunker system.' And they were fired upon. 'I got shrapnel to the leg and the shoulder, and we got extracted out.'

About three weeks later, Wilson returned to the spot where Crane had been hit, 'and they'd refreshed all the bunker system and everything', said Wilson. 'I saw movement, just dashing out into the scrub, so I gave the "down", so everybody hit the ground. All of a sudden in front of us was a [man] coming up the track, and I'll never forget the eyes. He had an AK-47 slung across him. He must've been a courier bringing something into camp, and I'll never, ever forget those bloody eyes, because he knew he was gone. He just knew he was gone.'

It was rare for the SAS to suffer the loss of one of their own. 'Probably the worst thing that happened to me over there was the day we lost Brian Jones,' said Wilson. There were two men named BR Jones in 2SAS. 'There was a five-man patrol with a Brian Richard Jones – he was the patrol commander – and there was a patrol with a Barry Raymond Jones: me,' said Jones. 'And when we had a big job to do, they'd put two patrols together to make it into a fighting patrol.'

The two Joneses were out on a combined patrol on 10 April 1971. There were two teams on the ground and a backup patrol hovering above. 'I was in one of the choppers,' said Wilson, 'and we were listening to what was going on, and we heard Jones had been hit and we didn't know which one it bloody was.'

Second Lieutenant Jones had been shot by one of his own men, after he'd gone off to reconnoitre in one direction, then returned from another. 'It was in the papers "BR Jones of the SAS, killed in Vietnam"', said Jones. 'My family were very concerned, obviously.'

Lieutenant Jones was the regiment's last fatal casualty. 2SAS returned to Swanbourne in August 1971, and the SAS vanished from the war, leaving behind only a hill bearing their name. Two years' later, nobody left in Vietnam remembered even that.

34

THE MYTH OF THE VOLUNTEER

The most provocative and divisive question about national service in Australia remains whether any conscript was compelled to go to war. Some official and popular histories maintain every man either volunteered for overseas service by signing a declaration during corps training, or was offered 'a verbal exit'.[1] The issue dominated the letters pages of the RSL's *Reveille* magazine as recently as January 2009. An artillery gunner who had served in 1968 insisted, 'I did not volunteer and I was not consulted as to whether or not I wanted to go.'[2] A former soldier with the service corps in 1969 denied he had ever agreed to serve overseas. 'The standing joke at the time,' he wrote, 'was that we who had not volunteered were actually in country before most of those we knew who had volunteered.'[3] Others from Infantry and Artillery said they had signed a form or stepped forward.[4] In fact, a soldier was required to complete only a 'Declaration of Compassionate Circumstances for Retention in Australia', saying 'I . . . do hereby declare that I have NO compassionate circumstances requiring my retention in AUSTRALIA if I am posted to an overseas theatre.'[5] However, not all those who signed understood this as an agreement to go to Vietnam. And even if a soldier felt he was entitled to a compassionate exemption, there was no guarantee his argument would be accepted. To petition to stay at home, be rejected and then be required by law to go overseas is a singular form of volunteering. A man might be sent to Vietnam even if he were newly married, politically opposed to the war, threatening to go AWOL and claiming compassionate exemption: one soldier did all these things, and still found himself serving in Vung Tau in 1970–71.

David Wittner was born in Melbourne, where his father, who'd served through the Second World War in the Australian Army, had two pet shops. Wittner began training as a radiographer at RMIT. 'I knew there was a possibility I'd get called up,' he said. 'I put it to the back of my mind, hoping I wouldn't, because most people didn't. I thought maybe I could get out of it. I didn't believe in Australia's involvement.'

But his birthdate came out of the barrel, and he deferred his national service for three years while he finished his radiography diploma, 'hoping a Labor government and Whitlam would get in', he said. 'But it was 1970, still too early, and I couldn't do any more courses. They were putting pressure on me, so I just meekly went. I never thought I would go to Vietnam,' he said. 'It never entered my mind.'

He grudgingly slogged through recruit training at Puckapunyal. 'I could handle everything,' he said. 'I was into being fit before I went in the army, and in a perverse sort of way, I enjoyed all the running and marching and PT and climbing through things and climbing up things. I just didn't want to be there.' He joined the medical corps, as he always knew he would. 'They were desperate for radiographers,' he said, 'and if I'd said I didn't want to, they'd still have sent me there.' He learned basic field nursing at Healesville, then was posted as a radiographer to the 1st Military Hospital at Yeronga in Queensland. When he reported to the X-ray department, he was upbraided for not turning up in uniform. He hadn't even considered wearing his greens, he said. 'I wasn't really in the swing of the army.'

National serviceman Peter Carter was the radiographer sergeant in charge of the department, and Wittner shared an apartment in Brisbane with Carter and another conscript. 'They were pretty good days,' he said. But then he was called into the CO's office and told he was going to be sent to Vietnam. 'I said, "I don't believe in Australia's involvement, and I'm getting married in a couple of weeks,"' said Wittner. '"I'm not going to go." He said, "You'll have to go." I said, "Well, I won't. I'll just go AWOL." He said, "Well, you do that, but we'll catch you, and you'll spend the rest of your time in a military prison."

'I didn't like the idea of that,' said Wittner, 'and I went back to the X-ray department, had a word with Peter Carter, and he said, "Oh no, you don't have to go to Vietnam. All you have to do is write this letter to the minister for the army and explain you don't want to go, tell him the reasons, and you won't have to go." So I wrote this letter to Andrew Peacock, minister for the army, and explained the situation.' Wittner's letter remains tucked inside his service record. It reads: 'I was told only yesterday that I was to undertake a battle efficiency course, starting on the 20th August and then at a [sic] unspecified date after this, my services will be required in South Vietnam. However, I definitely do not want to serve overseas. I have written a letter giving my reasons to the commanding officer of my unit, and subsequently I have spoken to him about this matter . . . I have made arrangement to be married on the 21st August . . . I do not wish to be married and then leave my wife [after] only a few days to spend a twelve month period in Vietnam. I do not feel that this is very good grounding for a marriage . . . I am prepared to serve anywhere in Australia as long as I do not have to be separated from my wife to be . . . I feel very strongly about this and if necessary I am prepared to go AWOL . . . Another reason why I do not want to serve overseas is that I do not believe in Australia's commitment in South Vietnam.'[6]

On 31 July 1970, Peacock sent Wittner a reply which was in perfect concordance with government policy as stated from the beginning of the national service scheme: 'While the Army endeavours to employ every soldier in a location of his choice, this is not always possible and when the requirements of the Army and the soldier are at variance, the needs of the Service must take precedence . . . Careful consideration has been given to your case but it does not appear that the circumstances are such as to warrant your retention in Australia on compassionate grounds . . . retention may only be granted for the most pressing reason. I am, therefore, unable to accede to your request.'[7]

Of course, it's likely that Wittner, as a radiographer, was treated differently to an infantryman. Some troops were clearly given the chance to back out while others were not, but in September 1971, when Peacock finally announced national servicemen would no longer be obliged to serve in South Vietnam, he wasn't simply regularising an informal arrangement but signalling a change in government policy.

Wittner had his battle efficiency course deferred, was allowed to stay in Australia to get married and have a honeymoon, then sent to the 1st Australian Field Hospital, which had taken over from the 8th Field Ambulance, on 17 September 1970. Wittner had been given a promotion – it was inconceivable for a radiographer to be a private soldier – but, when he arrived at the hospital, the staff didn't believe he was Corporal Wittner. 'They said, "Where's your rank?"' he said. 'I didn't have my chevrons on with my two stripes. They said, "Why aren't you wearing it?" I said, "I don't believe in it." As I said, I wasn't really into the swing of the army in those days. They said, "Well, you have to wear it." And then they sent me to the adjutant's office, and he wanted to know my story so he sat me down at his desk – because he knew about me writing to Andrew Peacock – and he asked me what the situation was, and whether I was going to cause any trouble when I was there. I said no. He was really nice to me. He said, "Do you mind if I record this? I need to send it back to my headquarters in Melbourne." Then he just changed completely, from a nice guy to a major in the army. He was a little bit nasty and abrupt with me, so I started giving one- and two-word answers. I was still nice to him,

I just wasn't elaborating on the story at all. I said I was going to behave, and I did behave.'

At 1ALSG, Wittner had a phone next to his bed. Every time a helicopter came in, he was called to report to the Vampire Pad helicopter landing area. 'It wasn't always a proper dustoff,' he said. 'Sometimes it was just some officer flying around, trying to get from Vung Tau to Saigon or something. You'd have to get yourself down there anyway, to see if you were required.' He X-rayed most of the men who came in from the choppers, including VC prisoners – 'they'd get really good treatment, the same as Australian soldiers as far as I could see' – and Americans when the US Army hospital's X-ray machine broke down. The job could be harrowing, but the routine was familiar. 'What really used to upset me was national servicemen that'd been killed,' said Wittner. 'You'd see their number and know they were national serviceman, and know which state they came from.'

Wittner was Jewish, but came across no anti-Semitism in the army. At 2RTB, he said, 'There was hundreds of us, all lined up in one line, and they made an announcement for any Muslims or Jews to take a couple of steps forward, so I did that, and one other guy took a couple of steps forward. They came up to us and said, "Do you want to see a rabbi?" I said, "No." "Do you want any dietary considerations?" I said, "No." They said, "Okay, step back in the line." And then, for the ten weeks I was at Puckapunyal, one of the NCOs called me "Pork Chop", but I just regarded him as an ignorant sort of dickhead. That didn't worry me. He was a lance corporal and when I was in Vietnam he came in as a patient, and he noticed I had the two stripes. He acknowledged that and said, "Well done." He was harmless enough.'

Wittner came back to Australia on 16 September 1971, ten days before Andrew Peacock announced national servicemen would no longer be compelled to go to Vietnam. Wittner spent his final months in the army at Watsonia. 'But I was lucky,' he said, 'because, as I was a corporal, all I had to do was go in and tell them I was there, and I could leave straightaway. I was only at the camp ten minutes a day.' He did not work as a radiographer. 'They wouldn't've had X-ray equipment there,' he said. And if there was anywhere else the army could've used his skills, 'I don't know,' he said. 'I didn't enquire.'

David Roubin, the longest-serving Jewish nasho, made a career of the army, retiring as a major in October 1989. David was one of three brothers, all of whose birthdays were eventually drawn from the barrel. The next in line was Gary, who was studying veterinary science and had deferments that didn't expire until the war was over. But the youngest boy, Loris, went into national service in 1970. He found himself in Vietnam despite his opposition to the war, but in circumstances more ambiguous – and probably much more common – than Wittner's, and was eventually able to invoke 'compassionate circumstances' to get back home.

Loris had been studying for a business degree at the Queensland Institute of Technology. 'I was in with a group of fairly radical, hippy-type people,' he said. 'I was involved in different protests out the front of parliament, at the university, places like that. We were kids with placards, thinking that we were going to be noticed. I was very anti-conscription, anti-military, and yet my brother David was the apple of my mother's eye, he was the officer and the gentlemen. He'd done really, really well in the army, even the first couple of years. And there was five years between us, so I loathed everything that was associated with him and the army. It just wasn't where I was coming from. And maybe there was a bit of sibling rivalry. He'd made his mark in that direction, and I didn't want to.'

Loris assumed he would get a deferment like Gary, but failed part of his course and was automatically called up. David had strengthened an already solid military tradition in the Roubin family, and their mother urged Loris to go in without a fuss. But 'I pissed off', said Loris. 'I hitchhiked around Australia. I was trying to do the overland trip from Darwin through South-East Asia, and waiting to find some other guys who'd be happy to do it. I had this image of there being this underground railway, this network of clandestine conscientious objectors, finding their way to England or Canada, and I was going to join them. It was all bullshit. The whole thing was just a little boy's fantasy. I was holding out in Darwin, hungry and unshaven. I didn't meet other people wanting to do the same thing. I met some other guys who were in Darwin resisting national service, but they seemed quite happy just to stay in Darwin and not do anything.

'I got communications from a friend of the family who said my parents had been told if I didn't turn up in Brisbane for the next intake – it was already too late for that; it took weeks and weeks for the message to get to me – I'd go in jail. And I thought, Shit, I don't want to go to jail. So I started hitchhiking back.'

Roubin went to Singleton and 'even in recruit training I didn't really fit in with the group', he said. 'I had a strange name – Loris Roubin – I was singled out for being Jewish. I didn't go in for officer training. I didn't want to have any part of it. I kept thinking that I was a conscientious objector and I was going to get out of the army. I really wasn't interested in the government forcing me into a lifestyle I didn't agree with. Regimentation and discipline was not something I wanted. I was very aware of brainwashing. David had told me how it all worked, but I didn't want to experience it. Everyone was very keen to go and shoot a gun, and I was thinking, Why would I want to do that? It was against my principles and my ethics. And other people couldn't see what was happening: that they were being teased, being prepared, being groomed to become mechanical in their responses to expectations during the war as a soldier. And I was resisting all that.

'I got myself into a lot of trouble,' he said, 'missed out on quite a bit of leave. I was belligerent in a way. It wasn't so much that I was abusive, but I would question their authority, and they were as dumb as all shit.' Roubin's service record included a comment from his sergeant at 3RTB that he had 'too much to say', but it was also noted he was of a 'strong standard above normal'.[8] Roubin applied for the medical corps and was selected, but said he told the army he wanted to get out and be a conscientious objector. 'They said, "What do you object to?" I told them I objected to being put in a situation where it was my life or someone else's.'

Roubin enjoyed his corps training at Healesville and did very well in his medical orderly trade tests, scoring 99 per cent in preventative medicine and 96 per cent in anatomy and physiology. But, as a medic, he felt he might not be fit to be in the army as a childhood accident had left him without the full use of the fingers of his left hand. 'My parents had realised I wasn't very happy,' he said, and a question was raised in parliament about the propriety of calling up three boys from the same family, one of them possibly medically unfit. Roubin was ordered before the CO at 1st Military Hospital, told about his parents' complaint, and asked how he felt. He said he was fine. 'If I had've said, "I'm feeling shithouse. I'm finding all of this one hell of a burden," I reckon I'd've been out like that,' said Roubin. 'But I blew it.'

An officer asked Roubin if he would go to Vietnam. 'And he knew of David,' said Loris, 'so I explained again how I felt. I found myself justifying my moral stance and my ethics once again, in an individual interview. And he said, "How would you feel about it if you went over and did civil aid work with a group of army doctors and medics?" And I said, "I think that would be better than the alternatives, but I'm still not all that keen" . . . And the next thing I knew, I was off to Vietnam.

'I went out and I did one civil aid mission. I came back and I was told that I'd been assigned to the wards in the hospital. They moved me around for the rest of the time, from triage to surgical ward, medical ward, the aid post,' he said. 'Sometimes I'd be dressing wounds. Other times I'd be giving injections, or handing out meals. Sometimes I'd be scrubbing floors, mopping floors, wiping things down, other times I'd be seeing guys before they'd go to the doctor, and doing a preliminary assessment. Other times I was running out and carrying wounded and dead people from the helicopters into triage. There was a mechanical part to it, where you do it as part of a job that you're trained for, and there was this side of it that was just freaking me out. And it built up and got worse and worse and worse, and I did suffer some severe depression and I saw a psych while I was over there, because I was disassociating. I would turn off from what it was that I was supposed to be involved in.' He used his free time working at the civilian Le Loi Hospital in Vung Tau. 'I'd do anything I could,' he said. 'I'd give injections, I'd hand out medicines, mop floors, bandage patients, sit with families, and I'd run an English-language class at other times.'

In 1971, the first day of the Jewish festival of the Passover fell on 10 April. 'The chaplain had come down to visit me,' said Roubin. 'He said, "I believe your Passover is coming up in two days, and I was wondering if you'd like some special food." I hadn't asked for kosher. I was eating whatever they served. I said, "No, look, it's all right." He asked, "Is there anything else I could do for you?" The next thing I knew, he had told me to go to the airport at Vung Tau and find my way to Nui Dat. From Nui Dat I could hitch a lift to Saigon, and in Saigon there was a Passover service happening with some Americans in the Free World Building. I hadn't been to Saigon, I hadn't been to Nui Dat. I thought the Free World Building would be a hut somewhere, an American PX. But it was one of the biggest buildings I'd ever seen in my twenty-one years of life – I hadn't been very worldly anyway.

'I found the door and it was just on dark. I'd been running late, and I was wearing my Australian uniform with my slouch hat. I opened the door, and all I could see were lots of people sitting at tables. I felt really shy and intimidated, and I wasn't quite sure if I was even in the right place, and I could hear some Hebrew being sung. They were just about to do the Kiddush. And as I walked in, a couple of Americans closest to the door stood up and patted me on my back. And then some more stood up, and a couple started clapping, a slow clap, and then I realised I was the only Australian there. An Australian Jew at a Passover service in Vietnam! This was, like, mind-boggling. They were pushing me along and I was looking for a spare table to sit down on a seat and hide, and there wasn't one. They were pushing me further and further forward, and eventually everyone in this building was standing up and clapping me. The tears started rolling down my face, because Passover is a festival of freedom . . . All of a sudden, I was feeling Jewish for the first time in my life. I was feeling a unity with other people which I'd never felt. I grew up in the country, in Brisbane, and my Jewishness was really non-existent. There was this table of rabbis and all my life, I'd only ever seen one rabbi, and that was when I was being bar mitzvahed. People had come from the Philippines, Korea, all of Vietnam and Thailand. It was like I wasn't alone. It was the most amazing thing.

'I sat at the table with all the rabbis. I had really nice food, a great Seder service, and a lift back to the hotel where I stayed the night. Some of the Jewish officers I'd met showed me around. They came down to Vung Tau later on and they visited me. I went off to different places with them, and life was sort of different, but then the bastardisation increased, because I had alienated myself in the group dynamics of the unit by being Jewish and going to the Passover service and having a couple of days off when the others didn't. I'd alienated myself by not visiting the whorehouses, by not getting drunk in the boozer, by being involved in some humanitarian causes. I knew what was happening. I did nothing to promote my own cause. I made it worse.'

Roubin received a letter from a high-school friend, John Everingham, a Victorian photojournalist working in Vietnam, who later became famous when he smuggled his Laotian wife out of Laos under the Mekong River, using scuba equipment. 'The letter took weeks to get to me,' said Roubin, 'so I got all excited and rushed into town. I had a leave pass, but I realised I'd left it back at the camp. So I turned around, came back through the gate, and I was arrested for being absent without leave in a war zone. I thought this was a joke, because I already had a leave pass and, because I was laughing at the MPs, saying, "You can't be serious. I was just going back into the unit to get my piece of paper," they locked me up. I was marched up before the adjutant, and it was a formal charge reading, and then they said,

"Do you realise what the maximum penalty for being absent without leave in a war zone is?" And he said, "In some circumstances, you can be shot." I cracked up laughing. But the way they do it, they go, "Prisoner and escort, two paces forward, march! Escorts to the rear! Escorts to the ready!" and you hear them click their weapons and put a bullet in the bloody chamber. And here I was, a medic, in the medical corps, in a hospital unit, miles from a front line, and I've had some of my own troops poking me with a bayonet because I was laughing. It was so ridiculous, it didn't really seem real. Nervous laughter and fear, and I collapsed on the ground laughing hysterically. They thought I was laughing at them or the procedure, but I wasn't. I was so aware that this was people playing a game. Even though they were serious about playing the game, it doesn't justify the rules or the game they were playing. They were stupid.'

According to his service record, Roubin was charged on 4 July 1971 with being AWOL between 1400 and 1745 hours, and neglecting to obey a published order. He was sentenced to 'Summary CB (5 Days)'. 'I was doing field punishment,' said Roubin, 'in the medical corps. I was wearing full battledress, with a gun, digging a trench through solid rock, with a little Second World War entrenching tool. You hit the stone and go *boing! boing!* like a cartoon, and you get all this RSI up the arm, and you can't use your hands, and it was forty degrees and they had me doing that. After about four days, I thought I was hallucinating when this tall, blond-haired guy wearing a turban, an Indian kaftan, Jesus sandals and a string of cameras around his neck like hippy beads, turned up on the hill and started taking photos.' John Everingham had arrived.

'He came up to the parade ground where I was being punished,' said Roubin. 'I was doing this entrenching tool exercise – they'd had me polishing copper pipe with dry sand in my bare hands before that – and John reached into his knapsack, pulled out a joint, stuck it in my mouth and lit it. Now, I was in the army, and I was on a charge, and I was coughing and spluttering, to try and tell him, "Don't do this."

But anyway, I had a few tokes.' Everingham wasn't certain he passed Roubin a joint. 'I could well have done,' he said. 'To me, that wouldn't have meant very much. There were joints everywhere in Vietnam. Because I was a civilian, the military police couldn't bust me and I don't think the Vietnamese government knew what marijuana was.

'Loris had made contact with me when he knew he was coming to Vietnam,' said Everingham, 'so we arranged – which was in those days quite difficult, by letter back and forth – to go out and paint the town red. I was going to go to Vung Tau and he was going to get a few days off from the army.' Everingham suggested they rent a small apartment, and planned 'to have a lot of fun – smoke and drink and chase a lot of pretty girls around Vung Tau. When I actually got there, I turned up at the military base, showed my passport, got inside, got into one of the offices there and said, "Look, I've come to see Loris Roubin." And the guy immediately knew who Loris Roubin was, where Loris Roubin was, and the fact that he had a friend coming. He pointed outside, and there was this big fucking expanse of open dry dirt and rocky ground. There wasn't a single blade of grass. Out in the middle of this big, hot, baking-in-the-sun thing, there was one lone figure, swinging a pick, digging a trench. And it was Loris. I couldn't believe it.'

'They told me I had to go into town and look after John,' said Roubin, 'but not to let him back on the base.' The two men didn't have the great time they'd hoped for. 'But we did get out and do a little bit together,' said Everingham. 'I [feel] very warmly towards Loris. I knew him since I was nine or ten years old. We used to run around the bush together. He's a very genuine person, not the kind of guy you'd expect to want to go out and kill somebody. He was a very unhappy man. I think, at the time, Loris really regretted not having resisted the draft.'

Roubin came back from Vietnam in November 1971, having served more than eight months overseas. He was allowed to return for compassionate reasons, he said, when his father went blind. His homecoming was 'a real anticlimax', he said. 'I wanted to feel like my brother. I'd done a dedicated job. I'd been in a more humanitarian role. I wanted to feel proud about what I'd been doing, with Le Loi Hospital and the wounded: I was helping Viet Cong, Vietnamese regular army people, Americans, Australians, New Zealanders . . . I felt like I wanted to talk to people about that. Before I left Brisbane, I used to drink at the Regatta Hotel, near St Lucia. That was where most of my uni friends used to hang out. That was where the group told me to run away. I went back there looking for my friends. I'd forgotten that my life had stood still for over two years and now I was back, they'd all graduated and moved on. So I walked in with short hair, and I started to ask where some of the guys were. And someone said, "Where've you been?" and I told them, and that was a mistake. Because I then started to defend what I'd been doing, and telling some people that they didn't fucking understand, and even though I understood where they were coming from, they didn't understand where I was coming from. And you know all this bullshit you hear about people calling you babykillers? Well, it wasn't quite that I was called a babykiller, but I felt that I was a lot tougher than I really was, and I went and led with my chin.

'They didn't know how I felt, that I had somehow resisted the whole affair. I was a really confused little boy. I got caught up in the left-wing propaganda – and some of it was bullshit; I got caught up in the ideal of running away from the army. I often wonder how much of that was my own idea, and how much was the influence of the students' union. I was stupid. I was a kid. I don't think the army made a man of me. It just made me softer. It made me more compassionate. I've questioned things all the time in my life ever since.'

35

THE LAST DAYS

The army finally moved into the 1960s in October 1970, when the military board decided soldiers could grow their sideburns two-and-a-half centimetres longer than had previously been permitted. As the Melbourne *Sun* gleefully observed, this brought the army regulation 'sidelever' to about the same length as those worn by Andrew Peacock.[1] It was a small concession to the changing times, but the first Vietnam veteran elected to an Australian parliament wore his sideburns in the classic minimalist fashion. Twenty-four-year-old former national serviceman Tim Fischer campaigned for the Country Party in the seat of Sturt with the slogan 'His action packed life stands him well to capably represent Town and Country alike'.[2] Fischer became the youngest member of the NSW Legislative Assembly on 13 February 1971. 'There has been a lot of criticism directed at the rising generation in the mass media,' he said. 'There are, however, young people who have had considerable experience in man-management, human nature and also fighting for their country.' In the future, he said, politicians with battle experience would be available to make decisions about military action. He believed Australia was right to be in Vietnam but many mistakes had been made 'on both sides'.[3] On Anzac Day, he warned that 'society, while searching for scapegoats for the mistakes, the murders and the lack of a military victory, must not blame the returned servicemen from Vietnam'.[4]

Australia's Vietnam War was withering away. Early in 1971, Malcolm Fraser, whose sidelevers remained unexceptional, recommended cabinet should prepare for a further troop withdrawal in anticipation of yet another announcement from Nixon. This time the army would lose its tank squadron among other troops, and the RAAF and the RAN would also bring men home. While the announcement was still mooted but not yet made, the Australian military made its own plans to curtail any new civic action projects. Fraser had long felt these schemes to help the Vietnamese, by building village infrastructure such as drains and windmills, were not close to the army's heart or mind. He accused the military of independently abandoning the strategy and, in the scandal that followed, Fraser resigned as defence minister. Gorton announced a leadership spill, then stepped down when the vote of no confidence resulted in a tie. Billy McMahon was elected the new leader of the Liberal Party, and became Australia's twentieth prime minister on 10 March. That same day, the returned men of 7RAR marched through Sydney from the Domain to Hyde Park, clapped and cheered on a working Wednesday by a crowd four-deep, as they stepped through the customary barrage of confetti. The *Sydney Morning Herald* reported 'a small group of anti-war protesters outside the Town Hall' who were 'discouraged after police confiscated some of their placards'.[5]

On the other side of the Pacific Ocean, at the end of March 1971, William Calley was convicted at Fort Benning, Georgia, of the murder of eleven Vietnamese civilians at My Lai. The My Lai trials are often thought of as a turning point in Australian public opinion, after which diggers were libelled, lambasted and labelled rapists and babykillers. But a survey of public attitudes in Sydney in March–April 1971 showed 59 per cent of the sample believed the My Lai soldiers should be 'let off' if they were following orders, and 30 per cent agreed they themselves would shoot civilians if ordered to do so. (There were no questions asked about rape, and rape in war was barely a public issue until the publication of Susan Brownmiller's book *Against Our Will: Men, Women and Rape* in 1975.) Only 27 per cent of all the survey respondents, and only 31 per cent even of ALP supporters thought the soldiers should be punished if they'd been following orders. Far from blaming ordinary Australian troops for the war crimes of Americans, the majority of Australians did not even blame the American troops who'd committed those crimes.

Some of the apparent support for the soldiers may have come from respondents who believed the men at My Lai were being scapegoated for crimes whose responsibility lay with the US government. This was the attitude of anti-war US Vietnam veterans such as former Intelligence officer Michael Uhl, who came to Australia on a speaking tour in 1971, and told the Communist *Tribune* newspaper, 'We see Calley as a scapegoat. We hope to find a lull in the My Lai trial, when we can get some coverage and bring along a whole number of guys who were in Calley's regiment who will say: "Look, My Lai is a daily occurrence in Vietnam. It is the Pentagon and Washington that are guilty."'[6] Even in Australia, the press had become suspicious and began hunting for a homegrown atrocity story to match My Lai, as if that might atone for all the years of credulity.

The men at the Task Force grew despondent. Lance Bombardier Mick Rhode, a signaller with 12 Field Regiment, had arrived in Vietnam on 11 March 1971. 'We'd been there for a few months when they started to deliberately wind down,' he said, 'and we were given the orders we weren't to go out looking for [the enemy], we were in a defensive mode.' They patrolled largely to secure their own perimeter. 'We felt more like sitting ducks,' he said, 'because you were waiting for them to come in and have a go at you, whereas before you could pre-empt them, you could go out looking for them. And they knew you weren't going to go out looking for them, so they were more inclined to lay ambushes for you or come in furtive probing attacks.'

Mick Denley had been a boilermaker in the mines at Broken Hill before he was sent to 3RAR in Vietnam in February 1971. The regiment had a quiet eight-month tour. 'We never did the Long Hais, where all the landmines were,' said Denley. 'I think they were hiding us in the bloody jungle near the end.' In April, his company had lost its first casualty on Denley's first R&C, in Vung Tau: 'a lance corporal, pissed. The Land Rovers had the one steel round bar going back to the trailer. He tried to walk across that, and the trailer ran over his head when he fell off.' The second time Denley went to Vung Tau, 'They had a bloody great brawl,' he said. 'We thought it was with the gooks, but it was with the Koreans. There were flares going off and bricks and people getting hit in the head and MPs running around everywhere – and those Yankee MPs, they were cruel bastards, I'm glad I wasn't an American; they had those bloody great wallopers on them and they'd whack them in the knee and throw them in the back of the van. Basically I said to myself, after that [lance corporal] had died the first time, "You've got more chance of getting killed down here than you've got out in the bush."'

Jim Conley, who had found his place as a reinforcement with the Defence & Employment Platoon, arrived in country after several men from that platoon had been wounded by a mine. 'You could see they were still pretty shocked from that incident,' he said. Conley made a good soldier, and signed on for an extra six months' national service, 'and went from being 90 and a wakey to 270 and a wakey'. In June 1971 he became a ground team commander in the 1st Psychological Operations Unit. Conley moved tents at Nui Dat but returned at night to drink beer with his former section. 'We were playing cards,' he said, 'and I went back to my tent, and the next morning, they got ready reacted on an operation. They went out, and the APCs were going through the rubber plantation, and a satchel charge or an RPG hit one of the canisters full of Claymore mines. And half of my section were on that. There were seven people killed. Two of them, there was nothing to bury. But the guy that took over from me, he just lost his hearing. That was one of those moments where life changes for you. I remember thinking, It should've been me.'

In August 1971, *The Bulletin* published 'The Ten-Year War', a photo spread summarising Australia's experience in Vietnam. There were images of infantry on patrol; a soldier on a civic-action mission cradling a child; Centurion tanks at the Battle of Binh Ba; and confetti drifting down into a parade of saluting soldiers, captioned 'street parades of returning Vietnam veterans were becoming a regular part of city life'. There were no photographs of moratorium demonstrations. Nadine Jensen, the bride in blood, was nowhere to be seen. Instead, a firm-jawed soldier with an equivocal gaze illustrated the proposition 'the bush hat had replaced the slouch hat as a symbol of Australian nonchalance'.[7]

The Bulletin had maintained an amused interest in the protesters, and previously published an informed and comprehensive survey of student radicalism, rating the political heat on campuses from Monash ('hot') to Adelaide ('simmering') to New England ('cold') to Port Moresby in New Guinea ('frigid')[8] but the story of the dissidents belonged in the history of dissent. 'The Ten-Year War' was a record of a military campaign that had come to an end, which is how Vietnam looked to most people in 1971, before all the varnish and tarnish of decades to come. By the new year, there was a Vietnam exhibition installed at the Australian War Memorial and 'the speed involved in introducing this display may well have surprised Second World War veterans who had a long wait for galleries devoted to their war,' wrote the memorial's historian.[9]

Much of the media behaved as if the war were already over, but the last Australian battle took place at Nui Le on 21 September 1971. Four national servicemen and one regular soldier, all from 4RAR/NZ, died in a clash with NVA forces that had been building up in the north of Phuoc Tuy in anticipation of the Australian withdrawal. Ralph Niblett of Melbourne was the last national serviceman killed in Vietnam. He died of wounds before he could be loaded on to the dustoff chopper.

It was on 26 September that Minister for the Army Andrew Peacock finally announced national servicemen would no longer be posted to Vietnam if they objected to the war. 'It would be less than sensible to send someone to Vietnam who doesn't want to go,' he said on TV, as if the issue had been raised recently for the first time. By then, however, few fresh soldiers were being dispatched and among those taking the next flight to Tan Son Nhut were troops 'specialising in moving equipment and men out of Vietnam'.[10]

'We just weren't getting any reinforcements,' said Denley. 'In the end our section only had the gun group and me as the lance corporal, and two riflemen. That was all that was left.' Denley sailed home on the HMAS *Sydney* with 3RAR in October. The navy let them drag their mattresses up from the hold, he said, 'and we slept out in the cool breeze.'

The West Australians disembarked first, in their home state. 'They put the Customs on board,' said Denley, 'and there was every bastard throwing over their marijuana and flick-knives and porno cards, and all they were after was mud in the boots, for foot and mouth, and anything you'd bought that was in these containers that had wood in it, for some sort of wasp that bores and kills the pine forest. So they sprayed all that shit, and meanwhile all this porn was floating downstream, beside these flick-knives, .45 calibre pistols. Everyone was scared shitless they were going to go through our bags, but they never even went through them, just checked our boots, sprayed the bottoms of them. Somewhere off Rottnest Island, there's a great heap of scrap.'

When the *Sydney* docked in Port Adelaide at nine a.m. on 16 October 1971, the *Sunday Mail* reported that 'hundreds of impatient welcomers crammed on the wharf behind closed gates and jumped, shouted and waved with excitement as the ship made fast'. Once the troops disembarked, 'it was bedlam – kissing, hugging, back-slapping and hand pumping, tearful reunions by the score'.[11] At ten a.m., they were bussed to their homecoming parade in the city, where they met more than two hundred men from the battalion's advance and rear parties who had flown back earlier, and marched along King William Street to the Torrens Parade Ground. At the town hall, they took the salute from Lieutenant Governor Sir Mellis Napier. Channel Seven broadcast a fifteen-minute film report of their arrival in the harbour and a direct telecast of the march.

With no fanfare, the term of national service was cut to eighteen months, a reduction which applied to men currently serving in Vietnam – if their time was up, they could go home. When Nui Dat began to close down in October, Rhode had already been in the army for more than a year and a half. 'They asked for volunteers to sign on for the extra time to go home with the regiment,' he said, 'which was only about a month later. They got all us January 1970 intake out onto the parade ground and said, "All those who are willing to do it, take a step forward." There was not a man moved. So [the officer] said, "You gutless nasho bastards," and just walked off. None of us would've signed on. We wouldn't've even contemplated signing on.

'Two years later, I signed on for six.'

Task Force troops left Nui Dat for Vung Tau, then departed Vietnam for Australia. Owen Pettingill of D Company 4RAR, formerly a junior clerk and salesmen at Elders, watched from SAS Hill as the ARVN came in and took over Nui Dat. 'They were a pretty casual mob,' he said, 'pretty second rate.' The last days at Vung Tau were 'a bit of shindig' with 'plenty of parties'. 4RAR was an Anzac battalion and 'the Maoris hated a party', he said. 'We were very carefree. Well, not carefree but cared less. We were in a mess where one American dollar could buy nine tins of beer and a packet of smokes. What else could you wish for?'

The last Australian concert parties in Vietnam included a performance at Vung Tau in November 1971. It was headlined by Lorrae

Desmond, and the bill once again featured Sean and Sonja. Sean Cullip was among the first men balloted into national service, and among the last men at 1ALSG. 'Lorrae put together a show,' said Cullip. 'We'd all do our individual things, she would close the show, then she'd start singing, 'We've Got to Get Out of This Place', which was the theme song. And one by the one, the acts would come out and join in. Then each act would do an encore and the others stood in the background, then we came out and did the whole finale again. So the finale lasted about twenty-five minutes. Things were so much easier at that stage in Vietnam. We were allowed to go out and eat in restaurants and walk on the streets. There was no protection. We didn't need it any more.'

Gary Treeve, a boilermaker from Tamworth who had come to 1ALSG as a conscript in the RAEME, signed up to stay on with the regulars in January 1972, and was one of the troops on the last boat out in February. They did not feel like a defeated army. 'We never won and we never lost,' said Treeve. 'We didn't really know. As far as we were concerned, our part was finished and we were going home okay. We probably thought the Americans have got control of it now and they were sort of winning.

'We worked nearly twenty-four-hour shifts on a steam cleaner,' he said, 'cleaning carriers and other equipment from the workshop. And other units were doing the same, cleaning their stuff and packing it up, getting it all prepared to go home. It kept us fully occupied, but we'd still do piquets of a night. We were still on full alert the whole time. The carriers used to go along the beach and do patrols.

'We dug a lot of big holes with B66 loaders to throw all the rations and a lot of old stuff like webbing and some old greens. We just threw range fuel in and – *woof!* – it went up. In a few hours it was all burned, and they just covered it over. The dirt they dug out they put back in. A lot of the established buildings – the huts that we lived in and the beautiful big, steel-structured workshop, the Kevin Wheatley Stadium, the Peter Badcoe Club, the swimming pool, all those facilities were still there. They were empty and we just walked out and left them all,' said Treeve.

'Our platoon jumped on APCs to get to Front Beach to meet the barges to go out to the *Sydney*,' said Pentingill. 'I remember driving through Vungers just on the outside of APCs. Kids, women, disappointed that we were leaving, were throwing rocks and cans.'

'All of our armoury stuff and our personal weapons were loaded into a container and put down in the bulk of the ship,' said Treeve. 'Quite a few carriers were on the flight deck, and some trucks and Land Rovers and recovery vehicles.' HMAS *Sydney* arrived back in Garden Island from Vietnam for the last time on 12 March 1972, to salutes from the ships in Sydney Harbour, and a band playing 'Waltzing Matilda' on the dockside. The troops were met by 'a large crowd of relatives and friends and hundreds of children' and were welcomed home by the new minister for army, Bob Katter, who had served as an army officer for ten months during the Second World War, but had his appointment terminated on medical grounds before he could go overseas. Katter thanked the troops from the flight deck and told them they'd done a tremendous job. Only one in one thousand had suffered emotional illness, he said, and 'this extremely low rate is not to be bettered by any other Army in the world'.[12]

At the end of Australia's Vietnam War, national service was still more popular than either the government or the opposition. A *Sydney Morning Herald* survey published in April showed nearly two-thirds of respondents were in favour of the continuation of some kind of national service scheme, although fewer than one-quarter thought conscripts should be sent overseas.[13]

On 25 April 1972, the RSL honoured men returned from Vietnam by inviting them to lead the Anzac Day parade through Sydney. One hundred and fifty thousand people turned up to watch the march, vastly outnumbering the attendance of any demonstration against the war anywhere in Australia ever. 'The proud figures of 600 Vietnam war veterans . . . instilled a new enthusiasm into the crowds lining the street,' reported the *Sydney Morning Herald*. 'Australia's newest veterans received generous applause amidst cries of "welcome back, boys," and "good on you, fellers." And the feeling seeped through as old servicemen from South African campaigns and World War I received their full quota of recognition.'

But the start of the march had to be delayed for two minutes when a timer-detonated flare went off among the wreaths around the cenotaph, and mourning flowers caught flame.[14]

36

NATIONAL SERVICE WITHOUT A WAR

Australia, which had not conscripted men in the First World War, now had a national service scheme in peace time.

In many ways, not much had changed since the first conscripts had marched into the recruit training battalions. Victorians were still concerned when their footballers were taken by the army: two Footscray players, Bernie Quinlan and Peter Walsh, were photographed at Swan Street on 26 January. The Melbourne *Herald* presented its usual feel-good story about the first intake of the year. This time, a man from Sunshine enjoyed a champagne breakfast on the banks of the Yarra before passing through the depot gates. In March, an international sportsman was found to be insufficiently fit for the Australian Army when Queensland tennis player Ross Case was excluded on medical grounds. One day after his exemption was decided, he flew with the Australian Davis Cup team to Hong Kong. He went on to win grand-slam doubles titles at the Australian Open in 1974 and Wimbledon in 1977. Case's treatment raised the old doubts about the way the scheme was run, but the DLNS rolled out a luckless assistant secretary to explain, 'Those we reject are not necessarily unfit for normal activity, including sport. Last year we rejected an international rugby star because he was slightly deaf. It didn't affect his performance on the field, but it could have been fatal on a military operation.' He scorned the suggestion that a person who was fit for normal activity might be given an office job. 'We don't consider it worth disrupting a man's life for 18 months just to put him behind an Army desk,'[1] he said. Later in the year, a football club for the first time pronounced itself 'happy' a player had been called up. When Richmond ruck-rover Greg Hollick was drafted, club secretary Alan Schwab said, 'The discipline should do him the world of good.' Hollick had played ten times in the season but, when he was dropped to the reserves, he declared himself unavailable and went back to his parents' home for a holiday before starting his national service training.[2]

The *Sydney Morning Herald* sent journalist Gavin Souter to talk to national servicemen about life in a peacetime army. Souter had anticipated they would grumble, he wrote, but 'these complaints were more bitter than I expected'. Seven years after all the assurances that Australian soldiers would no longer work in camp kitchens, a former bank officer from Taree, NSW, told him, 'If you get a battalion you do a lot of general duties – working in the kitchen, guard duty and so on.' An APC driver at Holsworthy said, 'I've been here eight months . . . In that time I've done 10 weeks' training, of which only three weeks were in the bush. Since the war is over, and we aren't doing much training, what are we doing here?'

Another cavalryman said, 'The other day we took five APCs out to the Task Force maintenance area. That's in the bush. We cut down a couple of trees, we played cards, we played a bit of cricket. Then we came home. Don't ask me why we were out there.' The army, which had never claimed to be perfect – only had those assertions made on its behalf by cheerleading journalists – admitted there was no system 'in or out of the Army, which can keep a man fully occupied one hundred per cent of his time'.[3]

Nothing much had altered for the protesters either. Demonstrators from SOS and the Draft Resisters Union blocked the gates at Swan Street on 19 April, shouting, 'Don't go through the gates. It is not too late to change your mind. You can still become a conscientious objector.' The conscripts, their family and friends, as usual, jeered and booed them. The untiring SOS activist Jean McLean, who'd accepted the chrysanthemums from a national serviceman when she'd stood vigil for Errol Noack, was there with her loudhailer.[4]

With Australia's military commitment in Vietnam all but over, the anti-war marches of April 1972 were smaller but more frenzied than earlier protests, and aimed more squarely at the US. In Melbourne, there were attacks on the US Consulate and the Pan Am building. Tim Fischer warned against overreacting to the new street violence. 'I have no brief for the demonstrators,' he said, 'who enjoy a freedom in Australia non-existent in their beloved Hanoi and who have no idea of the bloodshed and atrocities which the Communist takeover would bring in Vietnam. However, I respect their right to peacefully demonstrate within the scope of sufficient but not excessive government control.'[5]

Draft resistance continued, even without the threat of war. In April, hundreds of Sydney University students freed from arrest a well-known evader, Mike Matteson, shearing his handcuffs with bolt-cutters. In July, Matteson turned up at Melbourne University and spoke to a crowd of about three hundred and fifty demonstrators before they marched on the DLNS offices in the Century Building on Swanston Street, converging below its relentless vertical lines and sentinel cupola, chanting, 'Smash the draft!' Matteson was at Melbourne University again to address a protest which laid a wreath on the foot of the steps to the Shrine of Remembrance, with the inscription, 'To the unwilling led by the unqualified to do the unnecessary'.

In the absence of a war, even previously loyal establishment voices expressed scepticism about the need for national service. The annual conference of the Australian Legion of Ex-Service Clubs unanimously agreed that conscription in Australia was 'absolutely abhorrent'.[6] Even the minister for the army, Bob Katter, said he didn't like the ballot system, 'But damn it all, how else can you get an army of 40000?' He took refuge in the Menzies-era calumny that the policy had been formed by experts. 'I've accepted the fact the men who have had it under close scrutiny believe it's the most suitable system for Australia,' he said.[7]

In August, the governor of New South Wales, Sir Roden Cutler, who, as honorary colonel of the Sydney University Regiment, had once been the target of a messy student demonstration, told the state conference of the RSL he had 'doubts about the need for national service' and was certainly 'doubtful about its efficacy'.[8] The government's argument that the scheme was absolutely necessary to keep the army at its required size was undermined when the army was revealed to be already over-strength by 1773 men, as a result of a worsening civilian job market and increases in services pay. But Lieutenant General Sir Thomas Daly, the widely respected former chief of general staff, warned the army would lose five of its nine battalions if conscription were to come to an end, and that many of the best officers would resign rather than face the uncertainty of the future. He said improved pay and conditions helped to keep men in the army, but questioned whether this was any great benefit. 'A professional army is no place for old men, certainly not for old private soldiers,' he said. Daly suggested an all-volunteer army might be not only undesirable but immoral, and the abolition of national service would result in 'economic conscription'.[9] At the *Sydney Morning Herald*, the years of bloodshed and protest, the Vietnam War, the massacre at My Lai, lost lives and social disruption – and even the recent pronouncements of the great and good – had not shifted the newspaper's ideas one millimetre. Daly, the paper editorialised, had made 'what any reasonable Australian must consider an un-answerable case for the continuation of National Service'.[10]

The government struggled to combat the false impression that draft resistance had become commonplace. 'Since the beginning of

1968,' said McMahon's minister for defence David Fairburn, 'only 13 men persisted in their non-compliance to the point where they were imprisoned for failing to obey a call-up notice compared with some 38,000 men who were called up and enlisted. These figures speak for themselves and bear out what the Government has said on a number of occasions regarding the level of acceptance of National Service among the young men affected.'[11] Draft resisters were conspicuous in part because they were so very rare.

But a kind of anomic sickness seemed to be spreading through the ranks of conscripts – or perhaps it had always been there but was only now acknowledged, when the stakes were low. On 21 September, South Australian Senator Jim Cavanagh, who had worked as a plasterer through the Second World War, said three national servicemen had attempted suicide at Puckapunyal recently, and called on the government to investigate. There had always been whispers about self-harm in the RTBs, and perhaps some of them were furphies, bedtime stories for the barracks. However, during the week that followed Cavanagh's statement, the army proved the senator wrong: it wasn't three national servicemen who'd tried to kill themselves, it was five, including one young man who had eaten rat poison and drank petrol. Lieutenant Colonel Stan Maizey, the CO at 2RTB, said in the previous three months there had been three wrist-slashings and an attempted hanging. 'All the incidents were attempts by recruits to draw attention to their own emotional shortcomings,' said Maizey, 'rather than genuine suicide attempts.'[12] There was no bastardisation at the camp, because Maizey wouldn't abide it. He had discovered that two of the men had tried to kill themselves before they'd been conscripted. 'Basically,' he said, 'some chaps, because of their psychological makeup, are going to do this sort of thing whether they are in the army or not.'[13] Lieutenant Colonel John Bennett from army PR described the environment at Puckapunyal as 'perhaps like the nursing profession',[14] to which some men just hadn't adjusted. Brigadier Ian Gilmore said some national servicemen suffered from a lack of purpose since Australia's commitment to Vietnam had ended, and blamed the protesters: because national service had been a subject of controversy, he said, 'recruits came into the army with varying degrees of intention to co-operate'.[15]

The thirteenth and last national service ballot was drawn by former Australian Test cricket captain Ian Johnson, to select four thousand two hundred men to go into the army in January 1973. None ever did. On 2 December 1972, Gough Whitlam drew to a close Labor's twenty-three years in opposition when the ALP won the federal election with a nine-seat majority over the Coalition.

Donald Chipp, the Liberal MP who had been present at the first national service ballot, retained the Victorian seat of Hotham, which had been contested by the ALP's Barry Johnston, a draft evader on the run, for whose integrity and courage Chipp had expressed admiration. Hotham aside, national service was barely an issue in the election – the ALP campaigned on 'cities, schools and hospitals' – but as soon as Whitlam took office he fulfilled his pledge to end the scheme. Conscription ceased in far greater haste even than it had begun. The call-up was abolished as the first act of the new government, outstanding charges were dropped against all draft resisters, convicted and currently imprisoned evaders were released, and any man was free to leave the CMF. The last conscripts in uniform had the choice of completing their eighteen months' national service, transferring to the regular army, or being released pending discharge.

This was the government of the new, heralding most of the changes it was once hoped national service might forestall. In the campaign, Whitlam had posed with a pop star – Little Pattie, the darling of Long Tan – and worn a T-shirt with his suit. He was fashionable, almost a fop, and he stood for a new, soft, feminised Australia. The manly virtues would be pushed aside. The death penalty would be abolished. Women would have equal pay in the public service. Long-haired, bearded students would see their fees abolished, while short-haired, clean-shaven diggers watched their battalions amalgamate. Communist China would be recognised. The old ways were routed.

On 11 December, a 'steady stream of national servicemen' handed back their kit to the quartermaster's store at the 101 Transport Company in Randwick, Sydney. The company second-in-command, Captain KW Barlow, said about a third of the national servicemen at the base had opted to remain in uniform. There were still a small number of Australian troops in Vietnam, including the AATTV, which was immediately withdrawn, before the US, North and South Vietnam and the Viet Cong signed an agreement ending the war on 27 January 1973. The only Australian unit left behind was the Australian Embassy Guard Platoon Saigon, which included three men who had entered the army as national servicemen, the last of whom, Lance Corporal Robin Wybrow, came home on 30 June 1973.

It wasn't until 22 November 1974 that the last of the 63740 national servicemen was discharged from the army. Private PB Stapleton of the combined 5th/7th Battalion had entered the army in July 1972. He should have been discharged by January 1974, but he broke his ankle horseriding while on his final leave. The army could not let him go until he was medically fit, so he performed light duties at Holsworthy for almost a year until his injury was fully healed. Stapleton said he felt unlucky not to have had a chance to go to Vietnam, and he'd grown to like the military life. 'The pay is good,' he said, 'and the conditions are getting better.' On the afternoon of the day he was discharged, the last national serviceman signed up to join the regular army.

When the last Australian troops had pulled out of Vietnam, there were two hundred national servicemen dead. Although they had only ever made up 37 per cent of the army, they numbered 42 per cent of its fatal casualties. If the thirty-six regular soldiers who died before the national servicemen arrived in Vietnam are taken from the equation then, for the six years in which national servicemen fought the war, they comprised 45 per cent of the dead. Each dead man's parents received a visit from an army officer and a religious minister, and a telegram from the government, expressing its regret. A little later, almost every family also took delivery of an envelope addressed by hand, containing the commiserations of a stranger who understood their sorrow knew no depths, their grieving would have no end.

It was a personal note from Walter Noack, still mourning his terrific kid.[16]

AFTERWORD

'We didn't sort of fit in. You can imagine coming back to a place where you knew a lot of people and all of a sudden they had their own interests and you weren't included. You were lost completely . . . The only place we could meet was in pubs; and I drank too much. Everyone was established, their lives were running smoothly, and you were an intrusion.' – FRANK BAKER

'When we first got back there seemed to be this wall of almost wilful incomprehension. We were all, they said in effect, mad as hatters, and it was dangerous to let us rattle on. So we would start talking about what had happened and instantly people were busy changing the subject, looking bored as all hell.' – RUSSELL BRADDON[1]

The evening after I finished the first draft of *The Nashos' War*, I met a middle-aged journalist friend at a book launch. She'd probably driven from Sydney's eastern suburbs, but it seemed to me she'd come down from the skies as a gift from the god of afterwords. I told her I'd been writing about national servicemen in the Vietnam War, and she replied, 'They were treated like pariahs when they came home, weren't they?' Well, some of them were by some people in some places at some times, but to allow that to become the entire story of 15 381 men who fought in a foreign war is naive, almost obscene.

This book barely touches on what happened to national servicemen after they left the army. I talked with a few veterans who spoke of angry challenges in hotels, snide comments at parties, of being personally abused or spat at – although the spitting often seemed to represent a collective, symbolic experience of men who felt rejected. Many more remembered a mood of indifference and incomprehension. Yet the real experiences of social alienation of men who once had been among the most conformist and well-integrated in society have been drowned in the spit and blood of more sensational stories, many of which, in the judgement of the *Official History*, 'may have been exaggerated or imported from American experience'.[2]

The fixation with the reception faced by some veterans has all but obscured the hardship and heroism of the war as it was fought by men who, in most cases, felt they had no choice but to go into the army. It has also allowed all manner of strange statements to stand unchallenged. On 18 August 2012, a veteran incorrectly named in his local newspaper as both 'Colonel Bill Glassick (retired)' and 'Colonel Bill Glassic' addressed a Vietnam Veterans' Day service on the Sunshine Coast. 'Glassick' used the occasion to criticise politicians for not attending the funerals of servicepeople killed in Vietnam, as 'our government of the day did not see it as fitting to return those killed in action to Australia'.[3] In fact, until the Vietnam War, almost every Anzac who fell on foreign ground was buried in foreign soil, as the vast European war cemeteries mutely attest. Two hundred and ninety-one Australian casualties of the Korean War are interred in the United Nations Memorial Cemetery in Tanggok, Busan. Most of the Australians who died in the Malayan Emergency are buried at Christian cemeteries in Taiping and Penang, with one further Australian grave in the military cemetery at Terendak, Malacca. A scattering lie at Kranji in Singapore, alongside the serried ranks of soldiers who died defending the island from the Japanese in the Second World War, and their comrades subsequently murdered while prisoners of the emperor. The reason there are cenotaphs standing like upturned railway spikes at the crossroads of so many city suburbs and country towns is the bereaved had nowhere but the monuments to grieve. As Ken Inglis, the historian of memorials wrote, in fact the Vietnam War marked 'the first time Australians dead on service abroad were mourned at actual and not just surrogate funerals'.[4] But there seems a small taste for truth in the memory of Vietnam, and omnivorous appetite for insult, even in death. In 1991, 6RAR volunteer national serviceman Robin Harris wrote of the 'eternal shame' of those who 'turned up at the funerals of servicemen to wave placards', although there are no reported instances of this occurring, and the idea only appears in secondary literature when sourced back to Harris.[5]

The idea that radicals rode roughshod over everything has been fed by what historian Jeffrey Grey called a 'military "urban myth"' that General Daly ordered desk-bound troops in Australia to dress in civilian clothes to avoid trouble with protesters. In fact, wrote Grey, 'the move to have officers in Army Headquarters in Canberra (and at St Kilda Barracks in Melbourne) wear suits to work rather than uniforms seems to have been a pragmatic one since officers were not allowed to wear uniform in social or commercial settings, and this was clearly an inconvenience in a place like Canberra out of hours.'[6]

The fable of an omnipresent, dominant peace movement, with an influence on every aspect of public life, works for everyone. To the left, the story proves that patient propagandising and mass demonstrations can bring about irreversible cultural change and the end of a war. To the right, it's a cautionary tale of what happens when people dare to protest against military action – it's only the enemy who benefit and the soldiers who suffer.

In August 2006, Prime Minister John Howard apologised in parliament to Vietnam veterans. He did not say he was sorry they had been sent to a war in which hundreds of young Australians had died and thousands been severely wounded. He showed no regret for the government's use of national servicemen to fight a foreign war. He was without remorse that many of the dead had been chosen by ballot. He was unrepentant that Robert Menzies had erroneously identified Chinese expansionism as the force behind Vietnamese Communism and mischievously labelled it a 'direct military threat to Australia'. And although Howard was only twenty-six years old in 1965, he certainly was not apologising for not having joined the army and fought what he believed to be a just war. Howard was only sorry the returned men 'were not welcomed back as they should have been'.[7] But as Max Teichmann wrote in the conservative *Quadrant* magazine in 2008, 'Conscription would not have been necessary had the young men among the DLP and the Liberals been ready to do what, in their opinion, others should be forced to do. Namely, *they* should have taken the Queen's shilling, joined up, and helped keep the Reds out and Australia white. But our poltroons of the Right, in the main, *didn't* join up.'[8]

In part, those who came back from Vietnam believe they met with an apathy unknown to other veterans because the history of earlier returned men is rarely told. A movie on a loop at the excellent National Vietnam Veterans Museum in Victoria includes the commentary, 'Following World War One, World War Two and the Korean War, our troops were welcomed home with flags, cheers, hugs and kisses.' As this book has attempted to show, many Vietnam veterans met with precisely this reception. And, the truth is, many diggers from previous wars did not. As Grey has written of the first AIF, 'The earlier shiploads of men marched in triumph through city streets, but later contingents received more muted welcomes, or none at all. The same thing applied in the aftermath of the next world war.'[9] And, as Grey pointed out, 'soldiers "from the wars returning" have always caused fear and apprehension in the wider societies which have spawned them'.[10] The homecoming has eternally been a part of the story. Only in the Vietnam War – and only since the 1980s – has it become the dominant part.

There were so many other comments my friend at the book launch could have made about national servicemen, from, 'They were the unlucky ones, weren't they?' to, 'What a great adventure that must have been.' She could have asked, 'Didn't they hold the line at Long Tan?' or, 'Didn't they charge like Anzacs on Operation Bribie?' She could have called them dupes or heroes. She could have denounced them as babykillers, although that barely seems thinkable today. To reduce the national service experience to nothing but a half-imagined protester's placard is like saying of the 2nd AIF, 'They built the Thai–Burma Railway, didn't they?'

And the quotations at the opening of this afterword are not from Vietnam veterans. They are the words of former prisoners of the Japanese, struggling to describe what it was like to return to civilian life at the end of the Second World War.

NOTES

Preface

1 Edwards, Peter, *A Nation at War: Australian politics, society and diplomacy during the Vietnam War 1965–1975*, Allen & Unwin and Australian War Memorial, St Leonards, 1997, 353

Prologue

1 *The Sun-Herald*, 22 August 1965
2 *The Sun* (Sydney), 15 December 1965
3 Hazlehurst, Cameron, 'Young Menzies', Cameron Hazlehurst (ed.), *Australian Conservatism*, Australian National University Press, Canberra, 1979, 10–11
4 Final Geneva Declaration, 21 July 1954
5 Eisenhower, Dwight D, *The White House Years: Mandate for change, 1953–56*, Doubleday, New York, 1963, 372
6 Commonwealth of Australia, Parliamentary debates: House of Representatives: official Hansard, No. 17, 29 April 1965, 1061
7 *The Australian*, 30 April 1965

The Errol Noack Letters

1 Langley, Greg, *A Decade of Dissent: Vietnam and the conflict on the Australian homefront*, Allen & Unwin, North Sydney, 1992, 49
2 State Library of SA, PRG 1452/5, yabby log book of Errol Noack
3 The *Canberra Times*, 11 March 1965
4 Guy, Bill, *A Life on the Left: A biography of Clyde Cameron*, Wakefield Press, Kent Town, 1999, 260
5 The *Sydney Morning Herald*, 26 May 1966
6 National Australian Archives (NAA), B2458/4717546, Department of Labour and National Service Personal Data Sheet for Errol Noack, 12 May 1965
7 Letter to Mr EW Noack from the National Service Registration Office, Adelaide, 3 June 1965
8 'Circular to National Servicemen' from the brigadier at Central Command Keswick Barracks, 9 June 1965

9 The *Sydney Morning Herald*, 7 August 1964
10 The *Sydney Morning Herald*, 1 August 1964
11 Letter to Mr Noack from major officer commanding company at Puckapunyal, 5 July 1965
12 National Vietnam Veterans Museum, letter from Errol Noack to Loris Noack, circa July 1965
13 *The Age*, 9 August 1965
14 NAA, B2458/4717546, Errol Noack's 'Psychological Assessment', 1 September 1965
15 Letter from Errol Noack to BH Mattner, date unclear
16 National Vietnam Veterans Museum, letter from Errol Noack to Herb and Loris Noack, undated
17 National Vietnam Veterans Museum, letter from Errol Noack to Herb Noack, 9 October 1965

The Friends of Errol Noack

1 *The Sun*, 16 June 1965
2 NAA, B2458/4717546, 2/66 Cadre Course Report, 18 May 1966
3 National Vietnam Veterans Museum, letter from Errol Noack to Loris Noack, undated
4 Ibid.

The Body of Errol Noack

1 Mackay, Ian, *Australians in Vietnam*, Rigby, Adelaide, 1968, 134
2 *The Age*, 30 April 2005
3 White, Tony, *Starlight: An Australian Army doctor in Vietnam*, CopyRight Publishing, Brisbane, 2011, 39
4 O'Neill, Robert J, *Vietnam Task: The 5th Battalion, the Royal Australian Regiment, 1966–67*, Cassell Australia, Melbourne, 1968, 38
5 White, *Starlight*, 39
6 Langley, *Decade of Dissent*, 49
7 White, *Starlight*, 39
8 *The Advertiser*, 27 May 1966
9 National Vietnam Veterans Museum, cable from Malcolm Fraser to Mr W Noack
10 Frame, Tom, *The Life and Death of Harold Holt*, Allen & Unwin, Crows Nest, 2005, 180
11 Fraser, Malcolm & Simons, Margaret, *Malcolm Fraser: The political memoirs*, Melbourne University Publishing, Carlton, 2009, 137

12 *The Age*, 26 May 1966

13 National Vietnam Veterans Museum, letter from General Westmoreland to Mr W Noack

14 The *Sydney Morning Herald*, 26 May 1966

15 *The Age*, 26 May 1966

16 *The Advertiser*, 26 May 1966

17 The *Canberra Times*, 30 May 1966

18 *The Advertiser*, 26 May 1966

19 *The Advertiser*, 27 May 1966

20 *The Sun*, 27 May 1966

21 *News* (Adelaide), 26 May 1966

22 AWM, PR03142 Private Record of Noack, Errol Wayne

23 *Daily News* (Perth), 30 May 1966

24 NAA, B2458/4717546, DADPR Minute in Noack, Errol Wayne, 31 May 1966

The Reality of National Service

1 Forell, Claude, 'Conscription: Part 2. Volunteers are Really Cheaper', *The Age*, 24 December 1970

2 The *Sydney Morning Herald*, 23 September 1964

3 The *Sydney Morning Herald*, 28 October 1964

4 NAA, A4940 C162, Part 2 'National Service – Policy, 1964–1967', 'Submission No. 521. For Cabinet. Services Manpower Review', November 1964

5 Ibid.

6 Ibid.

7 Howson, Peter, & Aitkin, Don (eds.), *The Howson Diaries: The life of politics*, Penguin, Ringwood, 1984, 121

8 Brass, Ken, 'Veterans Count Cost of Hearts Hurt at Home', *The Australian*, 4 May 1987

9 NAA, A4940 C162, Part 2 'National Service – Policy, 1964–1967', Cabinet Minute, Canberra, 4–5 November 1964

10 Brass, 'Veterans Count Cost'

11 Howson, *Howson Diaries*, 121

12 NAA, A463 1964/5143, Part 1, 'National Service Training Scheme – Policy, 1964', speech by R Menzies on Defence Review, 10 November 1964

13 *The Age*, 10 November 1964

14 NAA, A463 1964/5143, Part 1, 'National Service Training Scheme –Policy, 1964', letter from HA Bland to FW Jennings, 22 February 1965

15 NAA, A463 1964/5143, Part 1, 'National Service Training Scheme – Policy, 1964', 'Notes on National Service', 18 November 1964

16 Naughton, Kevin, ' "We had to bring it in": defending conscription, 50 years on', *Crikey,* 8 January 2014. Retrieved from http://www.crikey.com.au/2014/01/08/we-had-to-bring-it-in-defending-conscription-50-years-on/
17 NAA, letter from HA Bland to FW Jennings, 22 February 1965
18 *The Sun*, 2 July 1965
19 *The Sun*, 29 June 1965
20 Menzies, Robert Gordon, Sir, *The Measure of the Years*, Cassell Australia, North Melbourne, 1970, 75
21 *The Sun*, 2 June 1965

The Myths and Meaning of National Service

1 *The Herald*, 29 June 1965
2 NAA, Part 1, 18 November 1964
3 *The Sun-Herald*, 15 November 1964
4 NAA, A4940 C162, Part 2, 'National Service – Policy, 1964–1967', from Department of Labour and National Service, 'An Account of the Administrative Processes involved in the National Service Scheme up to the Stage of Call-up', 15 April 1966
5 NAA, A4940 C162, Part 2, 'National Service – Policy, 1964–1967', letter from HA Bland to Sir John Bunting, Prime Minister's Department, 18 April 1966
6 The *Sydney Morning Herald*, 18 June 1965
7 *The Australian*, 7 September 1965
8 *The Telegraph*, 19 August 1965
9 The *Sydney Morning Herald*, 27 July 1965
10 The *Sydney Morning Herald*, 17 August 1965
11 *The Herald*, 24 September 1965

The Happy Media

1 The *Sunday Herald*, 22 July 1951
2 The *Sunday Herald*, 29 July 1951
3 James, Clive, *Unreliable Memoirs*, Jonathan Cape, London, 1980, 141
4 Ibid., 147
5 The *Sydney Morning Herald*, 22 July 1953
6 Hay, David, 'Total Recoil: The Australian military and the national service training debate', *Limina: A journal of historical and cultural studies*, University of Western Australia, Nedlands, 1990, 86
7 The *Daily Telegraph,* 10 September 1955
8 Hay, 'Total Recoil', 88

9 Shields, Neville, T, 'National Service Training, 1950–59', Forward, Roy & Reece, Bob (eds.), *Conscription in Australia*, University of Queensland Press, Brisbane, 1968
10 Johnson, Bob, '8 Weeks to the Big Ballot', *The Sun-Herald*, 17 January 1965
11 *The Sun*, 17 June 1965
12 *The Sun*, 13 May 1965
13 The *Sydney Morning Herald*, 1 July 1965
14 *The Age*, 1 July 1965
15 Johnson, Bob, 'This Is Your Army, Digger', *The Sun-Herald*, 4 July 1965
16 *The Herald*, 29 June 1965
17 *The Herald*, 30 June 1965
18 *The Sun*, 1 July 1965
19 *The Age*, 1 July 1965
20 The *Sydney Morning Herald*, 2 July 1965
21 *The Herald*, 1 July 1965
22 Coleman, Robert, 'You Name It, They Have It', *The Herald*, 3 July 1965

Silver City

1 Gilfoyle, John & Robbins, John, *You'd Better Bloody Believe It!*, John & Lurelle Gilfoyle, Arana Hills, 2011, 1
2 Johnson, Dick & Sykes, Stuart, *Don't Tell Me I Can't Do That: An autobiography*, Ironbark, Chippendale, 1999, 48
3 Parr, Alan, *Memories of Vietnam*, Alan Parr, Nemingha, 2006, 8
4 Lipski, Sam, 'The Pucka Recruits', *The Bulletin*, 17 July 1965, 24
5 *The Age*, 6 September 1965
6 Australian Army, 'Information Booklet For National Servicemen', Australian Army, Australia, 1965
7 Australian Army Headquarters, ' "It's Like This–" Army Leaders Guide on Service Conditions', Australian Army, Canberra, 1960
8 Johnson, *Don't Tell Me*, 49
9 Lipski, Sam, 'The Crash-Programme Army', *The Bulletin*, 25 September 1965, 40

Officer Training

1 The *Sydney Morning Herald*, 4 July 1965
2 Lipski, 'Crash-Programme Army', 40
3 Fall, Bernard, *Street Without Joy*, Stackpole, Mechanicsburg, 1964, 381
4 Lipski, 'Crash-Programme Army', 40

5 Pynt, Gerald (ed.) & Epstein, Jack, *Australian Jewry's Book of Honour World War II*, Griffin Press, Netley, 1974, 34

Ready to Go

1 Commonwealth of Australia, Parliamentary debates: House of Representatives: official Hansard, No. 19, 13 May 1966, 1891
2 *The Age*, 9 March 1966
3 *The Age*, 10 March 1966
4 The *Sydney Morning Herald*, 31 March 1966
5 The *Daily Mirror*, 12 April 1966
6 *The Sun-Herald*, 24 April 1966
7 Jones, Geoff, 'Morale High at Puckapunyal', *The Sun*, 11 March 1966
8 Gilfoyle, *Better Bloody Believe It*, 16–17
9 The *Sydney Morning Herald*, 21 April 1966
10 The *Northern Daily Leader*, 14 May 1966
11 *The Australian*, 9 June 1966
12 The *Sydney Morning Herald*, 9 June 1966
13 Ibid.

In Country

1 Conley, Jenny, 'Dear Mum and Dad', *The Age*, 13 August 1993
2 The *Sydney Morning Herald*, 12 August 1966
3 Burgess, Pat, 'The Village of Hidden Hate', *The Bulletin*, 21 August 1976, 16
4 Conley, 'Mum and Dad'
5 Burgess, Pat, 'A Correspondent's Report', *War: Australia and Vietnam*, Maddock, Kenneth & Wright, Barry (eds.), Harper & Row, Sydney, 1987, 104–105
6 The *Sydney Morning Herald*, 22 June 1966
7 Ibid.
8 'The Mosman Shooting', *The Bulletin*, 2 July 1966, 5
9 Samuel, Peter, 'After the Viet Cong Collapse', *The Bulletin*, 2 July 1966, 16
10 Burgess, Pat, '6th Battalion in Baptism of Fire', The *Sydney Morning Herald*, 1 August 1966
11 *The News*, 18 August 1966

The Battle of Long Tan

1 *The Examiner*, 22 August 1966
2 Conley, 'Mum and Dad'
3 Parr, *Memories of Vietnam*, 49

4 McAulay, Lex, *The Battle of Long Tan*, Arrow Books, Milsons Point, 1987, 132–3
5 The *Sydney Morning Herald*, 23–24 August 1966
6 The *Sydney Morning Herald*, 24 August 1966
7 Baker, Mark, 'At Last, Susanne Says Farewell For Us All', The *Sydney Morning Herald*, 16 August 1996
8 *The Sun-Herald*, 21 August 1966
9 The *Sunday Mail*, 6 July 1986
10 The *Northern Daily Leader*, 5 December 2009
11 The *Northern Daily Leader*, 6 September 1966

Operation Bribie

1 *The Age*, 20 February 1967
2 The *Sydney Morning Herald*, 20 February 1967

The Changing of the Guard

1 The *Sydney Morning Herald*, 13 May 1967
2 *The Courier-Mail*, 15 June 1967
3 Brisbane *Telegraph*, 14 June 1967
4 Grey, Jeffrey, 'In Every War But One? Myth, History and Vietnam', Stockings, Craig (ed.), *Zombie Myths of Australian Military History*, University of New South Wales Press, Sydney, 2010, 200
5 The *Sydney Morning Herald*, 28 June 1967
6 The *Sydney Morning Herald*, 5 April 1967

The Unwilling

1 NAA, B2458/3789907, Henderson, Alwyn James, 'Individual Training – Progress Record', 13 December 1966
2 *The Peacemaker*, June–July 1967
3 *The Peacemaker*, August–September 1967
4 NAA, B2458/3789907, Henderson, Alwyn James, report by L. Preston, psychiatrist, 22 September 1967
5 *The Sun*, 23 August 1967

The Willing

1 *The Sun*, 19 April 1966
2 The *Sydney Morning Herald*, 21 April 1966
3 *The Sun*, 20 April 1966
4 *The Sun*, 13 November 1967

5 Walters, Doug, & Laws, Ken, *The Doug Walters Story*, Rigby, Adelaide, 1981, 41
6 Walters & Laws, *Doug Walters*, 44
7 The *Daily Mirror*, 15 December 1965
8 The *Daily Telegraph*, 18 June 1966
9 *The Sun-Herald*, 11 September 1966
10 *The Sun*, 14 April 1967
11 The *Daily Mirror*, 29 May 1967
12 *People*, 14 June 1967
13 *The Sun*, 26 June 1967
14 The *Daily Mirror*, 10 December 1967
15 Taylor, Ken, transcript of tape ten, side one – 'Parliamentary Library Interview with Sir Allen Fairhall', 3 September 1983

Love, War and Pogos in Vung Tau

1 Fall, Bernard, letter to Dorothy Fall, quoted in Fall, Dorothy & Halberstam, David, *Bernard Fall: Memories of a soldier-scholar*, Potomac Books, Washington DC, 2006, 115
2 McAulay, Lex, 'Myths of the Vietnam War', in *Wartime*, Australian War Memorial, Media Marketing Group, Canberra, Issue 20, October 2002, 23
3 *The Herald*, 1 August 1967
4 Ponting, Derek, '*Dear Mam–': Letters and memories of a Liverpool soldier in Vietnam 1966–67*, Countyvise Ltd, Birkenhead, 2011, 98
5 Montesini, Lorenzo, *My Life And Other Misdemeanours*, Penguin, Melbourne, 1999, pp 159–160
6 Montesini, *My Life*, 163
7 Montesini, *My Life*, 164–167

Pigs and Mines in the Year of the Goat

1 Australian War Memorial (AWM), PR00353 Private Record of Renshaw, Terence James, Letter from Renshaw to his parents, 19 May 1967
2 AWM, PR00353 Private Record of Renshaw, Terence James, Letter from Renshaw to 'Buckle, Jan, Mark & Tracy', 21 May 1967
3 AWM, PR00353 Private Record of Renshaw, Terence James, Letters from LS Sempel, undated
4 AWM, PR00353 Private Record of Renshaw, Terence James, Statement by the Minister for the Army, Malcolm Fraser, 16 June 1967
5 Beckett, Richard, 'Australian Fence Hits Viet Cong', *Herald*, 7 June 1967
6 Heard, Barry, *Well Done, Those Men: Memoirs of a Vietnam veteran*, Scribe, Carlton North, 2005, 157–158

Call Up the Police

1 NAA, A463 1964/5143, Part 2, 'National Service Training Scheme – Policy', Letter to Mrs S Emery from Harold Holt, 26 October 1967
2 *The Herald*, 2 June 1965
3 *The Age*, 3 June 1965
4 NAA, A1209 1975/2165, 'National Service Training Scheme Policy 1969', Letter from AG Rylah to Mr Holt, 11 August 1967
5 NAA, A463 1964/5143, Part 2, 'National Service Training Scheme – Policy', Note for Prime Minister, 16 August 1966
6 Archbold, Jim, letter home, 6 April 1968

Tet

1 *The Age*, 2 February 1968
2 *The Age*, 3 February 1968
3 *The Australian*, 5 February 1968
4 *The Herald*, 8 February 1968
5 *Daily Telegraph*, 8 February 1968
6 *The Australian*, 21 February 1968
7 Russ, Martin, *Happy Hunting Ground*, Atheneum, New York, 1968, 185
8 *The Herald*, 8 March 1968
9 Mcrae, Toni, 'Confession of a Digger', *Fraser Coast Chronicle*, 17 April 2010
10 Burstall, Terry, *A Soldier Returns: A Long Tan veteran discovers the other side of Vietnam*, University of Queensland Press, St Lucia, 1990

The Battle of Coral

1 *The Herald*, 10 May 1969
2 The *Sydney Morning Herald*, 14 May 1968
3 The *Sydney Morning Herald*, 15 May 1968
4 Weekes, Neil, unpublished manuscript
5 Ibid.
6 Ibid.
7 Ibid.
8 Rees, Peter, *The Boy from Boree Creek: The Tim Fischer story*, Allen & Unwin, Crows Nest, 2001, 64
9 The *Sydney Morning Herald*, 18 May 1968
10 Archbold, Jim, letter home, 22 May 1968
11 Archbold, Jim, letter to his mother, undated

Objection Overruled

1 Pepper, William, 'The Children of Vietnam', *Ramparts*, January 1967, 55
2 *The Peacemaker*, October–November 1967
3 *National U*, 10 June 1968
4 *The Telegraph*, 10 January 1969
5 Goot, Murray & Tiffen, Rodney, 'Public Opinion and the Politics of the Polls', Peter King (ed.), *Australia's Vietnam: Australia in the Second Indo-China War*, Allen & Unwin, North Sydney, 1983, 135
6 *The Herald*, 29 January 1969

Normie Goes To War, Many Don't

1 NAA, B2458/3793130, Rowe, Norman John, 'Australian Military Forces: Course Report', 31 May 1968
2 The *Daily Mirror*, 21 June 1968
3 *People*, 26 February 1969
4 The *Daily Telegraph*, 14 January 1969
5 The *Sydney Morning Herald*, 14 January 1969
6 *The Sun*, 18 April 1969
7 The *Daily Telegraph*, 9 September 1969
8 The *Daily Telegraph*, 20 December 1969
9 *The Herald-Sun*, 4 June 2013
10 Thompson, Peter, transcript of radio interview, *Talking Heads*, ABC, 19 May 2008. Retrieved from http://www.abc.net.au/tv/talkingheads/txt/s2242030.htm
11 Hart, Royce, *The Royce Hart Story*, Thomas Nelson, Melbourne, 1970, 53
12 *The Sun*, 28 June 1967
13 Anderson, Jon, 'Keith Gent's Stolen Dream', *The Herald-Sun*, 25 April 2007
14 Dapin, Mark, 'Two of Us: Leon and Henry Nissen', *Good Weekend*, 28 June 2003, 16
15 Ibid.
16 Ryan, Michael, 'Henry Right, Father Left, Leon Middle', *The Age*, 26 August 1969

The Battle of Binh Ba

1 The *Canberra Times*, 24 August 1966
2 Strathdee, Robin, 'Binh Ba – Village of the Dead', The *Sydney Morning Herald*, 9 June 1969

The Day Mankind Kicked the Moon

1 The *Sydney Morning Herald*, 22 July 1969

The Myth of the Sixties

1 TV interview with Mike Sheahan, *Open Mike*, Fox Footy channel, 19 August 2013
2 *Stateline South Australia*, 'The Inside Story of the Cornes Family', ABC TV, 29 August 2003
3 *Open Mike*, Fox Footy
4 *Stateline South Australia*, 'Inside Story'
5 *Open Mike*, Fox Footy
6 *Stateline South Australia*, 'Inside Story'
7 *The Sun*, 8 March 1969
8 *The Herald*, 7 March 1969
9 The *Sydney Morning Herald*, 23 April 1969
10 *The Courier-Mail*, 31 May 1969
11 The *Sydney Morning Herald*, 5 July 1969
12 Jones, Evan, personal diary, 17 November 1969
13 *The Australian*, 6 August 1969
14 The *Sydney Morning Herald*, 21 October 1969
15 Ibid.
16 Jones, Evan, personal diary, 2 November 1969
17 Doherty, John, 'Welcome Marred Melee As Troops Parade', *The Advertiser*, 10 December 1969
18 Stewart, Elizabeth, 'Welcome Home: Vietnam Vets Return from War', *SIT-REP*, December 2009
19 Giblett, Noel (ed.), *Homecomings: Stories from Australian Vietnam veterans and their wives*, Australian Govt. Pub. Service, Canberra, 1990, 23
20 Harcourt, David, *Everybody Wants to be Fuehrer: National Socialism in Australia and New Zealand*, Borchardt Library, Bundoora, 1985, 57
21 The *Sydney Morning Herald*, 24 March 1971

The Myth of the Moratorium

1 Winter, Peter, *The Year I Said Goodbye*, Wakefield Press, Kent Town, 2003, 70
2 Ibid., 130
3 Ibid., 141
4 NAA, A1209 1975/2165, 'National Service Training Scheme policy 1969', Department of External Affairs Inward Cablegram from Australian Embassy, Washington, 24 February 1970
5 *The Advertiser*, 9 May 1970
6 Edwards, *A Nation at War*, 271
7 *The Advertiser*, 9 May 1970

8 AWM, Lewis, Bob, (Lewis, Bob, Harvey, Trevor and Horan, John eds.,) *Then There was Nine: 9 Platoon, 3RAR, 1969–2001*, 2001, 21

9 Wells, Greg and Hann, Adrian, 'Adelaide', *Revolution*, June 1–July 1 1970

10 *The Bulletin*, 16 May 1970

11 Edwards, *A Nation at War*, 247

12 *The Telegraph*, 7 July 1970

13 The *Sydney Morning Herald*, 26 September 1970

14 The *Sydney Morning Herald*, 29 September 1970

2RAR's Words of War

1 Collyer, David, *From Fishnets to Foxholes and Back Again*, The Author, Ballarat, 2001, 7

2 Ibid., 9–10

3 Sloman, Des, personal diary, 2 May 1970

4 Ibid., 12 and 16 May 1970

5 Ibid., 13 May 1970

6 Ibid., 17 May 1970

7 Ibid., 23 June 1970

8 Ibid., 16 August 1970

9 Collyer, *Fishnets to Foxholes*, 52

10 Donohoe, Frank, personal letter to Des Sloman, 3 February 1971

Rebels in the Ranks

1 State Library of Victoria, MS 12326, Papers of Maxwell Keith Costello, 21 April 1968

2 Ibid., 16 December 1968

3 The *Tribune*, 11 November 1970

The Myth of the Volunteer

1 David Horner & Jean Bou (eds.) in *Duty First: A history of the Royal Australian Regiment* (Allen & Unwin, Crows Nest, 2008, 190) maintain 'The national serviceman had to specifically volunteer for overseas service by signing a declaration during Corps training, and thus all national servicemen who served in Vietnam volunteered to do so.' The same wording appears in Paul Ham's book *Vietnam: The Australian War* (HarperCollins, Pymble, 2007, 170), as a quote from a letter to Horner from Brigadier Colin Khan, formerly of 5RAR, to which Ham adds the caveat, 'Many conscripts do not recall being asked to sign a form, but in practice they were all offered a verbal exit.'

2 Dougherty, David, *Reveille*, January–February 2009, 4

3 Russell, Ronald D, *Reveille*, January–February 2009, 4
4 McDowell, David J, & Elder, Bruce A, *Reveille*, March–April 2009, 6–7
5 Appears in Battle, Brian, *Nashos in Australia 1965–1973*, Raby, 2008, 82, and several army service records.
6 NAA, B2458/3798268, Wittner, David Maurice, Letter to Andrew Peacock, 11 July 1970
7 NAA, B2458/3798268, Wittner, David Maurice, Letter from Andrew Peacock to Private Wittner, 31 July 1970
8 NAA, B2458/1736660, Roubin, Loris, Record of Service

The Last Days

1 *The Sun*, 20 October 1970
2 The *Daily Advertiser*, 23 January 1971
3 The *Sydney Morning Herald*, 17 February 1971
4 The *Sydney Morning Herald*, 26 April 1971
5 The *Sydney Morning Herald*, 11 March 1971
6 *Tribune*, 3 October 1971
7 'The Ten-Year War', *The Bulletin*, 28 August 1971
8 'The Trouble with Students', *The Bulletin*, 5 July 1969
9 McKernan, Michael, *Here is their Spirit: A history of the Australian War Memorial 1917–1990*, University of Queensland Press and Australian War Memorial, St Lucia, 1991, 264
10 The *Canberra Times*, 27 September 1971
11 The *Sunday Mail*, 16 October 1971
12 The *Sydney Morning Herald*, 13 March 1972
13 The *Sydney Morning Herald*, 3 April 1972
14 The *Sydney Morning Herald*, 26 April 1972

National Service Without a War

1 The *Sydney Morning Herald*, 25 March 1972
2 *The Herald*, 29 June 1972
3 Souter, Gavin, 'What motivation will replace the Vietnam War?', The *Sydney Morning Herald*, 3 April 1972
4 *The Herald*, 19 April 1972
5 The *Sydney Morning Herald*, 18 May 1972
6 The *Sydney Morning Herald*, 27 March 1972
7 *The Australian*, 11 August 1972
8 The *Sydney Morning Herald*, 9 August 1972
9 *The Age*, 16 August 1972

10 The *Sydney Morning Herald*, 17 August 1972
11 The *Sydney Morning Herald*, 4 September 1972
12 The *Sydney Morning Herald*, 21 September 1972
13 The *Sydney Morning Herald*, 22 September 1972
14 *The Age*, 22 September 1972
15 *The Telegraph*, 24 September 1972
16 Letters of acknowledgement to Walter Noack from the families of the dead, sighted by the author at the home of Grant Collins

Afterword

1 Nelson, Hank, *Prisoners of War: Australians under Nippon*, ABC Enterprises for the Australian Broadcasting Corporation, Crows Nest, 1990, 211
2 Edwards, Peter, *Australia and the Vietnam War*, NewSouth Publishing and Australian War Memorial, Sydney, 2014, 278
3 Brand, Anthony, 'Funerals Used by Pollies', *Sunshine Coast Daily*, 19 August 2012
4 Inglis, KS & Brazier, Jan, *Sacred Places: War memorials in the Australian landscape*, Melbourne University Press, Carlton, 2008, 362
5 Harris, Robin, 'The New Breed', Maddock, Kenneth (ed.), *Memories of Vietnam*, Random House, Milsons Point, 1991, 67
6 Grey, Jeffrey, *A Soldier's Soldier: A biography of Lieutenant General Sir Thomas Daly*, Cambridge University Press, Port Melbourne, 2012, 133
7 Commonwealth of Australia, Parliamentary debates: House of Representatives: official Hansard, No. 11, 17 August 2006, 62
8 Teichmann, Max, 'The Cut-Lunch Commandos', *Quadrant*, April 2008, 73–74
9 Grey, Jeffrey, 'Vietnam, Anzac and the Veteran', Pierce, Peter, Grey, Jeffrey & Doyle, Jeff, *Vietnam Days*, Penguin, Maryborough, 1991, 87
10 Ibid., 63

BIBLIOGRAPHY

Notes

All interviews not cited were conducted by the author. Additional biographical information not otherwise attributed is from the *Australian Dictionary of Biography*. Poll data not cited is from Gallup polls. Statistics not otherwise attributed are from the various volumes of the *Official History of Australia's Involvement in Southeast Asian Conflicts 1948–1975*. Extracts from parliamentary debates are from Hansard. Additional material on 7RAR comes from *Conscripts and Regulars* (O'Brien, Michael, Allen & Unwin, St Leonards, 1995). For a broader historical perspective see *Vietnam: A History* (Karnow, Stanley, Penguin, Harmondsworth, 1984).

Australian Army publications

Australian Army, 'Information Booklet For National Servicemen', Australian Army, Australia, 1965

Australian Army Headquarters, '"It's Like This–" Army Leaders Guide on Service Conditions', Australian Army, Canberra, 1960

Australian Army, *Pocketbook: South Vietnam*, Dept. of Defence, Canberra, 1967

Collections in Australian libraries

Australian War Memorial Research Library, Private Records of PR00353 Renshaw, Terence James and PR03142 Noack, Errol Wayne

State Library of Victoria, MS 12326, Papers of Maxwell Keith Costello

State Library of South Australia, PRG 1452, Noack family

University of New England, Saunders Collection, Anti-Vietnam Movement in Australia

National Archives of Australia (NAA)

A463 1962/3685 Part 1, Prime Minister's Department correspondence files, National Service Training Scheme – General representations, 1962–1966

A463 1964/5143 Parts 1 & 2, Prime Minister's Department correspondence files, National Service Training Scheme – Policy, 1964–1968

A1209 1975/2165, Prime Minister's Department correspondence files, National Service Training Scheme Policy 1969, 1969–1975

A4940 C162 Parts 1 & 2, Menzies and Holt Ministries – Cabinet files, National service – Policy, 1950–1967

B2458, Central Army Records Office, selected Army Personnel Files

National Vietnam Veterans Museum

Letters and papers of Noack family

Select list of books

Battle, Brian, *Nashos in Australia 1965–1973*, Raby, 2008

Benko, Frank, *730 and a Wakey*, Sid Harta Publishers, Glen Waverley, 2010

Brown, Wayne 'Sam', *Medic: Memoirs of an Australian infantry medic in Viet Nam 1968–69*, Wayne 'Sam' Brown, Palmwoods, 2002

Burstall, Terry, *A Soldier Returns: A Long Tan veteran discovers the other side of Vietnam*, University of Queensland Press, St Lucia, 1990

Collyer, David, *From Fishnets to Foxholes and Back Again*, The Author, Ballarat, 2001

Dapin, Mark, *The Penguin Book of Australian War Writing*, Penguin, Camberwell, 2011

Donnelly, Roger, *The Scheyville Experience: The Officer Training Unit Scheyville 1965–1973*, University of Queensland Press, St Lucia, 2001

Duncan, Bruce, *Crusade or Conspiracy?: Catholics and the anti-Communist struggle in Australia*, UNSW Press, Sydney, 2001

Edwards, Peter, *A Nation at War: Australian politics, society and diplomacy during the Vietnam War 1965–1975*, Allen & Unwin and Australian War Memorial, St Leonards, 1997

Edwards, Peter, *Australia and the Vietnam War*, NewSouth Publishing and Australian War Memorial, Sydney, 2014

Eisenhower, Dwight D, *The White House Years: Mandate for change, 1953–56*, Doubleday, New York, 1963

Ekins, Ashley & McNeill, Ian, *Fighting to the Finish: The Australian Army and the Vietnam War 1968–1975*, Allen & Unwin and Australian War Memorial, Crows Nest, 2012

English, Michael, *Brave Lads: 3RAR in South Vietnam 1967–1968*, Australian Military History Publications, Loftus, 2008

Fall, Bernard, *Street Without Joy*, Stackpole, Mechanicsburg, 1964

Fall, Dorothy & Halberstam, David, *Bernard Fall: Memories of a soldier-scholar*, Potomac Books, Washington DC, 2006

Frame, Tom, *The Life and Death of Harold Holt*, Allen & Unwin, Crows Nest, 2005

Fraser, Malcolm & Simons, Margaret, *Malcolm Fraser: The political memoirs*, Melbourne University Publishing, Carlton, 2009

Giblett, Noel (ed.), *Homecomings: Stories from Australian Vietnam veterans and their wives*, Australian Govt. Pub. Service, Canberra, 1990

Gilfoyle, John & Robbins, John, *You'd Better Bloody Believe It!*, John & Lurelle Gilfoyle, Arana Hills, 2011

Grey, Jeffrey, *A Military History of Australia*, Cambridge University Press, Melbourne, 1990

Grey, Jeffrey, *A Soldier's Soldier: A biography of Lieutenant General Sir Thomas Daly*, Cambridge University Press, Port Melbourne, 2012

Grey, Jeffrey, *Up Top: The Royal Australian Navy and Southeast Asian conflicts*, Allen & Unwin and Australian War Memorial, St Leonards, 1998

Ham, Paul, *Vietnam: The Australian war*, HarperCollins, Pymble, 2007

Harcourt, David, *Everybody Wants to be Fuehrer: National Socialism in Australia and New Zealand*, Borchardt Library, Bundoora, 1985

Hart, Royce, *The Royce Hart Story*, Thomas Nelson, Melbourne, 1970

Heard, Barry, *Well Done, Those Men: Memoirs of a Vietnam veteran*, Scribe, Carlton North, 2005

Henderson, Gerard, *Menzies' Child: The Liberal Party of Australia, 1944–1994*, Allen & Unwin, St Leonards, 1994

Hodges, Ian, *Vietnam, 1968: The battle of Fire Support Bases Coral/Balmoral*, Dept. of Veterans' Affairs, Canberra, 2008

Horner, David & Bou, Jean (eds.), *Duty First: A history of the Royal Australian Regiment*, Allen & Unwin, Crows Nest, 2008

Horner, David, *SAS: Phantoms of the Jungle: A history of the Australian Special Air Service*, Allen & Unwin, Sydney, 1989

Howson, Peter & Aitkin, Don (eds.), *The Howson Diaries: The life of politics*, Penguin, Ringwood, 1984

Inglis, KS & Brazier, Jan, *Sacred Places: War memorials in the Australian landscape*, Melbourne University Publishing, Carlton, 2008

James, Clive, *Unreliable Memoirs*, Jonathan Cape, London, 1980

Johnson, Dick & Sykes, Stuart, *Don't Tell Me I Can't Do That: An autobiography*, Ironbark, Chippendale, 1999

Langley, Greg, *A Decade of Dissent: Vietnam and the conflict on the Australian homefront*, Allen & Unwin, North Sydney, 1992

Laurent, Rob, *With Anzacs in Vietnam*, BlueFlyer, Highfields, 2011

Lembcke, Jerry, *The Spitting Image: Myth, memory and the legacy of Vietnam*, New York University Press, New York, 1998

Lewis, Bob, Harvey, Trevor & Horan, John (eds), *Then There was Nine: 9 Platoon, 3RAR, 1969–2001*, 2001

Mackay, Ian, *Australians in Vietnam*, Rigby, Adelaide, 1968

Maddock, Kenneth (ed.), *Memories of Vietnam*, Random House, Milsons Point, 1991

McAulay, Lex, *The Battle of Long Tan*, Arrow Books, Milsons Point, 1987

McDowell, David, *Soldier, Soldier: A national serviceman in Vietnam 1969–70*, David J McDowell, Berowra, 2009

McFarlane, Brain, *We Band of Brothers: A true Australian adventure story*, BW McFarlane, Bowral, 2000

McKay, Gary, *Delta Four: Australian riflemen in Vietnam*, Allen & Unwin, St Leonards, 1996

McKernan, Michael, *Here is their Spirit: A history of the Australian War Memorial 1917–1990*, University of Queensland Press and Australian War Memorial, St Lucia, 1991

McNeill, Ian, *To Long Tan: The Australian Army and the Vietnam War 1950–1966*, Allen & Unwin and Australian War Memorial, St Leonards, 1993

McNeill, Ian & Ekins, Ashley, *On the Offensive: The Australian Army in the Vietnam War, January 1967–June 1968*, Allen & Unwin and Australian War Memorial, St Leonards, 1993

Menzies, Robert Gordon, Sir, *The Measure of the Years*, Cassell Australia, North Melbourne, 1970

Montesini, Lorenzo, *My Life And Other Misdemeanours*, Penguin, Melbourne, 1999

Murphy, John, *Harvest of Fear: A history of Australia's Vietnam War*, Allen & Unwin, St Leonards, 1993

Nelson, Hank, *Prisoners of War: Australians under Nippon*, ABC Enterprises for the Australian Broadcasting Corporation, Crows Nest, 1990

O'Neill, Robert, *Vietnam Task: The 5th Battalion, the Royal Australian Regiment, 1966–67*, Cassell Australia, Melbourne, 1968

Parr, Alan, *Memories of Vietnam*, Alan Parr, Nemingha, 2006

Payne, Trish, *War and Words: The Australian press and the Vietnam War*, Melbourne University Publishing and Informit, Carlton, 2007

Pemberton, Gregory (ed.), *Vietnam Remembered*, Weldon, Willoughby, 1990

Ponting, Derek, *'Dear Mam–': Letters and memories of a Liverpool soldier in Vietnam 1966–67*, Countyvise Ltd, Birkenhead, 2011

Pynt, Gerald (ed.) & Epstein, Jack, *Australian Jewry's Book of Honour World War II*, Griffin Press, Netley, 1974

Rees, Peter, *The Boy from Boree Creek: The Tim Fischer story*, Allen & Unwin, Crows Nest, 2001

Russ, Martin, *Happy Hunting Ground*, Atheneum, New York, 1968

Taylor, Jerry, *Last Out: 4RAR/NZ (ANZAC) Battalion's second tour in Vietnam*, Allen & Unwin, Crows Nest, 2001

Thomson, Jimmy & MacGregor, Sandy, *Tunnel Rats*, Allen & Unwin, Crows Nest, 2011

Walters, Doug & Laws, Ken, *The Doug Walters Story*, Rigby, Adelaide, 1981

White, Tony, *Starlight: An Australian Army doctor in Vietnam*, CopyRight Publishing, Brisbane, 2011

Whittaker, Bob, *Jellybeans in the Jungle*, EIEIO, Toowoomba, 2011

Williams, Jean R, *The Devil's Rainbow: Conscripts, chemicals, catastrophe*, Homecoming Publications, Nambour, 1999

Winter, Peter, *The Year I Said Goodbye*, Wakefield Press, Kent Town, 2003

Essays, chapters and articles

Burgess, Pat, 'A Correspondent's Report', Maddock, Kenneth & Wright, Barry (eds.), *War: Australia and Vietnam*, Harper & Row, Sydney, 1987

Conley, Jenny, 'Dear Mum and Dad', *The Age*, 13 August 1993

Curthoys, Ann, 'Vietnam: Public Memory of an Anti-War Movement', Hamilton, Paula & Darian-Smith, Kate (eds.), *Memory and History in Twentieth-Century Australia*, Oxford University Press, Melbourne, 1994

Goot, Murray & Tiffen, Rodney, 'Public Opinion and the Politics of the Polls', King, Peter (ed.), *Australia's Vietnam: Australia in the Second Indo-China War*, Allen & Unwin, North Sydney, 1983

Grey, Jeffrey, 'Diggers and Kiwis', Wiest, Andrew (ed.), *Rolling Thunder in a Gentle Land: The Vietnam War revisited*, Osprey, Oxford, 2006

Grey, Jeffrey, 'Vietnam, Anzac and the Veteran', Pierce, Peter, Grey, Jeffrey & Doyle, Jeff (eds.), *Vietnam Days*, Penguin, Maryborough, 1991

Grey, Jeffrey, 'In Every War But One? Myth, History and Vietnam', Stockings, Craig (ed.), *Zombie Myths of Australian Military History*, University of New South Wales Press, Sydney, 2010

Harris, Robin, 'The New Breed', Maddock, Kenneth (ed.), *Memories of Vietnam*, Random House, Milsons Point, 1991

Hay, David, 'Total Recoil: The Australian military and the national service training debate', *Limina: A journal of historical and cultural studies*, University of Western Australia, Nedlands, 1990

Hazlehurst, Cameron, 'Young Menzies', Hazlehurst, Cameron (ed.), *Australian Conservatism*, Australian National University Press, Canberra, 1979

Jordens, Ann-Mari, 'An Administrative Nightmare: Aboriginal Conscription 1965–72', *Aboriginal History*, Australian National University, Canberra, 1989

McNeill, Ian, 'The Australian Army and the Vietnam War', Pierce, Peter, Grey, Jeffrey & Doyle, Jeff (eds.), *Vietnam Days*, Penguin, Maryborough, 1991

Richardson, Kate, 'Tim Fischer: the Promise of Personalised Representation', Charles Sturt University, 2009

Shields, Neville, T, 'National Service Training, 1950–59', Forward, Roy & Reece, Bob (eds.), *Conscription in Australia,* University of Queensland Press, Brisbane, 1968

Private letters and papers (outside public collections)

Archbold, Jim, letters

Conley, Jim, *The Vietnam Years*, unpublished manuscript, 2007

Donohoe, Frank, letters

Jones, Evan, diary entries

Mattner, Binny, letters

Sloman, Des, diary entries

Weekes, Neil, unpublished manuscript

Periodicals

The Advertiser, The Age, The Australian, Brisbane *Telegraph, The Bulletin,* The *Canberra Times, The Courier-Mail,* The *Daily Advertiser,* The *Daily Mirror,* The *Daily Telegraph, The Examiner, Fraser Coast Chronicle, Good Weekend, The Herald, The Herald-Sun, National U, The News,* The *Northern Daily Leader, The Peacemaker, People,* Perth *Daily News, Quadrant, Ramparts, Reveille, Revolution, SIT-REP, The Sun,* The *Sunday Mail, The Sun-Herald, Sunshine Coast Daily,* The *Sydney Morning Herald, The Telegraph, The Tribune, Wartime: The Official Magazine of the Australian War Memorial*

Video, audio and websites

Crikey (crikey.com.au)

Open Mike (Fox Footy)

Stateline South Australia (ABC TV)

Talking Heads (ABC Radio)

Taylor, Ken, 'Parliamentary Library Interview with Sir Allen Fairhall', 3 September 1983, courtesy of Allen Fairhall Jnr

Wotherspoon, Norm, 'Journey of an Ordinary Man' blog (journeyofanordinaryman.blogspot.com.au)

ACKNOWLEDGEMENTS

Hundreds of people helped me with this book. To individually acknowledge each of them would add another chapter to the manuscript, which would not necessarily endear me to the publisher. But first of all, I am enormously grateful to every veteran who answered the phone to a stranger calling out of the blue and asking them to recall events that took place fifty years earlier. Astonishingly, almost every person I canvassed was happy to help, and many acted as if they had been expecting the call, or this kind of thing happened to them every day. To those who invited me into their homes, and shared with me their photographs, diaries and letters, I cannot sufficiently express my gratitude. I need to thank every man whose words appear in this book: in every case where a quote is not referenced, it comes from the record of a personal interview. Please accept my usage of your memories as my appreciation for your time.

It seems churlish to single out a few men from the many but, reading back through the manuscript, my two early interviews with Grant Collins helped shape the book more thoroughly than I could have imagined at the time – so, thanks, Grant. And thanks to Penny Debelle at the Adelaide *Advertiser* for putting me in touch with Grant, and to Roy Eccleston of the *Advertiser* for putting me in touch with Penny. None of these things happen easily. One long interview with the encyclopaedic Dave Sabben also yielded more information than a chat with any one person might reasonably be expected. Norm Wotherspoon – an unacknowledged poet of the Vietnam War – was extremely helpful, both in word and deed. I also owe John O'Halloran for all his time and patience. The two Alan Parrs – from 6RAR and 1RAR – were also a great help. Barry Heard was extremely encouraging. Evan Jones provided an interview, diaries, photographs and a cover. He could hardly be expected to do more. Similarly, thanks to Jim Archbold for his photos, letters and time. Normie Rowe was wonderful. Graham Cornes was an early inspiration. Dave Sturmer, a fine painter, was fantastic. Bernard Clancy, an overlooked novelist of the war, helped arrange several interviews for me. Des Sloman's lyrical diaries were a great find. Lorenzo Montesini's published memoir offers a unique and poetic perspective on national service. Thanks to David Wittner for his letter from Andrew Peacock, and the Roubin brothers for everything.

For perspectives from the anti-war movement I'd like to thank the ever-helpful Dave Nadel, Ken Mansell and Hall Greenland, and also Brian Laver. Denis O'Donnell was also a great help, not least in pointing me towards Jerry Lembcke's book *The Spitting Image*, which helped clarify my thinking about the 'home front' after confusion had all but overwhelmed me. Thanks to Paul Ham for vigorously arguing the opposing position on these issues.

It is of sadness to me that I had to leave some fantastic material unused. Noel Turnbull, whose insightful comments inspired this book in the first place, somehow does not appear in its pages, and nor does his fellow Scheyville graduate Geoff Schuberg, who gave me a sprawling, fascinating, honest interview. Two other former provosts, Stewart Nuss and Chris Furlong, should also have made the cut, as should so many others, including Patrick Fiddler, a sapper with civic affairs, and 5RAR's John Burridge. Some of those men I spoke to but did not ultimately quote – such as Wayne 'Sam' Brown and Walter Beattie – contributed a huge amount of background material. As did Wayne's mum, Jean Williams.

Initially, I had planned for this book to cover national servicemen in every theatre, including Malaysia and Papua New Guinea. Ultimately, however, I had to narrow my focus and so (once again) overlook the fascinating experiences of Ian Freeman in the Pacific Islands Regiment, and I also couldn't use the Malaysian stories of Don McNaught and others.

Thanks to Bill Hartley for agreeing to grace the cover of a book he hadn't read. Thanks to Jenny and Jim Conley for everything. Thanks to Peter Haran. Thanks to Greg Ivey. Thanks to Philip Mendes. Thanks to Alan Kitchen. Thanks to Gary Townsend. Thanks to John Schumann. Thanks to the journalist at the *Townsville Bulletin* whose name I have shamefully mislaid, Greg Ray at the *Newcastle Herald*, Jim Hope at *Good Weekend*, and Zoe Curtis at the *Herald-Sun*. And thanks to the people of South Australia who responded to my appeal for information about the life of Errol Noack, especially Binny Mattner. Thanks to the excellent Australian Vietnam Veterans Museum for permission to use Errol's letters.

For taking me to Vietnam, thanks to China Southern Airways and Bill Gray (this is just one of the things I owe to Bill). For showing me around the country, and later reading the book proofs and sharing his contacts and opinions, Walter Pearson was a priceless guide. Also thanks to Jimmy Thomson and Sandy MacGregor for hosting me on an earlier trip to Australian war sites in Phuoc Tuy.

It feels as though I should thank all librarians everywhere, but especially Andrew Sergeant at the Petherick Library, Sharon Polkinghorn at the Adelaide *Advertiser*'s newspaper library, the staff of the *Herald-Sun*'s library, the staff at the Australian War Memorial and the National Archives in both Melbourne and Canberra. The librarians at the state libraries of New South Wales, Queensland and South Australia were particularly helpful.

Australia fought a small war in Vietnam over a limited area, and it was well documented by the military. Most of the Australian troops who survived the fighting are alive today. Australia in the 1960s had a small population, few large cities and many local newspapers. It should be easy to establish what really happened, both in Vietnam and at home, and yet aspects of the public memory of national service and the Vietnam War differ wildly from the historical record. There have been several attempts by academics and former soldiers to bridge this gap. For his guidance and encouragement, Professor Jeffrey Grey at ADFA was peerless, and his essay, 'Vietnam, Anzac and the Veteran' provides much of the underpinning for this book, although he might not recognise some of his perspectives through my distorting mirror. Similarly, I owe a debt to Mike O'Brien for (among other things) his study of 7RAR, *Conscripts and Regulars*, and to Professor Bob Hall for his study of 8RAR, *Combat Battalion*. Anybody who writes a book about the Vietnam War today is extraordinarily lucky to have *The Official History of Australia's Involvement in Southeast Asian Conflicts 1948–1975* as a reference, and I am thankful the final volume was released halfway through my research for this book.

Thanks to Neil Weekes for permission to quote from his unpublished manuscript, and Alan Parr, David Collyer, Barry Heard and Lorenzo Montesini for allowing me to quote from their published work.

Last of all, I'd like to thank Claire Waddell for all her incredibly hard work as assistant on this book, Lesley Waddell for helping type it, Ben Ball for commissioning it, Deborah Callaghan for agenting it, Arwen Summers for editing it (with incredible patience), Nikki Lusk for proofreading it, Jeanne Rudd for indexing it, Rebecca Bauert for her beyond-the-call-of-duty editorial assistance. And you for buying it.

INDEX